Positive Perspectives 2
Know Your Dog, Train Your Dog

Pat Miller
CPDT, CDBC

Dogwise™
Publishing

Wenatchee, Washington U.S.A.

D1210698

Positive Perspectives 2
Know Your Dog, Train Your Dog
Pat Miller

Dogwise Publishing
A Division of Direct Book Service, Inc.
403 South Mission Street, Wenatchee, Washington 98801
1-509-663-9115, 1-800-776-2665
www.dogwisepublishing.com / info@dogwisepublishing.com
© 2008 Pat Miller

Graphic Design: Nathan Woodward
Indexing: Cheryl Smith
Photos: Nancy Kerns, Pat Miller

Portions of this book previously appeared in *The Whole Dog Journal* and *Your Dog*. Used with Permission.

Library of Congress Cataloging-in-Publication Data

Miller, Pat, 1951 Oct. 14-
  Positive perspectives : know your dog, train your dog / Pat Miller.
    p. cm.
  ISBN 978-1-929242-50-4
  1. Dogs--Training. 2. Dogs--Behavior. I. Title.

SF431.M5515 2007
636.7'0887--dc22

                              2007041119

ISBN13: 978-1-929242-50-4

Printed in the U.S.A.

Contents

Dedication

To Paul—my beloved husband, my bff, and my hero.

And to Tucker—a great dog who never wore a choke chain on his big furry neck.

April 25, 1993 - May 3, 2007

Acknowledgements

I know it's customary to use this section of a book to thank everyone who has helped the book get written, edited, published, etc., and indeed I am grateful to all who have participated in that process, especially Nate and the other fine folks at Dogwise who prompted me to proceed with a second Positive Perspectives volume.

I'd like to step outside the norm, however, and recognize some voices from the past who have served as models for me, not only in their passion for writing about animals, but in caring about them as well.

When I was bedridden for several months as a small child with a serious illness, I discovered a book titled *Beautiful Joe: An Autobiography*. I read and re-read this book so many times the cover fell off, and I could recite the entire first chapter from memory. Written in 1893 by Marshall (Margaret) Saunders and the winner of the ASPCA's writing competition that year, the book is a fictionalized presentation of the true story of an abused dog who was rescued from his cruel master by a young woman, Laura. Laura was a champion of animal protection in the very early days of that societal movement. I have no doubt that my admiration for Laura and my love for this book have had a strong influence on my life. Although my path has meandered, it has always centered around sharing my life and my work with animals.

Beautiful Joe is a canine version of *Black Beauty: The Autobiography of a Horse*, another book that grasped my imagination and reinforced my love for animals at an early age. Marshall Saunders used Joe's voice to speak out on behalf of dogs in the same way Anna Sewell had Beauty speak for horses sixteen years earlier. I am enamored of both these books to this day—our bookshelves are lines with various editions of both works, from first edition copies to a paperback version of *Beautiful Joe* published very recently.

Fellow animal loving readers will no doubt share my fondness for other authors of classic animal stories: Eric Knight, author of *Lassie Come Home* and Albert Payson Terhune, who wrote numerous dog books, mostly about Rough Collies. These two writers fueled desire to own one of these magnificently loyal dogs, and as a result, for many of my childhood years this was my family's breed of choice. I *will* share my life with a Rough Collie again, one of these days.

Marguerite Henry and Walter Farley round out the equine side of my early literary animal obsession. Henry, prolific author of 59 books including *Misty of Chincoteague*, provided steady fodder for my unquenchable drive to read. Reading about her life after her death in 1997, I was bemused to discover that her first published work came at the age of eleven; a short story about a Collie. Farley authored some 25 volumes, most of which were part of the beloved story that began with Alex Ramsey and his beautiful horse being rescued following a shipwreck, in *The Black Stallion* series.

To all of these, and the countless other writers who have fed my hunger for animal stories over the years, I thank you for your gifts.

For those of you who, like me, fell in love with Beautiful Joe at some point in your lives, I only recently discovered that there is a Beautiful Joe Heritage Society, a Beautiful Joe Park, and a website for him, at: www.beautifuljoe.org.

Cast of Characters

I refer to my own dogs (along with their good points and their not-so-good points) frequently in this book. Rather than introducing the dogs over and over again as they appear in the following chapters, here is a brief description of my dogs who you will get to know through the course of the book.

Current Dogs

Dubhy (pronounced "Duffy," meaning "Dark" in Gaelic). Presently 7 years old, neutered male dark brindle Scottish Terrier we found as a stray at age 6 months in Chattanooga, Tennessee. Has a large repertoire of wonderful tricks (Say Your Prayers, Push a Baby Buggy, Pups in a Blanket, Ride a Skateboard, Play an Electronic Keyboard), and more—and is also dog reactive.

Lucy (Footloose and Fancy Free). 3-year-old spayed female brindle-and-white Cardigan Welsh Corgi, adopted from the Humane Society of Washington County (Hagerstown, Maryland) at age 7 months. High energy with some isolation distress behaviors, she has typical herding dog control behaviors that sometimes conflict with Katie's herding dog control behaviors. Loves to play tug and do barn chores.

Bonnie (Bonnie Wee Lass). 2-year-old spayed female black Scottie/Corgi/Poodle mix, adopted from the Humane Society of Washington County at age 5 months. Has a wonderfully soft, sweet, appeasing personality (and submissively urinates)—as a result both high-ranking Katie and Lucy let her do things they would never tolerate from many other dogs.

Dogs Who Are (Sadly) No Longer With Me

Josie. My heart dog; this wonderful Terrier mix was the love of my life, and the one who showed me how much better positive training methods are than the old-fashioned coercive methods I used previously. She had several titles in Mixed Breed obedience, and was one of the first 27 dogs in the world to obtain a title in APDT Rally. We found her at age 6 months in San Jose, California, in 1987, while we were doing undercover cockfighting surveillance, and said our sad good-byes 15 years later.

Dusty. A purebred 8-pound Pomeranian we adopted at age 10 months from the Marin Humane Society in Novato, California, where I worked at the time, Dusty taught me to love and appreciate small dogs. His heart was every bit as big as the largest Great Dane, and when we went hiking and camping he always kept up with the big dogs. Also titled in obedience and APDT Rally, we lost him at age 14 in June of 2004, shortly after we moved to Maryland.

Tucker. We adopted our Cattle Dog mix, Tucker from the Marin Humane Society as a 12-week-old pup. My husband and I could never agree on the other part of his mix—I said German Shepherd, Paul said Bernese Mountain Dog. But we fully agreed that he was all wonderful. We let him go in May of 2007, at age 14, after a year-long struggle with prostate cancer. As Nancy Kerns said in a tribute to him in *Whole Dog Journal*, "He was a good, good dog."

Katie. Matriarch of our canine family until September of 2007, Katie was an Australian Kelpie—a breed uncommon in the US, but quite popular in its native country, as we found during a trip to Australia in the fall of 2006. They are high energy dogs, bred to work until they drop. At age 15, with her hearing, vision and hind legs failing, we finally, reluctantly, said our sad farewells.

Introduction

It's a tribute to the importance of our canine companions in our lives that we never run out of things to say about dogs. A few years ago, I teamed up with Dogwise to publish *Positive Perspectives, Love Your Dog, Train Your Dog* composed of a collection of well-received articles from publications that I write for, primarily *Whole Dog Journal* and Tufts University's *Your Dog*.

Now, several years and dozens more articles later, we've done it again. Like the last book, this one again emphasizes the importance of training with methods and philosophies that support relationships between dogs and humans based on mutual trust, respect and co-operation.

Positive training has come a long way. At one time the poor step-child of the training profession, it is now widely accepted as the most humane and effective way to accomplish training goals, whether those goals are about shaving half-seconds off agility times, achieving perfectly straight sits in the obedience ring, having fun and earning titles in Rally obedience, or simply the honorable and admirable goal of helping your furry pal become a well-behaved, loving companion for life.

This book picks up where the first one left off. As before, the chapters of this book can stand alone as resources for quick reference on a variety of topics. I offer considerably more information in these pages on working with problem behaviors, including aggression. Taken and read as a whole, however, it will introduce you to some of the more advanced—and exciting—training techniques we're using in the positive training world, such as shaping, as well as provide a consistent and effective approach to behavior modification that is well-grounded in the science of behavior and learning.

So read on, and as always, love your dog and train your dog. If you find useful information here that helps you actualize a lifelong loving relationship with your dog, then I've accomplished my goal. Read on, and enjoy!

Part One
READING YOUR DOG

You will learn that recognizing your dog's communication signals is key to achieving your training goals and building a mutually rewarding relationship. Because dogs are primarily body-language communicators, the more skilled you are at observing and interpreting your dog's subtle and sometimes not-so-subtle signals, the more you'll appreciate and successfully influence his behavior. Part One will help you have a better understanding of what your dog is trying to say to you, and how to best respond. Be careful—dog owners who start spending more time analyzing their dogs' body language find it a fascinating topic. Once you realize the richness and depth of your dog's language, you may get hooked on reading *all* dogs! Not only does this enhance your relationship with your own four-legged friend, it also helps you keep him safe in the presence of other dogs, and makes *your* interactions with other dogs safer and more successful as well.

Fluent in Body Language

How to avoid inadvertent miscommunication with your dog

We are in Week Three of our training class, working on "verbal downs"—getting the dogs to lie down on just a verbal cue. Diane and her exceptionally sweet and compliant eight-month-old Great Dane, Gable, aren't succeeding. I ask her if I can try.

"Sure!" she says cheerfully. A lazy wag of Gable's long tail signals his willingness, as Diane passes me his leash. I wait for Gable to offer a sit, which he does as promptly as his gangly, adolescent body allows.

Arms relaxed by my sides, I say "Down" in a clear and happy voice. He stares adoringly into my eyes, and remains sitting. I wait three seconds, then lure him down with the treat hidden in my right hand. He follows the lure to the floor; I click the clicker in my left hand, and pop the treat in his mouth. We repeat this a couple more times, with a Click! and treat each time.

I ask for the down again, and give an almost imperceptible nod of my head. He drops halfway to the floor and glances up at me, eyes bright. I give an enthusiastic "Good boy!" and quickly lure him the rest of the way down, then Click and treat. On the fifth trial, I give the verbal down cue without moving. He stares into my eyes for a heartbeat, and then sinks all the way to the floor. Click! and **jackpot** (a cascade of treats).

Body Language

Dogs are, first and foremost, body language communicators. While they do have a limited ability to communicate vocally, they are much more articulate with their subtle body movements, and much more intuitively able to understand ours. As Patricia McConnell says in the introduction of her excellent book, *The Other End of the Leash*, "All dogs are brilliant at perceiving the slightest movement that we make, and they assume that each tiny movement has meaning."

Watching my students (the human ones) in class, I can see that those who tend to be most successful are those who are most consistent with their body movements. Consistency allows the dog to attach a consistent meaning (and response) to the movement. The more inconsistent the movement, the harder it is for the dog to connect the human's random motions to a specific behavioral response.

Gable was able to do a verbal "Down" for me in just five repetitions because:

- Diane had done three weeks of work with him luring the down (and some work on the verbal cue "Down"), so he was very familiar with the cue and the behavior. I just had to fade the lure.

- On the first three attempts, I separated the verbal cue from the motion of the lure, so he had the opportunity to process the word separately from the lure.

- On the fourth repetition I gave the verbal cue, along with a body language cue to help him translate, then gave him a few seconds to process it. His half-down was a question—"Is this right?" My "Good boy!" lure and Click! and treat constituted a big "YES!" answer to his question. Dog owners often miss their dogs' questions, or fail to answer them.

- By the fifth iteration, it was clear to Gable that the verbal "Down!" meant the same thing as the lure. The tiny movement of my head served to bridge the gap between the verbal cue and the behavior for him. We had successfully translated the body language into spoken English.

It is *because* of a dog's use of body movement as a first language that we can train so successfully using lure-and-reward methods, and easily teach hands signals. However, the importance of understanding and responding appropriately to our dogs' body language goes far beyond formal training. Body talk can make everyday life with your dog easier, enhance your relationship, and overcome some of the canine behaviors that are giving you grief.

Cross-species Communication

One of the reasons humans and canines co-exist so beautifully is that we are both social species—we live in groups and create social rankings within those groups. Both species intuitively understand the concept of a "group leader" (Alpha Dog = Head of Household, Employer, President of the US); both species have members in their various groups who lead more naturally than others; and in both groups, ranking (or status) is fluid. You might be the head of your household, but subordinate to your boss at work, or to a colonel in the Army, or the Queen of England. Your dog might be the leader of your dog pack, but have very low status among the regular canine visitors at your local dog park.

However, canine and primate body talk have very different vocabularies, which can cause serious conflict between our species. For example:

- Humans meet face-to-face and hug. Dogs tend to meet obliquely, and a dog who puts his chin or paws over another's shoulders in greeting is probably making an assertive statement about his rank—which may well elicit an aggressive response. This is why dogs have a tendency to bite when kids (or adults) hug them.

- It is considered polite by humans in the Western world to make direct eye contact. Failure to do so is considered evidence of lack of character—disrespectful, shifty, or outright untruthfulness. However, this is not true in some other human cultures, where direct eye contact is considered rude.

In the canine dictionary, direct eye contact is an assertion or a threat. The dog on the receiving end either looks away, a sign of submission—in order to avoid a fight—or takes offense and engages in aggressive behavior in response. The other dog backs off, or a fight occurs. This is one reason why so many children are bitten. They tend to stare at dogs anyway, and the more strangely (aggressively) the dog behaves, the more a child stares. Adults who insist on direct eye contact with strange dogs also tend to get bitten.

- We naturally face another person that we are speaking to, and our force-based culture encourages us to get more strident if a subordinate fails to comply with our requests. We were once taught to call our dogs by standing squarely facing them, arms at our sides, and saying "Come!" in a commanding tone of voice. Our voices got louder, more insistent, perhaps even angry, if our dogs fail to come. Dogs see a full-frontal communication as a threat, and loud, firm, angry vocalizations as aggressive. Their natural response is to turn away in appeasement, or at best, to approach slowly, in a submissive curve, rather than the speedy, enthusiastic straight line that we strive for.

- We often reach for our dogs' collars over the top of their heads. They see this as a direct threat; they duck away in submission (or they bite), and learn to avoid us when we are trying to catch them. We follow or chase them, intimidating them further or, alternatively, teaching them that if they take the lead, we follow. The more we try to catch them, the more they avoid us.

- We bend over them to pet them on the tops of their heads, or to cuddle them. Again, we are unwittingly offering a posture of threat and intimidation. Primate "hovering" is a very off-putting posture for dogs. Dogs back away in fear or submission, or worse, bite in an aggressive response. Prompted by ill-advised old-fashioned thinking, some humans still use force (alpha-rolls and scruff shakes) to overpower and dominate their dogs. Most dog body language is very subtle and in large part ritualistic, including the "belly-up" position which is usually offered voluntarily by the subordinate pack member, not forced by the higher ranking one. Dogs experience the alpha roll as a violent, terrifying attack, and some will respond out of a likely belief that they are fighting for their very lives.

This man was mystified when the dog, who was romping loose at a dog park, suddenly shied away from him, growling and raising the hair on his back. All the man did to elicit this response was to bend over, staring at and calling to the dog. See the next chapter to find out what happens next!

The Good News

If you think about it, it's surprising that we get along with our dogs as well as we do! The good news is that both of our species are pretty darned adaptable. We can teach our dogs to appreciate some of our bizarre primate behaviors, and we can learn to use canine body talk to our advantage.

We humans pretty much insist on hugging our dogs. Touch is so important to us that as much as we may intellectually understand our dogs' resistance to such close body contact, our hearts overpower our heads and we just have to hug them. When a dog reacts badly to being hugged, it's often an innate response, not a conscious decision. The dog doesn't sit next to the hugger, ponder his options and make a deliberate decision to bite. Rather, the hug triggers a subconscious response—"Threat! Fight or Flee!!" If the dog can't flee—because he is being hugged—or is one of those dogs whose fight response is stronger than his flight response, he bites.

It's easiest to teach a dog to accept hugging if you start associating gentle restraint with something yummy when he is very young. Using **counter-conditioning** and **desensitization** to change his natural association with close contact from bad (Danger! Run Away!), to good (Oh Yay! Cheese!), you can convince the part of his brain that reacts subconsciously, that being hugged is a very good thing.

To do this, hold the dog at a level of restraint with which he is very comfortable—perhaps just a light touch of your hand on his back. Feed him a tiny tidbit of something wonderful, and remove your hand. Repeat this step until he turns his head eagerly toward you in anticipation of his tidbit when he feels your hand touch his back.

Now, very slightly increase the intensity of your touch, either by holding your hand on his back longer and feeding him several treats in a row, perhaps by pressing a tiny bit harder on his back, or by moving your arm a little farther over his back, so your hand brushes his ribs on the other side. The more your dog accepts your touch, the quicker you will be able to move through the counter-conditioning and desensitization process.

Be careful to increase intensity of only one stimulus at a time. For example, work on length of time until he is perfectly comfortable with long "hand-rests," then shorten the time while you work on increased pressure. When he is comfortable with each new stimulus, add them together. When he can handle more pressure happily, start doing more pressure for longer periods of time. Then ease up on both of these while you work on moving more of your arm over his back.

At the same time, of course, it is vitally important to teach children (and uninitiated adults) not to hug dogs unless they know the dog very well and are totally confident that the dog is fully comfortable with such intimate contact. Even then, young children should never be left unattended with *any* dog.

The same approach used to teach your dog to appreciate a hug works with many "culture clash" behaviors. If you want your dog to love having his collar grabbed, pair the action with cheese, or hot dog, or chicken. This particular exercise should be taught to every dog. Perhaps *you* know that the safest way to take hold of a dog's collar is gently, under the chin. But if a friend tries to grab the collar over your dog's head, it would be nice if she doesn't get bitten for her primate behavior, because your dog has learned to accept it.

You can also teach your dog that eye contact is a good thing, by encouraging him to look into your eyes, and rewarding him when he does. The clicker is very useful here. Have your dog practice this with other humans as well, if you want him to be comfortable with that pervasive and offensive primate penchant for staring rudely into canine eyes. And, again, teach your children *not* to stare into a dog's eyes.

A Two Way Street

While you are teaching your dog to understand and accept primate language, you can also learn and use canine body language. This will greatly enhance your relationship and your training program, since your dog can respond very quickly when he realizes you are speaking Dog.

McConnell describes a process that she calls "body blocking," which simply means taking up a space to prevent your dog from doing so. Let's say your dog Tess is on a Sit/Stay while you are cooking in the kitchen, and you drop a fried drumstick on the floor. Tess starts to get up to get it. Rather than grabbing at her or yelling "STAY!" simply step forward into the space she was about to occupy. Like magic, she settles back into her Sit/Stay. McConnell reminds us that the *sooner* you react the better, and says that once you get good at it, you can simply lean forward an inch or two to express your intent to occupy the space.

You can also use body blocking with dogs who jump on you. Next time you are sitting in a chair and your wild Westie makes a running charge for your lap, clasp your hands against your stomach and lean slightly forward, blocking the space with your shoulder or elbow. It also helps to look away, rather than make eye contact. You may have to do several repetitions of this, especially if your dog has had a lot of practice lap-leaping, but it can be very effective if you are consistent. He can learn to wait for permission to jump up on your lap or on the sofa next to you.

I used body blocking for years without thinking about it or defining it as clearly as McConnell does. When our four dogs are all doing "Wait" at the door, I can release them one by one, by name, in part because I use subtle body blocking movements to indicate which dogs are to remain in place. As with the "Stay" blocking, the more you do it, the more subtle the movements can become, because dogs are so good at reading tiny body language signals.

This is just one example of the many ways you can make the canine/primate difference work *for* you as you build a relationship with your dog based on mutual trust and respect, and as you encounter other dogs. Move (run!) *away* from your dog when you want her to come rather than moving toward her. She will follow the leader, instead of moving away from an intimidating direct approach. Look away from the challenging stare of an aggressive dog instead of sending your own direct-eye-contact challenge back, and you are more likely to escape from the experience bite-free.

We, as the supposedly more intelligent species, should be able to understand and forgive canine behaviors that clash with our human social expectations. It seems that our dogs are pretty darned good at understanding and forgiving ours, thank goodness. As you and your dog journey together through life, each translating primate to canine and vice versa, appreciate the great value of this cultural diversity.

Puppy Restraint

Positive trainers the world over teach their clients the importance of having their pups accept handling and restraint. There are two methods primarily in use, and while they look similar on the surface and both are considered by many trainers to be positive, there is a subtle difference that makes one more positive than the other.

Method #1: Positive Reinforcement

When we use positive reinforcement (+R) in training, the dog's behavior makes something good happen. In +R restraint, the puppy is touched, or gently restrained, and fed a wonderful treat. He learns that when he is touched, eventually restrained (hugged), he gets good stuff—yummy treats, human attention, scratches under the ears. He comes to love being touched, handled, even hugged, because he has come to associate those things with very good stuff.

Method #2: Negative Reinforcement

When we use negative reinforcement (-R) in training, the dog's behavior makes something "bad," or uncomfortable, go away. In –R training, the puppy is gently restrained, and if he struggles, is held until he stops struggling, and is then released. He learns that he can make the restraint go away if he doesn't struggle. He learns to tolerate being handled or restrained, because struggling makes it last longer. He still thinks being held is not a pleasant thing, and he does what he needs to do to make it go away as quickly as possible.

Both methods can teach puppies to accept being held, hugged, and otherwise restrained and handled. Which would you prefer for your puppy?

Say What?

Learn to understand and recognize your dog's body language

Play bows. Averted eyes. Tail wags. Flattened ears. Our dogs are not only masters at reading *our* body language, but also experts at *sending* messages with an incredibly expressive tool—their own bodies. If we humans were half as good at reading their signals as they are at reading ours, there would be a lot less miscommunication between our two species.

The fact is, most dog owners don't *see,* much less *recognize* the basic grammar of dog body language. That's why, when owners call me asking for help with their dog following a bite, they often say "The bite just happened out of the blue—there was *no* warning!" In most (if not all) cases when I meet the dog, I see him giving *plenty* of indications that he's stressed and/or uncomfortable, signs that to a more knowledgeable canine observer are obvious warnings that a bite may emerge in that dog's near future.

What's worse, many owners who would recognize the more overt warning signs—growls and snaps, for example—have successfully suppressed those signs by previously punishing the dog when they occurred. So, in a way, they're right—the dog didn't hang up a flashing neon sign that he was about to bite, because he had already learned that it wasn't safe to do so.

Let Me Hear Your Body Talk

The more you learn about your dog's subtle body language communications, the better you'll be at reading him so you can better manage his environment to prevent trouble. Is he tensing up, readying himself for a battle to defend himself against a perceived threat? Or is he playfully anticipating a romp with a canine pal he enjoys roughhousing with?

It's important that you not focus on just *one* piece of the message. The various parts of your dog's body work together to tell the complete story, and unless you read them all, you'll be missing out on important elements of the equation. You want to be especially aware of the ears, eyes, mouth, tail, and the dog's body posture as important pieces of the whole puzzle.

Because canine communication is a constant flow of information, it's sometimes difficult to pick out small signals until you've become an educated observer. You can start by studying photographs of dog body language, then watching videos that you can rewind and watch repeatedly, and finally honing your skills on live dogs. Dog parks, doggie daycare centers, and training class playgroups are ideal places to practice your observation skills.

I'll help get you started with some photographs to analyze. For each of the pictures provided, cover the analysis, jot down your observations of the key body parts visible, using the accompanying grammar key, then compare your answers to mine.

A note about the photos: Most were taken at dog parks. Some of the dogs are wearing types of collars, harnesses or other training gear I don't like. In fact, it's a good idea to remove any extra gear on dogs who are playing in groups—it's too easy for them to get caught in each other's gear.

Ready to get started? Go!

Canine Body Parts: Basic Grammar

Conventional wisdom has it wrong—a wagging tail does *not* always mean a happy dog. The following abridged Canine/English dictionary can help you become a skilled translator. Keep in mind that breed characteristics can foil your interpretation (and even confuse other *dogs*!). Relaxed ears and tail for an Akita (a prick-eared dog, tail curled over his back) look very different from relaxed ears and tail for a Golden Retriever (a drop-eared dog with a long, low tail).

Canine conversation is fluid and ongoing. A moment's freeze or hard look from one dog will mean, "I'm having fun but *watch* it," and is often answered by an equally transitory appeasing expression from his play partner, "Sorry! I'll be more careful. Now let's play!"

That said, please note that if a dog's body language vacillates it can indicate ambivalence, which *may* precede a choice toward aggression.

Ears

- **Pinned back:** Submissive/appeasing, deference or fearful
- **Back and relaxed:** Calm, relaxed, friendly
- **Forward and relaxed:** Aware, friendly
- **Pricked forward:** Alert, excitement, arousal, assertive; could be play arousal or aggression arousal

Eyes

- **Averted, no eye contact:** Submissive/appeasing, deference or fearful; may be a subtle flick of the eyes, or may turn entire head away
- **Squinting, or eyes closed:** Submissive/appeasing, happy greeting
- **Soft, direct eye contact:** Calm, relaxed, friendly
- **Eyes open wide:** Confident, assertive
- **Hard stare:** Alert, excitement, arousal; could be play arousal or aggression arousal

Mouth

- **Lips pulled back:** Submissive/appeasing or fearful (may also be lifted in "submissive grin" or "aggressive grin")
- **Licking lips, yawning:** Stressed, fearful (or tired!)
- **Lips relaxed:** Calm, relaxed, friendly
- **Lips puckered forward, may be lifted (snarl):** Assertive, threat

Tail

- **Tucked under:** Submissive/appeasing, deference or fearful
- **Low and still:** Calm, relaxed
- **Low to medium carriage, gently waving:** Relaxed, friendly
- **Low to medium carriage, fast wag:** Submissive/appeasing or happy, friendly
- **High carriage, still/vibrating or fast wag:** Tension, arousal, excitement; could be play arousal *or* aggression arousal

Body Posture

- **Behind vertical, lowered; hackles may be raised:** Submissive/appeasing or fearful
- **Vertical, full height:** Confident, relaxed
- **Ahead of vertical, standing tall; hackles may be raised:** Assertive, alert, excitement, arousal, possibly play arousal or aggressive arousal
- **Shoulders lowered, hindquarters elevated:** A play bow—clear invitation to play; dog sending a message that behavior that might otherwise look like aggression is intended in play

Analysis of Photos

You may notice a theme in these first three photos shown below. In each picture there are body language expressions that to a novice observer might have indicated pending serious aggression: tails stiffly raised, mouths agape with teeth bared, tension in body posture—however the moment frozen in time precedes the onset or continuation of clear and appropriate social behavior rather than aggressive expression.

It's not uncommon for humans to misread perfectly normal play behavior and interrupt/separate dogs who are having a rousing good time together. At the end of Week 2 of my group good manners classes—and every week thereafter—we have play sessions where the dogs get to play with their canine classmates. In each new class there is at least one owner, often more, who is very tense about her dog's play behavior. I narrate body language descriptions and explanations as the dogs play, and watch owner stress levels diminish as they come to understand what their dogs are really saying to each other.

A good technique to use when looking at body language is to analyze first, draw conclusions second. Let's do that now, with Photos 1, 2 and 3:

Analysis of Photo #1

Dog #1—German Shepherd on the left: Ears are back, eyes are rolled sideways, lips are pulled back, mouth is open but relaxed with teeth covered, tail is relaxed at medium carriage, and although he's stretched out running, at this moment his body posture is lowered, slightly behind vertical.

Dog #2—Bully-type dog on the right: Ears are back, eyes are squinting, lips are forward, mouth is open wide with teeth bared, and tail is high but appears still. Again, although he's running, at this moment his body posture is tall and ahead of vertical.

Conclusions

The Bully-type dog appears the more assertive of the two—his body expressions are more intense and aroused, with his raised tail and bared teeth. Still, the interaction is clearly play—the Shepherd is not intimidated by the Bully's display—he's offering deference behaviors but having a rousing good time; his facial expression is high good humor. The Bully's squinty eyes and flattened ears speak "friendly" and belie the pseudo aggressiveness of his teeth and tail. If his ears were pricked sharply forward and he was giving the Shepherd direct eye contact with a hard stare, I'd be concerned—and likely so would the other dog!

Analysis of Photo #2

Dog #1—Pharaoh Hound on the left: Ears are back slightly, can't see the eyes, mouth is open slightly with lips forward and teeth bared, tail is high and waving, body posture is hard to tell but appears tall and vertical.

Dog #2—Shepherd mix on the right: Ears are back slightly, eyes are fully open but slightly averted, mouth is slightly open and relaxed, tail is high and waving, body posture is tall and slightly behind vertical.

Note: I don't condone the use of prong collars as shown on Dog #2 on the right.

Conclusions

There is a little more mutual tension in this encounter than in Photo #1, but still not alarmingly so. Both tails are high but appear to be gently waving, and while both dogs are standing up fairly straight, ears are not pricked forward and there's no direct eye contact. While the Pharaoh Hound is offering more assertive behaviors they are not excessively so, and the Shepherd is clearly more deferent, avoiding any potential conflict. This is far more social than aggressive. I would watch these two closely, but expect to see something occur any second to relieve the tension.

Analysis of Photo #3

Dog #1—Lab on the left: Ears are somewhat back but a little raised, eyes are direct but soft, mouth is closed with lips pulled forward, tail is high but not stiff, body is clearly behind vertical.

Dog #2—German Shorthair Pointer on the right: Ears are raised (that's "pricked" for a drop-eared dog), making strong direct eye contact, mouth is closed with lips forward, can't see the tail, body posture is tall and slightly forward.

Conclusions

This is the most worrisome of the three photos. While the Lab is the more deferential of the two with his behind-vertical posture, he may not be deferential enough for the Pointer, who could take offense to the Lab's direct eye contact, forward commisure (corner of the lips) and raised tail. Her expressions are more serious than playful, and the outcome of this encounter likely depends a lot on whether the Lab backs off…which fortunately for him, he does. In the next photo he's dropped into a play bow, his ears are back, his lips are pulled back and he's sending very clear "No Offense, Ma'am!" messages. The appeasement messages are received: the Pointer, while still not convinced she wants to romp and roll with this upstart, has softened her expressions in return—her ears are also back, her gaze is now over his head instead of directly into his eyes, and she has rocked back slightly behind the vertical. Phew!

Just a Little More...

Now let's look at three photos in a series, this time of a dog-human interaction. Dog-human interactions can be more difficult than dog-dog ones, since our native languages are so different. This series of three photos depicts a classic conflict between a canine and a human; the two are strangers and neither really understands what the other is communicating. Similar interactions are played out every day in communities across the country, in which well-intentioned humans do all the wrong things in their efforts to be friendly with dogs. Far too often, the failure of dog and human to understand each other and react appropriately results in a bite—or several.

Ready to give it a whirl? Do your analysis, draw your conclusions, and then compare them to my comments.

Analysis of Photo #4

Remember the photo from the previous chapter of a man encountering a strange dog in a dog park? Now let's find out how this seemingly innocent meeting turns out.

Man—The man is bent over from the waist, directly facing the strange dog, making direct eye contact. He has observed the dog growling and barking at him, and is probably saying something like, "Here, boy!"

Dog—Tail is stiffly erect, ears appear pricked forward, commisure (corner of lips) appears forward, body posture is tall and forward, and the dog is also making direct eye contact.

Conclusions

The man would like to meet and greet the dog, and is using appropriate *primate* body language to do so.

Bending at the waist is a human invitation to come closer. In our culture, a face-to-face greeting that includes direct eye contact indicates honesty, friendliness and sincerity. The man is doing his best to entice the dog to come see him.

However, in the canine world, a full-front, bent-forward posture with direct eye contact is a strongly assertive threat, and the dog is reacting accordingly with defensive aggression. He may not be sure what the man is up to, but he's sure he wants no part of it!

Analysis of Photo #5

Man—Our human has straightened to full height and is stepping forward, still maintaining direct eye contact with the dog.

Dog—Has moved off to the side, still carrying his tail high and keeping direct eye contact with the man. His ears are pricked and his mouth appears puckered forward. Hard to tell for sure because of the angle, but his body posture still appears tall and forward.

Conclusions

The man has recognized that the dog is rejecting his advances, and is choosing to walk on. He has properly interpreted the dog's aggressive posturing and has wisely given up making friends. While the human's upright posture is less of a threat to the dog than his bent-over position in Photo #1, he is still making direct eye contact. The stick in his right hand is raised slightly. I'm curious as to whether he's aware he did this—if he made this defensive gesture consciously, or if it was an automatic self-protection response.

The dog is still clearly aroused—keeping his eye on the man and his defenses up to see if the dangerous human poses any further threat.

Analysis of Photo #6

Man—Has ceased interacting with the dog and walked forward, stick still slightly raised.

Dog—In contrast, the dog continues to engage. He has circled behind the man and continues to show tension in his markedly forward posture, intense stare and sharply pricked ears.

Conclusions

While the man appears to have dismissed the unfriendly dog and moved on, the dog isn't done yet with this once-threatening human. Actually, the man is probably at the greatest risk at this moment in the interaction—defensively-aggressive dogs are most likely to bite from behind or if cornered, and this one looks likely to run up behind the man for a stealth attack. Something about the man's posture suggests he may be more aware of the potentially threatening dog than it seems at first glance. Perhaps he has belatedly realized that his eye contact was exacerbating the dog's aggression.

Fortunately, this interaction ended without a bite. The man's decision to break eye contact and move on worked. If he's ever in a similar situation again, it might be wiser to stand still, turning slowly if necessary to keep his eye on the dog without making strong direct eye contact, until the dog relaxes and leaves, or relaxes enough that the man can leave more safely.

I Submit!

These canine gestures are intended to do more than just "calm" others

Katie, our cranky, creaky, geriatric Australian Kelpie, is grumpy with just about every other member of the canine species. I was at least a little concerned when we brought home our most recent family member, Bonnie, a Scottie/Corgi/Whatever-mix.

At age five months, Bonnie came with a personality that was one of the softest and sweetest I've seen in ages. In fact, I suspect she was surrendered to the shelter by her owner of just one week in large part due to the fact that she urinated submissively the instant anyone spoke to or touched her. I worried that Katie's gruff admonitions would be too much for her sensitive nature.

Quite to the contrary, Bonnie's willingness to defer to Katie with obviously submissive body language at every turn has averted any potential conflict. In fact, Bonnie gets along with Katie—and the rest of our pack—better than any of our other dogs simply *because* she's so appeasing. I was surprised and immensely delighted when I looked out my office window one day last week to see Bonnie and Katie playing—no, *romping*—together in the back yard!

Reading Dogs

Paradigm shifts in the dog-training world in the last decade have led dog owners and trainers to pay closer attention to the observation, interpretation and understanding of canine body language. Norwegian dog trainer Turid Rugaas, in her book *On Talking Terms with Dogs,* identified more than 30 body gestures that dogs make in social settings—whether with members of their own species or with humans—that, she postulated, demonstrated intent to get along with other "pack members." Rugaas coined the term **calming signals**, to collectively describe these gestures and their purpose, and the term has found acceptance and everyday use as dog owners and trainers discuss dog behavior. Clumped behind that deceptively simple phrase, however, is a complex constellation of behaviors that accomplish many more purposes than just "calming."

Rugaas has asserted that dogs purposely use calming signals to calm the other being with whom the dog is interacting. The suggestion is that the behaviors brought under this broad umbrella are deliberate.

Today, many ethologists (people who study animal behavior) speculate that the communications now popularly identified as calming signals are often hardwired, automatic responses rather than deliberate ones, and are far more complicated than a simple attempt to *calm* a dog's social partners. They likely have more to do with the presenter's own state of mind and/or an end goal to affect the *behavior* of the other dog or human for the purpose of self-preservation—rather than a necessarily deliberate intent to change the *state of mind* of the other being.

Communicative behaviors are adaptive in nature—helping canids maintain peaceful pack relationships without resorting to violence. Ethologists suggest that non-threat canine behaviors are more important in keeping the peace in packs than are dominance behaviors— that relations are primarily maintained by deference behaviors exhibited by subordinates toward high ranking members, not dominance displays by the alpha member. Canine social groups may more appropriately be described as deference hierarchies rather than dominance hierarchies.

As such, the dozens of behaviors that have been dubbed calming signals might more appropriately be separated into several subgroups called **appeasement** (active submission), **deference** (passive submission), **displacement**, **stress signs**, and **threat** (dominance) **displays**.

By observing dogs, learning to recognize and respond to the various behaviors in this constellation, your relationships with canines will become richer, and your translations of dogspeak more accurate. Let's start by taking a closer look at the submissive/subordinate behaviors.

Please Appease Me

As stated above, subordinate behaviors can be grouped into two general categories—active submission (appeasement)—characterized by increased activity and diminished posture, and passive submission (deference)—denoted by decreased activity and lowered body posture. The difference lies in whether the dog offering the submissive behavior desires attention from the higher-ranking individual, or would prefer that the attention he's receiving go away.

Active submission may also be identified as attention-seeking behavior: nuzzling, licking (including licking ears and lips), jumping up, paw lifts and pawing motions, "smiling," teeth clacking, crouching, pretzeling, and play-bows. Ears may be pulled back, and tail may be wagging expressively—wide, sweeping movements or circles. These behaviors can often be seen during greetings between dog and owner, or between friendly, compatible dogs.

"Nothing to see here, sir…Please go away so I can breathe again!" Even though the Shepherd-mix looks friendly enough, the black dog is younger, less socially experienced, and lower-ranking. He freezes, keeping his tail low, and keeps his gaze averted in an attempt to disappear from the other dog's radar.

Passive submission usually involves a dramatic reduction in activity with a goal of diverting attention, and is most often seen in a lower-ranking dog when threats are directed toward him by a higher-ranking member of the social group—dog or human. The dog's ears may be pressed flat against the head, with his tail tucked between legs. The subordinate dog often freezes, averting eye contact, lowering head and body, sometimes to the point of going "belly-up" on the ground. Passive submission may also be accompanied by submissive urination.

Below are descriptions of several common submissive behaviors and suggestions for appropriate responses when the behavior is directed toward humans. When directed toward dogs, submissive behaviors usually elicit appropriate responses from the other canine. Situations where they don't are material for a different book!

Active Submission (Appeasement)

Some of the gestures exhibited by a dog who is demonstrating active submission can be obnoxious to us humans. The important thing to remember is that, with these behaviors, the dog is communicating his recognition that you are his leader, a higher-ranking individual. Be a good leader and let him know how he can best appease you by redirecting his behavior into something less bothersome.

Nuzzling

Dog pushes muzzle against you, perhaps under your arm or hand. If you respond by giving the dog attention (petting, making eye contact, speaking to dog) you are positively reinforcing the behavior and it will continue or increase. This is fine if you like the behavior—and some people do. It can, however, become annoying if the dog is very persistent.

You may prefer to extinguish the behavior using **negative punishment**. When the dog nuzzles you, turn away or even walk away. The dog is seeking attention. If nuzzling consistently evokes the opposite response—attention goes away—the behavior will stop. Of course, you must educate all family members and visitors to respond in the same way, or the behavior will be randomly reinforced and will persist.

Another option is to put the behavior on cue, and teach the dog that nudging only works to elicit attention when you ask for it. You can also pre-empt nuzzling by consistently asking the dog for an incompatible behavior that gains him the attention he seeks. A "Sit" or "Down" can serve as incompatible and polite attention-seeking behaviors if you consistently give your dog attention for those.

Licking

Dog licks body parts and clothes, including lip-licking, ear-licking and nose-licking. Again, if you like this behavior, you can encourage it with positive reinforcement—giving your dog the attention he seeks when he licks. If you don't enjoy your dog's licking, use negative punishment (licking makes you go away) and install an incompatible behavior in its place. Having your dog hold a toy in mouth when he approaches people is a great attention-eliciting behavior that's incompatible with licking.

Jumping Up

Dog puts paws on human body, often projecting body against human with some force. A lot of small-dog owners don't seem to object to jumping up as an attention-getter, and a lot of small dogs are incorrigible jump-uppers as a result. Not all people with small dogs like this, however, and most people who cohabitate with medium-to-large dogs much prefer four-on-the-floor.

Jumping as an attention-getting behavior is positively reinforced by attention, even behavior that dog owners may offer to try to reduce jumping up, such as pushing the dog away, or telling him to get down. Once again, removing yourself from contact with the dog—taking the attention away—will reduce the behavior, especially if you replace it by reinforcing an incompatible behavior such as sit or down. See the pattern yet?

Paw Lifts and Pawing Motions

Dog lifts paw or paws at human. While uncontrolled pawing behavior can be annoying, a simple paw lift is a lovely behavior to put on cue and turn into a series of fun and useful behaviors. A paw lift on cue can become "Shake," "Wave," "High five," and "Salute," and pawing motions can be useful for turning appliances on and off, indicating found objects for dogs doing scent and search work, pushing a ball (canine soccer!) and playing an electronic keyboard. Persistent, annoying pawing is best extinguished by ignoring the behavior and putting an incompatible behavior on cue, such as four on the floor, or a gentle paw lift.

Teeth Clacking

Dog's teeth click or chatter. This is an innocuous behavior, and one that you can simply ignore—unless you're an avid trainer and want to encourage it by clicking and treating when the dog offers it, then putting it on cue.

Crouching

Dog lowers his body closer to the ground. This is also an innocuous attention-seeking behavior. If it bothers you, ignore it, and reinforce your dog when he approaches you standing taller. Training, using positive methods, will also increase your dog's confidence and decrease incidents where he feels compelled to make himself smaller.

When a dog "slinks," with lowered body posture and averted eyes, she exhibits her deference to you, not guilt.

Pretzeling

Dog corkscrews his body into a "C" shape. This is also a harmless, kind of cute behavior that I'd be tempted to reinforce and put on cue!

Play-Bow

Dog lowers his forequarters while keeping his hindquarters elevated. This is a lovely behavior, and I can't imagine someone wanting to extinguish it. I'd reinforce and put it on cue.

Smiling

Dog lifts his lips into a grimace that is unaccompanied by other behaviors that would indicate at threat. I see no reason to try to make this behavior go away as long as humans around the dog understand that it's not an aggressive behavior. I think it's quite cute—I'd encourage it by clicking and treating when the dog offers a smile, and then put it on cue!

The yellow Lab signals his active submission to the older female Pointer by pretzeling his body, lowering his forequarters and head, lifting a paw, keeping his tail waving big and low, and holding his ears back.

Passive Submission (Deference)

Deference behaviors are offered by the dog in response to a *perceived* threat—there doesn't have to be any intent to threaten on the part of the person interacting with the dog. For all of the deference behaviors listed below, the appropriate response is to determine how/why the dog perceives a human or humans as threatening, then working to change the dog's perception through consistent positive associations with the perceived threat(s).

Human behaviors that can be perceived as threatening by a dog (thereby eliciting deference behaviors) include direct eye contact, a full-frontal approach, a loud voice, bending over the dog, and patting him on top of the head. Punishing or "correcting" a dog for offering a deference behavior is the worst thing you can do if you hope to modify the behavior. He will only intensify his deference in a futile attempt to convince you he's being subordinate. In a worst-case scenario, he may even become defensively aggressive if his deference signals aren't working. Instead, ignore the behaviors when they happen, and work to build your dog's confidence in relationships by being consistently non-threatening, and insisting others do the same. You can also build confidence through positive training—when the dog has a better understanding of how to influence and predict his environment, his confidence increases.

A dog's deference behaviors may include any or all of the following:

Tail Tucked

Dog pulls his tail tightly against his belly to cover and protect his vulnerable underparts. Even dogs with "gay" tails or tails that curl over their backs can do this when sufficiently threatened.

Freeze
Dog ceases all motion as he attempts to convey his submission to the party threatening him—usually in conjunction with averting eyes.

Averting Eye Contact
Dog shifts eyes to avoid making eye contact, or actually turns head away.

Lowering Head and Body
Dog ducks head and/or crouches closer to the ground.

Belly-Up
Dog rolls over on back and exposes vulnerable underparts. This can also be a simple invitation for a tummy rub when not accompanied by other deference behaviors.

Submissive Urination
Dog urinates in response to perceived threat (not necessarily an actual threat) in a person's voice, touch or approach.

It's been a joy to watch Bonnie develop over the past three months. Training and a consistent lack of threats or intimidation in her relationship with us and other humans in her life have increased her level of confidence. While she still offers appropriate appeasement and deference behaviors to Katie and the other members of the Miller pack, her submissive urination with humans has ceased. Like many pups who offer this behavior, maturity and a consistent, kind and predictable environment has helped her outgrow it—it's been weeks since a pat on her head has created a puddle on the floor.

Major Misunderstanding

Humans have long misunderstood submissive behaviors in both categories, and reacted inappropriately as a result. In many human cultures, failure to make eye contact is a sign of someone who is untruthful, shifty and sneaky. Dogs displaying submissive behaviors such as averting eyes and lowering body posture ("slinking") are often perceived as wimpy, cowardly, sneaky, manipulative, guilty, and disobedient—misinterpretations based on our familiarity with primate body language.

Unless wise to the ways of canid communication, humans tend to assume a dog offering lowered body-posture deference behaviors is expressing guilt—when in fact he's only responding to a perceived threat in his human's body language.

Sometimes, the more the dog acts guilty, the more righteously angry his human gets, the more submissive (guiltier) the dog acts, the angrier the human—a lose-lose cycle if there ever was one.

Submissive urination is another classic case in point. Dog owners who still live in the old-fashioned punishment dog-training paradigm may attempt to physically or verbally "correct" a pup for peeing submissively—the exact wrong thing to do.

A pup urinates submissively in response to a perceived threat—the assertive approach of a higher-ranking member of the social group. In the dog pack, this is a useful survival mechanism that effectively averts the wrath of most adult dogs who could otherwise do serious harm to a young subordinate.

Unfortunately, when the higher-ranking member is a human, the behavior (urination) that should avert wrath often initiates or escalates anger in the human.

The pup's response is to urinate more—not less. The human gets angrier, the pup pees more, the human gets even angrier, the pup pees even more in a desperate attempt to turn off the anger—and another lose-lose cycle is born.

Even the submissive grin is misunderstood. Sadly, it can be mistaken for a snarl, and a dog may be labeled as aggressive who is actually anything but. It's also often perceived as a doggy version of a happy smile—a less damaging interpretation, but still a misperception of a clearly subordinate display.

Interestingly, the submissive grin is believed to be an imitation of the human smile, since dogs don't normally display this behavior to each other, only to humans.

While some behaviorists consider the grin to be an attention-seeking appeasement gesture, others consider it more of a threat-averting deference signal. In any case, it's important to understand that the dog who grins is making a status statement—your rank is higher than his—exhibiting neither an aggressive threat nor a relaxed, contented smile.

Stress Signals

Learn to recognize signs of your dog's stress

Recently, there was a video clip of a two-legged dog making the e-mail rounds. Faith, a gold-colored Lab mix, is missing her front legs from birth, due to a congenital deformity. Several people sent me the clip with their comments about how wonderful it was that the dog could walk and hop around on her two hind legs and lead a relatively normal life.

I watched the clip a number of times, and found the footage more disturbing than uplifting. I was concerned that *every person* who sent me the clip thought Faith looked "happy." I wondered if we were watching entirely different videos! What *I* saw was a dog who was noticeably stressed in almost every bit of the footage, with the exception of a few seconds showing Faith lying under the covers in bed with her owner.

I suspect the people who sent me the video saw the heartwarming miracle of a dog who survived against all odds. I saw a dog who was stress-panting, ears pinned back against her head, eyes large, anxious whenever her owner walked away from her, and avoiding contact when admiring members of the public reached out to touch her. Why was there such a huge difference between our interpretations of the dog's behavior?

Please note: I'm not saying Faith appeared to be on the verge of biting someone, or had any tendency at all toward aggression. But she certainly did appear to be stressed—at least when she's been filmed.

Many of the folks who sent Faith's clip to me are above-average dog people. They read *Whole Dog Journal*, frequent good training e-mail lists, and read the right books. If *they* missed a package of behaviors that signaled to me that Faith was not calm and relaxed, it's not surprising that so many *average* (and worse) dog owners are fairly poor at recognizing signs of stress.

The smart, aware owner is always on the alert for signs that her dog is stressed, so she can alleviate tension when it occurs. Those whose dogs are easily stressed often become hyper-vigilant, watching closely for tiny signs that presage more obvious stress-related behaviors, in order to forestall those unpleasant reactions.

It's difficult to see in black and white, but what looks a bit like an icicle drooping out of this little dog's mouth is, in fact, a long rope of drool. He had planted himself by the gate of a dog park and was clearly ready to leave, although his owner hadn't noticed.

If more owners were aware of the subtle signs of stress, fewer dogs would bite. That would be a very good thing.

Why De-stressing Helps

There are many reasons why it's important to pay attention to stress indicators, including the following:

- Stress is a universal underlying cause of aggression.
- Stress can have a negative impact on the dog's health.
- The dog's ability to learn is impaired when she's stressed.
- Dogs respond poorly to cues when stressed.
- Negative classical conditioning can occur as a result of stress.

For all of these reasons, and more, it's worthwhile to monitor your dog for signs of stress, and take appropriate steps to make his life a little easier.

Listed below are some stress behaviors that are often overlooked. With each behavior the appropriate immediate course of action is to identify the stressor(s) and figure out how to decrease the intensity of that stressful stimulus. In many cases that's by increasing the distance between your dog and the stressor—be it a child, another dog, a noisy street sweeper, a person in uniform, men with beards…

If possible, remove the stressor from your dog's environment entirely. If, for example, he's stressed by harsh verbal corrections, shock collars and NASCAR races on TV, you can probably simply stop exposing him to them. For stressors that can't be eliminated, a long-term program of counter-conditioning and desensitization can change the dog's association with a stressor from negative to positive, removing one more trigger for stress signals and possible aggression.

Signs of Stress

Anorexia

Stress causes the appetite to shut down. A dog who won't eat moderate to high-value treats may just be distracted or simply not hungry, but this is more often an indicator of stress.

Appeasement/Deference Signals

These don't always indicate stress. Appeasement and deference are important everyday communication tools for keeping peace in social hierarchies, and are often presented in calm, stress-free interactions.

Appeasement and deference signals are generally offered by a lower ranking dog to a higher-ranking member in a social group to promote the tranquility of the group and the safety of the lower ranking member. When offered in conjunction with other behaviors, they can be an indicator of stress as well. Appeasement and deference signals include:

- **Slow movement:** Lower ranking dog appears to be moving in slow-motion.
- **Lip Licking:** Lower ranking dog lips at the mouth of the higher ranking member of the social group
- **Sitting/Lying Down/Exposing Underside:** Lower ranking dog offers submission by lowering body posture, exposing vulnerable parts
- **Turning Head Away, Averting Eyes:** Lower ranking dog avoids eye contact, exposes neck.

Avoidance
Dog turns away; shuts down; evades handler's touch and treats.

Brow Ridges
Furrows or muscle ridges in the dog's forehead and around the eyes.

Digestive Disturbances
Vomiting and diarrhea can be a sign of illness—or of stress; the digestive system reacts strongly to stress. Carsickness is often a stress reaction.

Displacement Behaviors
These are behaviors performed in an effort to resolve an internal stress conflict for the dog, not related to hierarchy. They may be observed in a dog who is stressed and in isolation (for example a dog left alone in an exam room in a veterinary hospital), differentiating them from behaviors related to relationship or hierarchy.

Displacement behaviors include:

- **Blinking.** Eyes blink at a rate that is faster than normal.
- **Nose Licking.** Dog's tongue flicks out once or multiple times.
- **Chattering Teeth.**
- **Scratching.**
- **Shaking off.** As if wet, but dog is dry.
- **Yawning.**

Drooling
May be an indication of stress—or a response to the presence of food, or an indication of a mouth injury.

Excessive Grooming
Dog may lick or chew paws, legs, flank, tail, and genital areas, even to the point of self-mutilation.

Hyperactivity
Frantic behavior, restless pacing, sometimes misinterpreted as ignoring or "blowing off" owner.

Immune System Disorders
Long-term stress weakens the immune system. Immune related problems improve if the dog's overall levels of stress are reduced.

Lack of Attention/Focus
The brain has difficulty processing information when stressed.

Leaning/Clinging
The stressed dog seeks contact with human as reassurance.

Lowered Body Posture
"Slinking," acting "guilty" or "sneaky" (all misinterpretations of dog body language) can be indicators of stress.

Mouthing
Willingness to use mouth on human skin—can be puppy exploration or adult poor manners, but can also be an expression of stress, ranging from gentle nibbling (flea biting) to hard taking of treats, to painfully hard mouthing, snapping, or biting.

Obsessive-Compulsive Disorders
These include compulsive imaginary fly-snapping, light and shadow chasing, tail chasing, pica (eating non-food objects), flank-sucking, self-mutilation and more. While OCDs probably have a strong genetic component, the behavior itself is usually triggered by stress.

Panting
Rapid shallow or heavy breathing in the absence of the dog being warm or having just been exercising.

Stiff Movement
Tension can cause a noticeable stiffness in leg, body and tail movements.

Stretching
To relax stress-related tension in muscles, many dogs perform elaborate, deep stretches (may also occur after sleeping or staying in one place for extended period).

Sweaty Paws
Damp footprints can be seen on floors, exam tables, or rubber mats.

Trembling
May be due to stress (or cold!).

Whining
This high-pitched vocalization, irritating to most humans, is an indication of stress. While some may interpret it as excitement, a dog who is excited to the point of whining is also stressed.

Yawning
Especially when the dog does not appear otherwise fatigued.

A portrait of three stress cases, from left to right. Paws is whining. Cooper is stress-panting, even though it is not hot. Rupert keeps licking his nose.

As I reread this list, I find myself making note of my own dogs' signs of stress, past and present. I recall the time my dearly-missed Dusty was earning the third leg of his Companion Dog degree. As I released him from the three-minute Long Down I noticed tiny, sweaty paw prints on the rubber show ring mats where his little paws had rested. Only in that moment did I realize how stressful that exercise must have been for him.

Our sound-sensitive Lucy trembles violently with the approach of a thunderstorm, long before I can hear the distant booming, while Tucker just comes and leans against me—also well before I can hear the storm. With dogs like those two, who needs weather forecasters? Dubhy normally takes treats with exceptional gentleness—except when he's stressed in the presence of another dog. Then its fingers beware!

Even we humans succumb to the natural biological need to use body language to express and relieve stress. I used to show hunters and jumpers (horses). Every time I sat on my horse outside the over-fences classes waiting for my turn to go jump, I would be afflicted with the incontrollable need to yawn—and yawn—and yawn. Only recently did I realize why. Stress! It affects us all.

Without Provocation

Almost every "Dog Mauls Toddler" headline is followed by an article that includes, among other things, these two phrases:

1. "The dog was always good with children," and,

2. "The bite was unprovoked."

Both statements make me cringe. Most people who think their dogs are "good with children" don't realize that many dogs only *tolerate* children—the dogs are actually stressed in the presence of children, at least to some degree. These dogs usually show low level signs of stress that would warn an observant owner that they really don't think little humans are all that great after all. Dogs who are truly "good with children" *adore* them; they don't just tolerate them. They are delighted to see children, and, with wriggling body, wagging tail and squinty eyes, can't wait to go see them. Anything less than this joyful response is mere tolerance.

With the very rare exception of **idiopathic** aggression—aggression for which there is no discernible cause—every bite is provoked *from the dog's perspective.* We, as humans, may feel the bite wasn't justified or appropriate, but rest assured the *dog* felt justified in biting. In many cases the provocation is pretty apparent from the news article: the dog was kept on a chain; the dog had a litter of puppies; the toddler was left outside in the back yard with a dog who had just been fed. In each case, the dog was stressed beyond his or her ability to control his bite.

Raise your stress awareness. Examine news reports about dog attacks to see if you can identify the possible stressors and provocation in each incident. Then be sure to protect your own dog from those potential bite-causing circumstances.

Part Two
ADVANCED TRAINING AND BEHAVIOR CONCEPTS

We have come so far from the days when choke chains and collar corrections were the norm in every training class. Part Two will introduce you to some of the many concepts that are part of the new paradigm in dog training and behavior: you *don't* have to use force and intimidation to be a benevolent leader; there are lots of effective, nonviolent ways to accomplish your training goals; and dog training should be fun for you and your canine pal, not a source of stress and conflict. At one time, training was a "method" that applied equally to all dogs. If the method didn't work, the dog was labeled defective. Today, modern trainers recognize that every dog requires individualized training and management; if something isn't working, it's not the dog's fault, and we can try something else. One of the best new things to come along in the dog training world is the technique called "shaping"—a process that really empowers the dog in training. Have fun with it!

The Crossover Challenge

Understand your dog's behavior as you switch to positive training

Please bear with me for a moment while I brag on Dubhy. From the time we found him as a stray puppy at age six months, we have trained using him using methods and management tools consistent with my positive training philosophies. He is the first of our canine family members to be trained completely with modern, non-coercive methods.

Last weekend, we put up a brand new set of agility equipment in our back yard. As my husband was tightening the last bolt, I dashed into the house to get Dubhy, who had never seen an agility course. To my delight—but not surprise—he happily and willingly traversed even the most daunting of the obstacles on the first go-round. Well, the closed tunnel gave him pause for a moment—when he couldn't see his way through the collapsed chute he jumped on top of the barrel instead, and perched there happily, sending me a cheerful "Is this what you wanted?" query from his sparkling eyes. When I invited him off the barrel and opened the chute to show him the way through, that obstacle, too, was quickly conquered.

I've had other dogs who were just as smart as Dubhy, but until the feisty Scottie came along, I had not yet owned a dog that I trained completely without compulsion. No "ear pinches," yanks on the collar, knees in the chest, stepped-on toes, or any other physical "corrections" whatsoever. And oh! What a difference it can make.

Don't get me wrong—I have not used coercive training techniques for more than twelve years. I was totally and completely converted to "positive-only" training following a moral, professional crisis with another one of my dogs a dozen years ago. Since then I've used only "dog-friendly" training methods with thousands of dogs and seen ample proof that these effective methods encourage and foster a strong, trusting bond between dogs and their owners.

However, until Dubhy, I had never so clearly seen the difference between a **crossover** dog—one who was initially trained with force-based methods and then switched to positive training—and a dog who had *never* experienced scary, hurtful, or force-based training. They are, as the saying goes, completely different animals.

Dogs who have been trained with positive methods from puppyhood tend to show more volunteerism; they raptly observe their handlers, looking for opportunities to offer behaviors that may be rewarded.

Take, for example, Josie, the canine love of my life. The Terrier mix was a joyful and willing worker, and we accomplished a lot together, including titles in competitive obedience and Rally. Josie was also my first crossover dog. Until she was three years old, I had trained her with conventional force-based methods. Josie prompted my conversion one day when she hid under the deck and unhappily refused to come out when she saw me getting out a set of scent articles in preparation for a training session. (I had been working with her retrieve using a conventional coercive training method, the ear-pinch.)

After this incident, I took a two year time-out from training to learn about modern, positive methods that are grounded in the science of behavior and learning. Only then did I begin training Josie again. This time, I used only dog-friendly methods, and she responded beautifully. Our accomplishments continued apace.

But throughout the rest of her life, Josie's response to new training situations or requests was very different from Dubhy's eager and creative volunteerism. The best way I can describe this is that when faced with something new, she waited to be shown what to do—as do many crossover dogs. My guess is that her fear or anxiety about doing the *wrong* thing was stronger than any impulse she might have had to try to guess what I wanted—even though for the last twelve years of her life she was never punished for doing the wrong thing.

In other words, faced with a unique training request, crossover dogs like Josie tend to do nothing, or they offer a safe behavior that they already know.

Why Positive Methods Work

In contrast, Dubhy and other dogs who were encouraged since infancy to "offer" novel behaviors in response to new training requests, joyfully go to work trying to solve the puzzle. The modern methods of training teach, foster, and capitalize on this initiative; the dog's volunteerism is what makes it work so well.

In positive training, the goal is to help the dog do the right thing and then reward him for it, rather than punishing him for doing the wrong thing. If he makes a mistake, the behavior is ignored, or excused with an "Oops, try again!" to encourage the dog to do something else. Using "Oops!" as a **no-reward marker** teaches the dog that the behavior he just offered didn't earn a reward, but another one will. So he tries again, and learns to keep trying until he gets it right, without fear of punishment.

In early training, he only needs to get it a "little bit right" to earn a Click! and reward; the goal is always to help the dog succeed, to keep him confident and willing to play the training game. In the beginning, for example, the dog is rewarded for walking in the general area of "heel" position, in order to learn to walk politely on his leash. If competition heeling is desired, this can be **shaped** later for more precision by clicking closer and closer approximations to "perfect" heel position. He learns where he needs to be to make good stuff happen through repetition and rewards, and volunteers to be there because he likes the good stuff.

In contract, force-based training teaches the dog to heel by administration of a sharp jerk (pop) on the leash any time the dog steps out of heel position. He learns where he needs to be in order to avoid bad stuff through repetition and punishment, and stays in heel position because he doesn't want to get hurt.

Both methods can teach dogs to be well-behaved. The force-trained dog learns to watch and read people, in large part in order to avoid the negative consequences that occur when he makes a mistake. The praise and rewards that sometimes follow a correction are rarely enough to overcome the learned caution of trying some new behavior that might be punished. The positive dog also learns to watch and read the humans around him, so that he can take advantage of opportunities to offer rewardable behaviors that are likely to result in good stuff. He has no fear of offering behaviors, because he has no anticipation of a painful consequence.

Obedient But Inhibited

Despite twelve years of positive training and relationship-building, I know that Josie would not have addressed the agility course with the aplomb that Dubhy demonstrated. She surely would not have hopped on top of a slippery barrel to see if *that* might be an alternative rewardable behavior. This is due at least in part, I believe, to their different personalities. Dubhy is sturdy and stalwart, and possesses the typical terrier "no-fear" attitude. Josie was soft, sensitive, and cautious.

I am also sure that Josie's lack of confidence about trying new things was equally due to her early training experiences, when she learned that unasked for behaviors often got punished, and that the safest course of action was to wait told be told or shown what to do.

Dubhy, on the other hand, has consistently been encouraged and rewarded for offering behaviors. Give him a new object, and he immediately sets to work trying to figure out what he is supposed to do with it. Give him a whole agility course, and he immediately tries to figure out what he is supposed to do with each of the various pieces of equipment.

Crossover History

Of course, I'm not the only one who has witnessed the vast differences between crossover dogs and those started from scratch with positive training.

The phrase "crossover dog" was actually coined in the 1990s as a result of the large influx of trainers who found themselves switching over from old-fashioned methods to more positive training. In her landmark book, *Don't Shoot the Dog*, former marine mammal trainer Karen Pryor introduced the dog-training world to the exquisite method of positive training known as clicker training. As dog trainers learned about the effectiveness of the techniques, many of them, too, "crossed over" to positive training methods. As Pryor has said, "In the early 90s, I could count the number of clicker trainers on one hand. Now there are thousands of us!"

Crossing With Your Dog

As trainers cross over—professional and non-professional dog owners alike—they encounter the challenge of teaching their crossover dogs a whole new approach to training. The phenomenon that I observed with Josie—her reluctance to freely offer new behaviors—is often discussed among professional positive trainers. I asked several well-known trainers to share their thoughts on the challenges of working with crossover dogs—*and* humans. Here's what they said:

Deborah A. Jones (PhD, Assistant Professor of Psychology, Kent State University, Ohio)

Dr. Jones is a college professor, author, producer of the excellent *Click & Go* DVD series, and a positive dog trainer. Her first performance dog was an adult rescue Labrador Retriever. Katie came to Jones with the pejorative label of "stubborn." Fortunately for the dog, Jones understood that Katie had simply learned to tune out and withstand unpleasant training techniques by shutting down and doing nothing.

In Jones's hands (and clicker), Katie's whole attitude and demeanor changed; she competed happily and successfully in obedience, and became a fantastic therapy dog.

Jones agrees that the differences between crossover dogs and positive-trained dogs are easy to see. She says, "Usually, crossover dogs have learned from their training that 'when in doubt, it's best to do nothing.' If they have been punished for making mistakes in the past, they have learned the concept that trying new things gets you in trouble."

"Dogs who have been exposed only to positive methods, however, are willing and eager to try new things. They are active in the training process, rather than waiting for explicit instructions. They also tend to be creative, which is a great asset when trying to shape or capture new behaviors."

Jones estimates that 95% of her human and canine clients are crossovers, and that people are eager to find ways to train that don't involve force and compulsion. While Jones herself never used old-fashioned methods, she watches her human clients struggle with crossing over, in part because old habits are hard to break, but also because they had accepted the old myth that effective dog training requires the use of force, compulsion and intimidation. "But as soon as they see that there is another way," she says, "most are very willing to give it a try, and are happy with the results."

Jean Donaldson (Founder/Instructor, The San Francisco SPCA Academy for Dog Trainers)

Jean Donaldson is the author of the highly regarded *The Culture Clash*, as well as *Dogs Are From Neptune*, and *MINE! A Guide to Resource Guarding in Dogs*. She lectures extensively in the U.S., Canada, and abroad.

Donaldson agrees that crossover dogs are generally less willing to take risks, and suggests that they can even display "learned helplessness." This is characterized by apathy, immobility, and non-response to stimuli in cases where the dog cannot avoid—or does not know how to avoid—the aversive (punishment) that is applied by the trainer. "So," she says, "when the trainer crosses over, a training session has a great deal of baggage and it may take time for the dog to learn that aversives are no longer forthcoming."

She even sees fallout from dogs trained with lots of luring and physical prompts (as opposed to **free-shaping**—waiting for the dog to perform a behavior and then click-rewarding it). Donaldson also suggest that these dogs may be less willing to offer behavior, as the lured and prompted dog has learned to wait for the trainer to show him what the answer is, rather than offering behaviors to figure it out himself.

Contemplating the crossover question, Donaldson muses, "Isn't it hard to imagine how anyone... has *not* crossed over, given the track record of positive reinforcement training, and readily available information on it?"

Leslie Nelson (Tails-U-Win! Canine Center, Tolland, Connecticut)

Leslie Nelson was one of the early icons in positive training, and continues to supervise more than 50 classes a week as director of her "Tails-U-Win!" training center. She feels that dogs adjust more easily to crossing over than many humans do, and recalls her own crossing-over struggle. "I can remember well, many years ago, when I made the decision to switch to all positive training," she says. "In the beginning I had to work totally without a leash [in order to resist making leash corrections]. Old habits die hard."

Nelson finds that most crossover dogs respond enthusiastically to positive training, although they can have some difficulty with pure clicker training and shaping, and may find the new approach stressful at first.

"They can be very reluctant to offer new behaviors for fear of being wrong," says Nelson. "Fortunately," she adds, "positive reinforcement training offers a variety of choices and can be adapted to meet the needs of each dog. Crossover dogs can be very successful when trained using a combination of luring (using a treat to get the dog to offer the behavior), targeting (teaching the dog to touch his nose to a designated target) and modeling (using gentle physical assistance to help the dog into the desired position)."

Karen Overall (MA, VMD, Ph.D., ABS Certified Animal Behaviorist, University of Pennsylvania, Philadelphia, Pennsylvania)

Dr. Overall is an internationally renowned researcher, author, speaker and behaviorist whose best-selling textbook, *Clinical Behavioral Medicine for Small Animals*, is a bible for many trainers who do behavior work.

True to her academic background, Overall was reluctant to speculate without solid research to back up her opinions. She offered that because dogs learn so well from context, they probably cope better with crossing over than most humans do.

According to Overall, dogs rely so much on non-verbal signaling (body language) backed up with olfactory communication (sense of smell), that we can't lie to them easily. Thus, when we humans truly commit to positive training, our whole non-violent message is clearly communicated to our dogs.

Beware, however. As Nelson says, "Old habits die hard." We sometimes send mixed messages when we inadvertently or deliberately fall back on old-fashioned punishment methods that worked for us before.

Overall suggests that dogs closer to the edge—the more uncertain, anxious, roughly-handled ones—will have more difficulty with crossing over. She says, "It likely all comes down to how well the dog can read the rules, and how damaged they are. The longer I go on the more I am convinced that 'normal' is defined by how well you recover."

Patience Begets Progress

The trainers I interviewed all seemed to agree (as do I) that punishment-based training causes damage (mental if not always physical) and that crossover dogs must recover from that damage as part of the crossing over process. The degree of success in that recovery varies, depending on a number of factors including the dog's personality, the amount of damage done, and the skill and consistency the owner/trainer demonstrates in her commitment to and application of positive methods.

Dr. Jones offers some final words of wisdom for humans who embark on the crossover journey. "Be patient," she counsels. "Your dog has to unlearn old information before he can completely participate in your new way of training. Progress should occur on the dog's timetable, not yours. Let him discover that trying new things is reinforced, not punished. Let go of the idea that you control the training process, and let your dog be an active participant."

A year ago, my husband and I said our heart wrenching good-byes to my first crossover dog, Josie, when she let us know that her 15-year-old body was too tired to carry on in this world. I am eternally grateful to her for showing me the way to be a more compassionate trainer and human. And I will always regret the three years of measured punishment I inflicted on her, using the methods I had been taught before I learned a better way. If I could change just one thing in my life, I would take back the three years of collar corrections, verbal aversives and ear pinches that I imposed on my beloved Josie, before she taught me a better way. I can see Josie in my mind's eye even now, running the agility course in our back yard next to Dubhy, sharing his joy, confidence and faith in a positive world.

Theory and Practice

Every new dog requires individual training and management

The decision to add a new dog to the pack shouldn't be taken lightly. I counsel prospective owners of new dogs to be clear about their needs and preferences rather than making spur-of-the-moment rash decisions, because their success at integrating a new dog into an existing "pack" so often depends on their ability to make informed decisions. These choices include what kind of dog to adopt, how to prepare their home to accommodate the new dog, how to introduce the new dog to the existing members, and how to incorporate her into family routines.

Bringing a new dog into the family can be fraught with unexpected developments, no matter how experienced a dog owner is, how well her home is prepared, and how good-natured the dogs are that she already owns. I've incorporated a new dog into my family dozens of times in my lifetime, counseled hundreds of clients about how to do it, and written a number of articles about it, and I *still* am surprised by the issues that can arise when a new dog comes home. However, with preparation, flexibility, and dedication to principles of positive training and behavior management, most dog owners can get through the adjustment period with peace in the pack.

Adoption Choices Should Be Made With the Brain as Well as the Heart

I recently had the chance to practice what I preach when the loss of Dusty, our valiant 8-pound Pomeranian, left a vacant spot in our pack last spring. Dusty had been my almost constant companion for close to 15 years, and though it's been nearly five months since we euthanized him, the pain of his passing is still very close to the surface. I often tear up as I think of his dear little fox face and boundless good cheer.

One of the things I do to help ease the overwhelming hurt of losing a close companion is to remind myself that it also means there's room in our family for another. Without actively looking, I know that a new furry face will one day draw my attention and grab my heart, as surely as if I had hung out a "Vacancy" sign. So it was early this summer, while I was doing behavioral assessments at the Humane Society of Washington County, where my husband, Paul, serves as the executive director.

As is my custom on the day that I do assessments, I made a quick pass through the kennels before picking up paperwork for the day's list of dogs. In one ward, a brindle-and-white pixie with huge stand-up ears, a low-rider body and an excessively generous tail with one decisive curl in the middle captured my attention. A Corgi pup? I glanced at her kennel card. Sure enough—a 5-month-old Corgi, and a Cardigan at that. (Pembrokes are the Corgis with short tails, Cardigans have long tails.)

I have long been enchanted by Corgis, and occasionally fancied adding one to the family some day. Perhaps this was the time?

Dashing back to the Operations Center, I placed the Corgi's paperwork on the top of the stack. I was determined not to make *too* rash a decision—we would at least evaluate her before I lost my heart.

I recently had the opportunity to take (and test!) my own advice about bringing a new dog home. This is Lucy, the newest member of my household.

Develop a List of Desired Traits

In my case, I knew that I was looking for a small to medium-sized dog, with a preference for a short-coated female. With three other dogs in our home already, smaller would be a better space-fit than larger, and with a male dog (neutered) at home who could sometimes be aggressive with other male dogs, estrogen seemed like a wiser choice than testosterone. I lean toward the herding and working breeds; I like their genetically-programmed work ethic. As much as I adore the most recent addition to our canine family (Dubhy), I really wanted a dog who was more hard-wired to work closely with people, and one who would (I hope) grow up to be highly social with people and other dogs. And I like to adopt dogs who are 5-10 months old—past the worst of the puppy stuff, but still young enough to be programmable. With that checklist in mind, the young Corgi seemed to fit the bill—so far.

The results of her assessment were mixed. On the positive side:

1. She was highly social; she couldn't get enough of the humans on the assessment team—so much so that I was confident she'd be a good off-leash hiking partner on the farm.

2. She was very bright and trainable; she quickly learned to offer sits during the training portion of the process.

3. She was resilient and non-assertive, responded well to the startle test, and offered appeasement signals rather than aggression during the "stranger danger" test.

In the negative column:

1. She did pretty persistent tail-chasing during the evaluation. Uh-oh…a dog with obsessive-compulsive behaviors at the tender age of 5 months. That's a red flag!

2. She never stopped moving. This little girl is clearly more energetic than the average dog.

3. She was very vocal—and her voice was very shrill.

Despite my intent to make an unemotional clear-headed decision, I was smitten. I carried her into Paul's office and set her on the floor. He looked at her, glanced at my face, smiled, and said, "When are we doing the paperwork?"

We weren't quite that foolhardy. We were confident that Tucker and Katie could manage to live with her, but knowing that Dubhy can be selective about his canine friends, we arranged to bring him in to meet her. If he gave the nod of approval, we would adopt. One week later, Lucy (short for "Footloose and Fancy Free"), joined the Miller family.

As we set about assimilating Lucy into our social group, I was humbled by the reminder of how challenging it really can be to adopt a young dog in sore need of good manners training. There's nothing like having to use the suggestions and instructions yourself that you routinely offer your clients to give you a much better appreciation for how well they sometimes work—and sometimes don't.

Modify to the Individual

There are exceptions to every rule. No matter how well a technique may work with *most* dogs, there are *some* dogs who require their owners to stay flexible and be willing to tailor the technique to their needs.

Case in point: I frequently use tethering in my training center and often offer it as a solution for dogs whose behaviors need to be under better management and control in the home. Such a simple, elegant solution—what could possibly go wrong? I was about to find out.

Lucy's initial introduction to the rest of the pack was easy. We let them meet in the back yard, where the open space was more conducive to successful relationships. As we had expected, she offered appropriate appeasement behaviors to Katie, "the Kelpie Queen" and was permitted to exist. She and Dubhy had already met, and seemed to remember each other. She wriggled her way up Tucker and he accepted her annoying puppy presence easily.

Indoors, however, we discovered that at the tender age of five months she was already a dedicated cat-chaser. Perfect time for a tether, I thought—and quickly discovered that she still charged the cats when they entered the room, only to hit the end of the tether at full speed, moving a very heavy coffee table several feet, and risking injury to her neck. Tethered in my office, she promptly began guarding the entire space as her own with ear-splitting barks and ugly faces.

She also gave shrill voice any time she was left tethered by herself in a room for even a brief moment. Leaving her a stuffed Kong™ or other valuable chew toy simply elicited serious resource-guarding behavior toward the other dogs. Too much tether time also triggered the obsessive/compulsive tail-chasing that worried me during her evaluation. Life quickly became very stressful. I experienced more than a few "What have I done?" moments.

Ultimately—as in *four months later!*—I finally succeeded in getting Lucy to lie by my chair rather than chase the cats. To accomplish this I had to use less tethering and more counter-conditioning and desensitization ("Cats make *really* good treats happen!"). Our cats can again tread softly into the living room to spend the evening on our laps without fear of a Corgi attack.

Appreciate the Successes

On the bright side, Lucy was everything I had hoped for in other areas. Our first day home, we went for a long hike with the rest of the pack. Halfway through I took a deep breath, crossed my fingers and unclipped her leash. As I had hoped, she stayed with the other dogs, and came flying back when I called her.

I smiled to see her bounding through hayfields, leaping after the butterflies that scattered in her path. She quickly learned to paddle in the pond and stick her head down ground-hog holes with the other dogs. She will even happily traipse alongside my horse as we ride the trails—an even better energy diffuser than hikes with the pack! The daily exercise did wonders for her tail chasing, which vanished in less than a week, returned when we had to restrict her activity following spay surgery, and vanished again as soon as she could run in the fields.

Feeding time was another challenge. Lucy's propensity to resource-guard gave rise to a few dramatic meals, but the other dogs solved this one for me. Dubhy, a skilled resource-guarder in his own right, quickly set her straight about intruding on *his* dinner, and Lucy decided that she was best off with her nose in her own bowl. I knew that the commonly offered solution of feeding in crates wouldn't work for her. She already guarded her crate space from the other dogs. Adding food to the crate equation would have been a disaster!

Lucy also came with some other behavior challenges. When taking treats, her hard mouth—"sharky"—actually drew blood from my fingers during our first few weeks together. This time, the advice I usually give worked, although it took longer than I expected, and it was even more difficult in the presence of the other dogs.

It took more time with her than it usually takes with other dogs, but Lucy learned to gently take treats from my hand.

I began offering treats to her enclosed in my fist. If she bit hard enough to hurt, I said "Ouch!" and kept my fist closed until her mouth softened. When she was gentle, I opened my hand and fed her the treat. It was a delight to feel her begin to deliberately soften her bite, even in the presence of the other dogs or with a very high value reward. Now, five months later, I realize I haven't "Ouched" for several weeks. Progress does happen!

Think Outside the Box

When a tried-and-true approach doesn't work, don't persist in hammering that square peg into a round hole. Instead, be creative and try to adopt your favored approach to your dog's situation.

Lucy decided early on that she doesn't like going out the back door to the fenced yard. She quickly learned the back door means she'll be out in the back yard for a while with the other dogs. She much prefers the side door, which means either hikes in the field, stall-cleaning time, or off to the training center—all of which she adores.

All my first responses to the problem only made it worse. The door is at the end of a narrow hallway, so calling her, walking down the hall and turning to face her, only made her less interested in going out. I tried continuing through the door onto the back deck myself, with no luck. Luring with treats worked twice; she got wise to that very quickly. Even though she is pack-oriented, she never fell for the trick of chasing the rest of the dogs enthusiastically out the door. Reaching for her collar to lead her out made her wary of my hands moving toward her.

We finally found two strategies that worked, and continue to use them both in hopes of getting her *happy* about going out the door rather than just tolerating it:

- Fetch! Lucy *loves* retrieving, so I have made it a point to frequently pair going out the back door with an energy-eating round of fetch the doggie disc.
- Leash! While Lucy quickly learned to avoid my reaching for her collar, she is perfectly happy to munch a treat from one hand while I slide a slip lead over her head with the other. Once leashed, she follows willingly out the back door and stands while I feed another treat and slip the leash off her head.

It took several months, but Lucy learned how to accept her time on a tether rather calmly.

Patience Pays Off

I counsel owners not to adopt a second dog until the first is trained, because the difficulties encountered when trying to train two at once are more than most people can successfully take on. It's challenging enough to train one dog—and it's even harder to get much done if two or more dogs are out of control at the same time.

Although my other dogs are reasonably well trained, I made it a point to work with Lucy separately, at least at first, until she knew a new behavior, before I asked her to do it in the company of her canine companions. I had the luxury of a separate training center to work in, but even if I hadn't, I could have worked with Lucy outside while the others were in, or vice versa. I could have trained Lucy in one room while the other dogs were shut in another part of the house, or crated them with yummy food-stuffed Kongs so they didn't feel deprived while I focused my attentions on the new kid. A dog can even learn to sit quietly in his own spot while watching another in training, knowing that the reward of his own turn is coming soon.

Lucy is nowhere near perfect. While she heels beautifully in the training center, she'll still pull on leash outside unless she's wearing a front-clip no-pull harness. I found myself losing my patience with her pulling until I started using the harness. Now we both have more fun when she has to walk on a leash. We both prefer the off-leash hikes, of course.

She still jumps up, but not nearly as much as she did at first. Our persistence in ignoring the jumping up and rewarding polite greetings is paying off. She still has a shrill voice, but doesn't use it quite as often as she used to. I must constantly remind myself—and Paul—to redirect her behavior when she's barking, rather than falling into the natural trap of yelling at her to be quiet.

She now spends a lot of time lying quietly on my office floor instead of traumatizing kitties, hasn't chased her tail in months, and chews only on toys provided for that purpose. She hasn't had an accident in the house for several weeks now, and although she and Katie have small arguments almost daily, I don't usually have to intervene.

Last night, as Paul and I sat watching TV, I looked up at all the dogs sleeping quietly on their beds, and realized that it's been quite some time since I've had one of those "What have we done?!" moments. She has become a full-fledged member of the pack. She will never be Dusty, but she is Lucy, and that's all she needs to be to stake her own claim to my heart. I hope your next adoption goes as well.

Be a Benevolent Leader

Why you shouldn't worry about
being "dominant" to your dog pack

Dominance has become something of a dirty word in many dog-training circles, and for good cause. Behaviorists once used the word to appropriately define a relationship between two individuals in a social group. However, over recent decades, the word has been warped and twisted to inappropriately describe an assertive dog's personality. It is also often applied to misinterpretations of normal, non-assertive dog behavior.

Sadly, "dominance" has been used as justification to inflict a litany of punishments on dogs, especially those dogs who react defensively to force-based training methods. In the past, if a dog responded to compulsion-based training or punishment by defending himself with a growl or a snap, this was interpreted as "dominance" and defiance. In addition, many natural, normal dog behaviors such as the desire to sleep on soft surfaces (beds and sofas), jumping up in greeting, and an eagerness to dash through doorways to get to the great outdoors, were also interpreted by some people as "dominant" behaviors that needed correcting.

According to these outdated theories, a dog's *owners* should be the only dominant figures in the household, and they were exhorted to establish dominance over their dogs by being forceful. We were cautioned by our trainers and by the dog-training books of the day not to tolerate any of your dogs' resistance—and warned that if we failed to fiercely squash any opposition, disaster would ensue. We were urged to leap to the offense if a dog objected to our rough handling, and told to apply violent techniques such as scruff shakes and alpha rolls if our dogs dared resist.

Some trainers went even further, advocating extremely abusive methods such as hanging a dog by the choke chain and leash, "helicoptering" him in the air at the end of a chain and leash, or holding his head in a hole filled with water until unconsciousness for behaviors ranging from something as mild as digging to as serious as aggression.

We're Past That

Fortunately for dogs, modern behavioral science has moved past the simplistic notion that a dog owner's absolute dominance will solve all (or any) of a dog's behavior or training issues. This is especially true in cases involving a dog who "fights back" when physically hurt or frightened. Severe physical punishments may force a dog to fear the person meting out the punishment, or become violent in return.

Today's positive trainers recognize the importance of the relationship between dogs and their owners, and realize that, while force-based methods *can* effectively train dogs, they also risk damaging the relationship between dog and owner, sometimes beyond repair.

Gentle, humane training methods are as effective as pain-based techniques (if not more so), and can accomplish the same training goals without force and the attendant risk of negative reactions such as fear and aggression that are possible whenever force is applied.

Ideally your dog feels secure and confident with your leadership, in a friendly and mutually beneficial relationship. He "works" for you because it gets him what he wants.

Learning to Lead

A good leader doesn't need to be violent—she simply needs to create an environment where it is easy and rewarding for her followers to comply with her wishes, and difficult for them to make mistakes. She helps them succeed. Attending a positive training class with your dog is a good place to start establishing yourself as a benevolent leader to your dog. A training class helps you and your dog understand each other better, and your trainer can help the two of you problem solve if the road gets bumpy along the way.

A successful leader/owner controls valuable resources (food, toys) and shares them with her dogs generously and judiciously. Appropriate behaviors earn rewards. Inappropriate behaviors do not. If resources are consistently awarded on the basis of desirable behaviors, and withheld in the presence of undesirable behaviors, what dog in his right mind would not choose to be well-behaved? It's no different than teaching a toddler that he has to say "Please" to get a cookie rather than scream "Gimme!" at the top of his lungs while his face turns blue.

Dominance Myths

When the "you have to dominate your dog" concept was in vogue, many trainers instructed their clients to establish "dominance" (used incorrectly here) over their dogs. This was supposed to be accomplished by, among other things, eating before the dog eats, going through doorways before the dog, and routinely rolling the dog on his back in a show of force.

Fortunately, current and in-depth behavior studies have shown that in wild *and* domesticated dogs it's *not true* that the pack leader always eats first, goes through doorways first, or routinely rolls other pack members onto their backs to keep them in line. She may be *able* to do all those things if she wants, but it really is in the pack's best interest—and hers—to be in a state of equilibrium that doesn't involve a constant show of force.

When there is plenty of food to go around, there is no need for the pack leader to assert herself at the feed trough. If she is eager to go through a door, she may *choose* to go first, in which case lower-ranking pack members defer to her.

And anyone who has ever watched a group of dogs greeting and interacting quickly realizes that a "belly-up" posture on the part of a subordinate dog is usually voluntary. In fact, this voluntary submission posture normally triggers a response in the more assertive dog to call a truce. If one dog violently forces another onto his back and/or ignores the subordinate dog's voluntary attempt at appeasement, the "underdog" is probably fighting for his life.

Similarly, the dog who is being alpha rolled by an owner may also fear for his life and, terrified by his owner's inexplicable violence, fight back accordingly.

Lower-ranking pack members show their deference to the leader with a number of body-language behaviors. Dubhy has learned the fine art of appeasing our very assertive Kelpie by keeping his eyes averted to avoid Katie's intense Kelpie glare. As long as he avoids eye-contact, she lets him pass without comment. He has, in essence, learned to say "please."

Teaching Your Dog to Ask

Your dog need not physically submit to you by offering his vulnerable underside—he only needs to *defer*. There are a number of quick and easy exercises you can insert painlessly into your daily routine to remind your dog that *you* are in charge of the resources, and he receives them thanks to your benevolence.

- **Say Please for meals:** It is perfectly okay to feed your dog *before* you eat your own meal—as long as you remind your dog that you control the food bowl. For starters there should be no free-feeding. If your dog can pick from his dish whenever he wants, you allow him to believe that *he* controls the very valuable food-bowl resource, and you miss a golden opportunity to reinforce deference one or more times a day. (I feed my adult dogs twice a day.)

  Each mealtime, after preparing your dog's food, lift the bowl off the counter with his meal in it, and hold it at your chest. Wait for him to sit. If necessary, move the bowl over his head to lure the sit, or ask him to sit verbally. When he sits, tell him he's a good boy and lower the bowl toward the floor. If he starts to get up, say "Oops" and lift the bowl to chest level again. Keep doing this until you can set the bowl on the floor without him moving. Then tell him "Okay!" and encourage him to eat.

  This is actually engaging in a little friendly food-guarding, a concept his canine brain should grasp easily. You are saying, "This food is really mine, because, as leader, all things belong to me, but because I'm nice I'm letting you have some of *my* food."

- **Say Please to go outside:** Anytime you are going to open a door to the outside world, ask your dog to "Wait." Open the door a crack, and if he starts to go through, say "Oops" and gently close the door. *Caution: do not slam the door on his nose!* Then tell him "Wait!" and open the door a crack again. If he stays still, tell him he's a good boy and close the door again. Gradually work up until you can open the door wide and he doesn't go through unless you tell him he can.

  Sometimes you will release him with an "Okay" so he can run out the door into his fenced yard; sometimes you will go through the door and then invite him out; and sometimes you will go through and close it behind you, leaving him in the house.

You are telling him, "This is *my* door. I get to decide who goes through, and when. Sometimes you can go first, sometimes I go first, and sometimes you don't get to go through at all."

If you have more than one dog, vary the order in which you release them so that each goes first some of the time.

- **Say Please for treats:** Take advantage of every opportunity to instill "Sit" as a default behavior—the thing the dog will do when he's not sure what to do. Instead of popping a treat in his mouth just because he's cute and you love him, wait for a sit—then pop the treat in his mouth.

  You are telling him, "These are *my* treats, and I will share them with you if I feel like it. You can make me feel like it by sitting." A gratuitous treat is a missed opportunity to reinforce sit as his default behavior.

- **Say Please for greeting:** When your dog runs up to greet you, all excited because he hasn't seen you for at least three full minutes, watch him closely. If he gathers himself to jump on you, say "Oops!" and turn your back. Watch him over your shoulder, and when he settles solidly on all fours, or even better, sits (because that has become his default behavior) say "Yes!" and turn back to greet him. If he jumps up, turn away again. Keep repeating until he will sit politely to be greeted.

  You are telling him, "I am the leader, and as leader, my greeting is a valuable resource that I only give to dogs who are sitting."

- **Say Please for fun:** Does your dog like to chase the ball? Play tug-o-war? Visit with his canine pals at the park? Go for a ride in the car? A walk on the leash? A swim in the pond? Precede all his favorite activities with a polite sit. "Sit" makes the ball go. "Sit" brings the tug toy to dog-mouth level. "Sit" gets the leash attached for a walk, or removed for a romp in the park. "Sit" elicits the release cue for a dive into the lake. "Sit" makes all good things happen.

  If you want to take it a step further, "Sit" makes the ball go, but the dog can only go when you give him an "Okay!" or "Go" release cue. Similarly, "Sit" lowers the tug toy to mouth level, but he can only grab it when you say, "Take it!" You are telling him, "I control all these wonderful resources—you can have access to them at my whim and pleasure, when I decide you can, and not before."

- **Say Please for attention:** Rather than allowing your dog to demand your attention, make him ask by—you guessed it—sitting. If he is a big dog and you are sitting in a chair or on the sofa, a "Down" is an even better way to Say Please for attention.

  You are telling him that this very valuable resource—your attention—must be earned with a sit or a down; he doesn't get it on demand.

Kindly Controlling

You should be getting the picture by now. The more assertive your dog's personality, the more important it is that you control as many available resources as possible, and be consistent about paying them out for appropriate behavior. Whatever your dog's personality, the better you are at controlling resources and awarding them for desirable behavior, the better behaved your dog is likely to be.

The benevolent leader concept comes naturally for some people. These are the folks who always seem to end up with well-mannered dogs without appearing to think much about it—it just happens. Either they were born with good "animal instincts," or they had good human models to imitate from an early age. If it doesn't come to you naturally, don't despair, you can learn—just start asking your dog to Say Please for everything you can think of.

Positive, Not Permissive

Don't make the mistake of thinking that "positive" equates with "permissiveness." Advocates of old-fashioned methods insist that if dogs aren't taught that there are "bad" consequences for "bad" behavior, then they will never learn to be well-behaved. These people envision a generation of ill-mannered dogs running rampant because they have never been put in their place. Nothing could be further from the truth.

Certainly, some dog owners have difficulty providing the consistency and structure necessary to develop well-behaved dogs through positive training. These are most likely the very same owners who would be incapable of administering corrections consistently and effectively—the owners who would probably end up with out-of-control dogs *regardless* of what training method they chose.

Positive trainers *do* use punishment—negative punishment, that is—as a back-up for positive reinforcement that rewards desirable behaviors. Positively trained dogs learn that there are consequences for inappropriate or unwanted behaviors, but the consequences don't involve pain.

In behavioral terms, "punishment" is simply an action that decreases the likelihood that an organism will continue to perform a behavior. It doesn't have to be violent or involve pain. "Negative punishment" simply means that the dog's behavior makes a good thing go away.

Negative punishment works like this: If your dog tries to grab a food-stuffed Kong from your hand, say, "Oops!" and whisk it behind your back. His behavior has caused a good thing to go away. If his grabbing behavior causes him to lose the desired object every time he grabs, he'll quickly learn not to grab thereby decreasing grabbing behavior.

Used in combination with positive reinforcement, this is a powerful tool. When your dog realizes that grabbing doesn't get him the Kong, he will do something else, like sit (especially if you have consistently rewarded sit in the past). When he sits, say, "Yes!" and hand him the Kong, reinforcing the polite sitting behavior. You may need to prompt him to sit at first, but when he realizes that a sit gets the Kong, he will happily offer sits instead of grabbing whenever he sees something he covets in your hand.

Dogs do what works. In fact, all living things repeat behaviors that are found rewarding, and behaviors that are not rewarded tend to be extinguished (go away).

Biscuits, Not Rolls

Why you should never use the "Alpha Roll"

Teddy's owners were distraught as they explained to me on the phone why they had called. Their veterinarian had told them that their nine-week-old Golden Retriever puppy was "dominant aggressive" because he was biting their hands. He had advised them to alpha roll the pup every time he tried to bite or otherwise challenge their authority. They'd been following the vet's instructions for a week, and Teddy's aggression was getting seriously worse. They feared they would have to euthanize their pup. We made an emergency same-day appointment for a behavior consultation.

I found Teddy to be a somewhat assertive puppy, who enjoyed actively exploring the world with his mouth, as normal puppies do. Like many assertive, excitable pups, Teddy also got increasingly aroused when his owners protested his needle-sharp-toothed explorations on their skin. The more they protested, the more excited (and mouthier) he got. Hence the veterinarian's all-too-common misdiagnosis of "dominance aggression" and his woefully inappropriate prescription of alpha rolling the pup to put him in his place.

Rolling the Dice

The **alpha roll** consists of physically rolling a dog onto his side or back and holding him there until he stops resisting or struggling, supposedly submitting to your superior authority. Popularized by the Monks of New Skete in their dog-training books (such as *How to Be Your Dog's Best Friend*) in the 1980s, the technique is a truly unfortunate and dangerous interpretation of a normal canine social behavior. When approached by a higher-status dog, a lower-ranking member of the pack may first avert and lower his head and shoulders, then voluntarily lie down on the ground and perhaps roll onto his side or back as an appeasement or deference gesture. Typically, when an appeasement gesture is used, the higher-ranking canine has no need to assert himself by forcibly flattening the lower-ranking dog to the ground; the subordinate is already there!

In a real alpha roll, the dog is physically forced and pinned to the ground until he goes limp and "gives up." We've staged a mock "alpha roll" with a playful dog who was actually enjoying having his belly rubbed; however, note his tense expression when we held him firmly for even just a moment. This is a vulnerable position for a dog.

Job Michael Evans, one of the New Skete monks responsible for writing *How to Be Your Dog's Best Friend,* later left the order, and subsequently stated he regretted including the now-controversial technique in the book. While he didn't go as far as to say the alpha roll was ineffective or inappropriate, he did say he felt it wasn't safe for use by the general public.

Modern behavior professionals who are well-educated in the science of behavior and learning go much further, denouncing the risky technique along with other methods based on faulty dominance theory.

The most obvious negative consequence of techniques that encourage owners to physically overpower and intimidate their canine companions is the possibility of scaring or coercing the dog into defending himself. He reacts aggressively in return, angering or frightening his owner, who often responds by escalating his own level of violence. Before you know it, the relationship between the two is seriously, sometimes irreparably, damaged.

Despite compelling evidence that physical intimidation does more harm than good, some trainers today (indeed, some very high-profile ones) are stubbornly attached to the forced roll-over, cloaking it in new-age terms and turning a blind eye to the damage done to relationships between dogs and their humans in the process.

Questions of appropriateness aside, it takes someone skilled in handling dogs to be able to alpha roll a dog without significant risk to human safety—which is at least in part why one television show where the technique is frequently used includes a "Don't try this at home" style disclaimer. It's also why trainers who employ methods such as the alpha roll talk about being bitten as "part of the job," while those who use more appropriate, non-confrontational approaches are more likely to keep their skins intact.

Canine as a Second Language

Again, the alpha roll is supposed to mimic the behavior of the "top dog" in a pack, and send the message, "I'm the boss of you!" But one huge error in alpha roll logic is the belief that we can successfully pretend to be dogs in our interactions with our canine companions. Dogs know we're not dogs, and any attempt on our part to mimic their language is doomed to failure.

Dogs are masters at speaking and reading canine body language. Their communications with each other are often subtle and nuanced, a furry ballet designed to keep peace in the pack. Our efforts to use canine body communications are oafish in comparison—and I imagine that our dogs are alternately amused, confused, nonplussed, and terrified by our clumsy attempts to speak their language.

Violence occurs between dogs within established social groups when the communication system breaks down; it's a sign of an unhealthy pack relationship. Ethology studies from the 1970s and 1980s suggest that canine social structure holds together because appeasement behaviors are *offered* by subordinate members, not because higher-ranking members aggressively demand subservience. Instead, successful pack leaders were observed to calmly control the good stuff—an approach frequently suggested by today's modern, positive trainers as a much safer, more appropriate, and effective method for creating a harmonious mixed-species social group.

In her book, *Clinical Behavioral Medicine for Small Animals,* Dr. Karen Overall agrees, stating, "The behavior of the lower status individuals, *not* the higher ranking one, is what determines the relative hierarchical rank. Truly high-ranking animals are tolerant of lower-ranking ones."

Methods that encourage dogs to offer deference behaviors, and then reward them for it, are a much closer approximation of actual pack behavior—and easier for us to emulate successfully—than any application of force. Use biscuits (training treats), not (alpha) rolls!

Establishing Leadership

The Monks, and others like them, didn't have it *all* wrong. It *is* important that your dog perceive his humans as higher-ranking member of your collective multi-species social group. It is far better, safer, and ultimately more effective, however, to accomplish this through offered deference rather than forced dominance.

In his text, *Handbook of Applied Dog Behavior and Training, Volume Two: Etiology and Assessment of Behavior Problems,* Steven R. Lindsay, a dog behavior consultant in Philadelphia, says, "A wise lupine leader avoids unnecessary dominance contests and assertions of authority."

Lindsay also cites a 1988 study (E. Fonberg, "Dominance and Aggression"), noting that dominance that is established without resorting to aggression appears to be more stable than dominance that is maintained by constant vigilance and displays of strength.

There is a multitude of ways to establish appropriate social hierarchy without resorting to aggression. No, you don't have to go through all doorways first, nor do you have to eat before your dog does. You can simply wait for and/or encourage your dog to offer deference behaviors in order to make good stuff happen, while at the same time you make sure that pushy behavior doesn't result in him getting good stuff.

Your dog's driving ambition in life is to get good stuff. Some owners and trainers express concern that teaching the dog that he can get you to Click! and give him a treat by offering certain behaviors elevate his status because *he's* controlling *you.* In reality, a dog's psychological response to deference behaviors appears to so hardwired that if a dog repeatedly performs them, he *becomes* deferent. It's not just a role he's playing, like an actor. If he *does* deference, he *is* deferent. He can't help it.

Deference behaviors you can use to your relationship advantage include:

- **Wait at the door.** Dog sits and waits to go through a door, even a wide open one, until you give him permission to move forward (good stuff = go out and have fun).

- **Wait for your dinner.** Dog sits and waits to eat his meal until you give him permission to eat (good stuff = eat food!).

- **Wait to get in car.** Dog sits and waits outside car while door is opened, hatchback is lifted, or tailgate lowered, until you give him permission to jump in (good stuff = go somewhere in the car and have fun).

- **Wait to get out of the car.** Dog sits and waits in vehicle while car door is opened, hatchback is lifted, or tailgate lowered, until you give him permission to jump out (good stuff = get out of car and have fun).

- **Wait to get out of kennel, crate, or exercise pen.** Dog sits quietly waiting to be let out (good stuff = get out of kennel, crate, or pen and get attention and have fun.)

- **Sit for your leash.** Dog sits calmly to go out for a walk while leash is attached to collar (good stuff = go for walk).

- **Ask to be petted.** Dog sits and waits politely at your feet to be petted rather than jumping up, pawing, or nudging you for attention (good stuff = petting and attention).

- **Ask for permission to jump on sofa or bed.** Dog sits and waits to be invited onto furniture instead of jumping up uninvited (good stuff = lying on soft, comfortable surface and getting attention).

In each case, the dog learns to offer deference behavior in order to get the desired "good stuff" result. Appropriate (deference) behavior moves him closer to his goal; inappropriate behavior makes the good stuff go away.

Happy Endings

That phone call from Teddy's owners came almost 10 years ago, early in my career as a professional behavior consultant. Although I had handled many aggressive dogs during the 20 years I worked at the Marin Humane Society, I had not yet worked with a lot of aggression-modification cases professionally. I agreed to see Teddy, with the understanding that I would refer him to someone more experienced if I felt I wasn't capable of handling his case.

He turned out to be one of the simplest aggression cases I've ever worked with. He just needed his people to stop frightening him with their unpredictable eruptions of violence so he could stop having to defend himself.

We began training with clicks and treats. Teddy loved the clicker game, and caught on very quickly to the concept that a "Click!" equals "treat"—and even better, that he could *make* the Click! happen by offering one of a growing list of desirable behaviors. We used a tether to restrain Teddy during training so if he *did* do inappropriate mouthing we could simply say "Oops!" and step out of reach of his nasty-sharp baby teeth.

In the very first session his arousal and biting lessened noticeably. By the time I returned for the second session, the mouthing problem was 95 percent resolved, Teddy's owners were tearfully grateful, and we happily moved on with his basic training.

Since Teddy, I've lost count of the number of "aggression" cases I've handled where the alpha roll was the clear and present *cause* of a dog's increasing aggression. A frightening number of puppy/dog owners are still counseled by their veterinarians, trainers, other animal professionals, and well-intentioned friends to alpha roll their uncooperative canines.

It's always better to get your dog to voluntarily buy into your desired behaviors than to try to force him. That's the challenge, the joy, and the excitement of positive training. As the supposedly more intelligent species, we should be able to figure out how to get dogs to want to do what we want, including being deferent to us, without the use of force. Biscuits, not rolls!

Your Pet's Pet Peeves

Five ways you annoy and confuse your dog

Eavesdrop on a group of dog owners discussing their dogs, and along with a lot of brags about newly-trained behaviors and hard-won trophies and titles, you're likely to hear a fair number of complaints about the annoying things their canine companions do. Well guess what? If you could eavesdrop on a pack of dogs at the dog park, you might well hear a litany of things that humans do to annoy their dogs!

Of course, dogs can't talk, and, aside from a few animal psychics we can't claim to really know what they're thinking, but we can make some pretty good guesses. If we *could* take a survey, compile the results and list our dogs' top five pet peeves, I'm guessing here's what they might tell us.

1. They Treat Me Like a Monkey!

Dogs are canids; humans are primates. Our two species have hardwired behaviors that make us what and who we are. The physical differences are obvious—dogs have fur and tails, and walk on four legs. We are naked and tailless, walk on two-legs, and have opposable thumbs.

The behavioral differences aren't always as noticeable, but they are well-documented. To their credit, dogs are far better at observing, analyzing and manipulating the behavior of humans than most humans are of dogs. For example, current thinking about the history of the dog-human relationship now holds that rather than humans deliberately domesticating dogs, it's more likely that dogs adopted humans, recognizing early man's leftovers and garbage as a reliable source of food, with the boldest and tamest members of the dog packs self-selecting for ever-bolder-and-tamer genes in their pups. Eventually, Dog was sleeping at the hearth of Man.

Still, they are dogs, not furry, four-legged humans, and as dogs, they have an inherited package of social behaviors that differs significantly from ours. We approach other humans head-on, make direct eye contact, and reach out to shake hands, hug and kiss. Dogs generally approach each other from the side, avoid direct eye contact unless they intend to challenge, and if one dog puts a paw "around" another it's probably an aggressive move (unless done in mutually agreeable play).

Yet we insist on imposing our primate greetings on dogs. Not just on our *own* dogs, who might reasonably be expected to tolerate rude behavior from their own humans, but even on strange dogs we encounter. Watch any random group of humans greet dogs that they don't know. From very young children all the way to senior citizens, the majority will try to pat dogs on top of the head, gaze meaningfully into their eyes, even hug and kiss them.

Even those of us who know better do this… I hug and kiss our dogs—especially Dubhy, who is most tolerant of my monkey-ness. I can't help it—he's *so huggable!* He puts up with my attentions in exchange for the pleasure of lying on his back in my lap and getting a tummy rub—which he adores. I used **classical conditioning**—associating the joy of tummy rubbing with the less desirable hugging—to get him to accept, perhaps even enjoy human arms around his fuzzy body and human lips on the top of his head and the tip of his nose. I'm much more careful to use appropriate greetings with dogs I don't know, however!

You have a couple of options if you want to avoid annoying dogs with primate social behaviors. With strange dogs, your best bet is to avoid direct eye contact, offer a hand slowly, palm up, and reach under the chin to scratch rather than over the head to pat, kneel to greet rather than bending over from the waist, and *don't hug or kiss*!

You should resist hugging and/or kissing dogs unless you know them very well, and you have worked to condition them to tolerate, or better yet, enjoy this type of contact. Does this dog look happy?

With your own dogs, you can either avoid egregiously primate behavior, or condition your dog to enjoy pats, hugs and kisses by associating them with really good stuff—like tummy rubs, treats, ear scratches, toys, and play.

Remember, this is not just about greeting. If your dog barely suffers your head-pats, and you think you're rewarding him for a desirable behavior by patting him on the head, think again—you could actually be punishing him, thereby decreasing the behavior rather than reinforcing it. Watch him the next time you reach to pat his head. Does he close his eyes blissfully and lean into your hand? If so, then he really likes it! But if he moves away, flattens his ears, ducks his head or otherwise looks less than joyful, it's time to rethink your primate behaviors.

2. They Leave Me Alone Too Often!

Canids and primates are both social species; it's one of the reasons we get along with each other as well as we do. In addition to the need for food, water and some amount of shelter from the elements, we share an inborm need for close and regular interaction with others from our social group.

My husband and I moved to Maryland from a state whose culture held the common view that dogs belong in the back yard, preferably in a pen. My husband, who was director of the city animal services division, was taken aback by the number of calls he got from owners asking for help catching *their own dogs*. In each case, the dog had escaped from his pen and, although still in a fenced back yard, could not be recaptured by the owner. Paul finally asked one caller why he even *had* a dog, if all he did was keep it in a pen in the yard. The owner answered, "I just like looking out the window and seeing him there."

Keeping a dog in a pen 24/7 falls woefully short of meeting a dog's needs for mental and physical stimulation. I doubt there are any well informed readers who would consider a pen in a yard to be an adequate environment for a canine companion. Still, I would bet that many otherwise responsible dog guardians fall somewhat short of meetings their dogs' needs. If your dog is crated at night and lies around on his foam dog bed all day waiting for you to come home from work, you'd best be setting aside some quality morning and evening time for Rover.

A walk-on-leash around the block is an exercise *hors d'oeurve* for many dogs. Barring physical infirmity or other frailty, every dog deserves a good aerobic workout—if not every day, at least every other day. If you don't feel like a hike in the hills with your dog frolicking on a long-line, or off leash with a solid recall, at least give him a good round of Frisbee™ or tennis ball retrieves in the back yard on a reliably frequent basis. Not only will he be healthier, but it will help with behavior problems as well. A tired dog is a well-behaved dog.

While you're at it, don't forget mental exercise. When's the last time you and Rover learned something new together? Maybe it's time the two of you signed up for a Freestyle class or Rally obedience. Other brainteasers? Find a good book on teaching tricks and start having more fun with your dog while challenging canine and human brain cells.

Next time your dog brings you his leash or a toy, and says he wants to go for a walk or play with you, don't dismiss him in annoyance and promise him a walk on the weekend. If you just want something to look at, get a picture of a dog and hang it on your wall. Life is short—play now!

3. They Ignore Me When I'm Good!

Dogs may not be able to articulate the principles of **operant conditioning**, but they understand them perfectly—especially the part about "Behaviors that are reinforced will increase." The flip side of that says, "Behaviors that are not reinforced will decrease and eventually extinguish."

We are a busy culture. We tend to ignore our dogs when they are behaving themselves, and pay attention when they are being difficult. By doing so, in essence we are punishing appropriate behaviors, and reinforcing inappropriate behaviors. That's backwards!

Dogs must find it frustrating when they perform a beautifully appropriate and rewardable behavior (such as sitting to greet you) and you are oblivious.

"Hey!" your dog thinks. "I'm sitting! Don't I get a Click! and treat? Or at least a word of praise and a scratch behind the ear?" Preoccupied with planning dinner, or tomorrow's budget meeting, you walk right past your sitting dog. "'Scuse me," your dog says as he puts his paws up on your $400 business suit and snags a thread. "Aren't you supposed to reward me for sitting to greet you?" "Not now, Rover!" you snap as you push him away. "Well," he sighs, "at least she spoke to me and touched me. I'll have to try jumping up again next time."

It's easy to forget to pay attention to good behavior. You're busy on your computer keyboard, and he's sleeping quietly in the corner. He's finally calm, and you don't want to rile him up again. Just quietly croon to him, "Goooooood boy," in a low voice. Or lean over and gently drop a treat in front of his nose. Make a pledge to notice (and reinforce) your dog's good behavior at least three times a day. You'll be surprised by how easy it really is.

Make it a point frequently to "catch" your dog when he's doing what you'd like him to do with-out being told to do it, such as settling himself down and lying quietly near you while you work. Occasionally reward the behavior with praise and a treat.

4. Humans Are So Inconsistent!

Dogs don't understand special occasions, or "just this once." They do best with structure and consistency. If you let Rover up on the sofa today, don't be surprised if he jumps up and makes himself at home tomorrow while you're off at work. The best-behaved dogs are generally those who live in structured, consistent environments—where they can learn early on what works, and what doesn't.

The best way to avoid confusing your dog with lack of consistency is to set clear house rules and make sure the whole family follows them. Some of the things you may want to address in your family "Dog Rules" meeting might include:

- Is Rover allowed on any furniture? Some furniture? All furniture?
- Where will the dog sleep? In a crate? On someone's bed? In whose room?
- When and where is he fed? Who is responsible for making sure he gets fed?
- Where is his bathroom? In the back yard? Anywhere in the back yard, or in a designated spot? Who is his bathroom monitor?
- Who will train him? One person? The whole family? How do we make sure everyone is using the same training methods, philosophies and cues?
- What games are okay to play? What are the "rules" of the games?
- What do we do about undesirable behavior? What if we "catch" him having an accident in the house? What if he tries to nip? What if he barks too much? What if he chews something? What if he chases the cat?
- Who will walk him? Exercise him?

Keep notes at the meeting, and write up the results. Post a list on the refrigerator of agreed-upon rules so everyone can remember to be consistent with the dog. If something isn't working, discuss it and modify rules as needed.

Then remember that every time you are with your dog, you are training him. Make mental notes of behaviors he does that you like, and figure out how to consistently reinforce those. Make note of those you don't like, and devise a plan to manage the behaviors so he can't get rewarded for them. When he tries, divert him to a more acceptable, incompatible behavior. For example, if he jumps up, consistently reinforce sitting instead—he can't jump up and sit at the same time.

The more consistent you can be with your reinforcements and your management, the sooner your dog's world will make sense to him and the easier life will be for you both.

5. Human Expectations Are So Unreasonable!

Imagine how upsetting it would be if your spouse announced one day that you were going to be his training partner for preparing to run the Boston Marathon—and you have bad knees and asthma. It's not any different than if you decided you wanted your English Bulldog to start training for world-class competitive agility—especially if his favorite activity is napping with you on your recliner. Certainly, a Bulldog could have fun doing agility, but if you expect him to outrun Border Collies, you'll *both* end up upset and frustrated.

Your relationship with your dog will be much more rewarding for the two of you if you know and understand your dog's talents and limitations, and work with them. If you have a Beagle or a Bloodhound, rather than being annoyed that his nose is always on the ground, get excited about a future in tracking. Maybe you can do Search and Rescue together, or develop a new career finding missing pets! If your Australian Kelpie drives you crazy chasing things that move, don't lose your cool over your herding fool—get yourself a flock of sheep or Indian Runner ducks for her to round up and give her a meaningful job to do. Compatible cats may do, in a pinch.

Your Pomeranian may never win the Iditarod, but he could be a lovely Freestyle partner, or the "size" dog on a Flyball team. Be open to whatever gifts your dog has to share with you, and let them guide you to activities that you can find mutually rewarding. As Leslie Nelson, noted author and trainer, said at the recent Association of Pet Dog Trainers conference, "Appreciate (and love) the dog you have, not the one you wish you had."

If you are successful at fixing the things you do to annoy your dog, you may be pleasantly surprised to find that he does fewer things to annoy you as well. Then, next time you're standing around with a group of dog owners who are complaining about their dog's annoying behaviors, you'll happily have nothing to contribute. Wouldn't that be nice!

What You Can Do

- Make a commitment to improve your relationship with your own dogs by fixing the things you do that annoy them.

- Be aware of your body language around strange dogs—don't annoy them with rude primate behaviors.

- Read *The Other End of the Leash* by Patricia McConnell to advance your understanding of the relationship between canids and primates.

Fun and Games

*Build your relationship, solidify your
dog's obedience, and have a blast*

Training is about relationship. While basic good manners and other more complex lessons are undeniably an important part of training, the most successful dog/owner teams are those who have cultivated the relationship at the same time they are learning the ins and outs of "Sit," "Down," "Stay," and all the other things a dog needs to know. In other words, the best teams are those who remember to have fun together along the way.

By the way: Just about everything presented here regarding dogs also applies to puppies— it *especially* applies to pups! That's because puppies are irrepressible fun machines. They romp, they play, they chase, they chew, they wrestle—in fact for a good part of your first six to 12 months with your new pup you will probably spend a lot of time trying to convince him to have a little less fun!

Be careful that you don't go overboard. If you insist that he be *too* serious, he'll *forget* how to play, and you'll end up with a lump of overweight canine who doesn't even want to accompany you on your walks around the block. Instead, engage your pup—and later, your dog—in structured games that direct his play-energy into appropriate channels, reinforce his play behaviors, reward his sense of humor, and keep the relationship flames burning bright.

Fun games for Fido go far beyond fetching a tennis ball or a Frisbee™. I'm going to assume you know the old stand-bys, and introduce you to some that you may not have thought of. There are games you and Fido can play together, games the whole family can play, and games you and Fido can play with your friends and their dogs. Some of the best games also have practical applications, but don't let the practical aspects override the play. Have fun!

Find It!

Ever wonder how those drug dogs do what they do? You can teach your dog to find stuff with his nose and wow your friends with his prowess. A dog's nose is a bazillion times more sensitive than ours, so this is easy for Fido, once he understands what you want. Here's how:

Step 1: Have Fido wait and watch while you "hide" a strong-smelling treat in plain view, 5-10 feet away from him. Return to his side, tell him to "Find it!" and encourage him to go get the treat. Repeat this a few times until he seems to have the idea. Most dogs catch onto this pretty quickly.

Step 2: Have Fido wait and watch you hide the treat in a less obvious place, such as behind a chair leg, under the edge of a cushion, or next to a toy. Return to his side, tell him to "Find it!" and encourage him to go get the treat. When he can do this, hide several treats while he watches, and keep encouraging him to "Find it!" until he has found them all. Repeat this until he is doing it easily. If he has trouble, *don't* show him where the treats are—you will teach him to wait for you to point them out, rather than use his nose to find them himself! Move in the general direction of the hidden treat, but don't show it to him.

Step 3: Have Fido wait where he can't see you. Hide several treats in the same places you hid them before. Bring him into the room and tell him to "Find it!" Keep encouraging him until he has found them all. If he has trouble, move in the general direction of the treat, but don't show it to him.

Step 4: Try "Find it!" with other things—a ball, or a favorite chew toy. Show your dog the ball, have him wait and watch while you hide it in an easy place, and then tell him "Find the ball!" Once he gets the idea, hide it without him watching, and tell him to "Find the ball!"

Practical Applications: Are you forever forgetting where you left you car keys, or the remote control? Let Fido find them for you. Teach him to find your kids, other family members, and friends! Our dog Josie learned how to find lost turtles; we didn't even realize we were teaching her, but it sure came in handy when our turtles escaped!

If you have a dog who exhibits mild separation anxiety when you leave, you can hide several treats and a stuffed Kong™ or two. Ask her to "Find it!" just before you leave, and she will be too busy looking for hidden goodies to worry about you leaving. If Junior gets lost in the woods, what could be more anxiety-relieving than know Fido can find him for you?

Caution: Don't hide treats in places that will encourage your dog to dig into carpets or cushions or chew furniture to get to them.

Bloodhounds aren't the only canines with good noses; any dog can be trained to search for items or people using his sense of smell. And training your dog to find your kids is a potentially lifesaving skill.

Jumping Jacks

When I was a kid, my favorite game was to put mop handles and broomsticks across chairs and run through the house jumping over them with my white Collie. Great exercise for both of us!

You may not choose to jump over the jumps with your dog (although you might be surprised to discover how much fun it is), but you can create jumps from broomsticks, scraps of woods, boxes, and other household items. You can buy materials and build simple jumps if you are handy, or splurge and buy a set of Agility or Flyball jumps to play with—as long as you promise not to get all serious just because you paid real money for them!

Step 1: Set up one low jump. If your dog is very cautious, just lay the bar on the floor and encourage your dog to step over it by luring with a treat. As he gets braver, toss treats on one side of the low jump, then the other, until he is jumping it easily. Use lots of verbal praise as well, to keep it cheerful, exciting and fun.

Step 2: When he is jumping the low jump smoothly, add a verbal cue such as "Jump!" or "Hup!" or "Over!" Start using the cue just before you toss the treat.

Step 3: To fade the use of the treat, make a motion with your hand as if you were tossing the treat, then give the verbal cue. After your dog jumps, *then* toss the treat. Eventually move to random reinforcement, where he gets a treat sometimes, but not every time he jumps. Remember to use verbal praise—your excitement will keep him enthusiastic about jumping!

Step 4: Gradually raise the jump to a height that is suitable for your dog. Vary the location and type of jumps, so your dog is very jump-versatile. You can hang towels or jackets over jump bars to change the look, put flower pots or children's toys under them—be creative!

Practical Application: Hopping over small obstacles when you are hiking in the woods; and hey, Lassie jumped over fences when she ran home to tell everyone that Timmy was in the well!

Caution: Puppies should not jump too much or too high—it can damage their soft baby bones and joints. Even adult dogs should jump primarily on giving surfaces (grass, not cement) with good traction to avoid injury and arthritis, and should not be asked to jump higher than is comfortable and safe for them. Ask your veterinarian how much jumping your dog should do.

Hide and Seek

This is easy and great fun, especially if you start with a young puppy who is still very dependent on you.

Step 1: Take your dog for a walk in an area with some trees and other objects you can hide behind. When he is busy sniffing or bird watching, hide behind a tree. Be quiet and still, but peek out so you can watch him.

Step 2: When he notices that you are gone, he should start searching for you. Let him search and find you, then make a big fuss over him with lots of yummy treats, tug with a tug toy, chase a ball, or whatever other reward is very meaningful to him. If he can't find you or doesn't look for you, help him—but just a little—by calling his name softly or making some other small sound that will get him started in the right direction.

Practical Application: This game teaches your dog to keep his eye on you—he never knows when you might disappear! It also teaches him to look for and find you if you *do* happen to get separated accidentally.

Caution: Some dogs panic if they can't find you, especially dogs prone to separation anxiety. Remember to watch your dog, and help him if he is looking anxious, *before* full-fledged panic sets in. Also, some dogs could care less about where you are. If you think your dog might just run off into the woods when you play this game, keep him on a long line when you hide so you can prevent him from leaving.

Group Games

Most of the following games can be played with the whole family, or are games you and Fido can play with your friends and their dogs. If your family has just one dog, pass him from one person to the next. Or get a group of your friends together with their dogs! Some of the following games are great party activities for 4-H or dog training club get-togethers.

Sit Around the World

This game is not only fun, but it also practices that all-important "coming when called" behavior and reinforces polite greetings.

Step 1: Arrange all available human players in a large circle in a safely enclosed area. Begin with Fido sitting in front of one person.

Step 2: Have the next person in the circle call the dog with a cheerful, enthusiastic, "Fido, Come!" You can use toys and squeakers initially, if necessary, to get Fido excited about playing the game. When Fido comes, he must sit before he gets his treat reward. Lure the sit, rather than giving the "Sit" cue, so he learns to sit in greeting without being asked.

Step 3: Have the next person in the circle call him.

Step 4: When Fido is really good about coming around the circle, you can start calling him randomly *across* the circle.

Step 5: To play this game as a competition, be sure the humans are equally spaced, and then use a stopwatch to keep track of the time it takes for Fido to come and sit for each person. The person with the fastest time, or fastest average times, is the winner.

Practical Application: Coming when called and polite greetings—how much more practical can you get! If you are a multi-dog household, try this with two or more dogs at a time, after each dog has learned the game individually.

Caution: If Fido is large and tends to jump up, small children may not be able to play this game until the dog understands the rules.

Musical Sits

For a group of dog people, this is way more fun than the human-only version of musical chairs. It can be played on several different levels, from beginner to advanced. As another variation, each game can be played only with downs instead of sits.

Easy Version: Have dogs and handlers walk to the music around orange cones in a large circle. When the music stops, all players ask the dogs to sit. Luring with treats is allowed; physically forcing the dogs to sit is not. First dog to sit wins! Repeat until everyone has had enough play.

Intermediate Version: Space rug sample squares evenly around a large circle, one fewer rug than there are dog/handler teams. Have dogs and handlers walk to the music, outside the circle of rugs. When the music stops, players must proceed to the next available rug square and have their dogs sit. The team that doesn't get a rug is out. Repeat until one team wins.

Advanced Version: Set out a double line of chairs back to back, in the center of the room, one less chair than dog/handler teams. Put rug sample squares in a large circle around the chairs, one rug per team. Have dog and handlers walk to the music outside the circle of rugs. When the music stops, players must proceed to the next available rug, put their dogs on a sit-stay, and run for a chair. Player who doesn't get a chair is out. *However,* if a dog breaks his sit-stay, the player must return to the dog, re-establish the sit-stay, and then return to her chair. Meanwhile, of course, another player can sit in the chair.

Practical Application: Great opportunity to practice leash-walking in groups, fast sits, downs, and reliable stays with *lots* of distractions.

Caution: Players can get pretty enthusiastic with this game. You may need to establish safety rules based on the surface footing of the play area and the energy level, size and strength of various players.

Diving For Dogs

Our Pomeranian loves this one so much that he starts trembling with joy and anticipation when he sees us setting it up!

Step 1: Slice several hot dogs into an equal number of thin pennies.

Step 2: Put 2 to 12 inches of water in a pan or tub. Small dogs will require a shallower "pool."

Step 3: Drop five hot dog pennies into the pan. Let the dog watch you do this. Be sure he knows they are hot dogs.

Step 4: With your stopwatch in hand, say, "Ready, Set, Go!" and start the stopwatch. On "Go," the handler releases the dog and encourages him to get the hot dogs out of the water and eat them. The dog who eats all his hot dog pieces the fastest wins.

Practical Application: None that I can think of, but is sure is fun, the dogs love it, and it's a *great* spectator sport! Actually, if you want to teach your dog to retrieve under water, this can get him started.

Caution: I have never seen it happen, but you might want to watch for a dog who risks drowning himself while "diving for dogs." Stop the game if a dog starts sputtering.

The canine (hot dog) version of "bobbing for apples" has no real training applications; it's just fun to watch!

Personal Preferences

Different types of games appeal to different human and canine personalities. There are many more games to be played than the ones I have described for you here, although I hope you found some that you liked. Talk to your dog friends and see what ideas they have. Look up "dog training games" on the Internet and see if you can find more. Pick out the ones you and your dog are most likely to enjoy, gather the equipment you need to set them up—and then go play in the yard.

Now You See It...

*How to "fade" the prompts and
lures you use to cue your dog's behavior*

Old-fashioned trainers—those who use physical corrections as a moderate-to-significant part of their training programs—often criticize positive training, saying that "foodies" (positive trainers) have to bribe their dogs to get them to do things. This is a shallow, shortsighted view of a powerful, effective tool.

It's true that in the beginning stages of positive training we do use treats, also known as lures, to show the dog what we want him to do. Some positive trainers also use visual signals and gentle physical assistance as "prompts" to communicate to the dog.

But in a good training program, as soon as the dog performs a behavior easily for a prompt or lure, the trainer proceeds to put the behavior on **cue**. A cue is the primary signal or stimulus you use to ask your dog to perform a behavior. When a dog performs a behavior on cue, quickly, anywhere, and under a wide variety of conditions, the behavior is said to be under **stimulus control**.

Many novice dog owners never make it past luring and prompting. As long as they're satisfied with that level of training, it's perfectly okay that they will always have to point, clap, or use a treat to get their dogs to perform. It's their relationship, and their choice as to how well and clearly they want to be able to communicate with their dogs.

It's impressive when you can get your dog to sit, lie down, or walk calmly at your heel with just a word or hand signal. More importantly, this accomplishment demonstrates that your dog really does understand your cue; he's not dependent on a certain context or combination of conditions and body language to "guess at" your intent.

However, there is a huge advantage to working with your dog, gradually **fading** your lures and prompts and teaching your dog to respond to verbal cues or hand signals, until she can reliably perform certain behaviors on cue. Having your dog respond to cues without prompts gives you more security and versatility in your training; your dog will respond even if she can't see you, or if your arms are full of groceries. With enough practice, your dog will even be able to respond appropriately to your cue while "tuning out" potentially dangerous distractions—say, a squirrel chattering at the foot of a tree across a busy street.

If you would like to move on to the next level of training and communication to your dog, by working to "fade" your lures and prompts and teach your dog to respond to verbal cues or hand signals, read on!

Taking It to the Next Level

Your dog is pretty well trained. You point to the floor and say "Down!" Your dog instantly drops to the floor. You ask her to sit as you touch her on her back, and she happily responds by settling onto her haunches. You hold a piece of hot dog over her head and say "Up!" and she lifts her front paws off the ground in a lovely performance of "Sit Pretty." Your friends and family are in awe of your training prowess, and comment on how well-trained your dog is. But is she, really?

From one perspective, she certainly is. She knows how to perform a long list of behaviors, and will oblige you by doing them when you ask her to.

But from another perspective, she's not. For each behavior, you're relying on back-up information to help your dog understand the cue and perform the behavior. You are using **prompts**.

Prompts are vitally important dog-training tools. We use them all the time when we train a new behavior. A **lure** is something the dog wants—a treat or toy—that you can use to demonstrate to the dog what you want her to do, by moving it and having her follow. Because dogs are not native speakers of our language, you can use a piece of hot dog or some other tasty tidbit as a "translator" to explain the behavior you want. Because dogs *are* natural body language communicators, they respond easily to physical and visual prompts.

Anything you use to back up your initial cue is considered a prompt. A food lure is a very obvious prompt. Gentle physical assistance (for example, a light touch on the dog's back to tell her to sit) is a less obvious but still very visible prompt. Hand signals are cues if they are the initial request for a behavior, but prompts if they *follow* or closely accompany the initial verbal cue, such as pointing at the floor when you ask your dog to lie down. Consciously or unconsciously, all of us also use many more subtle prompts, such as eye contact (or lack of eye contact), the way we stand or move, the position in which we hold our hands or tilt our heads—all of these can be back-up communications to our dogs when we give them a verbal cue.

The important thing to keep in mind when using lures and prompts is that the longer you continue to use them after your dog has learned a new behavior, the more dependent you both become on them, and the harder it will be to teach her to respond to a verbal cue alone.

Do Fade Away

In order to fade a prompt, whether it's a lure or a physical or visual prompt, you need to help your dog fully understand the meaning of the cue itself. At this point in your training the verbal cue is often irrelevant to the dog. It makes *you* feel good to say "Down," when you point to the floor, and you may *think* your dog "knows" the word, but here's an experiment you can try to see if your dog really understands. Point to the floor without speaking. Chances are your dog will lie down. Now say "Down" without pointing to the floor. Chances are your dog will stand there with a happy look on her face, waiting for you to translate. She really *doesn't* understand the word.

If she lies down without the point, then she *does* understand the word, and you don't *need to* point to the floor every time you ask her to lie down. You can fade your prompt just by discontinuing its use, and/or you can also use the "point" as your primary hand signal cue for down, and disassociate its use from the word.

Let's assume your dog didn't lie down on your verbal cue. Right now, she knows and understands the "point to the floor" cue as the stimulus for the behavior of "lie down." In order to give meaning to a new cue, the new cue must consistently *precede* the known cue. That means every time you ask her to down, you'll need to use your verbal "Down" cue *first*, give her a few seconds to think and respond, and then use your "point" cue if she doesn't respond to the verbal. It's as if you're saying, in canine shorthand, "Dog, the word 'Down' means the same thing as when I point to the floor."

Some dogs catch onto this translation very quickly, others take some time. If you don't feel you are making good progress try these two things:

- Wait longer after you give the verbal cue before you give the prompt. As long as she's still focused on you and the wheels seem to be turning in her doggie brain, have patience, and give her time to think it through. If you lose her attention, try again with another verbal cue, but don't wait as long to prompt. Experiment with varying waiting times before giving the prompt. The longer you've been prompting, the more repetitions and practice sessions it may take her to catch on to the new concept.

- Gradually fade the prompt itself. Give your verbal cue, wait a few seconds, then point, but point *less* than you normally do. If your pointing finger usually ends up nine inches from the floor, stop 12 inches from the floor and see if she lies down. If she does, do several repetitions at 12 inches, then try stopping your point 15 inches from the floor. Gradually diminish your point until you are no longer pointing at all.

You can follow this fading program for any of the prompts you are using. If you get your dog to sit by touching her back, say "Sit" *first,* then give her time to think and respond. If she doesn't sit, go ahead and touch her back, but more lightly than normal, to elicit the sit. You're saying, "Dog, the word 'Sit' means the same thing as this touch on your back." Gradually fade the amount of pressure in the touch until you aren't touching her at all.

Is This It?

When you're fading your prompts, remember that your dog doesn't *know* the word—she only knows the *prompt.* Dogs communicate primarily through body language, and it can be difficult for them to learn words, especially at first. It's easy to get frustrated—spoken language seems so simple to us—but have patience. She'll get it. Once you work through a couple of prompt-fading exercises it will come more and more easily with each new cue you teach her. I often wonder how frustrated our dogs get with *us* because we're so dim-witted about understanding *their* body language!

In fact, if you watch your dog closely, she may give you body language clues that she's beginning to understand the word. Many dogs, when they are starting to grasp the concept of "Down," will glance at the floor when they hear the verbal cue, as if they are saying "I know that word has something to do with 'down there,' but I'm not exactly sure what." Take heart, your message is getting through!

When you see her glance at the floor, tell her "Good Girl!" and help her with your prompt. You're telling her "That's it!" Remember that it will speed her learning if you use a marker, such as a Click! of a clicker or a verbal "Yes!"—and give a her a treat when she lies down, even if you had to prompt.

Another body language message she may send you is to go partway down and stop, then look up at you. She's saying. "Is this it? Is this what you mean?" Again, you'll speed her learning if you acknowledge her question with a "Good Girl!" and a prompt to help her lie down the rest of the way. Then Click! and treat. *Note: It's important not to Click! and treat until she is all the way down. Your "Good Girl" tells her she's on the right path, the Click! and treat marks the performance of the complete behavior. If you Click! the partway behavior, she may think she is only supposed to go partway.*

Unintentional Prompts

Anything you do as a regular part of a behavior cue is an unintentional prompt. If you always have your dog facing you when you ask her to sit, then she'll think facing you is part of the "Sit" ritual; your position is a prompt. If you always bend your knees and lean forward slightly when you ask your dog to lie down, those movements will be unintentional prompts that help to translate the verbal "down" cue to your dog.

If you took the "Sit Test" below and learned that your dog is highly reliant on unintentional prompts, you now know how well your dog *really* knows the "Sit" cue. You can create similar tests for other behaviors such as "Down" and "Come," to help you discern whether your dog's behaviors are really under good stimulus control.

Most dogs think the cue for "Sit" is a combination of a person standing in front of them with treats in her hands, looking right at them, speaking loudly, gesturing strangely, perhaps only in the house.

Another helpful exercise is to have someone videotape you while you're doing a normal training session with your dog. Watch the video afterwards, and pick out several body movements or positions that you consistently use with some of your commonly used cues. Now go back and work with your dog again, making a conscious effort to eliminate two or three of those cues. See if your dog is less responsive to your verbal cues when you take away your unintentional prompts.

If your dog doesn't sit when you ask but seems otherwise focused on your training exercises, it's likely that you've made a subtle change in your prompt. Many people in this situation jump to the erroneous conclusion that their dogs have chosen to deliberately defy them, and they give their hapless companions a "correction" for their "disobedience." Poor dogs! If your dog stops performing a behavior that you think she "knows," examine your unintentional prompts and see what you might have changed.

Subtle prompts are not a bad thing, just something to be aware of. In fact, obedience competitors make good use of a wide variety of prompts to back up their legal obedience ring cues. Some make it a point to always start off on one foot if they are asking the dog to heel with them, the other foot if the dog has been asked to stay. Many competitors fold their arms across their chests to emphasize their stay "commands" from across the ring, while their arms are relaxed at their sides as required by obedience regulations for a recall from a stay. You may decide to use prompts deliberately on certain occasions as well—nothing wrong with that!

Fading Treats

Using treats in training is *not* bribery. In early stages of training as described above, treats are lures. After a dog knows how to perform a behavior, treats are rewards when given after the fact to reinforce the behavior.

Still, there's value in minimizing the use of treats so your dog doesn't expect one *every* time she performs. When your dog gets a treat every time she sits (called a **continuous schedule of reinforcement**), she comes to *expect* one every time she sits. Ask her to sit a few times without a reinforcer, and she may stop sitting on cue because it's no longer rewarding to her to do so. When an animal stops performing a behavior due to the removal of reinforcement, it's called **extinction.**

When you gradually reduce the frequency of treats so that she gets them randomly and occasionally but not every time (an **intermittent schedule of reinforcement**) she'll keep sitting when you ask because she knows it will pay off eventually—like putting quarters in a slot machine. Putting a behavior on an intermittent schedule makes it very resistant to extinction, and makes it more likely that your dog will respond when you need her to, even if you've run out of treats.

That said, I always try to have treats in my pockets so I can intermittently reward my dogs for giving me behaviors that I ask for. They don't get discouraged if they don't receive a reward for one or two or even a bunch of behaviors, because they have learned that they can count on me to eventually reward them in some way...

Karen Pryor's Four Rules of Stimulus Control

From the book *Don't Shoot The Dog; The New Art of Teaching and Training*

1. The behavior always occurs immediately upon presentation of the conditioned stimulus (the dog sits when told to).

2. The behavior never occurs in the absence of the stimulus (during a training or work session the dog never sits spontaneously).

3. The behavior never occurs in response to some other stimulus (if you say "Lie down," the dog does not offer the sit instead).

4. No other behavior occurs in response to this stimulus (when you say "Sit," the dog does not respond by lying down or by leaping up and licking your face).

Take the Sit Test

Originally developed by Ian Dunbar, the purpose of the Sit Test is to provide an objective assessment of performance reliability for basic behavior cues. This helps to remind us that while we think our dog "knows" a behavior, it's likely that our dog knows the behavior reliably in response to our cue (under stimulus control) in a relatively limited scope. The following Sit Test is *not* the same as the one originally developed by Ian, but serves a similar purpose.

1. Front sit: dog sits on cue facing handler.

2. Side sit: dog sits on cue at handler's side.

3. Chair sit: dog sits on cue with handler sitting in chair.

4. Floor/Back sit: dog sits on cue with handler sitting on floor with back to the dog.

5. Handler down/sit: dog sits with handler lying down on floor.

6. Down-Sit: handler tells dog to down and stay, steps 6 feet away, cues dog to sit.

7. Across-the-room sit: helper takes leash, walks dog across room away from handler and drops leash. Handler cues dog to sit.

8. Come-Sit: helper takes leash and walks dog across room away from handler and drops leash. Handler calls dog, cues dog to sit when dog reaches halfway point.

Perfect Score: 200 points (each exercise worth 25 points). Deduct 5 points for each additional cue. Deduct 5 points for each dog-length moved before the dog sat.

The Bowl Game

How and why to use your dog's food bowl to your advantage

You may think of it simply as a convenient vessel, useful for keeping your dog's food gathered in one place, off the floor. Your dog probably has a very different perspective. For him, the bowl is likely to be a high value object of great import, especially if he's a hearty eater. In this magical dish, one or more times a day, *food* appears.

Mealtime carries great significance for most dogs. It can be fraught with excitement, arousal, and stress. A wise dog owner understands the importance of mealtime, and uses it to her advantage. Your dog's feeding ritual can be used to reinforce good manners, practice deference exercises, and encourage a positive association with food, food bowls, feeding, and the presence of humans in the vicinity of his hallowed feeding vessel.

If you just dump food in Buster's bowl and deposit it on the floor, you miss a golden training opportunity—and you might actually reinforce undesirable behaviors.

Meals Versus Free Feeding

I cringe internally when a client tells me she **free-feeds** her dog—that is, keeps the bowl on the floor filled with kibble all the time. I'm a strong believer in feeding meals for a number of reasons, in addition to the medical fact that a dog's digestive system is designed more to gorge than to graze. There are numerous advantages to feeding your dog specific amounts of food at specific times:

- You can monitor intake. If you feed meals, you'll know the instant Buster goes off his feed—sometimes the first sign that he's not feeling well. If you just keep the bowl topped off, it may be a day or two before you realize he's not eating.

- You minimize your dog's opportunities to guard his food. If there's always food in the bowl, your dog might just decide he needs to protect his valuable resource and the territory around it. If the food bowl is picked up when it's empty, the feeding zone becomes more neutral.

- You can utilize feeding time as training time. Teach him good manners and impulse control by reinforcing a "Sit/Wait" behavior while you place the bowl on the floor, then give him the cue to eat. (See "Wait Training" pg. 71.)

- You can take advantage of feeding time to reinforce your role as the higher-ranking member of your social group. You can't be the "alpha dog"—your dog knows you're not a dog—but you *are* a member of his social group. The leader controls the "good stuff," and dinner is definitely "good stuff." If food is available all the time, your dog controls it. If you, as benevolent leader, choose to share some of *your* food with him out of the goodness of your heart, and he performs a deference behavior such as sit, or down, to get you to share, you're reinforcing a healthy relationship.

- You know when he's full, and when he's empty. Your training sessions are more likely to be successful if you train when Buster's stomach is empty rather than full.

- You can use his meals as training treats. This is particularly useful for building a relationship with a dog who is not convinced he needs you. If all good things, including meals, come directly from your hand, he's more likely to decide you're important in his life.

- You can control your dog's weight. Is he looking a tad too prosperous? Cut back a few calories from his portions. Looking a little ribby? Add an extra half-cup to his bowl.

- You may spark his appetite. People with fussy eaters often make the mistake of leaving food out constantly. The dog grazes all day and never gets hungry, thus never gets eager for food. Offering food, leaving it down for 10-15 minutes, then picking it up, can teach a picky eater to take advantage when he can—or wait for the next meal.

If you have multiple dogs, free feeding can be even more problematic. One dog may eat more than his share and plump up, while another dog goes hungry. You're even *less* likely to notice if one dog is off his feed, since the other is still eating and the food's still disappearing. Tensions may escalate around the bowl, and fights can occur.

Of course, there are plenty of dogs who can share food resources amicably. Yours might share nicely, but you're still missing out on all the other benefits of meals.

Not all dogs are capable of eating peacefully right next to another dog, but these dogs understand that it's a rule at this house that there is no guarding or trading bowls allowed. If someone breaks the rule, they lose the balance of that meal.

The Feeding Ritual

There was a time when trainers recommended following routines that supported the status of the higher-ranking dog in the pack. Feed the "alpha dog" first, they said, and move on down the line. That thinking has changed.

Since I'm the highest-ranking member of the social group in my home, I get to make the rules, and I can decide if the rules change. Today, I might choose to feed a lower-ranking dog first, and move up the line. Or start in the middle, and move toward the ends. Or randomly select appropriate behaviors to reinforce with the food bowl. Of course, since we now know that pack hierarchy is more fluid than once thought, I might be guessing wrong about who's higher ranking on any given day, but that doesn't matter. I'm still the leader, and I get to decide with whom I share food, and when.

In my canine group, Katie the crazy Kelpie often obsesses about Tucker moving toward his food bowl. She'll stand behind him and bite his hocks if he moves. To help him out, I may invite Katie to eat first so Tucker can walk to his bowl without torment.

Lucy is convinced she should always eat first, and can barely contain herself if I feed someone else before her. So, of course, I do, so she can practice her self-control lessons. If she waits calmly on her mat, she may be next. If she's dancing around and whining for her breakfast, her bowl is slow to arrive.

Katie and Tucker, who has bad knees, are no longer required to sit and wait for their bowls, but Lucy and Dubhy are still reminded each meal that good manners and deference behaviors make food happen.

You get to decide what you want your particular mealtime rules to be, but in general, chaos is not acceptable and calm is good. Perhaps all dogs go to their respective place mats and wait for dinner to arrive. Maybe they just have to sit, lie down or stand around quietly to make food happen. Whatever your desired doggie dinner behavior, you can reinforce acceptable behaviors by continuing with your meal preparations when dogs are calm. If dogs get too excited, take a seat and read a magazine until calm returns, then continue on.

When Dusty the intrepid Pomeranian was still with us, he was convinced that barking made food happen. This is a classic example of **superstitious behavior**, where a dog believes that because a particular behavior—such as barking—occurred prior to an event of significance, that behavior can positively influence future outcomes, even though the two aren't really connected.

In Dusty's case we had to convince him that barking made food preparation *stop,* and *quiet* made food happen. We weren't entirely successful; ultimately we simply resorted to an outcome wherein barking made Dusty go outside, and quiet brought him back in to eat.

Food Fights

Food guarding is a natural, adaptive survival behavior for dogs. In the wild, if a dog doesn't lay claim to his valuable resources and defend that claim, he will likely starve to death. Wild canids who successfully defend their claims live to pass their genes on to their puppies.

While guarding from humans is a dangerous and unacceptable behavior, dogs should be able to reasonably protect their food from their canine peers. "Reasonably" means *appropriate* use of body language signals—some posturing, a glare or two, maybe even a raised lip. It doesn't mean launching, lunging, biting, fighting and/or causing punctures and lacerations.

If your multi-dog household erupts into all-out war during meals, it's time for a serious management plan. Depending on the intensity of the conflict, you can:

- Feed in opposite corners of the room and play referee—making sure one dog doesn't approach or threaten another, and picking up bowls when dinner's over to remove the high-value, guardable object.
- Feed in opposite corners of the room and put all dogs on tethers to ensure they don't threaten each other.
- Feed in different rooms with closed doors or baby gates in between to prevent conflict.
- Feed in crates, far enough apart that guarding isn't an issue.

You may also want to try to modify the behavior. This is best done with the guarder tethered, and a second person handling the other dog so the interaction is well controlled, while working your way through the following series of modification exercises:

Series #1

Step 1: With you standing next to Guarder, have the other person walk Dog #2 into the far side of the room on a leash. The instant Guarder notices the other dog, start feeding scrumptious treats, such as tidbits of chicken. When the other dog leaves, the chicken stops. You may want to have the other person feed treats to Dog #2 as well, to keep her attention focused on her handler, away from Guarder.

Step 2: Repeat Step 1 numerous times, until the presence of Dog #2 causes Guarder to look happily to you for bits of chicken.

Step 3: Gradually bring Dog #2 closer, watching for any stress/warning signs from Guarder. (See "Warning Signs of Stress" pg. 71.)

Step 4: Work at each new distance until you get a consistent "Where's my chicken?" response from Guarder, then decrease the distance another increment.

Series #2

When Dog #2 can come close—within 5 feet of the end of the tether—without eliciting stress/aggression signals from Guarder, go back and repeat Steps 1 through 4 with Guarder's empty food bowl on the floor next to him.

Series #3

When Dog #2 can come close with the empty food bowl on the floor, repeat Steps 1 through 4, but this time drop the bits of chicken into Guarder's empty bowl instead of hand feeding them.

Series #4

When Dog #2 can come close with chicken bits dropping into the bowl, repeat Steps 1 through 4, but this time start with some of Guarder's regular food in the bowl on the floor, adding bits of chicken as Dog #2 approaches.

If you've done your work well, by the time you reach the end of Series 4, Guarder should understand that when Dog #2 approaches, it *makes good stuff happen.* Continue to referee off-leash interactions at feeding time, watching for the recurrence of stress signals from Guarder that may indicate more practice sessions are needed.

As with all aggressive behaviors, if you feel the risk to your safety (or your other dog's safety) is high, or your modification work doesn't improve the behavior, I recommend seeking the assistance of a qualified trainer/behavior professional.

Guarding From Humans

Dogs who guard their food from humans are a significant threat. If the only thing the dog guards is his food bowl, you can manage the behavior by feeding him in a separate room, with the door closed, and inviting him out before you go in to pick up the empty bowl. If he generalizes his guarding to other high-value objects, the risk increases by leaps and bounds, especially if you can't predict what he may decide is valuable to him.

If you have a puppy, start early by associating your presence near his bowl with good stuff; drop yummy tidbits into his bowl as he's eating, so he doesn't feel threatened by your presence. Don't allow family members to tease or torment him at the food bowl, and if he does exhibit signs of guarding, *don't punish!* Punishment will only convince him that you're a threat to his food—you have to work harder to convince him you're not.

Jean Donaldson's excellent book, *Mine!*, offers a step-by-step program for modifying food-bowl guarding, but again, I advise you to heed the warning: if you feel the risk to your safety is high, or your modification work doesn't improve the behavior, seek the assistance of a qualified trainer/behavior professional.

Wait Training

Mealtime is a perfect opportunity for twice daily "Wait" training sessions, using two principles of operant conditioning: positive reinforcement and negative punishment. The positive reinforcement (dog's behavior makes a good thing happen) occurs each time you say "Yes!" and feed a tidbit. The negative punishment (dog's behavior makes a good thing go away) happens every time he gets up and you put the bowl back on the counter or lift it out of his reach.

1. Have your dog sit at his designated dinner spot. Tell him "Wait!" If he remains seated, say "Yes!" and feed him one tidbit from his bowl (which you have placed on the counter).

2. With your dog still sitting, say "Wait!" and lift his bowl off the counter. If he remains seated, say "Yes" and feed him a morsel (positive reinforcement). If he gets up, say "Oops!" and place the bowl back on the counter (negative punishment). Repeat until he stays seated when you pick up his bowl.

3. With your dog still sitting, say "Wait!" Lower the bowl halfway toward the floor, one to two feet in front of him. If he remains seated, say "Yes!" and feed him a tidbit from the bowl. Raise the bowl several inches and repeat a number of times until you're sure he'll remain seated. If he gets up, say "Oops!" and raise the bowl above the level of his head. Try again, and don't lower it quite so far this time.

4. With Buster still sitting, keep repeating the "Wait" exercise until you can lower the bowl all the way to the floor without him getting up. When he'll hold his sit with the bowl on the floor, tell him "Okay!" or "Get it!" and encourage him to eat.

Practice Buster's "Wait" training every time you feed him. You'll teach him a useful good manners behavior and remind him at every meal that you're the benevolent leader, controlling the good stuff, but happily sharing with him as long as he offers a deference behavior (sit) and minds his manners.

Warning Signs of Stress

It's important that you recognize subtle signs of food-bowl-related stress in your dog, as these are the precursors to more obvious signs of aggression. The sooner you can recognize your dog's discomfort, the earlier you can intervene, prevent aggression from happening, and be more successful at modifying the behavior. Here are some subtle signs to watch for:

• As you approach your dog at his bowl, he stops eating and freezes with his muzzle still buried in his food.

- As you approach he gives you a "whale eye"—with his nose still in his bowl, he rolls his eyes at you so you can see the whites around the edges.

- As you approach he eats faster.

- As you approach he blocks you with his body and keeps eating or tries to push the food bowl away from you.

Using a fake hand on a stick, one can test a dog's potential to guard. Note his "whale eye," snarling, stiffening…leading to SNAP! "I warned you."

Growling, snapping, lunging and actually biting are more obvious signs of food guarding. Some dogs will leap to the obvious signs without giving you more subtle warnings. Punishing subtle warning signs will make him *less* comfortable, and may suppress those signs so he jumps right to lunging and biting. Remember that your goal is to make him comfortable with you approaching his food. You can best accomplish this through a systematic program that changes his association with your presence at his bowl from "Uh-oh, she might steal my food" to "Yay! More chicken!"

Monkey See, Monkey Do?

Young or less experienced dogs can learn a lot from well-behaved dogs

The domestic dog is, inarguably, a social species. There is little scholarly disagreement over the fact that the dog's social dependency makes him exceptionally aware of the behavior of others, and contributes to his own behavior and learning abilities.

There is, however, ongoing discussion about how much, and how dogs can learn by interacting with each other—the question of "social learning" through contact, joining in the action, and pure observation without active participation.

You may have seen it yourself when you got a new puppy. You're positive ol' Spot taught little Junior where to go to the bathroom in the yard, how to find the water dish, and the importance of barking vociferously at strangers. Junior certainly came running hot on Spot's heels when you called the pair, thus learning the importance of the word "Come." It even seems like the new pup learned how to sit politely for a treat by watching Spot perform that well-practiced behavior. But did he really learn by watching Spot? Or was it all just coincidence?

Social Learning

The term "social learning" encompasses several closely-related concepts. Some clearly apply to the learning processes of dogs. Others are more debatable.

Allelomimetic behavior (mimicking), or group-coordinated behavior, relies on the hard-wired inclination of a social animal to follow and mimic members of the social group. Puppies are genetically programmed to follow and copy others of their kind. This is an important factor in early learning; it comes into play when Junior chases along when you call Spot, or when *you* run away from Junior and call him to chase after you.

Social facilitation is related to but different from allelomimesis. It refers to behaviors performed in a group, where the presence of another dog causes an *increase* in the intensity of the behavior. Two dogs acting in concert may run faster, bark louder, jump higher, eat more or eat faster than a dog performing alone. For this reason, trainers and behaviorists often caution *against* adopting a second dog for the primary purpose of resolving the behavior problems of Dog #1; you can easily end up with louder barking, or an increase in destructive behavior in *two* dogs, rather than the hoped-for *decrease* in undesirable behavior.

It is likely that the amplified magnitude of behavior is a result of an increased state of arousal, stimulated by the presence of one or more additional dogs. While the negatives of this effect are obvious, social facilitation can have positive effects as well, such as the increased speed and intensity of a competitive Flyball dog due to the presence of the running dog in the next lane.

The flip side of social facilitation is **social interference**—the irritating phenomenon that occurs when the presence of other dogs playing nearby interrupts your dog's ability to pay attention to your training session. This is known in training class as a "distraction." It's wise to teach Junior his new behaviors in a quiet environment, free from such social interference. Make sure he knows them well before you can expect him to be able to perform them in the face of major distractions.

Local enhancement includes pieces of social facilitation, but is different from true observational learning in that the dog actively participates in the behavior in the presence of the other dog and/or other environmental cues. Spot starts digging a hole—Junior joins in—and learns that digging holes is fun and rewarding as he follows Spot under the fence. Simply watching Spot dig the hole was not enough to inspire Junior to dig his way out of the yard; it was actually a combination of watching, participating, and enjoying the whole process that characterizes this as local enhancement.

Another example of local enhancement is when Junior learns to coordinate his clumsy puppy legs and jump into the car much more quickly by following behind Spot than he would by trying to climb in on his own. Junior's performance is enhanced by Spot's immediate example, and learning happens more quickly for Junior as a result.

New dog-walking clients learn how to behave in this complex situation through "local enhancement," which includes social facilitation, mimicking, and trial-and-error learning.

Just Watch

This brings us to the controversial question of true observational learning in dogs. Can our canine pals learn by simply watching?

"No" is an easy answer. Four necessary conditions for observational learning are attention, retention, motivation, and production. That is, the dog must pay attention to the dog performing the modeled behavior; retain the information gathered about the behavior during the observation; be motivated to reproduce the behavior in a time and place removed from the original; and finally, produce the behavior, or some reasonable facsimile thereof.

In training, for example, one dog could watch you through a window while you train another dog to lie down on cue. You could then take the observer dog to a new room and have him perform the behavior for you, on cue. Not likely!

If dogs were adept at observational learning, you could plop Junior in front of the television, pop in your favorite videotape about clicker training, leave him there while you head off to work, and come home to a trained dog. There would be no need for dog trainers, or dog training classes. Sometimes we *wish* it were that easy!

Still, some studies have determined that puppies, at least, have some capacity for observational learning. A 1997 study conducted by Slabbert and Rasa determined that pups between the ages of 9-12 weeks who were permitted to observe their narcotics-detecting mothers at work generally proved more capable of learning the same skills at six months of age than control puppies the same age who were not previously allowed to watch their mothers working.

A 1977 experiment by Adler and Adler found that puppies who watched other puppies learn to pull a food cart into their cages by an attached ribbon proved considerably faster at the task when later given the opportunity themselves. At 38 days of age, the "demonstrator" puppies took an average of 697 seconds to succeed, while the observers succeeded in an average of 9 seconds.

These are startling and exciting findings. While evidence of observational learning is scarce in adult dogs, the potential for it in puppies may change, yet again, our definition of a responsible breeder. One day, we may expect a good breeder to set her puppies on the sidelines so they can watch their mothers run through obedience routines, agility courses and service dog, search-and-rescue, or drug-sniffing jobs before they are placed in their new homes.

Put a Good Dog to Work

While we wait for more scientific information on observational learning in puppies, we can take advantage of social learning opportunities that we *know* can enhance our dogs' behaviors.

If your new dog is an only dog, you can still make use of his innate social mimicking behavior to encourage him to follow *you* while teaching him "Come."

If you do get a second dog, structure some training sessions so that he can learn from your more-experienced dog's knowledge of good manners and skills. For example, before you open the door to let your dogs out, wait for Spot to sit (we hope he has already learned this "good manners" behavior), and then calmly wait for Junior to do the same. Spot's calm behavior sets a good example for Junior to do the same. If Junior hasn't quite figured out the sit, that can come later; as soon as Junior is standing calmly, open the door and let them both out as their reward for calm.

Rather than chastising Junior for barking at a passing skateboarder when you're out playing in your fenced yard, grab Spot's ball and run with him away from the skateboarder, playing with him in loud excitement, to make use of social facilitation to turn Junior's unacceptable intense barking into acceptable intense play.

Finally, remember that you can utilize the presence of other dogs to amplify the magnitude of your dog's *desired* behaviors, while taking care to avoid those circumstances that might amplify *undesirable* ones. In other words, it might be wiser to spend more time with your new dog in the presence of well-mannered dogs at a daycare or training center than a pack of unruly, barking dogs at a dog park.

Training a dog is a big challenge—we can use all the social learning help we can get!

The Shape of Things to Come

This fun training technique can be used to teach your dog anything

Yard sales and flea markets are some of my favorite places to shop for dog training equipment. A couple of years ago I picked up a classic "Wizard of Oz" picnic basket with a lid that flips open—the kind Toto jumped out of while being dognapped on the Wicked Witch's bicycle. That basket sat in a corner of my training center for quite some time while I pondered what to do with it.

Finally one day while waiting for a client to arrive, I set about shaping Dubhy to flip the basket lid open with his nose. It took less than five minutes—and once again I was reminded how powerful this sometimes overlooked dog training technique can be.

Shaping, or as it's formally known, "shaping by successive approximations," simply means breaking a behavior down into tiny increments, and reinforcing the dog at each incremental step until you've achieved the full behavior. Some trainers believe that shaping is the ultimate approach to operant training, and that any steps that stray off the pure shaping path are detrimental to ultimate results. Others incorporate shaping as I do—as a valuable part of a multi-faceted training program.

The shaping process works because behavior is variable. In any series of repetitions of a behavior, your dog will give you variations in the manner that the behavior is performed—faster/slower, bigger/smaller, higher/lower, harder/softer, etc. If you wanted to shape your dog for a perfect obedience competition sit—straight, fast and in proper heel position, you'd break the behavior known as "Sit" into those three components and work on them one at a time, capitalizing on the variability of your dog's behavior for each one.

Perhaps you choose to start with speed. Your dog's average sit time might be three seconds. Your goal is a one second sit. In any given number of repetitions of "Sit," some will be faster than three seconds, some will be slower, and some will be right on the three second mark.

If you were to be scientific about your shaping program, you'd time the sits with a stopwatch, only Click! and treat (mark and reward) those that were three seconds or faster, and keep a written journal of your progress.

If you are less rigorous, you'd guesstimate the times and strive to click the faster sits. Over time, your dog's average elapsed sit speed time would decrease, perhaps to two seconds, as he realized that only faster sits get clicked, and deliberately tried to sit faster to make you click more often.

Now you raise the bar—only sits that are two seconds or faster get clicked. By breaking your goal of fast sits into smaller increments of time, you gradually shape your dog to do that lightning fast one second obedience ring sit that you covet.

Shaping is not just for the obedience ring. It has a number of important applications and benefits for all kinds of training, including:

- Accomplishing a behavior that your dog finds physically difficult or confusing, such as a teaching a Greyhound to sit.

- Encouraging your dog to perform a behavior that he finds mentally difficult or confusing, such as teaching a crate wary dog to enter his artificial doggie den.

- Fine tuning a behavior your dog can already do, such as teaching fast, straight, close sits.

- Helping your dog learn how to offer behaviors, try new things, and think creatively in order to solve problems, through shaping games such as "101 Things to Do With a Box" (see pg. 79).

Shaping Techniques

There are several different ways to shape a behavior. You can use "lure/prompt shaping" as a sort of hybrid technique: you're still showing the dog what you want him to do by luring with a treat, or prompting with a target or other body language, and reinforcing increments of progress to the final behavior.

Shaping "purists" tend to scoff at lure/prompt shaping, but it can be very effective at getting behaviors more quickly, although slower at teaching dogs to think creatively and offer behaviors freely. Dogs in basic good manners classes are often taught the "Down" with lure-shaping, by luring the dog's nose toward the floor with a treat, clicking and rewarding as the dog makes any progress toward the floor with his nose or other body parts.

You can use "basic shaping," where you have a goal behavior in mind and, without any prompting, reinforce small increments that the dog offers, such as described above for a faster sit. And you can "free shape"—by doing training exercises without any preconceived notion of where you want the behavior to go. Free shaping is the most difficult concept for novice trainers, who are often legitimately perplexed by the idea of training without knowing what behavior you're trying to train.

Lure/Prompt Shaping

Greyhounds are notoriously difficult to teach to sit. Theories abound as to why this is so; one theory has to do with the Greyhound's unique anatomy—a body shape that makes sitting an uncomfortable position. Whatever the reason, it does seem that while most dogs offer sits easily, these long, lean, muscular dogs are somewhat reluctant to do it.

"Lure/prompt" shaping can be used to quickly get a new behavior; however, it doesn't require the dog to figure out for herself what exactly it is that you want.

To lure shape a sit in a reluctant sitter, hold a treat at the tip of your dog's nose and lift it up slightly. If he lifts his nose to follow the tidbit, Click! and treat. Repeat this step, lifting the treat slightly higher and a little bit back over the head.

When each step seems easy for the dog, progress a little farther, continuing to move the treat back over the head. At the same time, watch for a bend in the hind legs. Be sure to click the slightest bend in the hocks, and when you start getting a consistent bend in the hocks, even a small one, keep luring, but only click the leg bend, not the head lifts. Reinforce gradually deeper bends in the legs until the dog is sitting.

Why not just push the dog into a sit, or "tuck" him into a sit by pressing in gently above the hocks? Certainly, some trainers do, and they teach the sit successfully in this manner. However, some dogs are reluctant to sit due to back or joint pain, and need to learn to find a way to move into a sit that doesn't hurt. Your push may cause excruciating pain.

Other dogs resent being physically manipulated. That may or may not be the reason I had a recent client whose Scottish Terrier caused serious injuries to his prior trainer when she tried to push him into a sit. He resisted her first two push-sit attempts, and on the third try went up her arm with his teeth.

Other dogs may have other reasons for failing to catch on quickly. A case in point is a shelter dog in my Intern Academy last summer—a beautiful English Pointer who had been purchased for hunting trial work but disqualified from competition due to a minor congenital rib deformity. At age four, he had never been asked to sit, and just didn't seem to understand what we were asking of him.

In fact, he was the classic example of a shut down dog—unwilling to offer any behavior at all. It took four days of the six day academy, but on Thursday when his trainer finally got him to sit, the whole class applauded wildly. Best of all, the dog got it! His eyes lit up, and he proudly offered sit after sit after sit. In the remaining two days of the course he and his trainer caught up on all the lessons that had been on hold while they worked on the sit, and both graduated with flying colors and big smiles.

Basic Shaping

Some trainers profess to teach their entire entry level classes using basic shaping only. I'll admit I'm not that brave, but I do introduce the concept of basic shaping with my "Go to Your Place" exercise. I explain to my class that shaping is a Zen exercise—it takes patience and close observation, and that we'll be **splitting** behavior rather than **lumping**. Lumping means to reinforce large chunks of behavior—capturing a sit, for example. In contrast, splitting means to look for the tiniest piece of movement, Click! and reinforce that, and build toward the final behavior. Splitting is the essence of shaping.

To shape a "Go to Your Place" behavior, set out a carpet square, dog bed, or blanket to designate "Place." You can actually do this without a physical object to mark the place, but it's easier for canine and human to succeed with a visual marker—and then you can generalize the behavior easily by moving the marker to another spot.

Now stand back several feet from the carpet square and watch your dog very closely. You're going to Click! and treat the tiniest motion toward "Place"—one step, a turn of the head, a flick of the ear—it doesn't even have to be directly toward the spot. In the general direction will do. If you've already reinforced your dog consistently for offered behaviors, he'll probably catch on quickly. As he starts repeatedly making deliberate movements toward the rug to get clicked, you'll hold out slightly longer to build more behavior. Just slightly! You want him to get a little frustrated and try harder (harder = bigger behavior) but if you hold out too long he may give up and quit offering behavior altogether.

As he gets closer to the mat you can move forward with him in order to keep delivering treats—but not ahead of him—that would be luring or prompting!

When he takes a step toward the mat, Click! and reset by tossing the treats behind you. Now he can step toward the mat again. The goal is to shape him to *go* to the mat, not just to *be* on the mat. When he's offering to go to the mat easily, start shaping him to lie down on it. The value of "Go to Your Place" is to be able to park your dog there for a while. When he's consistently offering to go lie down on his mat, you can add the verbal "Go to Your Place!" cue.

If your dog doesn't offer behaviors easily, it may take longer to shape the "Place" behavior. Be patient, and remember to split—look for the tiniest of movement to reinforce. If he only wants to gaze adoringly into your eyes, look at the rug instead of him. If he just lies down at your feet for a snooze, invite him up, reposition him, and look for movement to reinforce as he repositions. The more you can find to reinforce, the less likely he is to lie down for another nap.

Dedicated shapers may write out their complete shaping plan, carefully considering each potential step in the process, and measuring their progress against the written plan. Less scientifically disciplined trainers may work with just a mental picture of their shaping plan. You can do each shaping session for as long or as short as you like. Assuming your dog's happy to play the game, you can keep on playing! As with all training, try to end the session while the dog's still enthusiastic and successful.

Free Shaping

Free shaping is great for encouraging a dog who is somewhat shut down to offer behaviors, because he can't be wrong. *Anything* he does that even remotely relates to the exercise gets clicked and treated. Once the dog is easily offering random behaviors, *then* you can, if you choose, switch to basic shaping with a goal behavior. Here are a couple of free shaping exercises you can experiment with:

- **101 Things to Do With a Box.** You can use any ol' cardboard box for this, large or small, or it doesn't even have to be a box—you can play "101 Things to Do With Anything." Your dog can be on leash, or off if he'll stay and keep working with you. Set a chair a few feet back from the box or object, sit in the chair, and wait. As with the "Place" exercise, you're looking for tiny pieces of behavior to Click! and treat—*any behavior* that relates to the box—a look, a step, a sniff, a push…only this time you have no specific goal in mind, and you don't have to build up to a behavior—random behaviors are fine.

  If your dog gets hung up on one particular behavior you can stop clicking that one and wait for something else. The more confident your dog is about offering behaviors, the more easily you can just quit clicking one thing and wait for another. At some point, if you wish, you can decide on a goal behavior based on the ones your dog has offered, and shape it into something specific—front feet only in the box; hind feet only in the box; all four feet in the box, turn the box over; fetch the box; or…?

• **Body Parts.** Body Parts shaping helps your dog learn to offer behavior, and it also helps *you* realize how precise this process can be for shaping the tiniest of movements.

Sit in a chair with your dog facing you, and watch your dog closely for a movement in one of his body parts. Even a tiny movement will do. For example, you could watch for a flick of his ear, a turn of his head, the lift of a paw, or a tongue flicker.

When you have captured one of these movements with your Click! and treat, that's the one you'll continue to focus on. Sit and wait for another movement of that same body part. Click! and treat. Your goal is to reinforce that accidental behavior until your dog begins deliberately offering it. When he does, you can name it, incorporate it into a trick routine, or keep working with it to shape it into something bigger if you choose.

I really came to appreciate the power of shaping when I first purchased agility equipment, set it up in the back yard, and ran to get Dubhy to see what he'd do with it. To my delight, as I introduced him to each piece of equipment, he immediately started *doing stuff*—sniffing it, pawing at it, biting it, jumping on it, just trying out different things to see what he needed to do to get me to click. Made training a breeze!

Perhaps the greatest benefit of shape-training is that, through this technique, dogs learn to engage and offer novel behaviors when put in new situations.

Dubhy's Picnic

I decided to shape Dubhy to flip open a picnic basket with his nose. I could have used pure basic shaping, in which case the steps in our shaping plan might have looked something like the steps below. Because I'm doing basic shaping with a behavior goal in mind, not free shaping (i.e., waiting for a behavior to happen), I wouldn't click random offered behaviors that aren't in the shaping plan. Note that I would Click! and treat several times at each step, unless, of course, Dubhy took a quantum leap over several steps, in which case I'd be prepared to leap with him:

1. Looks at basket.

2. Moves toward basket.

3. Sniffs basket.

4. Sniffs basket closer to the lid corner where the opening is.

5. Sniffs basket at basket lid corner.

6. Nudges lid corner (here I might need to hold out to wait for stronger behavior to get the nudge). Nudges lid corner harder.

7. Nudges hard enough to move lid corner.

8. Nudges hard enough to lift up lid corner.

9. Nudges hard enough to lift lid corner higher.

10. Nudges hard enough to flip lid open.

When I actually trained Dubhy to do this, I chose to take a shortcut and do a little prompting with a target stick. That allowed us to skip steps 1-4 and go directly to step 5, sniffing the basket lid corner. From there, it only took a few minutes to get strong, reliable "open the basket" behavior.

Every piece of furniture is now a potential prop for Dubhy!

Now that we have reliability with the goal behavior of opening the basket, I could incorporate it into a trick routine—perhaps packing picnic supplies into the basket, or unpacking them and laying them out on a waiting picnic blanket. Or perhaps he could find a small "lost" dog who was trained to lie quietly hidden in the basket. Or…?

Karen Pryor's 10 Laws of Shaping

In her landmark book *Don't Shoot The Dog*, behavioral biologist and former dolphin trainer Karen Pryor says, "…a well-planned shaping program can minimize the required drilling and can make every moment of practice count, thus speeding up progress tremendously." She also tells us that the successful application of shaping principles makes the difference between shaping that is frustrating, slow, boring and disagreeable, and shaping that is happy, fast, and successful. Here are the 10 principles that Pryor suggests you follow for the most enjoyable and successful training:

1. Raise criteria in increments small enough that the subject always has a realistic chance for reinforcement.

2. Train one aspect of any particular behavior at a time; don't try to shape for two criteria simultaneously.

3. During shaping, put the current level of response onto a variable schedule of reinforcement before adding or raising the criteria.

4. When introducing a new criterion, or aspect of the behavioral skill, temporarily relax the old ones.

5. Stay ahead of your subject. Plan your shaping program completely so that if the subject makes sudden progress, you are aware of what to reinforce next.

6. Don't change trainers in midstream; you can have several trainers per trainee, but stick to one shaper per behavior.

7. If one shaping procedure is not eliciting progress, find another; there are as many ways to get behavior as there are trainers to think them up.

8. Don't interrupt a training session gratuitously; that constitutes punishment.

9. If behavior deteriorates, "go back to kindergarten"; quickly review the whole shaping process with a series of easily earned reinforces.

10. End each session on a high note, if possible, but in any case quit while you're ahead.

Part Three
TEACHING BEHAVIORS

Part Three will open your eyes to a variety of training possibilities that go beyond "Sit," "Down," "Stay," and "Heel." This section introduces new perspectives on some of the important old stand-by behaviors like coming when called, and suggests some tantalizing new opportunities, including "mind games" for the dog on restricted activity due to illness or injury, and new applications for scent work, such as my all time favorite—training your dog to find lost pets. If you have a giant breed or a toy, you'll also find useful information in this section on working with the special challenges—and rewards—that those dogs can offer you.

Higher Education

Training shouldn't stop at "Sit"—there is so much more your dog can do

There comes a time when dog and owner need to move past the basics to more advanced concepts of learning and behavior if they want to develop and enjoy their relationship to the fullest. Let's explore a few of the concepts that can take you and your dog beyond "Sit Happens!" to the hallowed halls of higher canine education.

Generalization

You will often hear trainers say that dogs don't **generalize** well. This means that just because Buddy learns to sit beautifully in your living room, he may not necessarily sit when you ask him to at the checkout counter of your favorite pet supply store. He thinks "Sit" means "sit in the comfort of my own living room." You may think he's being stubborn because he "knows" how to sit, when in fact he really only knows how to sit on cue at home—he hasn't learned to generalize the behavior.

The statement that "dogs don't generalize well" is actually only a half-truth. Most dog owners can tell stories of "one-trial" learning—where a single experience taught a dog to fear men with beards and hats, or to chase cats that run, or instilled some other high-arousal, strong behavioral response.

For the most part, behaviors that don't generalize well are those that involve **operant conditioning**, where the dog acts on the environment. Fido has to *learn* that he can make good things happen by sitting. Behaviors that involve a strong emotional response such as fear, or the chase instinct, are quite often learned in a single incident. Say a man with a hat and beard tripped over your dog and startled him, or a cat jumped out in front of him, hissing and spitting, tantalizingly close, and he gave adrenaline-pumping chase.

In these cases of **classical conditioning**, where the environment acts on the dog, Fido doesn't have to *learn* the emotional response, it just happens. It's easy for the response to happen the next time Fido sees a man with hat and beard, or a cat, even if the man doesn't trip over him or the cat doesn't jump up and run.

So how do you help your dog learn to generalize those operant behaviors (where the dog acts on the environment)? By doing exactly what your trainer told you to do: practice with your dog in as many different places as possible. In line at the bank. At the dog park. On your walks around the block. In the waiting room at the vet hospital. In the aisles of the pet supply store. In addition, if a dog has truly generalized his "Sit" cue, he will sit if you whisper it, yell it, if you're standing next to him, sitting on a chair, or lying on the floor across the room.

The more behaviors you help him generalize, the easier it becomes for him to generalize each new behavior. Before long, you'll have a dog who is as well-behaved in public as he is in the comfort of his own home.

Discrimination

Ah, the "D" word—a very bad word in employment or politics, but a very useful one in dog training.

In training, **discrimination** has nothing to do with skin color. It has to do with teaching your dog to differentiate between one or more *relevant* stimuli and all the other irrelevant stimuli in the environment at the time. That means that he sits when you say "Sit," and doesn't sit when you say "Down." He may learn to bark when he hears your doorbell, and generalize that to all doorbells, including the one on your favorite TV show. You could, if you wanted, teach him to discriminate, and only bark when he hears *your* doorbell, not any others.

In more complex discrimination exercises, you can teach your dog to distinguish one object from another. In Utility (upper level) obedience competitions, each dog must do a "scent discrimination" exercise. Using his nose, he must find the object that his handler touched amidst a pile of similar objects not touched by the handler, and bring the correct object back to his human.

There was a lovely example of discrimination on the television show *Pet Starz*, recently. A small, elderly Beagle correctly retrieved a half dozen items from a bag, one at a time, after being cued each time by his owner to get the item *by name*. The dog was letter perfect.

You can teach your dog discrimination with objects by asking him to bring you his toys, one-by-one, as you name them. This skill can be extended to your slippers, portable phone, car keys, etc. This is a vital skill for assistance dogs, and would be a useful behavior for the canine companions of any person who has limited mobility—or a tendency to lose things!

You can also teach your dog discrimination with locations by teaching him to go to different designated spots. For example, "Go to Bed" might mean you want him to lie down in his kennel, while "Go Settle" might mean lie down on his bed in the corner of the dining room.

You can even teach him discrimination with people, by teaching him the names of all your family members, and then asking him to "Find Timmy," Find Susie," Find Dad," etc. (See "Target Your Way to Discrimination" pg. 89.)

Salience

When we say something is **salient** to a dog, we mean it has noticeable significance to him. Your dog can learn to sit even in the face of distractions because the hot dog you are holding in front of his face is very salient. When you associate the hot dog with the verbal cue ("Sit!"), the cue itself becomes significant. The salient stimuli in the environment—you, your hot dogs, and the sit cue—are more significant than the distractions. They *overshadow* the dog barking across the street, the skateboarder whizzing by on the road, the slamming of a car door down the block. If your dog is too distracted to respond to the sit cue, then the distractions are more salient than you and your hot dogs. You either need to move your training to a less distracting environment, or find a way to make you, your treats, and your cues, more significant to your dog.

Blocking

Blocking refers to a phenomenon that occurs when the use of a known cue overrides the dog's ability to learn a new cue for the same behavior. Keep in mind that, while dogs can only learn one response to a particular cue ("Sit" must always mean sit, it can't sometimes mean lie down), they *can* learn several cues that all mean the same behavior.

Dubhy can lie down in response to the "Down" cue in English, French, Spanish, German and 2 different hand signals. This happened as a result of his role as a demo dog in some of my classes.

I use the down exercise to introduce my students to the importance of teaching their dogs to respond to verbal cues without body language assistance. We start by having the handlers lure the down, and as soon as their dogs will lie down easily by following the (treat) lure, we introduce the verbal cue; any new cue you are teaching must always *precede* the known cue. I use a demo dog to show them that the dog doesn't initially understand or respond to the word "Down", until we associate it with the luring motion that means "Down" to the dog. The motion is *salient* to the dog—the word is not.

I explain that in order for the dog to hear the word and learn that it also has significance, they must say the word *first,* then lure the dog down. If they give the verbal cue at the same time or after they lure, the lure *blocks* the dog's ability to learn the new cue.

With enough repetitions of the sequence—verbal cue, followed by lure and Click! (or another marker) and treat when the dog performs the behavior—the dog will learn that the verbal cue also has salience, and you will no longer need to lure him down; he will lie down when you give him the verbal cue.

As to Dubhy's multilingual talents? As soon as he learned a new verbal cue for "Down," I could no longer use that cue to show my students what to do when the dog hadn't yet learned the word; Dubhy would go down too quickly. I had to keep switching to new verbal cues in order to show them how to avoid blocking when adding a new cue for a known behavior.

Chaining and Backchaining

These are two important concepts that come into play when teaching your dog a complex sequence of behaviors. The behaviors are linked together so that each behavior is the signal for the next behavior in the chain. When a talented musician learns to play a piece by memory, she is **chaining**—each note or chord draws her forward to the next note or chord in the piece without her having to stop and think about what comes next.

"Chaining" is used to teach a dog a sequence of behaviors, such as going through a series of weave poles.

The competitive obedience retrieve is an example of a chained behavior. With her dog sitting at heel, the handler tosses the dumbbell, then gives the cue to "Take it!" Without any further instructions, the dog runs out to the dumbbell, picks it up, returns to his handler and sits in front of her, still holding the dumbbell, until the handler gives the cue to release it and return to heel position.

The "retrieve over high jump" is performed in the same manner, except the dog knows to sail over the jump *in both directions,* going out and coming back, again without further cues from the handler.

With **backchaining**, you begin by teaching the last behavior in the chain, and then add each step in reverse order, until the dog is performing the complete behavior. The theory is that when you teach the last thing first, your dog is always moving toward the thing he knows best, so he gains confidence as he learns the new links in the chain.

The song, "12 Days of Christmas," is a classic example of backchaining. You may forget how many "lords-a-leaping," or how many "maids a-milking" but I'd bet you never forget that partridge in the pear tree, and you get faster and more confident in your singing once you get to the five golden rings.

We recently placed a ramp over the three steps from our deck to our back yard so Dusty, our aging Pomeranian, could go up and down more easily. Dusty was afraid of the ramp. I tried luring him up, but he refused to set more than his front two feet on the surface. So we backchained. I set him on the top of the ramp, one body-length from the deck, and lured him up to safety. He did that easily, and after several repetitions I placed him a little farther down the ramp and lured him up to the deck. It took less than 15 minutes to get him confidently running up the ramp. Then we reversed it, and in just a few minutes he was running down the ramp as easily as he was running up.

Premack Principle

No, there is no Mack or Postmack, as one of my interns wondered recently. Premack is the scientist (first name David) who in the mid 1960s demonstrated that you can use a *more* rewarding behavior as the reinforcer for a *less* rewarding behavior, thereby improving the performance of the lesser behavior.

This principle is also sometimes called "Grandma's Law," as in, "You have to eat your vegetables before you can eat your dessert." If your dog would rather chase a squirrel than come when you call, you can use the **Premack principle** to teach him that he will get to chase a squirrel (sometimes) if he comes to you first. Start by applying Premack indoors in a controlled environment, and move outside when he's doing well.

Leave your dog on a sit-stay, and walk across the room. Position a helper with a plate of smelly treats halfway between you, slightly off to one side. The helper should also have a bowl, to cover the treats with when your dog tries to eat them. Now call your dog. If he stops to investigate the treats, the helper covers the bowl and doesn't let him have a taste. Keep calling your dog cheerfully and enthusiastically. When he comes to you, say "Good boy!" and "Go get it!" Race with your dog back to the treats, now uncovered, and let him have a few. Then cover the bowl and try again. Eventually—and surprisingly quickly, for some dogs—he will realize that he gets the treats if he comes to you *first,* and he will fly past the uncovered plate as fast as he can.

Premack exercise: To get the prize, the dog must pass it by and do something else first.

There are a couple of drawbacks to using Premack in real life: If the vegetables are too unpalatable, dessert may also lose its appeal; and you can't control the squirrels.

Habituation and Learned Irrelevance

These two concepts are quite similar. **Habituation** occurs when a dog learns to ignore an environmental stimulus, such as a startling noise, like the ringing of the telephone, or a disturbing sight, like a realistic statue of a dog. A dog who has never lived indoors may discover all sorts of disturbing stimuli if he's brought into a household.

Dubhy was six months old when we found him as a stray and brought him home to join our pack. He had clearly never lived in a house before, and when he saw his reflection in a full-length mirror he spent several minutes, on several occasions, peering behind the door to try to find the other dog. Eventually he habituated to the sight of the elusive Scottie and stopped looking.

Habituation is useful for training because dogs can learn to adapt to stimuli that are initially quite startling and distracting. However, sometimes the opposite effect occurs—**sensitization**. Some dogs, rather than habituating to a sound such as the telephone, become more and more reactive each time the stimulus occurs. Thunder phobia is a perfect example of this.

Learned irrelevance, while similar to habituation, applies to a dog who has learned to ignore a cue, rather than becoming accustomed to a startling stimulus. This is not deliberate defiance on the dog's part, but simply his response to a cue which has failed to have consistent and sufficiently strong significance attached to it. The cue becomes meaningless if it doesn't have a consequence. It's not salient.

"Come" is the most common example of this. Many dog owners use this word to call their dogs long before they ever take the time to actually *train* their dogs to come on cue. By the time they try to teach the dog to come, the dog has already learned that the word has no meaning.

The insidious thing about learned irrelevance is that once it has taken place, it's very difficult to instill salience to the cue. If your dog has learned that the word "Come" has no meaning, it will be easier for you to train him to come with a new cue than to try to make the old one significant. I have heard owners and trainers use words such as "Close," "Let's Go," and "Here" in place of an irrelevant "Come!"

Principle of Parsimony

This scientific principle applies to situations beyond dog behavior and training, but it's very applicable here too, and one of my favorites. It says, "Unless there is evidence to the contrary, you must account for a phenomenon with the simplest explanation available." Or, as one of my favorite radio personalities likes to say, "When you hear hoofbeats, think horses, not zebras."

If your adult dog has a single housetraining accident, the simplest behavioral explanation is that he had to relieve himself. Stress, bladder infections, and tumors are lower down the list, and "spite" doesn't even merit consideration. The appropriate response is to monitor his water intake and bathroom trips for a week or so to make sure he gets ample potty opportunities. If he continues to have accidents, then a more complex behavioral or medical cause would be suspect.

If your dog often pulls on the leash, the simple behavioral explanation is that he wants to go somewhere faster than you do. Dominance and defiance aren't even in the picture. If he normally walks politely on leash but suddenly starts pulling, simple explanations would be that something frightened him and he's trying to get away from it, or something very enticing is in front of him and he's trying to get to it. Again, dominance and other complex motives are unlikely.

As you can see, training can be a little more complicated than the basic "Sit," Click! and treat. The more you learn about the workings of your dog's brain, the better you'll understand how and why he does what he does, and the better prepared you are to respond appropriately. It can only enhance your already-wonderful relationship with your best friend.

Target Your Way to Discrimination

Targeting is very useful when you are teaching your dog to discriminate. If you have not already taught him it "Touch!" on cue, you'll want to start there. If he's already targeting to your hand, you're all set to teach him to identify—and find—family members.

Remind him of his "Touch!" behavior by having him target to your hand several times for clicks and treats. Now add Timmy (or some other family member), to the exercise. Have Timmy stand next to you, and instruct him to offer his hand as a target *immediately after* you say "Touch." With your dog on leash facing you both, say "Timmy, touch!" (It will be tempting to say "Touch Timmy," since this makes more sense to our human brains. Remember, to avoid blocking, the new cue must *precede* the known cue.) If your dog's targeting is strong—and most dogs *love* to target—he will recognize Timmy's body language cue when the boy offers his hand, and bump his cold wet nose into the offered target.

Repeat this several times until you're confident that your dog is targeting well to Timmy. Then have Timmy take a step away from you and continue your "Timmy, Touch!" cues, with your child offering his hand as the target. At this point have Timmy start making a less noticeable gesture with his target hand, until he can stand with his hands at this side and the dog will still target to him. You can also drop the "Touch" from the cue, since the word "Timmy" should have gained salience by now.

Gradually move Timmy farther and farther away from you and continue the exercises, starting each time with your dog next to you. Remember, the goal is to have him move away from you to the designated target—Timmy. Have Timmy treat him when you click, and then you Click! and treat when you call him back to you. *Note: It will probably take several sessions to accomplish this whole exercise. Always remember to stop the training before your dog's enthusiasm (or yours) starts to wane.*

When your dog will target to Timmy from across the room, have your child step out of the room, so the dog has to search for him. Add "Find" to your cue, so you are now asking your dog to "Find Timmy!" If you continue to increase the difficulty level, your dog will eventually be able to find Timmy when he's hidden in closets, behind trees, and in sheds. He might even find him some day when he's really lost!

But back to our discrimination exercise. When your dog targets well to Timmy, do the same thing with another family member, perhaps your spouse. (Of course, now you will use your spouse's name instead of "Timmy!") When your dog will target well to at least two family members, you can try your first discrimination exercise.

Have both family members with you, on opposite sides of the room. Stand in the middle with your dog by your side so you are both facing more toward Timmy, and say "Find Timmy!" If he targets to Timmy, Click! and treat. If he targets to your spouse, everyone just ignore him, until he decides to try Timmy. Then Click! and treat. If he loses interest in the challenge before he gets to Timmy, call him back to you and try again, but this time move closer to Timmy and face him more clearly.

Play with this step for a while, alternating randomly between your two family members, gradually using less of your own body language to help your dog make the right choice, and gradually moving your two targets closer together. When he can make the right choice eight out of ten times with Timmy and Spouse standing five feet apart, you're ready to add a third person.

Yes, it takes some work, but its *fun* work. It let's you enjoy the captivating experience of watching your dog think, while at the same time teaching him a useful skill. When he's good, you can have him carry messages to your family, like "Dinner's Ready!" or "Five minutes until the school bus arrives!"—and if Timmy ever falls down the well, your dog can find him!

Look At Me!

Paying attention to you is a vital skill for your dog
(and easy to learn)

One of the first things I teach people to teach their dogs in my basic "Good Manners" class is to respond to their names. We can't teach our dogs anything, I tell my students, unless we have their attention.

Getting attention is not enough, however. To be truly successful in training you must be able to *keep* a dog's attention once you have it. This is best accomplished by convincing her that it's in her best interest to offer attention of her own accord.

If you've ever watched an obedience competition and marveled at the dogs who gaze intently at their handlers' faces throughout the entire test, never once breaking eye contact, you know exactly what we're talking about. It speaks volumes about the relationship between dog and owner to have that kind of communication…or does it?

The Old Way

When I was first training my dogs seriously for obedience competition, I was disillusioned to discover exactly how that kind of attention was accomplished. My dogs and I learned two approaches: the force-based way and the hot dog way.

The force-based way was pretty brutal at times. We would stand with our dogs in the heel position, each of us exhorting our own dogs to "Watch me!" while training assistants, otherwise known as "distractions," would move among us, doing everything they could think of to get our dogs to look away—calling, clapping, whistling, offering hot dogs. If our dog took her eyes off us to look at a distraction, we were to say "Watch me!" and give a severe yank on the choke chain. Our dogs soon realized the price they paid for looking away, and kept their eyes glued on us for fear of the painful consequence of doing otherwise.

The Hot Dog Way

The hot dog way was more fun for all concerned. We humans would stuff our cheeks full of hot dog pieces (make mine a veggie dog!), which we would occasionally spit toward our canine partners as we heeled merrily around the training ring. Never knowing when the next hot dog "penny" might coming flying through the air, our dogs kept their eyes riveted on our faces. It was more eye-to-lip contact than eye-to-eye contact actually, but it kept them oriented toward us as the obedience genre expected, and sufficed to earn us high scores in the competitive obedience ring.

I much preferred the far more benign hot dog way, of course—and I'm sure my dogs did too—but it still left something to be desired in terms of positive training and relationship. My dogs looked at my face because they recognized that hot dogs appeared from that location, but I'm not sure they thought it was their intense gazes that *made* the hot dogs appear.

At the time, I didn't know that teaching dogs how to "make" us give them a reward for their behavior was a desirable goal. I had been taught the luring technique as a way to elicit the desired behavior; I was as yet unfamiliar with the concept of teaching dogs to *think* from an operant conditioning perspective.

Modern Methods

Today's positive trainer has a much more sophisticated approach to teaching the "Watch me!" exercise. We want the dog to actually *think* and understand that looking at her handler attentively makes good stuff happen, regardless of *where* the treats happen to be.

To that end, the first session of my classes I have the owners come without their dogs, and I explain that when they arrive with dogs the next week they will stand quietly, just holding their dogs' leashes and not asking for any behavior or soliciting attention. The instant their dogs look at them—or even look in their general direction—they are to Click! a clicker and give their dogs a treat. They are to continue clicking and handing over treats at a high rate of reinforcement as long as the dogs keep looking at them. If a dog looks away, her handler should stop the flow of treats, and wait for the dog to pay attention again. The intent of this exercise is to teach the dogs that voluntary attention is a highly rewardable behavior.

It takes only about five minutes for most or all of the dogs to be intently focused on their personal click-and-treat dispensers. Then the students can begin to ask their dogs for other behaviors they have practiced during their first week of training at home, such as sit, stand, and down. I tell the owners to use the dog's name for brief lapses of attention, but to continue to look for opportunities to Click! and reward voluntary attention.

If your dog tends to react to other dogs she sees when you are walking together, teach her to look at you when you see other dogs, and reward her for the attention.

As the dogs progress, I add distractions to the attention exercise, but rather than deliberately luring the dogs' attention away so the owners can punish them, I introduce distractions at a low level so the dogs can succeed in remaining focused on their owners and get rewarded for that behavior. They learn that keeping their attention on their owners even in the face of increasingly tempting distractions is highly rewarded.

"He's Just Looking at the Food!"

At some point during the six weeks of my "basic" class, some owners point out that their dogs are orienting on their treats—on bait bags, treat pockets, or treats-in-hand—rather than really making eye contact. I have them work on this by making the *treats* the distraction.

The owner starts by holding the treat up to her face to encourage eye contact. When the dog looks at her, she Clicks! and gives the dog the treat. Then she moves the treat a few inches to the side of her face and waits. Sooner or later the dog, who is watching the treat intently, will glance toward the owner's face as if to ask why the Click! is not forthcoming. *At that instant* the owner Clicks! and feeds the dog the treat. She repeats this until the dog is looking at her face quickly, and for increasingly long periods of time (up to several seconds) to elicit the Click! and treat.

Then she moves the treat a few inches farther from her face and continues the game. At this point she also adds the "Watch!" or "Pay attention!" cue that she will use to get the dog to maintain eye contact from then on. It is important to Click! consistently *before* the dog breaks eye contact while gradually lengthening the contact time, so the dog comes to understand that "Watch!" means "*maintain* eye contact until released."

Eventually, the treat can be anywhere, while the dog's gaze remains riveted to the owner's face for long periods. Voila! Now this dog/owner team can go into the obedience or Rally ring and achieve the kind of attention that spectators and other competitors envy. And this is accomplished *not* because the dog is waiting for a hot dog to shoot out of the handler's mouth, or avoiding a punishing jerk on the collar. It happens because the dog truly understands and happily performs the desired and rewardable behavior of maintaining eye contact and attention, even while in perfect heel position.

For "Regular" Dogs Too!

Treats need not be the only reward for paying attention. If your Border Collie is obsessed with her tennis ball (and what self-respecting Border Collie isn't?), teach her that eye contact, not bumping you with her nose or jumping up on you, is what makes you throw the ball. You can also teach your dog that sitting quietly near you and staring at you will earn her a chance to go play outside, go for a walk, or play a game with you.

Even though this skill is critical for competitors in the show ring, it's also a valuable behavior for "regular" dogs and owners.

A good "attention" cue can keep your reactive dog focused on you while other dogs (or other reaction-eliciting stimuli) pass nearby. It can keep your dog away from the Arrowroot™ biscuit in the nearby toddler's hand, or from the pile of unidentifiable rotting carcass on the side of the hiking trail.

Also, if you have visions of fame and fortune, it can keep her attentive to you when you make your grand debut on the *PetStarz* stage in front of distracting spotlights and a huge live audience. But whether you make it to Hollywood or not, the two of you will be stars in your own right if you can perfect the "Pay Attention" game and apply it to everyday life.

Name Response Exercise

There are certainly times when it's useful to be able to *get* your dog's attention if she's not choosing to offer it to you of her own accord. You can achieve this handy behavior by teaching her that her name means "Look at me and wait for further instructions," or in doggie shorthand, "Huh? Whaddya want?!"

It's an easy behavior to teach. Start by luring your dog's eyes toward yours with a tasty tidbit, and when her eyes meet yours, Click! a clicker and give her a treat. After a few repetitions, when you know you can lure her eyes to yours, say her name *first*, before you lure. Click! and give her a treat. It's okay if she's already (or still) looking into your eyes, say her name and Click! and treat anyway.

After a half-dozen repetitions of this, begin to "fade" the lure. Say her name and pause to see if she will look at you without the lure. If she does, Click! and treat. If not, make a sound (a kissy noise, for example), to attract her attention, then Click! and give her a treat.

Now that she's had ample opportunity to associate her name with the Click! and treat, wait until she looks away with mild interest at something else, then say her name. When she snaps her head back to look at you, Click! and jackpot! Give several treats, one after the other, making a big show over her great response. Continue to practice, with mild distractions at first, *gradually* increasing the intensity of the distraction until she will happily look back to you from the most enticing diversions.

It's very important to remember that you only use the cue—your dog's name—one time. If she doesn't look at you, then do something else to prompt the "Huh?" response: make a kissing noise, squeak a squeaky toy, clap your hands, bounce a ball. If necessary, move your training session to a location with fewer or less exciting distractions. If you keep repeating her name without getting the desired response, you teach her that her name has no meaning—a concept I call "learned irrelevance." It is more difficult to overcome a dog's learned irrelevance to a cue than to teach the dog a new cue, so if yours has already learned to ignore her name, you might consider a new nickname or "Huh?" cue; it will be easier to get the response you want.

Now you're prepared for all eventualities. If your dog offers her attention, use your "Pay Attention!" cue to tell her to keep focusing on you until you release her. If she's distracted, ask for her attention with her name, and when she makes eye contact, *then* ask her to "Pay Attention!"

Greetings and Salutations

*The process of teaching your dog to greet people
calmly starts at home*

During Week 2 of my Peaceable Paws Good Manners class, I ask the question, "How many of your dogs jump up on people?" Generally at least eighty percent of the dog owners in class raise their hands.

"Why do they jump up?" I ask.

I usually get at least one incorrect answer of "Dominance!" but most of my students realize their dogs jump up for attention. And because much of the time the behavior is successful, it's a challenging one to extinguish.

Be Consistent

Consistency is the cornerstone—and the bane—of training success. Consistent reinforcement of polite doggy greetings is reasonably easy. The tough part is ensuring that impolite greetings are consistently *not* reinforced. Even if *you* are very good at not reinforcing your dog's jumping up behaviors, the entire rest of the world is pretty crummy at it. If jumping up is reinforced randomly, it's very difficult to extinguish.

Paul (my husband) and I are very consistent at not reinforcing our Corgi for jumping up. Lucy is now very good at not jumping up—on us. She still wants to jump on everyone else she sees, so we work persistently on preventing her from being reinforced by everyone else.

I teach my students a three-step process for changing a behavior you don't want. It's perfect for applying to rude greetings:

Step 1: Visualize the behavior you *do* want. Instead of thinking, "I wish my dog wouldn't jump on people," have an image in your mind of the behavior you'd prefer to see: "I'd like my dog to greet people by sitting politely in front of them."

Step 2: Prevent your dog from being reinforced for the behavior you don't want. This means taking appropriate management steps to proactively intercede *before* Bounder plants his paws on a guest's shoulders. Your persistent removal of reinforcement for jumping isn't enough; you have to convince the entire rest of the world to follow suit.

Step 3: Generously and consistently reinforce the behavior you *do* want. Simply ignoring an undesirable behavior leaves a behavior vacuum. Unless you generously reinforce an alternative behavior, your dog will likely default to the behavior he knows, that has worked for him in the past. Constantly be on the lookout for polite greeting sits. Be sure to greet your dog when he offers them. It's human nature that we tend to overlook good behavior and respond to bad behavior. Turn that around.

Practice Makes Perfect

The three-step process sounds easy in principle. It's not always so easy in practice. You're most likely to encounter problems with greeting immediate family members, greeting guests in your home, and greeting people in public. Let's look at how you could apply the three-step process in each of these scenarios.

Greeting Family Members

In theory, this should be the easiest of the three scenarios, since family members are around very frequently and should be committed to helping you change the behavior. In reality, we know how hard those darned humans can be to train! (Remember that positive reinforcement works well with primates, too!)

You can try several different approaches with family members. First, all must agree to stop reinforcing your dog for jumping, and all must understand that *any attention at all* is reinforcement. Making eye contact with your dog when he jumps up is reinforcing him. By pushing him off, you've touched him—reinforcement! Asking him to "Off!" gives him attention by speaking to him. Reinforcement! In fact, just the fact that his paws touched you can be rewarding to your dog, even if you do nothing else.

To avoid reinforcing your dog for jumping up, he needs to get the opposite response. Rather than eliciting attention, a jump should make all attention go away. When Bounder starts his lift-off, say "Oops!" as you turn your back on him and step away. If he jumps again, turn and step away again. Keep an eye over your shoulder, and when he stops jumping (and, we hope, sits), turn back toward him and give him treats and/or attention.

Meanwhile, use a tether to *teach* him a more appropriate greeting. You can secure your dog with a leash, but a more durable tether consists of a four to five foot piece of plastic coated cable with sturdy snaps on both ends. Attach it to an adequately heavy piece of furniture, or create a tether station by screwing an eyebolt into a wall stud and clipping the tether to it. Alternatively, you can screw an eyebolt into a 2 x 4 block of wood, clip the tether to it, and slide it under a door that, when closed, holds your dog in place.

Use a tether to prevent your dog from jumping up on guests when they arrive. Generously reinforce his calm behavior.

With Bounder on his tether, approach from a distance. If he's leaping about in greeting, stand still until he's calm, then move forward. Anytime he starts to jump, stand still, or even take a step back. When you are close enough to reach out and touch him (but he still can't jump on you), stand still and wait for him to sit. You can help him get the idea by holding a treat at your chest a few times, but you'll want to fade the treat (stop using it) quickly so he learns to offer a sit in greeting without being lured. By the same token, don't *ask* him to sit—wait for him to offer it. You want him to volunteer the sit in greeting, not wait to be asked for it.

When he sits, mark the polite behavior with a "Yes!" or the Click! of a clicker, feed him a treat, and give him attention. Repeat this exercise until he sits promptly as soon as you head toward him.

Many dogs will immediately resume jumping up when petted, especially if they have been allowed to greet people boisterously in the past. If your dog starts to leap up as you reach for him or pet him, simply stand up, take a step backward (out of his range), and wait for him to sit again. You may have to withdraw and return several times in rapid succession before he realizes that leaping up makes the thing he wants (attention) go away, and sitting firmly on his bottom makes it return.

Teach your family not to reinforce the dog when he jumps up——rather they should quickly turn away.

Now have the rest of the family practice, all the way down to the toddler.

Of course, your dog won't always be on a tether, but when he has learned this exercise he'll be much quicker to offer you (and others) that highly reinforced "Sit" behavior in other scenarios as well.

Perhaps the most aroused greetings occur when you return home after a long day away. Bounder is clearly thrilled to see you, and it can be hard to turn your back on such a sincere display of love. Our human family members should greet us with this much enthusiasm day after day!

If you are reluctant to squelch your dog's welcome home enthusiasm, redirect it to a game you both can enjoy. Stash your dog's favorite toy—or several—in a box just outside the door. Walk into the house with the toy in your hand, and toss it for him to fetch. Even better, reinforce polite greetings by waiting for a sit before you toss. The "welcome home fetch game" allows your dog to be happy about your return, lets you reciprocate, and still keeps his energy controlled and directed into a productive and polite outlet. It's also easy to transfer to children and visitors!

You may have a family member who insists that he *wants* Bounder to be able to jump on him. Promise your body-slammer masochist that he can teach Bounder to jump up on cue—*after* the dog has learned to greet politely. That might motivate him to help with, rather than sabotage, Bounder's training. Then, when the two of you are ready to teach "Jump up!" be sure you select verbal and body language cues that are very distinctive, and not likely to be offered by accident by an unsuspecting dog greeter.

Greeting Guests in Your Home

Of course, it's too much to expect that visitors will know enough to turn their backs on your dog when he jumps up on them, so it's incumbent on *you* to make sure he doesn't have the opportunity. Your tether will come in handy here. When the doorbell rings, calmly clip him to his tether station, feed him a yummy treat, then go greet your guests. You don't have to worry about a door-darting dog, or one who blithely ruins your guest's nylons. Peace of mind. Over time, Bounder may even come to learn that the doorbell is the cue to go to his tether and wait for treats!

If necessary, leave a tab (a four to six inch piece of leash) or a house lead (a three to six foot light line) attached to your dog's collar so he's easy to gather up and tether. Be sure to remove these when you're not home, to prevent tangling accidents.

As your guests enter, hand them a few treats, and ask them to approach Bounder on his tether. Be sure they understand that they can feed him the treats and pet him *only when he is sitting*. Then supervise to be sure they follow directions.

When your dog's initial excitement subsides, you can release him to greet your guests off leash. By then, you will have had time to instruct them on how to properly reinforce his polite greeting, and how to avoid reinforcing him if he does try to jump.

You can also choose to play the "welcome fetch" game with visitors. Put a large sign on your door instructing visitors to take a toy from the box, bring it in the house with them, and throw it for Bounder when he sits. Dog loving visitors—the only kind who come to my house!—will enjoy this immensely. Remove the sign when you're not home, so burglars don't learn the trick of getting past your "guard" dog!

Greeting People in Public

In public, your leash is the tether. Hold the leash, giving your dog only about three feet of slack. As people approach, keep your distance and the leash at a length that prevents your dog from lunging forward and jumping up on the passerby. You can, of course, reinforce your dog if he offers a sit. If the approachers appear to have dog-petting on their minds, ask *(insist!)* that they wait for him to sit first. If they say, "That's okay, I don't mind if he jumps up," politely but firmly tell them that *you* mind, and that they need to wait until Bounder sits. If they ignore your instructions, turn and walk away with your dog, with a cheery "Oops! Sorry!"

If they are willing, you can hand them a couple of treats to feed when your dog sits. If they seem really interested, ask them if they'll help you train. Give them a handful of treats and ask them to do several approach-sit repetitions to give Bounder more practice at greeting strangers politely on the street.

Fearful Greetings

So far, we have presupposed an overenthusiastic greeter, whose behavior is best addressed with positive reinforcement and negative punishment principles of operant conditioning, where the dog's behavior (a polite sit) causes a good thing to happen (attention), and jumping up causes that same good thing to go away.

Some dog owners have the opposite problem—the dog who launches a volley of defensive fear-barking at the sound of the doorbell or the approach of a stranger on the street. This behavior is best modified through the use of **counter-conditioning**—changing the dog's association with visitors and strangers from "Bad! Scary!" to "Yay, treats are coming!"

You might begin by ringing the doorbell yourself, and immediately follow the sound with several tidbits of canned chicken (or something equally succulent and delicious), delivered to your dog's waiting jaws, *even if he's barking*. Repeat this exercise until the sound of the doorbell generates a "Yay! Where's my chicken?" response instead of wild barking.

Then have someone else ring the doorbell—someone your dog knows. Repeat the doorbell-chicken sequence until you're getting the positive response. Then have the person ring the bell and open the door. This is likely to elicit another round of defensive barking. Feed chicken. Then repeat, and continue repeating until the doorbell/door opening sequence consistently generates the "Where's my chicken?" response from your dog. Then have the person ring the bell, open the door, and step into the room.

Continue the progression, one small step at a time, feeding chicken at each step until you get the positive response at that level, then take the next step. When he's fine with the person he knows, try someone he doesn't know, or at least doesn't know as well, until he can maintain calm when anyone enters the house.

You can do a similar exercise with people on the street. Set yourself up a distance off the sidewalk so people aren't walking directly at your dog. The instant he notices someone walking in your direction, start feeding him bits of chicken. When the person has passed by, stop. Over time, as he associates people approaching with yummy chicken, his response should become calmer.

Important note: Do *not* have the *other* person feed treats to a fearful dog. His desire for the treat may overcome his caution, temporarily, but when the treat is gone and he realizes he's too close to a person who scares him, he may bite. You need to first change the association by feeding your dog the treats yourself. When your dog is happy to have visitors and strangers in close proximity, *then* you can ask the other person to drop treats, or offer them gently using very non-threatening body language: kneel sideways to the dog, hold the treat out to the side, not making direct eye contact, or any overt moves to reach for the dog.

If you are consistent and persistent, your dog can learn to greet people politely. In fact, he will soon run up to you and sit as hard and as fast as he can, with as much enthusiasm as he now displays when he jumps up on you. After all, dogs do what works. If you can manage matters so the behavior *you* want is the behavior that works for your dog, everybody wins!

Come Hither

A dependable recall provides off-leash freedom and safety

Taking advantage of a warm, sunny winter day, I went for a hike around the farm yesterday with our five dogs. It was a perfect opportunity to work on recalls.

Recall is the obedience ring term for "coming when called," an exceptionally useful canine behavior. With a solid recall, you can grant your dog off-leash privileges in unfenced dog parks, on dog-legal hiking trails, and at beaches where less accomplished dogs must remain tethered to their humans.

Your dog can enjoy the experience of unfettered canine freedom, wind whipping past his ears as he stretches his legs and runs doggy circles around you. You'll also benefit from his increased exercise when you return home—a tired dog is a well-behaved dog.

I was most interested in practicing with Bonnie, the newest member of our troupe. While I'd done some "Come" work with her in the house since we adopted her from the humane society in November, inclement winter weather had prevented us from doing much outside. At age six months, it was time for our Scottie-Corgi mix to learn to generalize the "Come" cue to the outside world.

No Popping the Leash

Much has changed in dog training since I trained my first Rough Collie in the 1960s. In those days, we introduced the recall exercise by leaving our dogs on a sit-stay, marching to the end of the leash, turning around, and calling "Come" in a commanding tone. The command was often accompanied by a solid "pop" on the leash, to convince the dog that "not coming" was not in his best interests.

"Come" *can* be a challenging behavior to train. In today's kinder, gentler world of positive training, we realize it's not necessary to jerk on leashes to compel dogs to come. We simply make the consequences of coming when called irresistibly delightful to convince the dog that coming when called is very wonderful indeed. We don't even use "commands" anymore; we use "cues" instead. (See "Cues v. Commands: What's In A Word?" pg. 105.)

A reliable recall depends on a strong, automatic conditioned response to the cue. When your dog hears you call him, you want him halfway back to you before his conscious brain even kicks in. You instill this automatic response by associating the cue with a very high value reward from the very beginning of his recall training. Here's how:

Step 1: Select a very high-value treat reward, such as chicken. Have your dog near you in a quiet room, on leash if necessary to keep him from wandering.

Step 2: Say your recall cue in the tone you would normally use to call your dog, and pop a bit of chicken in his mouth. Repeat this "Come!" and treat sequence several times in rapid succession. Your dog will probably glue his attention on you as soon as he realizes you're dispensing a high value treat. That's okay! You don't have to call him away from anything; at this point you're just associating the "Come!" cue with chicken.

Step 3: After several repetitions of Step 2, stand up, take a few running steps away from your dog and say "Come!" Then stop and feed chicken. Repeat this step until he's happily bounding after you as you run away. "Come!" now means "Run fast after my human to get chicken!" You're taking advantage of your dog's natural instinct to chase moving things to add enthusiasm and speed to his "Come!" response.

Step 4: As long as you're in a safely enclosed space you can take your dog's leash off for this step and beyond. Drop a few regular treats on the floor, and while your dog is eating, quietly move 10 to 15 feet away. The instant he finishes the treats on the floor, call "Come!" and run away fast. Stop and feed chicken when he gets to you. Repeat this step until you're confident he'll dash to you full speed every time you call. You can also add "Round Robin Recalls" at this step. Have other family members participate in games of "call the dog back and forth," with each person in turn calling the dog, running away, stopping and treating.

With your dog on-leash indoors, take a few running steps, call "Come!" rewarding him to keep up with you.

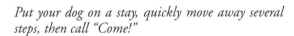

Put your dog on a stay, quickly move away several steps, then call "Come!"

Stop and feed your dog some high value chicken when he gets to you.

Step 5: Now add a collar touch. You want to be able to restrain your dog when he gets to you—not have him eat the treat and dance away. Repeat Step 4, and while your dog is eating treats from one hand, gently reach under his chin with your other hand and touch his collar. After several repetitions, when he's perfectly comfortable with the collar touch, gently take hold of it while you keep feeding treats.

When he's accustomed to having you grasp his collar, ask him to "Sit!" If necessary, lure him into a sit with a treat. If he sits easily, you can ask for the sit first, and then grasp the collar. Be sure to associate the collar-grasp with treats! This step will help him learn that "Come!" means "come and park," not "come and run away again."

Step 6: Look for opportunities to call him to you when he's not doing anything important—when he's wandering around the room sniffing, or lying calmly on his bed in the corner. Run away at least a few steps when you call, and reward with a high value treat when he responds. Repeat until he'll come happily every time you call him from these minor preoccupations. Regardless of what he's doing, when he hears you call, his head should instantly snap toward you and his feet should start moving. When he'll do this, the response is starting to become automatic.

You now have a reliable recall under ideal conditions—indoors, without distractions. It's time to raise the bar. Indoors, start adding distractions: small ones at first, then increasingly tempting ones. First it's the cat lying on the coffee table, or another family member sitting on the sofa. Next might be the cat walking across the room, or the family member munching popcorn on the sofa. When you're getting a consistent and reliable automatic "Come" response to these moderate distractions, you might graduate to having the cat dash across the room, a child bouncing a ball, or a family member eating a hamburger on the sofa.

In each case, work at whichever of the six steps is necessary for your dog to succeed.

When training outdoors, take advantage of your dog's instincts to chase.

Road Show

Meanwhile, start taking the recall show on the road—outdoors. With your dog on-leash, work in as low-distraction an environment as you can engineer. Outdoors is infinitely more distracting than indoors, even without joggers, skateboards, motorcycles, squirrels, and other dogs. A back yard with a solid wooden fence is ideal to minimize the inevitable exciting stimuli your dog may want to investigate.

Start at Step 2 of the program, and work there until you're getting a reliable automatic response. Then move up the steps, achieving a reliable response at each level before you move on. If at any time you've lost your dog's response, go back to the prior step and work there until you're ready to progress.

When your dog does reliable off-leash recalls in the fenced yard with major distractions, raise the bar higher. Go back on-leash, and work in more open areas where your distractions will be even less predictable.

You can control the unpredictable to some degree. If your dog will be highly aroused by a passing jogger or bicycle, work as far off the bike path as needed to succeed—20, 50, or 100 feet, if necessary. Gradually move closer to the path or road as your dog's recall response becomes automatic even in the presence of compelling distractions.

There's nothing wrong with *always* giving your dog high value treats to reinforce his recall. This keeps the automatic response strong and healthy.

Remember to *absolutely* keep your dog on-leash unless you're in a safely confined area. You can purchase long lines—leashes that are 20 to 50 feet long—for distance training in open areas. You can use retractable leashes for this purpose too, although I am not fond of them for general training and walking purposes—they can get you into too much trouble!

Take a Hike

When your dog is extremely reliable at long distances in open areas, consider taking him off-leash in safe, dog-legal hiking areas. Some dog owners are never willing to risk the possibility that their dog might disappear after a bounding deer in a wilderness area, perhaps never to be seen again. As a rule of thumb, herding, working and sporting breeds tend toward recall reliability more easily, while terriers and hounds can be more challenging—although there are plenty of exceptions on all counts. Carefully consider your dog's basic personality, level of training and reliability to his recall cue, and make a safe choice for him.

In our pack, Tucker and Katie are quite reliable, and have earned off-leash privileges in any safe dog-legal area. Lucy is strong-willed and independent, living up to her formal name of "Footloose and Fancy Free." She gets off-leash privileges here on the farm, but not yet elsewhere in polite society.

Dubhy does his part for the Terrier reputation—he has limited off-leash privileges under direct supervision, but will happily head off into the woods after groundhogs if my attention lapses. Once he's on a serious groundhog mission, his recall fails. Baby Bonnie, at 6 months of age, is a recall star. Despite her part-Scottie heritage, she has a soft personality and a strong connection to her humans. Her automatic recall response transferred almost instantly outside. She gained off-leash farm privileges her first trip out, although, of course, we continue to practice.

No matter how well trained my dogs are, I'll never intentionally have them off leash where traffic is nearby. I shudder every time I see an owner walking a dog off-leash along a busy road. There's no such thing as 100 percent reliability, regardless of the methods or tools you use to train. Even well-trained dogs make mistakes, just as we humans do, and I would hate to lose a beloved companion to the wheels of a speeding vehicle just because I was overconfident or complacent about his recall reliability.

Five Common Recall Mistakes

Your recall training will go more smoothly if you avoid these common mistakes:

Mistake #1—Not Training "Come": Because puppies are dependent on their humans and tend to stay close, it's easy to assume they've learned to come when called. An owner may get a rude awakening when a pup, reaching adolescence, starts to explore his world and assert his independence. Don't assume. Put in the training time, and if responses start to slip during adolescence, return to earlier training steps until the response becomes reliable again.

Mistake #2—Adding Distractions Too Soon: It's a mistake to call your dog to you before the recall response is solidly automatic, when he's doing something way more exciting than coming—like rolling in deer poop, romping with his pals, or chasing a fleeing squirrel. When you have a solidly trained recall in a low-distraction environment, add distractions gradually. Meanwhile, don't put your dog in an environment where you *have* to call him away from powerful distractions.

Mistake #3—Punishing Your Dog for Coming: A smart dog owner knows not to yell at or otherwise deliberately punish a wayward dog when he finally returns. Many owners don't realize they *inadvertently* punish their dogs for coming when called by doing something the dog finds undesirable. If you call your dog to you and start to clip his nails—and he hates nail trimming—you punished him for coming. Be sure "Come!" always results in a pleasant result. The not-so-wonderful stuff can happen a little later. A few minutes break between recall and nail trimming will be enough to avoid the negative association with the "Come!" cue.

Mistake #4—Failing to Generalize the "Come" Cue: It's easy to fall into the trap of training a terrific recall in your house or at your training class, and forgetting to generalize it to the outside world. Just because your dog makes a beeline for you when you call him in your living room doesn't mean he'll dash to you in an open field. Diligently practice the raised bar exercises beyond Step 6 in a wide range of environments to help your dog generalize his automatic "Come!" response to the rest of the world.

Mistake #5—Failing to Make "Come" Wonderfully Fun and Rewarding: An off-leash dog always has a choice to come when you call—or not. By making "Come!" a well-reinforced response, you'll help your dog consistently make the right choice when you call. In addition to high-value food rewards you can use other objects or activities your dog loves to reinforce a reliable recall. If your dog is nuts for a tennis ball, occasionally use a rousing game of "Fetch!" as his recall reward.

Cues vs. Commands: What's in a Word?

With the dog-training industry's shift toward more positive methods comes a parallel shift in vocabulary. The way you think guides the way you behave. One of the most striking examples is the trainer's choice of the word "cue" instead of "command." Another is their preference for saying "good manners" instead of "obedience." The change suggests a repertoire of useful, socially acceptable behaviors that go far beyond the rote performance of rigid, show-ring exercises.

The dictionary definition of "command" is: *To direct with authority; give orders to.* Indeed, owners and trainers who think in terms of "command" tend to bark orders to their dogs authoritatively and forcefully, often accompanied by intimidating body language. Because they expect orders to be obeyed, if the dog fails to comply they perceive him as recalcitrant, and may follow up the command with physical force or harsh verbal corrections.

In contrast, a "cue" is defined as: *A signal, such as a word or action, used to prompt another event in a performance.* A cue is a simple transfer of information—a request for a behavior rather than a demand. Owners who use cues with their dogs are more likely to offer them in a conversational tone of voice with relaxed body language. A failure to perform is more often viewed as a lack of understanding or attention than a deliberate disobedience.

By using more positive words to describe and define your dog and your training, you'll translate positive intent into positive action. Here are some of the vocabulary differences:

Old

Command
A demand for behavior which *will* be reinforced

Obedience
Strict, immediate responses to commands

Punish/Correct
"The dog is stubborn"

"The dog is sneaky"

"The dog is stupid"

"Make the dog obey"

New

Cue
A transfer of information

A request for a behavior

Good Manners
Appropriate social behaviors for a canine companion

Help the dog perform the behavior
"The dog is strong-willed and independent"

"The dog is creative and resourceful"

"The dog hasn't learned that yet"

"Help the dog perform the behavior"

Tug It!

This game <u>can</u> cause trouble if it's not well directed—but it can also teach your dog a number of important skills

Some trainers say you shouldn't play tug with your dog. Not me! Those of you who enjoy playing this energy eating aerobic activity with your dog will be pleased to know that I personally think it's a fine game to play, as long as you're using appropriate tug toys and playing with rules.

Tug, in case you've never had the pleasure of playing, is a fun and exciting game in which you hold one end of a tug object while your dog pulls with all his might on the other end. Variations include dog-dog tug, tug human around on a wheeled object (such as an office chair), and self-tug (in which the dog tugs an object such as a stuffed Kong™ that is secured to a sturdy post or tree).

Paws loves playing tug more than anything in the world. He growls and even barks (with his teeth clenched shut!) in a most fearsome manner, and he is incredibly strong.

Arguments Against Tug

Here are a few of the reasons you may have heard for *not* playing tug with your dog, followed my responses:

Reason: It encourages your dog to be dominant.

Response: It has nothing to do with dominance; it has to do with play and exercise. As with many other doggie games, you can easily create a structure that reminds your dog that you control the good stuff—in this case, the tug toy—which enhances your high-ranking position in the social structure, rather than undermining it.

Reason: It encourages your dog to be aggressive.

Response: Dogs can become very aroused playing tug. You can easily prevent this by stopping the game whenever your dog gets too excited. Use a phrase such as "That's all!" as you stop the game, and you will soon have a cue you can use in any situation where you want your dog to stop what he's doing and calm down.

Reason: It teaches your dog to put his teeth on your clothes and skin.

Response: Dogs *can* make poor decisions about where to put their teeth when they're engaged in a rousing game of tug. You can use this as a perfect opportunity to *decrease* the likelihood that your dog will bite in play by teaching him that teeth on human skin makes the fun stop. If you say something cheerfully (such as "Too bad!") and call a short time-out any time your dog's teeth stray into forbidden territory, you will teach your dog to keep his teeth to himself.

The game does not make him aggressive or "dominant" because he is allowed to play tug only if he adheres to the rules, especially the dictum against grabbing the toy without permission.

Arguments For Tug

- **Its great exercise:** It's a lovely indoor activity, perfect for relieving pent-up energy for a dog who's shut in on a stormy day or a sub-zero winter week. A low key version of the game is also useful for occupying a dog who is on physical restriction following surgery or an injury.

- **It can be used to teach retrieve:** A dog who is less-than-enthusiastic about putting retrieve objects in his mouth can sometimes be motivated to do so by encouraging him to play tug. When he gets aroused about tugging, you can take advantage of his enthusiasm to shape the retrieve.

- **It can be used to teach recalls:** Is your dog less-than-sterling about coming when called? Get him hooked on tug—then stick a tug toy in your pocket when you go hiking. When he's a short distance from you, call him, show him the toy and watch him beeline back to you for a short tug session. Stick the toy back in your pocket (or backpack), let him wander off a bit again and repeat. Stop before he's tired of tugging, so he's always strongly motivated to return. (Practice this on a long line at first, to be sure it will work for you!)

- **It's a useful distracter:** Lucy used to take delight in tormenting our Scottie, who hikes with me on a long line because his recall is not reliable. The long blue leash snaking through the grass would catch Lucy's eye, and she'd latch onto it and drag poor Dubhy around.

  A tug toy was perfect for redirecting her desire to grab and pull his leash. (I may, however, teach her to grab his leash and bring him back to me on those occasions when the recall doesn't work!)

- **It can be a stress reliever** Many dogs develop a very positive association with the tug game.

  One of my clients discovered a great application for tug while trying to do counter conditioning and desensitization (CC&D) exercises in public with her dog and people-reactive Briard. When the stimulus (a dog and/or person) occasionally and unexpectedly presented itself too closely, Jobie was too stressed to take treats. Terry discovered she could whip out a toy for a gentle game of tug and use her dog's positive association with the tug game to reduce his stress enough to the point he would eat treats and then resume the CC&D.

- **It's great for teaching self control**: As discussed in "arguments against," tug is a perfect activity for teaching your dog to control his energy and mouth placement, by teaching an "All done" cue to end the game, and using a "Too bad!" time out when canine teeth touch human skin or clothing.

- **It can be a "legal" outlet for roughhousing**: There is often at least one family member—usually male—who delights in playing rough physical games with the dog. Physical games that encourage body-slamming and mouthing *do* tend to reinforce inappropriate behaviors. Convince your roughhousing humans to play tug by the rules, and they'll help you reinforce desirable behaviors instead, while fulfilling their need to get physical with the dog.

- **It can build relationships**: Doing things with your dog that he loves helps build a strong bond between you. Playing tug with a dog who loves it can reinforce his focus on you, and his interest and pleasure in playing and training with you. While food rewards are an important part of positive training, life rewards—activities that are meaningful and reinforcing to the dog—strengthen the relationship and give you options for using other rewards in addition to treats.

Rules of the Game

These are general guidelines for making tug a positive training/relationship experience. The calmer and better behaved your dog is, the less necessary it is to follow the rules strictly. The more rowdy and out of control your dog, the more closely you will want to adhere to them. By the way, don't be alarmed by your dog's growls during tug—it's all part of the game. As long as his other behaviors are appropriate, let him growl his heart out!

Rule #1: You start the game. Keep the tug toy put away, and get it out when *you* want to play. It's perfectly okay to get it out when you know *he* is in the mood, but it's your choice to start the game. You control the good stuff.

Rule #2: No grabbing. Hold up the toy, and if your dog grabs or leaps for it, say "Oops!" and hide it behind your back. Then offer it again. When he is no longer leaping or grabbing, say "Take it" and offer his end to him. Then give him the cue to "Tug!" or "Pull!" and the game is on. You control the good stuff and allow him to have it out of the goodness of your heart.

Rule #3: You win most of the time. "Winning" means you end up with the toy and your dog doesn't. At first, you may need to offer him an irresistible treat as you say, "Give!" He'll have to drop the toy to eat the treat, and you've won! As soon as he devours the treat, say "Take it!" again and offer him his end of the toy. Now he got *two* rewards for letting go of it—he got the treat, and he gets the toy back! At least, he gets *his* end of the toy back.

Practice the "Give!" part of the game numerous times during each play session. Eventually you will be able to fade the use of the treat, as Bruiser realizes that the reward for "Give!" is more tug.

Rule #4: Use time outs as needed. If your dog gets too aroused and/or is putting his mouth on you or your clothing, use a "Too bad, Time out!" when his arousal level starts to escalate to an unacceptable level, or the *instant* his teeth touch forbidden surfaces. Put the toy high on a shelf and sit down for a few minutes. Then you can, if you want, retrieve the toy and play again.

If you have a dog who allows his teeth to stray into forbidden territory frequently by creeping his jaws up the length of the toy, use a tug object with a clear demarcation near his end of the toy—a change in texture or material—and do a time out immediately anytime his teeth cross that line. You control the good stuff, and his inappropriate behavior makes the good stuff go away.

Rule #5: Supervise Children. Very young children should not play tug with Bruiser unless and until the dog is impeccable about his self-control, and then only under direct supervision. Middle to older children can play with moderate supervision *if* they can be relied on to play by the rules, and *if* your dog is under reasonable self-control and not likely to get into trouble. Children can control the good stuff too!

Rule #6: You end the game. You get to decide when tug is over, not your dog. End the game with a "Give—all done!" cue and put the toy away on a high shelf or in a secure drawer. It'll be there, ready and waiting, when you decide to play tug again. You control the good stuff.

Variations on the Theme

The most common style of tug consists of a dog on one end of the toy, a human on the other. You don't have to stop there, however. If you have two compatible dogs who love to tug you can give them each one end of a toy and let them go at it with each other.

The key word here is *compatible*. Because tug *does* create a certain level of arousal, dogs who are prone to getting into fights should not be encouraged to tug together. Don't equate growling and snarling with fights, however—a lot of that will go on when compatible dogs play tug together.

If you have two dogs who can tug together, try two against one! Find a tug toy with one handle for the human and two ends for the dogs—a game the whole family can play!

At the other end of the spectrum, you can teach your dog to play tug by himself. Run a rope through a Kong and knot it so the knot is inside the Kong. Then stuff the Kong and suspend it from a tree branch so it's just barely within Bruiser's reach. Now he can tire *himself* out leaping and tugging at the Kong. There are also a number of toys on the market that are made with elastic bands, meant to encourage a tug-loving dog to pull harder and longer, even when there's just a tree or a post, not a playmate, on the other end of the toy. Of course, you lose the relationship value of tug with this variation of the game, but you might increase the exercise benefits!

What Makes a Good Tug Toy?

Tug toys can come in all shapes, sizes, colors and materials, but the best ones have these characteristics in common:

- They are long enough that your dog's teeth stay far away from your hand.
- They are made of a substance that invites your dog to grab and hold, and won't easily cause damage to teeth and gums.
- They are sturdy enough to withstand significant abuse.
- The "human end" has a comfortable handle or is otherwise easy to maintain a grip on.
- They are good value for the cost.

Remember, tug toys are *not* chew toys, and most won't stand up to unlimited gnawing. Remove them from your dog's reach when you are not supervising his play.

Making Scents

You can teach your dog how to use his nose for your benefit

What do Russian tigers, mold, lost pets, cancer cells, bomb-making equipment, illegal drugs, tortoises, termites, and knapweed have in common? They are all subjects of innovative training programs that work with dogs to seek out a growing list of unique targets for our benefit.

Humans have taken advantage of dogs' incredibly keen sense of smell over the ages for such uses as hunting, tracking lost and fugitive humans, and more recently, the detection of bombs, narcotics, and other contraband. It's well known that a dog's nose is many times sharper than our own—estimates range from 10,000 to 100,000 times superior to ours, with a far greater number and variety of scent receptors in their noses, more neurons linking the nose to the brain, and a greater proportion of their brains devoted to smell.

We accept this without question, as we routinely utilize our dogs' sense of smell to locate tennis balls we toss into deep grass in the dark; find treats and toys we stash around the house; search for us when we play hide-and-seek in the woods; and in Utility Obedience, where the dog is required to retrieve the one item that has been handled by the owner out of a pile of identical looking objects. Our dogs, if they ever thought about it, would have to conclude that we humans are seriously disabled in the nose department—we couldn't even begin to come close to duplicating the feats that they accomplish without thinking twice about it!

In addition to the now familiar uses for a dog's nose talent, trainers and researchers are only just starting to realize the best potential ways to make dog noses work for humans. For example, in 2002-2003, biologists in Russia trained dogs to help monitor a threatened species of tiger, the Amur Tiger, through a grant from the National Fish and Wildlife Foundation. The research team trained two dogs, not just to track tigers in general, but to actually identify *individual* tigers; one to 96% accuracy, the other to 89% accuracy.

Other new uses for dog noses include:

- Mold and termite detection for home repairs and sales.

- Searching out desert tortoises (a threatened species) in the U.S. to help preserve critical habitat.

- Locating an invasive, non-native noxious weed in Montana for eradication purposes.

- Sniffing out the deadly venomous brown tree snake in produce shipments from Asia to prevent accidental international transport.

- Detecting cancer cells in human urine for diagnosis and treatment.

- Locating leaks in pipe lines.

- Finding missing pets to prevent their suffering and allay human grief over the loss of beloved companions.

- Alerting Forest Service personnel to the presence of masses of gypsy moth eggs so the destructive pests can be eradicated before they mature, spread, and destroy forests.

What Kind of Dog?

According to Dr. Larry Myers, canine scent expert and professor of veterinary medicine at Auburn University in Alabama, *all* dogs have noses good enough to do scent work. However, trainability and interest in doing the job are important qualities; just because a dog can do scent work doesn't mean he *will*. For some kinds of work, size and coat length may determine suitability. A large, heavy-coated dog may not be the best candidate for working in the desert, for example.

While Bloodhounds are arguably the most famous scent dogs in the world, all dogs have a sense of smell that is thousands of times better than ours and are candidates for scent work.

Carole Schatz, CPDT, of San Diego, California, is the training director for a cancer detection study at Scripps Research Institute's General Clinical Research Center. Dogs selected for the Scripps study include Schatz's own Goldendoodle, a Border Collie mix, a Corgi, a Chihuahua mix, a Boxer, a Bernese Mountain Dog, an Italian Greyhound, German Shepherds, a Rhodesian Ridgeback, and an Aussie-Cocker mix. Schatz recruited the trainers for the program, and all the dogs are personal companions of the selected trainers.

In contrast is Hal Steiner, Bozeman, Montana, the owner of Rocky Mountain Command Dogs, a company that provides basic training services and also specializes in scent work. Steiner uses a specialized breed of dog that he created specifically for scent work purposes. He developed the "Rocky Mountain Shepherd" over decades, from Czech border patrol stock and hybrids of the red European wolf, and uses this breed almost exclusively for his scent work, although he does occasionally rescue dog of other breeds that might be suitable for his purposes.

David Latimer, of Vincent, Alabama, owns FSI K9 Academy. In addition to training bomb, arson, narcotics, and tracking dogs, Latimer trains dogs to detect water leaks, mold, and termites. He uses small to medium sized dogs such as Beagles, Rat Terriers and Border Collies for mold and termite work; they fit better into some of the confined spaces where their quarry is sought. Most come from local shelters and rescue groups and some are donated. He rarely purchases a dog.

"I look for dogs who have what I call a strong 'work ethic,'" says Latimer. "I want a dog with a high hunt drive and a high energy level coupled with a strong desire to please his handler. In addition, we look for dogs that are non-aggressive toward people and other animals."

Kat Albrecht, of Clovis, California, too, follows the eclectic approach to scent dog selection for her "pet detective" work. A former police detective and search dog trainer/handler, Albrecht began a new career finding lost pets when injuries sidelined her from police work. She now specializes in training what she has dubbed "Missing Animal Response" (MAR) search dogs who are trained and certified to locate various lost pets. Albrecht trains dogs for three types work: MAR Cat Detection K9s detect live and deceased cats; MAR Specific Scent K9s can detect the scent of any missing animal within a confined search area; and MAR Trailing K9s are trained to discriminate the scent of a lost dog and follow the scent trail to establish direction of travel in hope of finding the missing dog.

"Dogs best suited for MAR work are fixated on one of three things: cats, treats or other dogs," she says. "For cat detection dogs we look for dogs who absolutely *pine* for kitties and give a physical response (tail-wiggles, butt-wag, etc.) when they detect a cat's scent. For specific-scent dogs, we want dogs who will fixate their attention on a piece of hot dog and *do anything* for that hot dog, ignoring all distractions. For trailing dogs, we look for the "dog park" type of dog who *loves* to play with other dogs."

Since Albrecht's goal is to develop a system to train a massive corps of certified MAR K9 handlers around the world, she keeps an open mind about breed possibilities, with just a few limitations. Albrecht thinks that pug-nosed dogs (Pugs, Boxers, Pekingese, etc.), tiny dogs (Chihuahuas, Teacup Poodles, etc.) and giant breeds (Great Danes, Irish Wolfhounds, St. Bernards) are just not appropriate for MAR work due to their physical limitations. She also looks for dogs that are at least six months old and no older than eight years to enter the MAR training program.

Training Methods and History

While scent dogs are trained primarily with methods that focus on positive reinforcement, there is considerable variation as to how that operant principle is applied.

Cancer detection is a very new field of canine scent work. A study in England published in the *British Medical Journal* in September 2004 described how six pet dogs were trained to alert to the urine of patients with bladder cancer. The results of a double-blind test of the dogs at the conclusion of a seven-month period showed the dogs successfully alerted to the urine of patients with bladder cancer 41 percent of the time (14 percent would represent a random response).

The researchers involved with the study, including handlers from Hearing Dogs for Deaf People and medical researchers from the Erasmus Wilson Dermatological Research Fund, feel they have not only demonstrated the promise of this form of cancer detection, but also designed a successful training protocol and stringent controls in the testing phase suitable for extending the work. Their future goals are to optimize the experimental process and to study the potential for dogs to detect other types of cancer, particularly skin cancer.

A study that will be conducted in this country at Scripps Research Institute's General Clinical Research Center is still in the developmental stages. Trainer Carole Schatz and Dr. Robert Gordon are collaborating with Dr. Larry Myers at Auburn University. The study will attempt to teach 12 dogs to alert to an odor signature in the urine of patients with prostate and breast cancer. One of these dogs is Schatz' own two-year-old Golden Retriever/Poodle mix, Josie. Josie is already a certified assistance dog and registered therapy dog.

The dogs in the Scripps program will be trained with various positive methods.

"Every dog is an individual," says Dr. Robert Gordon, Principle Investigator of the Scripps study. "We have to learn which technique works best with each individual dog."

Dog trainers in the study are given latitude to experiment with their own training techniques to see what works best. Some are training their dogs to alert to the scent of vanilla. The alert signal is then transferred to the presence of the odor signature of cancer in urine. In a separate study being conducted by Myers at Auburn University, dogs are first trained to alert to the banana-like scent of n-amyl acetate, then transitioned to cancer cells.

One of the questions the researchers hope to answer is whether the cancer substances that are excreted in urine are universal to all cancers, or specific to individual cancers. For example, prostate cancer may be aggressive or non-aggressive, and there is currently no way to tell which is which. If dogs could be trained to distinguish the difference, it could make a big difference in how the cancers are treated.

"There is real scientific, humanistic value in this project," Gordon says excitedly. "If this project proves out, we could train teams to go places where modern diagnostic equipment isn't available. This could make a huge difference in the quality of peoples' lives."

In between training sessions, the cancer detection dogs live normal lives, or as Schatz says, "They are all pets."

Smelling Weeds for a Purpose

Kim Goodwin, a rangeland noxious weed specialist with Montana State University, contacted scent dog trainer Hal Steiner in 2003. She asked if he could train dogs to detect knapweed in the field, and Steiner agreed to give it a try. He selected a Rocky Mountain Shepherd (a breed he developed himself) to be the test dog for the project. The dog was so successful, he later named her "Knapweed Nightmare."

Phase 1 of the knapweed eradication program, also in experimental stages, was successfully completed and field-tested in the fall of 2004. At completion of the testing, Nightmare was finding the nonnative invasive plant with a 93 percent success rate. Steiner sold Nightmare to the university, which is now seeking funding to continue the work.

Steiner, while still using primarily positive training methods for the scent work, takes a different approach. From the time Steiner's professional working dogs are born, they never "play" the way a companion dog might.

"She's not a pet; she's not played with," Steiner says of Nightmare. "We start with basic obedience training, using corrections if necessary. Then using 'game theory,' we addict the dog to a certain type of toy, in Nightmare's case a towel or piece of plastic tubing with knapweed wrapped inside. When she's not working, she's in her pen."

Handlers in Steiner's program praise the dog—no food rewards—when she reacts to the scented toy. Steiner then places the toy where it is progressively harder to sniff out. As Nightmare becomes proficient, the trainers add distractions, to teach her to stay focused on her task.

The Rocky Mountain Shepherd was also trained to indicate her finds by digging at a spot of knapweed for 10 seconds so the Global Positioning System (GPS) attached to her collar could mark the location of a knapweed find.

"You don't want bomb dogs digging aggressively at a package of explosives," Steiner chuckles, "we want them to indicate finds gently. But Nightmare needed to stay in position for 10 seconds, and the easiest way to get her to do that was to encourage her to find aggressively, by digging at the spot for a bit, then moving on. Humans come check the spot later, to confirm the find."

Home Inspection

David Latimer tells me that dogs have been doing termite detection for at least 20-25 years in the United States. Mold detection developed originally in Europe about 10 years ago. Latimer uses positive reinforcement, and acknowledges the importance of timing when rewarding desired behaviors. He also subscribes to what he calls "fair and just discipline" as a part of training dependable working dogs.

Among other training exercises, Latimer uses a "scent board." This is a piece of 2x4 with eight, 4-to-6-inch sections of PVC pipe attached vertically, secured with screws to the board. Each section of pipe is capped with a screw-on cap to conceal the contents; the caps have small holes drilled through the center to release the scent. The target odor—termite-infested or moldy material—is placed inside one or two of the pipes, and distracting odors are placed in several of the other pipes. In order to earn a reward, the dog must correctly identify which pipe or pipes contain the target odor.

Pet Detecting

Kat Albrecht says that the use of dogs specifically for finding lost pets goes back to the 1970s, when a Bloodhound handler in Texas used his dogs to search for missing dogs. This trainer reportedly died in the early 1980's, and while an occasional search dog may have been used for this purpose since then, no one has attempted to do it on a large, formal scale.

Today Albrecht is the founder of Pet Hunters International, the world's first pet detective academy, and Missing Pet Partnership, a nonprofit organization that provides training for animal welfare organizations and conducts research into the behavioral patterns of missing pets. Albrecht is also the author of *Dog Detectives, Train Your Dog to Find Lost Pets,* a training book about her work.

For cat detection dogs, Albrecht conceals crated, gregarious, dog-friendly cats in shrubbery, and rewards dogs for responding to the scent of the cat. Dogs are reinforced for giving a physical alert to the presence of the cat, then encouraged to run back to and jump on the handler, then do a "re-find" by taking the handler back to the crated cat, where they are rewarded. The reward in this case is treats plus the opportunity to play with the uncrated, harnessed and leashed cat.

One of Kat Albrecht's "MAR Cat Detection dogs" plays with one of the training cats, her reward for finding the hidden cat.

For the specific scent training, Albrecht uses a clicker to teach dogs to search for treats by sniffing a sterile gauze pad that contains the matching treat scent. She progresses to hiding baby food jars with various scents, and uses the gauze pad to teach "smell this smell, find this smell."

Her dog-trailing dogs are trained using a modification of the method used to train Bloodhounds to follow the scent trail of a human, only using a scent article from a "target dog"—the dog used to lay the scent trail. The reward for the scent dog is to play with the dog he finds at the end of the trail!

Success Stories

David Latimer likes to tell about one of his handlers who was called to do a real estate purchase inspection on a lake house, and had the dog alert on an area outside the home.

"Upon investigation," Latimer relates, "the handler found that extensive termite damage had been cosmetically concealed prior to his arrival. Apparently another company had found the termite infestation on an earlier inspection, and the homeowner tried to conceal it from the handler in order to get a termite clearance letter." The handler would have cleared the house if his dog hadn't alerted.

Albrecht's favorite story included the participation of her cat, Yogi, as an impromptu pet detective. As Albrecht walked out of her house one morning, she noticed Yogi sniffing a spot in the road, unusual for the cat, who was normally terrified of the roadway. That evening, when her neighbor Andrea mentioned that her cat Rocky was missing, Albrecht remembered Yogi's unusual behavior.

Kat Albrecht took her Weimaraner, Rachel, a retired cadaver dog, out to look for blood in the roadway. Rachel squatted and urinated on the road—her somewhat unorthodox alert indicating that she'd found decomposing blood or tissue. Her find suggested to Albrecht that the cat was injured, not just lost or stolen, which prompted her to suggest the owner focus her search within the cat's territory.

"Sure enough," says Albrecht, "Andrea found Rocky under his deck, one back leg hanging by a thread, but alive. Rocky is now a happy three-legged kitty who was saved because of his curious neighbor cat and a trained search dog."

As these programs gain momentum, and as trainers develop more programs that use our dogs' incredible sense of smell, we will no doubt hear of more exciting ways that dogs can demonstrate their value. Most exciting to us is the comment of many trainers, that "any dog" can do scent work. That means you and your dog can do it too! Remember, if it has a scent, a dog can be trained to find it. The possibilities are endless.

Positive Training Techniques
Ideally Suited for Scent Work

All of the trainers we interviewed agreed that scent work was trained most effectively using reward-based, positive training methods, although there were differences of opinion over whether the reward should be food treats or "life rewards" such as the opportunity to play with a coveted toy.

As in every field of dog training, however, some of the trainers we spoke to still hold fast to the notion that corrections are necessary during training, especially during the foundation "obedience" phase, in order to achieve reliability. The idea that there must be unpleasant "consequences" for objectionable behaviors is difficult for many old-fashioned trainers to get past.

In contrast, we have found that the use of "negative punishment" (the removal of a desired object or outcome to decrease unwanted behavior) is a gentle but effective consequence that, in combination with positive reinforcement, produces dependable work dogs.

Carole Schatz, CPDT and training director for a study at the Scripps Research Institute's General Clinical Research center for canine detection of cancer, told us why she uses primarily positive reinforcement in her training and sought out trainers with a similar training philosophy to participate in the study:

"In the 1960s I was a reading teacher," Schatz says. "My kids learned the fastest because I bought pretzels. Each child was tested daily and if they learned the lesson, they earned a pretzel. My kids were always the first ones to learn to read. Thus, when I went into dog training in 1975, I was completely open to using positive rewards—goodies. It was lonely until I met Dr. Ian Dunbar in 1978 and traveled to his classes and seminars. Here was validation. "I love it when the dogs learn fast and have fun doing it. It also gives me great pleasure to see their happiness. It's win-win. Using punishment makes the dog fearful and unhappy and then I'm unhappy. It also takes longer because you have by-products of fear and confusion. The training methods involved in this study are no different than training anything else—ignore the wrong and reward what's right. My goal is happy dogs loving what they're doing and happy trainers. Alerting to cancer is frosting on the cake."

Mind Games

Occupy your dog's brain to get through
periods of restricted activity

We recently had our new Cardigan Welsh Corgi spayed. When we picked Lucy up from the vet hospital we were handed an instruction sheet that included the dreaded phrase, "Restrict activity for 10-14 days." In the few short weeks that this little dynamo had been a member of the Miller family, I had already realized how difficult it would be to keep Lucy under wraps.

We were lucky that it was only 10-14 days. Many canine injuries and ailments require much longer incarceration. Our 75-pound Cattle Dog mix had knee surgery (a tibial plateau leveling osteotomy—TPLO) several years ago. We had to keep Tucker quiet for a full six weeks following his operation! Fortunately, he was older and more settled than our adolescent Corgi, and our vet supplied us with tranquilizers to keep him quiet for the first few days, but it was still a large-scale challenge.

What *do* you do when your vet tells you your dog can't run around for a period of time? You get creative. You can, of course, arm yourself with an endless supply of stuffed Kongs™ and other such interactive toys, but even those get old after a while.

You can, and should, use calming massage techniques to help your dog adjust to confinement, but that's rarely enough.

You can beg your vet for tranquilizers (for the dog, not for you!) and she may give you a few to get you through the first critical days of a leg repair or other major surgery, but probably not enough to get you off the hook.

Eventually, you're likely to have to do something to tire your dog out. The good news is that mental gymnastics can be as tiring for a dog as physical exercise, and if you can keep your dog's brain occupied, you *can* make it through the torture of "restricted activity."

Free Shaping

Canine incarceration is the perfect opportunity to introduce your dog to some free shaping exercises. Shaping is the process of taking a complex behavior and breaking it into little pieces, then marking and rewarding each piece until you work up to the whole behavior.

With free shaping, you do no luring whatsoever. You simply take a behavior that the dog offers you and gradually shape it into something by marking (generally with an audible marker such as a Click! of a clicker or an exclamation such as "Yes!") and rewarding increasingly large, intense, or extended examples of the behavior.

Free shaping has several benefits in addition to exercising your dog's brain. It teaches you to be patient, gives you a real opportunity to watch your dog think and problem-solve, and it encourages your dog to offer behaviors.

You have to be a bit of a student of animal behavior to appreciate free shaping. I introduce it in my basic good manners classes but not everyone "gets it"—most dog owners need to be committed to training beyond basics in order to have the patience and understanding to do this. So let's get started!

Pick a Random Movement

This is a good exercise for dogs who are on total restriction. The goal is to get your dog to offer one of these behaviors on cue—Nose Lick, Head Turn, Ear Flick, or Paw Lift—without any luring or prompting on your part. Here's how:

1. Sit on a chair with your dog in front of you. If he wants to jump on you, put him on a tether and sit just beyond his reach.

2. Wait for him to offer one of the four behaviors.

3. When he does, Click! (or use some other reward marker such as a mouth click, or the word "Click!" or "Yes!") and then quickly give him a treat. Once you have clicked and treated one of the four behaviors, stay with that one—don't Click! and treat for any of the others.

4. Wait for him to repeat the chosen behavior. When he does, Click! and treat.

5. Keep doing this until you see him start to offer the chosen behavior deliberately, in order to make you Click! and treat.

6. Put the behavior on an "intermittent schedule of reinforcement." That is, Click! and treat most head turns, but occasionally skip one, then Click! and treat the next offered one. Gradually make your schedule longer and more random by skipping just one more frequently, and sometimes skipping two, then four, then one, then none, then three—so your dog never knows when the next Click! is coming.

   This makes the behavior very durable—resistant to extinction. Like playing a slot machine, your dog will keep offering the behavior because he knows it'll pay off one of these times! It's important to put the behavior on an intermittent schedule before raising the shaping criteria so he doesn't give up when you are no longer clicking each try.

7. Decide if the behavior is fine as is, or if you want to shape it into something bigger. A Paw Lift, for example, can be shaped into Paw On Your Knee, Shake, High Five, or even Salute. Head Turn can be shaped into a Spin. Ear Flick could become Injured Ear, while Nose Lick might become Stick Out Your Tongue.

8. Determine the "average" response your dog is giving you. If you want to shape Head Turn into Spin, envision a 360-degree circle around your dog. Perhaps your dog is offering head turns anywhere from 5 degrees to 75 degrees, but the average is 45 degrees. Now you are going to Click! and treat only those head turns of 45 degrees or better.

   Over time, your dog's average will move up as you Click! only the better attempts. When that happens, raise your criteria again—perhaps the range moves to 30-95 degrees, and now you'll click only those head turns that reach 60 degrees or better. Keep raising the criteria—gradually, so you don't lose your dog's interest—until you have a complete Spin.

9. Now give it a name ("Spin!") and start using the verbal cue just before your dog offers the behavior. Eventually you will be able to elicit a spin with the verbal cue—all by free shaping.

You can figure out how to do this with the other three behaviors. If your dog has to be kept confined for a long period, you might have time to teach all four, one after the other. Lucky you!

More Shut-In Games

There are a number of other low-activity games you can play with your shut-in dog, such as:

- **Targeting/Object Discrimination:** Teach your dog to target on cue by giving him a Click! and treat every time he touches his nose to a designated spot, such as the palm of your hand, or the end of a target stick. As soon as he can do that easily, add the cue "Touch!" just before his nose touches the target.

  When he will target on cue, transfer the targeting behavior to an object, by holding the object in your hand and asking him to "Touch." When he's targeting well to the object, give it a name: "Bell, Touch!" or "Ball, Touch!" When he knows the names of several different objects, you can have him pick out the one you ask for.

- **Take It:** This behavior is a piece of the retrieve, but you can do it without the run-after-and-retrieve part. It's also useful for having your dog learn to pick up dropped items and carry things for you around the house. Just show your dog something you know he'll want—like a treat or a favorite toy—and ask him to "Take it!" Odds are he will, and happily. When he's good at taking his favorite things, try a slightly less-beloved toy, and work your way down to non-toy objects. Remember to Click! and treat each "Take it!" When he's good at "Take it!" you can gradually extend the amount of time before you Click! and you'll begin teaching him to "Hold it!"

- **Give:** This is also part of the retrieve, and is useful for getting your dog to let go of "forbidden objects" without a fuss. Give your dog something he's *allowed* to have that he likes a lot, like his favorite toy. Then offer him a handful of yummy treats and say "Give!" When he drops the object to eat the treats, pay them out slowly and pick up the object with your *other* hand while he's occupied eating. Then, when he looks up, say "Take it!" and give him back the object. Double bonus—he gets the yummy treats *and* he gets his toy back! Practice this until he'll give up the object on cue. Next time he gets his chompers on a forbidden object, play the "Give" game and he'll give it up without playing keep-away. (*Note: If your dog is a resource guarder, this may not be a safe game to play. In that case, you'll need to modify the resource guarding behavior first.*)

- **Leave It:** This game teaches your dog to take his attention away from something *before* he has it in his mouth.

  Start with a "forbidden object" that you can hide under your shoe, such as a cube of freeze-dried liver. Show it to your dog, say "Leave it!" and place it securely under your foot so he knows it's there but can't get it. Let him dig, chew and claw at your foot to his heart's content (wear sturdy shoes!) until he loses interest. The *instant* he looks away, Click! and treat. As long as he's not trying to get the liver, keep clicking and treating. This is called "**differential reinforcement for other behavior**" (DRO)—you are rewarding any behavior *other than* trying to get the treat.

  When he's leaving your foot alone, uncover the liver cube slightly, and continue your DRO. If he tries to get the treat, just quietly (but quickly!) cover it back up with your foot and wait for him to remove his attention again.

  When he'll reliably leave liver on the floor and he's ready for more strenuous activities, generalize the behavior to other situations by using a leash to gently restrain him from real-life temptations while using DRO to reward him as soon as he removes his attention from the cookie in the toddler's hand, the ham sandwich on the coffee table, or the dog on leash on the other side of the street.

- **Puzzle Games:** There are a number of interactive toys on the market that require your dog to think and perform a mechanical puzzle-solving skill. Unlike stuffed Kongs and Buster Cubes™, your dog will need your active participation with these games. As soon as he solves the puzzle he'll need you to put the toy back together so he can do it again. They are great fun, and one more way to encourage your dog to quietly think, and tire his brain.

- **Tug:** Gentle games of Tug of War, with strict rules, may be a useful way to burn off some incarceration energy. Check with your veterinarian first to be sure this won't be a problem for your dog's particular condition.

Benefits of Down Time

There are lots of other low-activity exercises and games you can play with your dog to help pass the long hours and days of restricted activity. It's a great time to work on counter-conditioning and desensitization if he's at all touchy about nail trimming, grooming, or any other handling procedures.

You can also spend time transforming him into a tricks champion. Teach him Possum, Relax, Rest Your Head, Take a Bow, Crawl, Reverse, Speak, Count, Say Your Prayers, Kisses, Hugs… the list is virtually endless. If the two of you put your minds to it, at the end of a six-week lay-up, or even a shorter bout of nasty weather that keeps you shut indoors, you and your dog should be very well educated!

101 Things to Do With a Box

I first heard about this brain-teasing, free shaping exercise from Deb Jones, PhD, a wonderful positive trainer in Stow, Ohio.

Have your clicker ready. You are going to Click! and treat your dog for *any* behavior related to the box. With no preconceived idea about what behavior you want, set a cardboard box on the floor in front of your dog. Many dogs will sniff a new object with interest—Click! and treat when he does. Then watch him closely, and continue to Click! and treat any box-related behavior. See what your dog will give you!

If you're not getting a lot of box behavior, Click! and treat even tiny movements—looking at the box, moving toward or even looking in the general direction of the box.

Be careful you don't cheat! It's tempting to "help" your dog by pointing toward the box, or moving around it. Don't! You can help by looking at the box instead of looking at your dog, and you can stand on the opposite side of the box, but anything more than that is too much. Remember, you want your dog to learn to think—and he won't learn if you hold his paw and show him what to do; he'll just wait for you to bail him out.

"Crossover dogs" (dogs whose early training was force-based and whose later training was reward-based) can be particularly slow to offer behaviors because, when they were subject to punishment for doing the "wrong" thing, they learned it was easiest to stay out of trouble by doing nothing. Free shaping exercises are great for helping crossover dogs get over that inhibition—providing you don't help them too much, but rather let them think things out for themselves.

When your dog is offering a lot of box-related behavior, then you can decide to shape it into something "official" if you like. If you are more of a Type-A, goal-oriented kind of person, this may help you make more sense of the Box game. Be willing to think *outside* the box, though—there are lots of behaviors your dog can do beyond just jumping in and sitting in it—although, if that doesn't interfere with whatever physical condition your dog is recovering from, it sure is cute!

At first, Tater just looks at Sandi. Eventually, though, she gets bored and turns toward the box. Sandi clicks the clicker and gives Tater a treat. Ah! Immediately Tater understands there is something she is supposed to do with that box. She tries a number of things—walking around it, tipping it with her nose, scratching at it, looking in it. We liked Tater in the box best!

Size Matters

Secrets to training your small dog

There are two kinds of dog people in this world. Small dog people and dog people who haven't yet met and fallen in love with the right small dog.

I used to be a big dog person. I once owned a St. Bernard, and dreamed of owning an Irish Wolfhound. "Give me a big dog, a thumpin' dog," I used to say, referring to a dog who could withstand heavy patting. All my life, I looked disdainfully down on yappy little foo-foo dogs and the wimpy people who owned them.

Then, 13 years ago, a 10-month-old Pomeranian was surrendered by his owners to the shelter where I worked. I fell in love with—and adopted—Dusty. My whole perspective on the dog world shifted, as did some of my long-held paradigms on dog behavior, training, and management.

No longer did I scoff at people who snatched their tiny toys off the floor at the approach of a bigger dog. At a whopping eight pounds, Dusty had reached his full adult size, and I was constantly worried that I would step on him and break him, or that one of our bigger dogs might play with him too roughly and crush him. Or worse—some unknown dog with mayhem in mind could kill him instantly with one grab-and-shake move. Besides, it was just as easy—if not easier—to pick him up and carry him, so why not? The concept of "arm-dog" began to make perfect sense to me.

Big Advantages

Once you adopt a small dog you realize that, safety concerns aside, there are some huge advantages to sharing your life with a mini-canine.

For example, they don't take up as much room as a large dog—you can have several in the same space as one Great Dane. They share your bed without hogging it. They sit on your lap and still leave room for the newspaper. They don't eat as much, so they are less expensive to feed. You can get by with smaller yards, and often, lower fences. They require comparatively less grooming. Little dog poops are tiny and inoffensive, even in the house—you can pick up their mini-feces with a tissue and flush them down the toilet. As a corollary, the small dog is much more realistic to litter-box train than a Mastiff, if that suits your fancy.

You are much less likely to have to worry about counter-surfing with a little dog, nor is she as likely to knock over your 93-year-old Great Aunt Helen when she comes to visit (although a little dog *can* run under her feet and trip her up). The small dog is far more portable—you can fit her under an airline seat, in your shopping cart, or in a doggie backpack. Finally, she is less intimidating to people who are fearful of dogs, and more acceptable to landlords, hotels, motels, and other public places.

Of course, there are some disadvantages as well. Little dogs *do* break more easily, especially those with very fine bones, such as Chihuahuas and Papillons. Because of their small size, they can be mistakenly perceived as good pets for children. Some of them *can* be, but they are not automatically. It depends on the dog, good socialization, and the child's ability to respect the dog's small size. Their reputation as yappy and snappy is not entirely undeserved; they can become defensively aggressive if they feel threatened, and it's easy to feel threatened when you are surrounded by human giants who are anywhere from 10 to 60

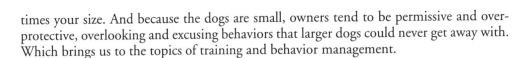

times your size. And because the dogs are small, owners tend to be permissive and over-protective, overlooking and excusing behaviors that larger dogs could never get away with. Which brings us to the topics of training and behavior management.

Small Dog House Manners

For optimum quality of life and relationship, it is every bit as important for the small dog to be trained as the large one.

Let's arbitrarily define the "small dog" as one who is 25 pounds or less. This encompasses a wide range of breeds, from the tiny, truly fragile 3-pound Chihuahua to the short and sturdy Scottish Terrier. It includes dogs with such varied personalities as the independent Jack Russell Terrier, amiable Pug, work-oriented Welsh Corgi, aloof Basenji, energetic Toy Poodle, and the relatively phlegmatic French Bulldog, to name just a few. That doesn't even take into consideration the infinite permutations of small mixed-breed dogs.

So forget any stereotype you may be holding of the "small dog" personality. The training challenges that small dog trainers face mirror to a large degree those faced by big dog trainers, and the same positive training methods work just as well.

There are some differences, however. The conventional wisdom that small dogs can be harder to housetrain is often a reality. There are several reasons why they are more likely to soil in the house, although it is *not* because they don't have the instinct to keep their den clean; they most certainly do. If your little dog's housetraining is giving you headaches, it may be because:

- Small dog signals are harder to see. If a Rottweiler sits and stares at your face while you are reading the paper, you probably notice. If a Pomeranian sits and stares at your ankle, it's easy to miss.

- Big dog owners may be more motivated. A tiny Yorkshire Terrier puddle behind the guest bed may not be discovered for weeks or months (or maybe never). The Great Dane lake in the kitchen is impossible to miss. It's a simple matter to pick up a teeny Terrier mistake, toss it in the toilet and dismiss the mistake. A moist, massive Mastiff mound is an entirely different matter.

- Small dogs have smaller holding capacities. Although you would expect their organ capacity to be proportionate to their size and intake, bottom line is they do seem to need to go out on a more frequent potty schedule.

- Small dog owners are more likely to supervise less, use crates that are too large (in which the toy puppy can poop and pee in one end and sleep and play happily in the other) or not crate at all. A little pup can't possibly be as much trouble as a big one, can she? Wrong! And besides, we want Midget to sleep with us!

- Small dog owners are more likely to paper-train and continue to rely on paper-training, sending a mixed message about inside elimination versus outside elimination.

- Small dogs, by virtue of their size, are more popular as pet store and puppy mill breeds—both environments where they are more likely to be over-crated. Thus they may have had their den-soiling inhibitions damaged by being left in crates too long. If a dog is required to live in her own excrement and urine, she comes to think that living in filth is normal, and she won't make an effort to "hold it" until she has access to a more suitable environment. This makes housetraining very difficult.

The answer to housetraining the small dog is scrupulous management. Constant supervision, through the *appropriate* use of leashes, crates, tethers, direct supervision, and regular trips to the outdoor bathroom spot—every hour on the hour, at first, if necessary. Pay close attention so you don't miss your dog's signals. All of the other regular housetraining tips also apply, of course. Feed regular meals instead of free-choice feeding; pick up water before bedtime; change crate substrate if necessary; and *clean* soiled spots with enzyme-based animal product cleaners.

The small dog owner often overlooks other house manners as well. Jumping up is much easier to accept when the dog is 5 pounds than 50, so lots of small dog owners don't bother to teach a polite greeting. Our four dogs range in size from 8 pounds to 80, and all of them know to greet people without jumping up. They also wait for permission before getting up on the sofa.

This can be accomplished with the small dog just as it is with the big dog, by preventing her from being rewarded by the behavior you don't want, and consistently and generously rewarding the behavior you *do* want with treats, attention, toys, or a nap on the sofa.

This means turning your back on the jumper and petting her (and/or giving a treat) when she sits. She will soon learn to sit to get your attention. Be sure you give it! It also means body-blocking your dog when you see the "sofa gleam" in her eye—by moving into the open sofa space and/or not making your lap available—until she sits, and then inviting her up (assuming she is allowed up). Be sure to notice when she sits, and invite her up when she does; as small as she is, she is easy to overlook when she is sitting politely. These two behaviors are actually much easier to accomplish with your small dog than a large one.

Your small dog also needs to be well socialized. Treat her like a dog! Lots of positive experiences from early puppyhood will help dispel the aggressive "arm-dog" image of the angry Pomeranian nestled in the ample and befurred bosom of the wealthy dowager. Your little dog needs to have her feet on the ground a good part of the time so she can learn to go up and down stairs, get into cars, and walk on grass, dirt, gravel, carpeting, and wood and tile floors.

Take her hiking. (In his younger days, Dusty could easily hold his own on an all day wilderness hike with the rest of our pack.) Have her meet lots of friendly people—all ages, shapes, sizes and races—armed with lots of tasty treats in lots of controlled circumstances. A good rule of thumb for socialization is to expose your pup to at least 100 *different* environments and types of people before she is four months old.

Basic Small Dog Training

It is true that there are lots of little dogs who strain on their leashes, don't come when called, and who think "sit" is something their owners do so the human can bend over and pet the dog. Yet the small dog is every bit as capable of learning basic and advanced training behaviors as a large dog—and it is just as important for their long term well-being and safety.

If you doubt a little dog's ability to learn, just watch any canine competition. You will be amazed by the number of diminutive canines who compete successfully in all levels of Obedience, Agility, Rally, Flyball, Canine Freestyle, and more. In fact, every Flyball competitor *wants* a small dog on her team, because the jump heights for the whole team are set at the proper height for the smallest dog in the group.

Positive training techniques are the same for all size dogs—they all have canine brains that respond similarly to the four principles of operant conditioning. There are some considerations for small dog owners that can make the relationship building/training process more successful. Whether your goal is a well mannered house dog or competition titles, if you keep the following concepts and tips in mind you and your small dog can both have more fun playing the training game together.

- **You are very big.** Primate body language (direct approach, looming over, eye contact, assertive gestures and voice) is intimidating to any dog who has not learned to read and interpret "human." In the dog world, these behaviors are considered rude and offensive. The smaller the dog, the more threatening our natural human body language can be. When you are training your small dog, at least at first until she learns to read and trust you, be very conscious of using soft eye contact, making your gestures and voice small and soft rather than large and effusive, turning slightly sideways to her, and squatting instead of looming over your dog to interact with her.

- **Your dog's stomach is very small.** I always remind dog owners to use small pieces of food treats and perhaps cut back on the size of their dog's regular meals, to prevent filling up before training is over and to avoid unwanted weight gain. Small dog treats must be *very* tiny and you may even need to eliminate some of your dog's meals.

- **Work on the floor.** If you always train your little dog when you are standing up, you are guaranteed to end up with a sore back. Exercises like puppy push-ups and luring the down can be especially backbreaking from full height. In the beginning, especially when teaching stationary exercises, sitting on the floor with your dog will save your back, and at the same time make you less intimidating to her. You can also work with your small dog while you sit on a chair, or you can put her on a raised surface where she is comfortable, such as a table, sofa or bed.

- **Stand up and use a target stick.** You also need to train your dog while you are standing up—at least of the time. She should learn to walk politely with you; even a small dog can damage her throat if she constantly strains at the leash. The better her leash manners the more fun it will be to take her places, and the less likely she will become an arm-dog. You can teach her to target and then use your target stick to help her learn to walk with you, *without* having to bend over. Simply put the target stick where you want her to be. You can also attach a soft treat to the stick for delivery to the little dog without having to bend over, or just drop treats on the floor.

- **Use appropriate-sized training tools.** Little dogs need lightweight collars and leashes. It's easy to underestimate the impact of a standard-weight leather leash if it accidentally bumps into your dog's face, or, worse, if you drop your end and it falls on her. Her training tools and toys should be scaled appropriately to her size—pet suppliers have gotten wonderfully creative with small dog products like toy-dog-size tennis balls and narrow, lightweight nylon leashes. Flyball boxes even have a spot that can pop out a mini-tennis ball for those toy-sized team members.

Training a small dog is easiest when you are closer to her level, as demonstrated by Sandi Thompson, a trainer with Sirius Puppy Training. Thompson was a "big dog person" until she met Tater, a Chihuahua-cross; she immediately became a "small dog person." These two have been together for more than 10 years.

Play It Safe and Smart

One of the reasons little dogs sometimes get an attitude about big dogs is that owners tend to panic when they see a big dog approaching. The owner's stress transmits to the small dog, who then becomes anxious herself. If you grab your dog every time another dog approaches, it will increase her stress and the potential for a confrontation.

Little dogs sometimes do get savaged by big dogs because their owners forget to think. "Be smart" means don't take your little dog places that you know are frequented by large, uncontrolled dogs. Only use your local dog park if there is a separate fenced area for small dogs.

If you are walking your dog on the street and you see someone approaching with a large dog, take evasive action—calmly cross the street while you practice good heeling so you can pass at a safe distance. If you see a loose dog approaching, look for an escape route—a place of business or fenced yard you can step into for safety. Carry an aversive spray such as Direct Stop™ that can thwart a persistent canine visitor. Only as a last resort should you pick your dog up—doing so also puts *you* at risk for injury if the approaching dog is intent on attacking.

Not that the risk of injury would stop any of us "small dog people" from protecting our beloved little ones. Like any dog owner worth her salt, our own safety is the last thing we think about when our canine family members are threatened. Their diminutive size only heightens the protective instinct that would cause us to risk life and limb for them.

Go ahead, big dog people, scoff at us if you want. It's only a matter of time before you meet the small dog who steals your heart.

Super-Sized

Keeping and training extra-large dogs can be a big challenge

Newfoundlands. St. Bernards. Irish Wolfhounds. Great Danes. They are the giants of the canine world, and it takes a special kind of person to appreciate their extra large appeal.

I think of a "big dog" as one whose normal weight exceeds the 100 pound mark. In addition to the above-mentioned breeds, this includes many of the Mastiff-type dogs, the Great Pyrenees, Scottish Deerhound, some (but not all) Rottweilers, and more. The only requirement for membership in this club is size. Everything about them is big, from their appetites (and by-products thereof) to the crates, collars, and other training equipment that they use, as well as the toys they play with. Pet supply companies offer giant-sized Kongs™, tennis balls, tug toys, and just about every other canine accessory you can think of. They know there's a "big" market out there.

Vet bills can be bigger too, since most surgeries are charged at least in part by the dog's weight. Larger dogs generally need more anesthesia.

Even finding homes can be more of a challenge for big-dog humans. Many landlords and hotels, if they allow dogs at all, accept pets who are 25 pounds or less. The next socially acceptable size increment seems to be around 70 to 75 pounds. Much bigger than that, and non-dog people tend to think your really are some kind of serious dog nut to want to share your life and home with a dog who outweighs many of the family members. Or dogs. Much to the consternation of big-dog humans, many of the giant breeds are listed on insurance company "do not insure" lists, making it almost impossible to find homeowners or renters insurance.

Finally, sadly, many of the giant breeds tend to have short life spans. A 10-year-old Great Dane is pretty ancient, while lots of 10-year-old small dogs are still in excellent condition and can look forward to 5 to 10 more years of life.

The Big Challenge

The awe-inspiring size of these dogs presents their human companions with a long list of training and management challenges not encountered by keepers of smaller dogs. Some are simple logistical challenges. Exactly how big a vehicle do you need to accommodate a couple of Great Dane crates? We could be talking motor home here, just to run to the local training class! Not to mention the extra space you need in your master bedroom if you plan to crate a few Newfies in your personal den. And imagine the ease with which a Wolfhound's tail can clear a coffee table, or swipe expensive porcelain statuettes from their display shelves.

Everything I've said in the past about prevention through management and training goes triple for big dogs. Teaching good manners when your wee one is a mere 15 to 20 pounds at age 10 weeks gives you a huge advantage over those who wait until 12 months, by which time the untrained, out-of-control, 150-pound Presa Canario may already be gearing up to maul an innocent neighbor. These dogs' forbidding size demands an early course in juvenile good manners. While your visiting aunt may be willing to tolerate the petite paw prints of a Pomeranian on her pantsuit, she is likely to frown on plate-sized mud-covered Wolfhound feet on the front of her cashmere sweater.

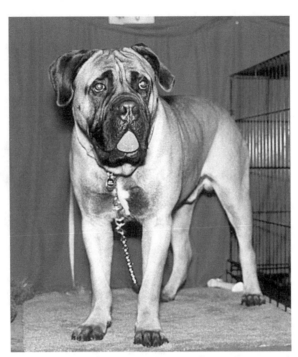

Most Mastiffs are good-natured, somewhat sedentary dogs. However, they still need regular exercise and socialization to keep them physically and emotionally healthy.

Socialization is another critically vital part of a large dog's educational experience. Many giant breeds have strongly developed guarding instincts. A poorly socialized, poorly trained large dog is a significant risk to the safety of the community. A well-socialized and trained dog will be able to turn on his protection behaviors if needed, but no matter his size, will be safe to have around your friends and family. A poorly socialized small dog is just as sad a statement about pet-owner irresponsibility as an unsocialized large dog, but is less of a risk to the community; a kamikaze Chihuahua can do far less damage on his worst day than a scud missile Neapolitan Mastiff on a minor bender.

Head halters——or head collars, as they are sometimes called——are a somewhat controversial training tool. While they can be useful for handling giant breeds, many dogs appear to find them quite aversive, and I recommend them only in very limited circumstances. I prefer to use front-clip harnesses when a control tool in needed.

Tall Training Tips

There are a number of good manners behaviors that are particularly important to teach your large dog while she is still small. Pay special attention to these if you have a big dog:

- **Polite Greeting**: As mentioned above, jumping up to greet humans is rude behavior for any canine, and especially intolerable for a large dog. Start when your puppy is small by avoiding the temptation to pick her up and cuddle her. (Cuddling teaches her that "up" is a very wonderful place to be.) Instead, designate a spot on the floor as "Cuddle Space," and get down on her level to do snuggle time. Teach "Sit" as a greeting/default behavior by consistently and generously rewarding your puppy for sitting, and turning away and stepping away anytime she jumps up. Insist that family members, visitors, and people on the street greet her only when she is sitting.

- **Loose Leash Walking**: If you begin teaching polite leash walking to your young pup, you will never find yourself being skijored down the street behind your Rottie was she takes off after an unexpected skateboarder. The keys to teaching good leash walking are: (1) a high rate of reinforcement (lots of Clicks! and treats); and (2) *very* high-value treats. You want to make sure it's more rewarding for your dog to pay attention to you than her surroundings. If you've already missed out on teaching this while your pup is small, consider using a front-clip control harness to maintain gentle control of your big dog while you retrain her leash behavior.

- **Say Please**: Also known as "No Free Lunch" or "Nothing in Life is Free," a "Say Please" program teaches your dog to ask for all good things in life by offering a sit in order to get what she wants. This prevents her from learning that she can push people around by virtue of her sheer weight and size. You can initially train and ask for the sit behavior, but your ultimate goal is for your dog to offer sits without being asked. If she is allowed on the furniture, she sits and waits to be invited, rather than just helping herself to the empty space on the sofa next to your visitor. Want to go outside? "Sit" makes the door open. Ready for dinner? "Sit" makes the dinner bowl descend to the floor.

- **Down**: A big-dog lover myself, I don't understand why some people don't fully appreciate the joy of having a Newfoundland drool in their laps, but it's still a fact—some just don't. A big dog is still plenty accessible for the occasional pat on the head if she is lying at your visitor's feet instead of panting in his face.

  Teach your dog that "lying at feet" is a highly rewardable behavior. Give her attention and treats on a variable schedule (sometimes close together, sometimes with longer pauses in between) when she lies down quietly. Give your guests a container full of treats and instruct them to reward the dog on a random schedule, too. Be sure to ignore any demand behavior, such as whining or barking, so the dog learns that the only behavior that gets rewarded is calm "lying at feet."

- **Off/Leave It:** It stands to reason that giant breeds have easier access to food-bearing surfaces such as tables and kitchen counters. One chance encounter with a roast beef sandwich can turn a dog into a dedicated counter-surfer. In addition to managing your big dog so she never has the opportunity to learn to counter-surf, a well-installed "Off" or "Leave It" cue, which tells the dog to back away from whatever she is looking at, can avert disaster when she has that "Mine!" gleam in her eye and is closer to the holiday turkey than you are.

- **Sharing With Others:** Like so many other things, resource guarding by a large dog can be infinitely more disastrous than the same behavior presented by her smaller counterparts. When your pup is small, teach her that having humans approach her when she is eating or otherwise occupied with a high-value possession makes *more* great stuff happen. When she is eating from her food bowl, occasionally approach and drop a few exquisite goodies into it. Before long she will *want* people to be around when she is eating.

  Caution: If you already have a serious resource guarding challenge with your dog, big or small, you will want to find a positive trainer/behavior specialist to help you modify this dangerous behavior.

- **Go to Your Spot**: A useful behavior for all dogs, this one is especially helpful if you have guests who don't appreciate super-sized canines. By repeatedly luring your dog to her "spot" or using targeting (or shaping) to send her to it, you can program a gentle "Go to your spot" cue that tells her to go lie down in her corner. If you use a portable throw rug to mark her "spot" you can take it with you—to the dining room during meals, the den for videos, even to the beach for a picnic and your friends' houses when you and your big dog go visiting.

- **Give**: The last thing you want to do is get into an argument with a big dog over something she has in her mouth. Take the time to teach your dog to "Give" by trading for treats.

  Most people make the mistake of only taking "forbidden objects" away from their dogs, which can teach the dog to object, since she learns that she'll never get it back. If you practice "Give" as a regular training exercise with a "legal" toy or chew object, you can repeatedly return the object in question after the dog gives it up for a treat. This way, she learns that she gets *two* rewards—the first for giving up the valuable object, the second when she gets the valuable object back again. Then, if she occasionally has to give up an "illegal" object that you can't return to her, it won't outweigh the positive impact of all the two-reward trades you have done with her.

- **Bite Inhibition**: Dogs bite. It's a natural canine behavior. Chances are that at some time in your dog's life, she may feel compelled to bite. If and when that happens, good bite inhibition could make the difference between a dent in the skin and plastic surgery. It could also determine whether your dog lives or dies, since dogs who bite and cause serious injury tend to not live long—especially *big* dogs who bite.

  You can instill good bite inhibition in a pup by gradually diminishing the force of her bite rather than punishing all bites. A puppy naturally learns to control the force of her teeth through playing with her siblings. If she bites softly, without causing undue pain, the other puppies will keep playing with her. If she bites too hard, the pup she's biting may yelp and run away, refusing to re-engage in play for a time.

  You can do the same thing. If your giant puppy bites softly, continue playing with her. If she bites hard enough to cause pain, calmly say "Ouch!" or "Oops!" and walk away from her. After a short time, begin playing with her again. She will learn to control her bite so that the fun can continue without interruption.

- **Think Positive:** If you think it's a good idea to force confrontations with your large dog, think again. First, it's not necessary, and second, the bigger the dog gets, the more likely you are to lose. In old-fashioned force-based training, owners were advised to dominate their dogs, and if the dogs offered to fight back, increase the level of human aggression until the dogs submitted. Dogs who refused to submit were labeled "vicious" and "incorrigible" and euthanized.

It takes two to fight. If you train with positive methods, you never set the dog up for conflict, and you teach her to willingly and happily respond to your behavior requests because good things happen when she does.

Big Bother?

If big dogs are such a challenge, why even bother with them? Some people like the look and feel of a big, solid dog by their sides. Many of these folks don't consider a canine to be a real dog unless they are at least 75 pounds. There is something very comforting about the bulk of an impressively large canine, especially if you are alone in a remote location, traveling through an unsavory part of town, or taking your dog for a late night walk in Central Park.

There is also much to be said for the big-dog personality. As a general rule, they are calmer than many of their smaller brethren—it's a lot of work to haul around that much bulk! Besides, a St. Bernard-sized dog with a Jack Russell Terrier's energy level probably wouldn't be around long—who could live with that?

If you want to think big, by all means go for it. Big rewards go along with those big challenges. Just be sure you are ready for the extra large responsibilities that go along with sharing your home and your heart with a supersized canine.

Big Ideas to Keep in Mind

- When you own a big dog, you must be ultra-responsible. Make sure you are prepared for the added responsibility of a super-sized dog before you bring one home. Don't be lured by the novelty of owning a giant breed unless you are honest with yourself about what you are getting into.

- Train and socialize early and often. Socialization must be reinforced throughout a dog's life, especially for dogs who are protective by nature. Training is more than a six-week beginner class; even old dogs can learn new tricks.

- Manage, manage, manage. Big dogs can get into bigger trouble than small dogs. Make a strong commitment to manage your dog's behavior so he doesn't get reinforced for undesirable behaviors, especially those that might put others at risk.

- Respect the feelings and fears of other people. Not everyone loves large dogs, and some people are terrified of them. Don't let your dog approach people unless and until you know that they are comfortable being greeted by a dog who may outweigh them. Warn them if your dog is likely to jump up or lick, even if you know your dog is only being affectionate.

Part Four
PROBLEM BEHAVIORS

No discussion of dog training is complete without paying some attention to the many and varied behavior challenges that these beloved furry creatures can present to their owners. Part Four addresses a broad sampling of these the hyperactive hound, indoor marking behavior, fear of household appliances, mounting, begging, escaping, barking, and more.

Crazy Owner, Crazy Dog?

Not necessarily—inconsistency is the decider

Several years ago when I went through a period of severe depression, my Terrier mix, Josie, was most empathetic. Her normally cheerful demeanor changed to match mine. She appeared sad, hung by my side, and cuddled next to me during my sobbing spells, her warm furry presence was a life-saving comfort.

Katie reacted entirely differently. She seemed to make a concerted effort to cheer me up with her bubbly personality, wriggling body and ridiculous "woo-woo" vocalizations—approaching with her eyes crinkled into beguiling squints, ears flattened against her head, hyperactive tongue ready to wash the tears from my cheeks. It often worked—her antics made me laugh, and helped to lift the dark cloud.

There's no doubt that our dogs pick up on our moods, and that our emotions and behaviors affect theirs. Sometimes this is good. One of the things we love about our canine companions is their steadfast presence—their ability to comfort us in hard times, and share the joys of our lives in better days.

It is comforting that dogs can reflect our moods——especially when we're enjoying quiet time.

But how does this affect them? Is it possible that human emotional instability can cause canine emotional instability? Are we making our dogs neurotic?

In his book, *Handbook of Applied Dog Behavior and Training,* behavior consultant Steven R. Lindsay defines neurosis as: "...an emotionally maladaptive and persistent habit or compulsion that resists modification through normal processes of learning."

Much experimentation has been done on animals in the study of neurotic behavior, led in the early 1900s by the Russian scientist Ivan Pavlov of bell-ringing, dog-salivating, classical-conditioning fame. Many—although not all—of those experiments involved stomach-turning applications of electric shock. As with humans, dogs are most likely develop neu-roses when they are unable to control and predict their environment. The unpredictable application of punishment, electric shock or otherwise, makes us—and our dogs—feel very much out of control.

Balanced Temperaments

Pavlov discovered that a dog's susceptibility to neurotic behavior was dependent on its temperament. Not surprisingly, he found that inactive, socially withdrawn dogs were the most strongly affected by neuroses-inducing environments, while those with the most bal-anced, extroverted, and flexible temperaments were least affected.

Scientific findings about neurotic behavior underscore the importance of consistency in dog training and management. Inconsistent application of reward and punishment create an environment in which the dog has no control.

This not only slows the dog's ability to learn, it can stop learning altogether. At some point the dog comes to realize he is damned if he does, and damned if he doesn't. All living things repeat behaviors that are rewarding to them and avoid behaviors that make bad stuff happen. If a dog can't predict whether his behaviors will result in a positive or negative consequence, he may simply choose to do nothing at all—a condition known as **learned helplessness**. He can't win.

Dogs who have been trained with old-fashioned force-based methods that focus on "cor-recting" inappropriate behaviors—using corporal punishment, choke chains, prong and/ or electric shock collars—often demonstrate this phenomenon in a milder form. This is especially true if the trainer is inconsistent with punishment, or has poor timing. Punish-ment-trained dogs may be reluctant to try new things, having learned that it's safer to do nothing.

Humane, positive trainers shy away from punishment tools, especially shock collars. Con-trast the force-trained dog with dogs trained using positive methods that focus on re-warding the dog for performing desirable behaviors. The positive-trained dogs are usually eager learners, willing to offer new behaviors as they look for the key to unlock the next reward.

Learned Helplessness

Poor timing of corrections in training contributes to learned helplessness because the dog can't understand which behavior is being punished, therefore he can't control whether the punishment happens or not. A common example is the irate owner who erroneously pun-ishes his dog for not coming when called—after the dog finally comes. The dog struggles with the conflict of responding to the cue to come—which sometimes gets rewarded—and his anxiety over the possibility of being punished when he does comply.

A more extreme example is what behaviorists call **non-contingent punishment**—punish-ing a dog *long* after the event. The owner who yells at his dog when he arrives home from work to discover the contents of the garbage can strewn across the kitchen floor is setting his dog up for neurosis because the dog can't connect his very rewarding garbage-play of several hours ago with his owner's unpredictable and dangerous behavior. Because the dog doesn't understand what is causing the owner's bizarre behavior, he can't control or predict it. A classic recipe for neurosis.

Remember that our definition of a neurosis says that it is:

1. Emotionally maladaptive;

2. A persistent habit or compulsion; and

3. Resists modification through normal processes of learning.

In other words, it's a behavior that doesn't help the dog adjust to his environment, and is darned hard to get rid of. Separation anxiety is a perfect example. So are canine obsessive-compulsive disorders such as spinning, self-mutilation, and shadow-chasing. Neuroses can also manifest as phobias, generalized anxiety and depression, and exaggerated attention-seeking behaviors.

A commonly held premise says that neurotic owners create neurotic dogs. True? Maybe—and maybe not. In fact the opposite can be true—mentally stable humans can—and do—frequently and inadvertently create neurotic dogs.

First it's important to differentiate between poorly behaved or "spoiled" dogs and truly neurotic ones. We tend to label a dog as neurotic because he's doing something that we wouldn't tolerate, like the irritating little Chihuahua who barks and snarls frenetically at every passer-by when cuddled in the depths of his owner's ample bosom. So we test it with our definition.

Persistent Habit

Is the barking and snarling behavior of the Chihuahua maladaptive? Maybe not, especially if the owner actually likes and encourages the behavior. Is it a persistent habit or compulsion? Persistent habit, surely, but compulsion? Perhaps not. And resistant to behavior modification through normal learning processes? Probably not, at least for many of these dogs who, if their owners chose to pursue a program of behavior modification, might easily stop the annoying behavior.

Second, we need to consider the environment of the dog who lives with the neurotic human. There are certainly humans with obsessive-compulsive neuroses who live very orderly, predictable lives. This kind of environment, in which a dog might feel quite able to control and predict events, would not likely give rise to a neurotic dog. There may also be neurotic humans whose lives are in disarray but who can maintain constancy in their reactions to and relationships with their dogs.

Again, this is not likely to give rise to canine neuroses. In fact, many humans with psychological disabilities find that their canine companions are the anchors that allow them to make some sense of the chaos of their lives—a very important role for some service dogs.

It is the inconsistent human—neurotic or not—who risks her dog's mental stability. There are legions of mentally sound dog owners whose lives are so chaotic, and their relationships with and responses to their dogs so unpredictable, that they are veritable Petri dishes for canine neuroses. If you invite your dog on the sofa sometimes—but yell at him for making himself comfortable at others, you are unpredictable and dangerous—he can't control your behavior by doing the "right" thing. If you hug him for jumping up on you when you're in blue jeans but knee him in the chest when you're in a suit, he can't control or predict his world.

What You Can Do to Help

No sane person wants a neurotic dog. Dogs who have separation anxiety are difficult, sometimes impossible, to live with. Imagine coming home from work every evening in anticipation of finding your house destroyed—it's enough to turn *you* into a neurotic wreck! It's painful to watch a dog in the obsessive-compulsive agonies of spinning, shadow-chasing or fly-snapping. It's irritating to live with a dog who constantly whines, nudges, or paws at you for attention. Neurotic behaviors can eat away at the human-animal bond that guarantees your dog a lifelong loving home with you, or with the next unfortunate adopter.

How do you avoid waking up one morning and finding yourself sharing your bed with a neurotic canine? Start by taking a hint from our Russian scientist friend. When you adopt a dog, look for one whose temperament is, as Pavlov labeled them "sanguine" or "phlegmatic" rather than "melancholic" or choleric." (See "Pavlov's Pooch Personalities" pg. 139). If you choose a dog whose personality leans more toward the less stable, know that you will need to be careful to avoid setting him up for neuroses.

Every dog—every living creature—is born with a genetic package that is the framework for his potential in life. Some of those genes are immutable. Dogs can't breathe under water, no matter how hard you try to train them. Nor can most fish survive on land. Tadpoles turn into frogs, not butterflies, and puppies grow up to be dogs.

Other pieces of the genetic package are more plastic, however, and to a great degree, we can mold our dogs' behaviors to our liking. You can avoid turning your Melancholy Collie into a Neurotic Nellie by providing the following:

- Consistency. Make sure *everyone* in the household understands the dog rules and agrees to follow them.

- Structure. Institute a "Say Please" program—also known as "Nothing in Life is Free." Teach your dog that she can make good things happen (control!) by offering a desirable behavior—usually a "Sit."

- Calm. Maintain a tranquil ambience in your household. Restrict uncontrolled human roughhousing to the back yard, and don't let your dog participate.

- Structured Play. While exercise can be quite helpful in lowering energy levels, unstructured play can increase arousal and chaos. Play games with consistent rules, such as "you must sit calmly to make me throw the ball," and "you must release the tug toy when I ask you to."

- Positive Training. Positive training, especially positive training that uses a reward marker such as a clicker, deliberately encourages a dog's sense of control over his environment. The absence of physical or harsh verbal punishment helps make the environment safer and more predictable.

If you have a dog who is poorly-trained and badly-behaved but not actually neurotic, these measures can help you, too.

The list for modifying neurotic behavior, not surprisingly, is very similar to the steps for preventing it. The critically important elements of bringing a dog back to sanity involve creating a milieu of consistency, structure, calm environment, structured play and positive training.

If you let your dog on the furniture sometimes, but not always, he can't help but be confused and anxious, unable to predict his world.

However, because one of the defining pieces of neurotic behavior is that it "resists modification through normal processes of behavior," you will likely need more than this. Behaviors such as separation anxiety and canine obsessive-compulsive disorders often require the assistance of a competent positive trainer/behavior consultant for successful modification.

Your behavior professional can observe your environment and help you implement the five steps on the list, as well as create a behavior modification program specific to your dog's neurosis. She can also work with you and your veterinarian if the two of you decide pharmaceutical intervention is in order—as is often the case with true neuroses.

Before you cringe at the thought of "drugging" your dog, know that modern pharmaceuticals for behavior modification are a far cry from the drugs of the past that left your dog in a stupor. The new classes of drugs, such as Clomicalm—commonly used in conjunction with behavior modification programs for separation anxiety—actually work to correct imbalances in brain chemistry.

Also know that these chemicals don't work all by themselves—they are intended to go hand-in-paw with a behavior modification program by opening a window of opportunity in the dog's brain that allows the modification protocols to be more effective.

I managed to survive my period of depression, with a lot of help from my canine friends. As far as I can tell, none of them became neurotic—at least not markedly so. Katie, being a Kelpie, was probably already playing with a certain amount of neurotic behavior, but it didn't seem to worsen during that time. I was, of course, already using positive training methods, and I suppose I managed to maintain a reasonable amount of structure in our lives despite my own troubles. After all, I *had* to get out of bed in the morning—I had dogs to feed!

Pavlov's Pooch Personalities

When conducting his experiments on neurotic behavior in dogs, Pavlov divided dogs temperaments into four broad types, two of which he believed to be particularly susceptible to neuroses. Of course, no dog falls into purely one set of characteristics, but when selecting for less potential for canine neuroses, look for dogs who are more sanguine or phlegmatic than melancholic or choleric. While certain breeds *tend* to fall into certain temperament types—I've indicated some examples below—don't be fooled; there *are* choleric Bassets and sanguine Chows out there. And remember, the plasticity of genetic material allows us to influence how strongly a dog displays some of his inherited tendencies.

Mixes of these breeds may or may not exhibit these temperaments, depending on how much of a gene package a particular mixed-breed happens to inherit. Just because he inherited the appearance genes for a breed doesn't mean he inherited the temperament genes.

The types:

- **Sanguine:** Friendly, responsive, focused, energetic: Golden Retriever, Labrador Retriever, Australian Shepherd, Papillion, American Staffordshire Terrier

- **Phlegmatic:** Passive, controlled, calm, balanced: Basset Hound, Chow Chow, English Bulldog, Mastiff, Pug

- **Melancholic:** Anxious, inhibited, unsociable, withdrawn: Chihuahua, Basenji, Shar Pei

- **Choleric (hot-tempered):** Touch sensitive, excitable, impulsive, aggressive: Australian Cattle Dog, Miniature Pinscher, Jack Russell Terrier, Australian Kelpie

Now—before anyone writes in protest to tell me they have a calm Jack Russell Terrier, or an outgoing Chihuahua, I *know* that such dogs exist. Remember that I said the genetic material is plastic. Someone has obviously done a good job with *your* dog to steer him away from the genetic tendencies of the breed.

Is Your Dog Spoiled?

*Living comfortably doesn't count;
being demanding and pushy does*

When a new client calls me seeking a private consultation, I often hear a litany of canine woes that include: barking, chewing, digging, counter surfing, house soiling, jumping up, biting, running away, and other destructive and inappropriate behaviors. With amazing consistency, clients conclude by confessing that they allow their dogs on the furniture and feed them people-food and then sheepishly claim, "I guess I've spoiled him." I always respond with, "My dogs are allowed on the furniture and I feed them people food. If allowing dogs on the bed and feeding them human food equals spoiling, then I passionately believe that dogs *should* be spoiled."

Contrary to what you may have read in some dog training books, letting your dog get on the sofa and feeding him real food does *not* mean he will turn into a raving dominant maniac-dog, nor does it teach him to drool at your dinner table. It simply means that you have made a conscious decision to grant him furniture privileges and provide him with a diet that goes beyond processed kibble. These deliberate choices on your part do not give rise to behavior problems. Spoiling a dog in a manner that leads to undesirable behaviors is something else entirely.

In her excellent book, *Click for Joy!*, author and clicker trainer Melissa Alexander says, "Spoiling occurs when you give something for nothing." I would add to her definition that spoiling also occurs when you allow behaviors to be rewarded that you will sooner or later come to regret. While a client who is calling me about behavior problems may indeed have "spoiled" her dog, the problems are far more likely a result of giving a dog the opportunity to practice and be rewarded for inappropriate behavior than they are a result of furniture privileges and dietary selections.

Some people see a "spoiled dog" in any canine who is not shivering outside on a chain. Most of us, however, recognize that a dog can enjoy a comfortable and even luxurious lifestyle without being "spoiled."

Who Controls the Goods?

Whenever you are with your dog, one of you is training the other. The healthiest dog/human relationships generally occur when the human is the trainer and the dog the trainee the vast majority of the time. This means that the human controls most of the "good stuff" in the dog's life, and decides when, where, and how the dog gets it. The dog can earn the good stuff by doing things that please the human.

Important note: The dog is not intrinsically trying to please the human. The dog is just doing whatever he needs to do to get the good stuff and thereby please himself. It is incidental to him that he pleases his human in the process.

I identify a "spoiled" dog as one who is allowed to be the trainer more often than he is the trainee and when the resulting behaviors are damaging to the relationship. The spoiled dog does things that don't please his human and he gets the good stuff anyway.

This is the dog who "demand-barks" to go out, come back in, get a treat or a toy—and the human gives him what he wants because she knows the barking will just escalate if she doesn't.

It's the dog who digs at his owner's arm for attention—and gets it. It's the dog who jumps up on the bed next to the wife and growls at the husband when he tries to get in on his side—especially if the result is the husband goes and sleeps on the sofa!

It's the dog who wakes up at 3:00 a.m., barks to go out—even though he is a healthy adult dog well able to "hold it" all night—and then whines and barks in his crate when he comes back in until his humans let him out to spend the rest of the night in the bed with them. It's the dog who drags his protesting owner around the block at the end of the leash, accosting every human, peeing on every bush and eating every bit of garbage he can find along the way. You get the idea.

Say Please

You may have a new dog or pup and are determined not to spoil her. Or perhaps you are realizing that you have already made some mistakes and now have a dog who is slightly or seriously spoiled. In any case, a "Say Please" program is a great way to either avoid or overcome the challenges of living with a spoiled dog.

Also known as "Nothing in Life is Free," or "No Free Lunch," a "Say Please" program teaches your dog that she must ask for good stuff—politely—by performing a desirable behavior, rather than by demanding—and getting—what she wants. "Sit" is the most versatile "Say Please" behavior, and by far the easiest to install. Most dogs can learn to offer sits in a few minutes or less.

As soon as your dog learns that sitting is a very rewarding behavior, it's a simple matter to wait for her to sit before bestowing good stuff on her. Breakfast time? Hold up her food dish and wait for her to sit; that's a "Say Please" behavior. Time for a walk? Sit gets you to attach the leash. Want to go out? Sitting politely makes the door open. Want to be petted? Dogs who sit get pets, treats, and attention.

You may be tempted to ask for the sit, but don't! Instead, use a little body language if necessary; hold a treat, the food bowl, or your hand, up near your chest—and wait until she offers the sit of her own accord. Then work quickly to *fade* (progressively eliminate) the treat and body language. You want your dog to realize that she has to initiate the request for the good stuff.

One of the goals of positive reinforcement training is to create dogs who learn to control their own behavior, so that you don't have to constantly tell them what to do. If you constantly *tell* your dog to sit, she won't learn to "Say Please" without being asked, and she won't generalize her polite "Say Please" behavior to other people and other situations.

Sit is not your only "Say Please" option. It doesn't matter so much *what* you ask her to do. What matters is that she learns she has to *earn* the good stuff, it doesn't just happen gratuitously. You can use any desirable behavior that your dog can do easily—or a variety of behaviors in a variety of situations. Dubhy used to grumble at me from my office doorway when he wanted to go outside. I found this a little pushy and annoying, so I taught him to "Say Please" instead, by coming into the office and sitting quietly at my feet. Tucker does a lovely "Say Please" play bow when he asks to go outside. And both of them "Say Please" again by sitting politely at the door when I go to let them out.

Stick to Your Guns

"Sounds simple," you may say, "but when I pick up my leash my dog Bonkers leaps and cavorts about, barks at the top of her lungs and body-slams me. She's not going to offer a sit!" At this point Bonkers thinks that cavorting is what causes the door to open. It's been working for a long time now, so why wouldn't she think that? It is certainly more challenging to reprogram an already-established undesirable behavior than it is to install the desirable one from the start, but it's not impossible.

You can make it easier by separating the environmental cues that tell her it's "walk-time." Perhaps you always keep the leash on the hook by the front door and put it on her collar in the entryway when you take her for her daily walk at 5:30 pm after you get home from work. Try moving the leash to the kitchen drawer. At 7:00 in the morning on a day when you don't have to rush off to work or school, take the leash out of the drawer and, using your "Sit" body language, help her to "Say Please." If she leaps and cavorts about uncontrollably, cheerfully say "Too bad!" set the leash on the counter and go about your morning kitchen business.

As soon as she calms down, pick up the leash again and try for another "Say Please." Every time she revs up, say "Too bad!" and set the leash down. Every time she calms down, restart the leash process. This teaches her that cavorting about makes the leash go away, and that sitting makes the leash happen. You will probably be surprised by how quickly she figures it out. This is the opposite of what she learned in the past, so be patient with her.

As soon as she will stay reasonably calm when you pick up the leash, encourage her to sit so you can attach it to her collar. If she leaps up again when you start to clip it on, give her another cheerful "Too bad!" and set the leash down again. When she will remain sitting calmly as you attach the leash, take her to a *different* door from the one you usually exit through with her, and help her "Say Please" at the door to make the door open. Take her out for at least a short walk as a reward.

Feel free to take breaks as needed during the reprogramming process. Training sessions are generally most productive if they last no more than 10-15 minutes at a stretch. Some dogs (and humans!) do best with sessions that last 5 minutes or less. Try to take your breaks following one or more successes, rather than waiting until you or Bonkers are so frustrated you can't take it any more. If you find yourself getting frustrated, ask Bonkers to do something that she loves and does really well, and take a break after that.

Bonkers may need several short sessions to understand that she needs to sit and stay sitting in order to get the good stuff (leash and walk), or she may get it in one session. When she will reliably sit for you in the kitchen for the leash and at the alternate door to make it open, continue to put the leash on in the kitchen, but return to using the door that you normally use to take her out, at her regularly scheduled walk time. When that part of the walk routine is reprogrammed, take the leash out of the kitchen drawer, but walk to the entryway and clip it on her collar—after she does a polite "Say Please" sit, of course. When she can do that calmly, hang the leash on its old hook by the door, and you're back in business!

The Art of Training

Most "spoiled" behaviors can be addressed by creating a reprogramming protocol similar to the one described above that teaches your dog to "Say Please" in order to get whatever the good stuff is that she wants at the moment. Keep in mind, however, that many dogs will exhibit a behavior known as an **extinction burst**, which is akin to the temper tantrum that a toddler might throw when she doesn't get her way.

For example, let's say your dog is in the habit of barking at you to get you to let her outside. In your new reprogramming mode, you carefully ignore her when she barks by turning away from her so that she is no longer rewarded for this undesirable behavior. Your dog *knows* that barking has gotten her what she wants in the past, and she can't figure out why, all of a sudden, it's not working now. So she tries harder, sure that if she just tries hard, loud, and long enough, it will work again.

Hearing the increased intensity and volume in the dog's voice, you may become convinced that the new training program isn't working and, tired of listening to the racket, open the door and let the dog out. You have just rewarded your dog's increased level of barking, reinforcing "louder and longer" and making it that much more difficult to reprogram the barking behavior.

Simply ignoring the dog's previously successful behavior leaves her frustrated and noisy, and stresses you both until you give in to her. This is where the "Say Please" program is so valuable. Teaching her an alternative successful behavior gives her something else to do—an acceptable way to make good stuff happen. However, if you respond to her barking by *asking* her to sit and *then* letting her out, you are simply teaching a **behavior chain** of, "I bark, I sit, and *then* the door opens." In order to avoid this dilemma, you must blend the science of behavior with the art of training.

Think About It

We tend to ignore our dogs when they are being polite, and we pay attention to them when they are being rude. That's how they get to be spoiled in the first place—they learn that they have to be pushy to get what they want. If you are working to unspoil your dog or to prevent spoiling, you must keep your eyes open, watch for the polite "Say Please" be-·havior to happen, and reward it a lot. When your dog does "Say Please," sometimes reward her with a pat on the head or a scratch behind the ear, sometimes with a yummy treat or a game of fetch, and sometimes by letting her out or giving her whatever other good stuff she is politely asking for.

However, this doesn't mean she always gets what she wants; the art of training is in finding the balance between controlling the good stuff and sharing it with your canine pal on *your* terms. In time, the new behaviors will be solidly programmed and you can reduce the rate of positive reinforcement without losing the new behaviors.

A "Say Please" program won't fix *all* behavior problems. The dog who doesn't let hubby on the bed can certainly benefit from learning to "Say Please," but his owners may also need the assistance of a trainer/behaviorist to resolve the bed guarding. It will, without a doubt *prevent* a lot of problems from ever occurring in the first place, and even implemented after-the-fact, can help make the trainer/behaviorist's job easier with the more challenging behavior problems.

If your dog doesn't know how to "Say Please," perhaps it's time to teach him. Then you can say, "Spoiled? Not *my* dog," as he sits politely on the sofa next to you, smiling and eating pieces of carrot and chicken.

The Social Scene

Dogs who are comfortable in public are born, not made

I just completed a private consultation with a client whose under-socialized Australian Shepherd recently bit their six year old daughter in the face, and nipped a friend of their nine year old son. I'm cursing a world that allows this to happen.

This well-meaning family adopted Blue from a shelter when he was 16 weeks old. He was "shy," they said—he hid under a chair in the get acquainted room when they met him. He had been at the shelter for two months—half his life. According to his paperwork he was the last of a litter of six and was timid when initially assessed.

In fact, all the pups were timid, but he was the worst—which was why he was the last one left when the Petersons went to the shelter to adopt last February. He was the only puppy in the shelter at the time, so they decided to take him despite his shyness. He'd come around, they thought, with love and attention.

Nature vs. Nurture

What they didn't know was that at 16 weeks, Blue was reaching the end of a pup's most important socialization period—the time in his life when he learns what is safe and good, and what is scary. In the wild, the lessons learned during the first few months of a pup's life are critical to his survival. As he ventures out of his den he learns to be bold where it counts—pouncing on prey, for example—and cautious where being prudent makes more sense. Pups who don't learn to avoid poisonous snakes, rushing floodwaters, and precipitous cliffs don't live to pass on their genes!

During this period, puppies who live with humans need to learn that the world is a good and safe place. Their general assumption then becomes that people, other animals, places, and things are okay unless proven otherwise.

An outdoor café can be an excellent place to find people to help you socialize your puppy. Look for a variety of people—old, young, big, small—and give volunteers a few delicious treats to feed to the pup.

In contrast, puppies who are not socialized are suspicious of everything except for a very narrow range of experiences they encounter in their very limited environment—someone's basement or back yard, for example. The rest of the world terrifies them, and any positive exposures they get later in life must struggle against this early, very strong programming.

A genetically sound pup has a better chance of recovering, at least to some degree, from a poor start in life. A pup who inherited poor genes for temperament and wasn't well socialized early is often a lost cause—or, at least, a huge challenge even for someone who is well-prepared, educated, and equipped to deal with him or her.

The fact that Blue and all his siblings were deemed to be "shy" when they were dropped off at the shelter indicated that they hadn't received adequate early socialization. Most shelters aren't ideal environments for remedial socialization, so by the time Blue was finally adopted, he was woefully behind in his "Life is Good" lessons—the lessons that, once missed, are very difficult (if not impossible) to make up.

The Petersons also didn't know that if they wanted to try to make up for lost time they had to immediately start super-socializing their new pup. By the time they brought Blue to me he was 11 months old, and the prognosis for successful behavior modification was dismal.

This dog's future is unknown. The Petersons want to try, and I will certainly try to help them, but they are facing a huge challenge. When children are involved and at risk, tolerance for error is low, and rightly so. I'm hoping to be pleasantly surprised by the outcome of this case.

Every dog is a product of the influence of his genes *and* his environment. If a pup comes from parents who have very genetically sound temperaments, then the pup can get by with an average amount of socialization—or even less. However, if Mom and Pop are genetically unstable, Pup needs to be ultra-socialized if he is to become a safe and friendly member of society.

The problem is, it's pretty hard to tell the difference. If you adopt a pup from a shelter, you rarely get to meet the parents. Even if you buy from a breeder, you can't tell if Mom and Dad are friendly because they're genetically sound, or because they were exceptionally well socialized. How do you know whether to give your new pup average socialization or the ultra package? You don't.

The answer to this conundrum is to socialize the heck out of every single puppy. Then you don't risk finding out later on that you had a pup who needed an extra boost in the social department—you already gave it to him!

Early Socialization

The best socialization programs begin while pups are still with their dams. A good breeder begins handling her pups gently and early, just as their eyes begin to open, giving them a positive association with human touch. As they get a little older (5-6 weeks) they should start meeting more humans—all shapes, colors, ages and sizes—who feed them treats and pet them gently. The breeder will need to supervise these interactions closely, as rough handling at this stage can have the opposite effect, teaching the pups that humans *aren't* safe to be around.

The mother dog's attitude is important at this stage too. If she is aggressive towards humans or even just stressed about having her pups handled, the pups can pick up on her attitude and learn this inappropriate behavior from her. If Mom is calm and relaxed around humans, pups are more likely to be, too.

By the time a pup is weaned at 7-8 weeks, he should already have a positive world view programmed into his little puppy brain. When you select your pup from a litter, whether you're at a breeder's home or a shelter—or picking one from a box of free puppies on a street corner—choose wisely. Resist the temptation to rescue the pup who hides in the corner. Select, instead, the pup who is outgoing without being overbearing—the one who seems to have a cheerful, "Life Is Good" attitude. Otherwise you risk finding yourself in the Peterson's shoes, with an 11-month-old dog who is biting children in the face.

Okay, you've adopted a friendly pup with a sound temperament. Good for you! That doesn't mean your job is done, however. You must continue your pup's socialization lessons assiduously until he is 16 weeks old, and then maintain his positive association to the world throughout his life. If you take an eight week old well-socialized pup and stick him alone in your back yard when has not had any previous outside exposure, the odds are good that you will end up with a problem.

The Health Dilemma

Puppy owners are often counseled by their veterinarians to keep their baby dogs cloistered safely at home until they are fully vaccinated at four to six months of age. Looking at the situation purely from a physical health perspective, this makes good sense. You certainly don't want to risk exposing your pup to nasty distemper or parvo bugs.

From a mental health perspective, however, it's horrible advice. You only have two to three more months to give your pup an unshakeable faith in the goodness of the world. You cannot afford to wait until those shots are done. During this period, you want to give your pup at least 100 new positive exposures and experiences, to "vaccinate" him against the possibility that he will feel compelled to bite someone, someday. (See "100 Exposures In 100 Days" pg. 148.) It's not a guarantee against biting, but it's by far your best chance of ending up with an adult dog who is friendly and safe.

Fear Periods

At one time in the last several decades, much ado was made about a pup's "critical fear periods." Behaviorists attempted to pinpoint those period of time in puppyhood during which a "bad experience" would scar a pup's psyche for life. More recently, we have come to realize that, although pups *do* seem to go through periods during which they are more fearful than others, that time can vary from one pup to the next. Rather than wrapping your pup in cotton wool for a designated period, it makes more sense to watch him closely and ensure that he has mostly good experiences, especially if he seems to be going through a cautious stage.

Even if something *does* frighten him, it's not the end of the world—you can set up a counter-conditioning and desensitization program to restore a positive association with that particular stimulus, and your pup should recover nicely.

Lifetime Socialization

Now your pup is 16 weeks old. You've reached the end of that magic socialization window, your "100 exposures" list is all checked off, and your pup loves the world. Are you done? Hardly.

Like your training efforts which continue on into adulthood and throughout your dog's entire life, you are never done with socialization. You've laid a very solid foundation; that's something to be proud of.

Much of that will be lost, however, if you toss your four-month-old pup into the back yard and cease all exposure. He still needs to meet and greet people, go places with you, and continue to share your world and your experiences, if you want him to continue to be the happy, friendly puppy he is today. And of course, that's what you want!

100 Exposures in 100 Days

Giving your pup 100 positive experiences in his first 100 days with you is not as daunting as it may sound. The most important thing to keep in mind is to control the circumstances so that the experience remains positive for your puppy. When introducing your pup to children, for example, put yourself between your pup and any overeager, rambunctious kids until you have a chance to tell the youngsters how they must behave if they want to meet the puppy. Don't let a baby clamp his hand onto any part of the puppy's anatomy, and don't hand off the pup to anyone who is in danger of dropping her.

It's also best to bring an ample supply of extra-tasty treats anywhere you take the pup. When someone sees your puppy and starts making the inevitable "Oh what a cute puppy!" approach, hand the person a couple of treats and ask if he would feed them to the pup as he pets her. Or bring along your puppy's favorite stuffed toy, and give it to the person so he can offer it to your puppy. Keep an eye on your pup's response; she should be happy, confident, and obviously pleased to see any and every new person approaching. If she appears frightened or overwhelmed, think about how you can make the interactions less threatening and more rewarding for her.

You'll find many opportunities in your own neighborhood to start your list of 100. You'll also want to get into the habit of taking your pup with you to as many *safe* places as possible, to enhance his socialization, and to start him on his path to being your well-behaved companion, welcome wherever you go.

I suggest you keep an actual written list of your pup's socialization exposures, with a goal of a minimum of one new exposure per day until you've reached the 100 mark. If you put a little effort into it, we're betting you'll get there well before your 100 days are up—more likely in half that time!

Here are some suggestions to start you off:

1. Your mail carrier. Snag him on his daily rounds and ask him to feed your pup a tidbit or two. Start an early positive association with this daily visitor to your home.

2. Your UPS or FedEx person. Add a little extra power to the positive association with uniforms to avoid trouble later.

3. Your neighbors. Actually, this can count as several, if you live in a diverse neighborhood. If your neighborhood is homogenous, try a park, or the bench in front of your local library: Look for (3) tall men, (4) short men, (5) tall women, (6) short women, (7) skinny men and (8) skinny women,

(9) portly men and (10) portly women, (11) babes-in-arms, (12) babies in strollers, (13) women pushing babies in strollers, (14) toddlers, (15) older children, (16) tweens and (17) teens, (18) men with beards, (19) men with hats, (20) people with backpacks, (21) women with hats, (22) people in wheelchairs, (23) people on walkers and crutches, (24) kids on bikes, (25) kids on skateboards, (26) kids on scooters, (27) kids playing basketball...

...and all of the above in various ethnic groups. Then add locations to your list, including your (28) bank, (29) vet's office, (30) pet supply store, (31) copy center, (32) hardware store, (33) puppy kindergarten class, (34) outdoor café, or (35) any place of business that doesn't have a "No Dogs" sign on the door.

Okay—you're one-third of the way there. You get the idea and you get to think up the rest. Be creative, and remember to control each interaction to keep it positive for your pup.

Places Not to Take Your Pup

While socialization is a wonderful thing, it's important to avoid places that pose a risk to your pup's physical and mental health and safety. Here are some places that are important to avoid:

- Off-leash dog parks, until he *is* fully immunized against the most common puppy diseases, or any places with accumulations of feces from unknown dogs.

- Any place where he is likely to encounter stray or sick dogs.

- Any place where he is likely to encounter aggressive dogs.

- Any place he is not welcome.

- Any place where he would have to be left unattended or in a hot car (no tying up outside the grocery store!).

- Any place where he will be uncomfortable (sitting in the full sun while you watch your son's Little League game).

- Any place where he is likely to encounter aggressive, rowdy, drunk, or otherwise inappropriate humans (this includes street fairs and festivals, parades, marches, and other public events).

- Any place where you won't be able to devote enough attention to him to ensure his safety, security and well being.

Crate Difficulties

Helping more dogs find contentment in the close quarters of a crate

The topic turned to crating on one of my trainer e-mail lists recently. I was horrified to read that some shelters and rescue groups refuse to allow prospective owners to adopt dogs who intend to use a crate with their dogs. What madness is this?

I first discovered crates some 30 years ago when they were relatively new to the dog scene. I was skeptical about putting my new Australian Kelpie puppy in a "cage," but since Keli was part of a Canine Field Agent program for the Marin Humane Society where I worked as a Humane Officer, I was determined to do everything perfectly right. I reluctantly decided to try crating.

On the third night, when I went to deposit Keli in her crate, I found Caper, my three-year-old Bull Terrier, happily curled up in the pup's den. Caper smiled up at me and thumped her tail in the blankets, clearly saying, "This is wonderful! Can I have one of my own? Please, can I?"

I bought Caper a crate of her own the next day, and have been a total crate advocate ever since. How could they now be perceived as a bad thing?

As I followed the discussion, I realized that the negative crate perspective stemmed from concerns of "overcrating." Apparently some owners crate their dogs all day while they're at work, let them out for a couple of hours when they come home, and then crate the dogs all night while everyone is sleeping. This, some shelters fear, is too much time in a crate for a dog's physical and mental health.

They're right.

The crate is an invaluable management tool. Like any training tool, it can be misused. Even when used properly, it's not necessarily the appropriate tool for every dog in every circumstance. The discussion that follows may help you decide when, and whether, it's the right choice for you and your canine pal.

In some homes, all the dogs sleep in their own crates, putting an end to middle of the night "arguments" over the fluffiest cushions or another dog's toys.

Overcrating

A properly used crate can be the answer to your housetraining prayers. I was astounded by the ease with which I was able to housetrain my Kelpie pup. I also, however, was in the enviable position of being able to take my baby dog to work with me, so I was never tempted—or compelled—to crate her for longer that she could "hold it."

If you're a normal person whose boss frowns on dogs at work, you simply can't crate your pup all day while you're gone. He'll be forced to eliminate in his crate, breaking down his inhibitions against soiling his own den—the very inhibitions you rely on to be able to accomplish housetraining.

A general rule of thumb is that puppies can "hold it" during the day for up to one hour longer than they are months old. In other words, your eight week old baby dog can be crated for perhaps up to three hours during the day. They can usually go somewhat longer at night because metabolism slows, but it's a rare two month old who can go through the night without a potty break.

So, you can only crate your pup during an 8-10 hour workday if you can arrange for at least *two* bathroom breaks. One quick run home at lunch won't be enough, at least not until he's five to six months old.

In addition to performing necessary bodily functions, a growing pup needs to move around in order to develop properly. Some runaround time during the day helps him develop mentally and physically, practicing skills and learning lessons he can't make up later in life.

Finally, a pup who spends his entire day in a crate stores up mental and physical energy. When an owner comes home exhausted after working all day, she's rarely in a state of mind to cope with pent-up puppy frenzies, or to provide adequate exercise and mental stimulation to make up for a day of relative deprivation. The relationship suffers, and the pup gets relegated to the back yard, alone, or worse—put back into the crate.

While adult dogs are more physically capable of "holding it" for extended periods than puppies, it's still not appropriate for a dog to be routinely crated for 10 hours. Hence, the concerns of adoption agencies.

Solution for Overcrating

Alternatives to crating include finding alternative confinement options, arranging for multiple bathroom breaks, or finding a daycare situation of some kind.

Some owners simply leave their dogs—including puppies—outside in a fenced yard during the day. This allows the dog total freedom to poop and pee at will. It also leaves him vulnerable to threats from the environment—theft, poisoning, accidental escape, snakes, raccoons, skunks, and coyotes. I even met a pup once with a huge scar across his back—souvenir of a brief flight, fortunately aborted, in the talons of a Golden Eagle.

Outdoor confinement also leaves the dog free to practice inappropriate behaviors such as digging, escaping, and barking, and exposes him to the extremes of weather.

It might be safer to confine your pup indoors, either in a small puppy-proofed room such as a bathroom, or in a secure exercise pen. This requires newspapering the floor, and perhaps encouraging the dog to use one of the commercial pee pad products or a litter box, essentially giving him permission to eliminate in the house.

This solution has risks as well. Your pup can learn to rip up vinyl flooring and chew on cabinets if he's loose in a bathroom. He may be able to knock over his exercise pen if it's not well secured, climb out (some come with lids), or get a leg caught between the bars. If you plan to use an ex-pen, get him used to it while you're home, to be sure none of these things are likely to happen.

Multiple bathroom breaks may be easier than you think. If there are two adults in the household, perhaps you can stagger your lunches—one at 11am, one at 1pm—to give him two breaks. If not, a commercial pet sitter can take a daily turn at potty breaks. Other options include friends, neighbors, or family members who live close enough to provide the service until the pup is older. You might even find a local teenage dog lover who would cherish the opportunity to earn some spending money.

Finally, Spot may just need to go somewhere else during the day. Commercial doggie daycare centers are increasingly popular and available. Generally not appropriate for very young puppies, a well-run daycare center may be the answer for a pup four months or older.

Crate Soiling

If Spot eliminates in his crate even when *not* overcrated, your first course of action is to rule out medical problems. Loose stools, a urinary tract infection, or other incontinence problems make it impossible for a dog to hold it for normal periods of time.

Assuming all is well, there are several other possible causes of crate soiling:

1. Your dog has been routinely overcrated in the past, and was forced to soil his crate. His inhibitions against soiling his den have been damaged. He now thinks the crate in an acceptable bathroom.
2. Your dog isn't eliminating outdoors before being crated.
3. Your dog has separation anxiety (SA) and is voiding his bladder and bowels during his SA panic attack.

Solution for Crate Soiling

Your approach to Spot's crate soiling behavior depends on the cause.

If he has learned to soil his crate, it may help to change his bedding, or remove bedding altogether until he's retrained. Bedding that absorbs fluids, such as a blanket, can make it more comfortable for your dog to be in his soiled crate. His current bedding also may have become his preferred substrate. Try newspaper instead, a square of heavy duty compressed foam rubber (the kind used for flooring), or no bedding. A tether may be a reasonable alternative to nighttime crating.

Make sure his crate is the correct size—big enough for him to stand up, turn around, and lie down comfortably. If it's too large, he can potty in one end and sleep in the other.

Perhaps you're just not making sure Spot eliminates outside before you crate him. In your morning rush to get to work on time, you let him out in the back yard and assume he empties before he comes back in. That may be an incorrect assumption. If it's cold or rainy, he may have huddled on the back porch, waiting to be let back in. Perhaps he was distracted digging for moles under a bush, or barking at the kids walking past the yard on their way to school. Maybe he gets a cookie for coming back into the house, so he's skipping the step where he's supposed to go pee on the grass first. It could be a substrate preference problem—he wants to pee on grass, and all he can find is snow!

Set your alarm to awaken you 15 minutes earlier than normal, so you can go out with Spot on leash before and after he eats his breakfast to make sure he's empty when you crate him. If he's reluctant to out in inclement weather, create a sheltered potty spot, so he doesn't have to eliminate with rain or snow dumping on his head, or strong winds buffeting him. Would *you* be able to "do your business" under those conditions?

If he's determined to go on grass, it's the dead of winter and there's no grass available, you may need to scrape snow away from the grass in his sheltered potty spot or provide indoor-grown grass until you can teach him a new substrate preference. Maybe artificial turf would work!

Refusing to Go Into the Crate

Dogs who refuse to enter their crates may have never been crate trained, or the crating process was somehow abused. Spot may have been overcrated and now resists entering a den he fears he'll be forced to soil. Perhaps someone previously used his crate as punishment, or forcibly crated him. He may have had a bad experience in a crate that may have been improperly secured and rolled with him in it, or by having loud noises or other fear-inducing stimuli occur while he was crated.

Learning to Love the Crate

Whatever the reason, you'll need to embark on a program of counter-conditioning and desensitization to change Spot's association from bad to good, and retrain his crating behavior.

Start by scattering yummy stuff around the outside of his crate, placing a couple of tidbits just inside the door so he can stick his head in to get them. Gradually toss more yummies inside the crate to entice him further in. When he's going in easily, start hand feeding tidbits while he's inside, to encourage him to stay in. If you use a clicker, you can now begin to Click! and give him a treat for going into the crate.

When he'll go in and stay calmly inside the crate while you feed treats, close the door gently, feed treats through the door, and then let him out. Gradually increase the length of time you keep the door closed, until he's quite comfortable with this step. Then take a step away from the crate, Click! and return to give him his treat. Continue this process until he is happy to enter and stay in his crate.

You can play another crating game to motivate your dog to "kennel." Take something scrumptious, like a meaty knucklebone, and put it in the crate. Show it to your dog, and then close the door with him *outside* the crate. Let him spend some time trying to get *into* the closed crate to get at the bone, then open the door allowing him to zoom in (and back out, if he wants) to claim his prize.

To keep crating fun for your dog, be sure to practice crating games often, not just when he's going to be crated for extended periods. You can also give him food-stuffed Kongs™ and other interactive toys to keep him happy in his crate.

If your dog absolutely refuses to enter the crate, get one that comes apart. Take the top off, and then start the counter-conditioning process.

Demand Barking in Crate

Sometimes barking happens because the dog really needs to go. While it's critically important to heed your dog's bathroom calls, it's equally important not to succumb to crate barking when it's simply his insistent plea to get out and play, or cuddle. The more often you let him out on demand, the more the behavior is reinforced, and the harder it will be to ever successfully train him to stay quietly in his crate.

Solution to Barking in Crate

If you're just starting your dog's crating lessons, be sure he empties his bowels and bladder before you begin, so you know he doesn't have to go. Ignore his barking, and let him out of the crate when he's quiet. At first, he may be quiet for just a few seconds. Mark the quiet with a "Yes!" or a Click! so he knows it's the quiet behavior that gets him out of the crate. Gradually increase the length of quiet time before you let him out.

If your dog has already learned to demand-bark to gain freedom you'll follow the same procedure as above. However, it will take longer to extinguish the behavior because it's been previously reinforced. Your dog is likely to go through an extinction burst—more and/or louder barking, as he tries to make this formerly successful behavior work again. Be strong; if you give in during an extinction burst you will reinforce your dog for an even *more* intense behavior, and it will be even harder to make it stop.

At first, listen for and reinforce even very brief pauses in barking. You have to show your dog what behavior *will* work—quiet—if you want him to offer more of it.

Panicking in the Crate

This is very different from demand barking. Some dogs, particularly many of those with SA, can't tolerate the close confinement of a crate. They experience a full-blown panic attack, and frantically try to escape from their prison.

A panicked dog's efforts to escape from his mental and emotional anguish may include hysterical, non-stop barking and howling—for hours and hours without pause; frantic attempts to bite and claw his way out—often breaking teeth and ripping out nails in the process; and stress-induced urination and defecation—which he proceeds to paint all over the walls of his crate as he thrashes around.

Solution to Panic: Don't Crate

You cannot subject a panicked dog to these conditions. You must address the SA problem through behavior modification, and *may* someday be able to use a crate with your dog, if you are successful in modifying the SA. In the meantime, look for doggie daycare-type management solutions.

Managing Aggression in Crate

Some dogs become ferocious in their crates, usually manifesting territorial aggression, fear aggression, or resource guarding. The behavior is alarming, especially to an unsuspecting passer-by—human, canine, feline, or other—who inadvertently walks too close to the crate and is greeted with a fierce roar and crash when the dog lunges into the side of his kennel.

Management is your best approach to this behavior, followed by behavior modification.

Dogs who are aggressive in their crates shouldn't be subjected to environments in which the behavior is constantly triggered. These dogs should not, for example, be left crated and unattended at canine sporting events. If children are in the household, they must not be allowed to approach Spot in his crate.

Some dogs will crate calmly if the crate is covered to reduce the stimuli that triggers their aggression. Others do well as long as there's nothing of high-value to be guarded in the crate, such as a favorite toy or stuffed Kong.

If Spot is fearful, taking refuge in his crate out of fear, be sure to do nothing to intimidate him while he's crated. No reaching in, for example, to remove bowls, toys, or dog from the crate. To avoid setting him up for crate aggression, you may do better to refrain from crating a fearful dog until he's become more confident with you.

To modify crate aggression, return to your old friends, counter-conditioning and desensitization. If your dog is aggressive to passers-by, arm yourself with a large supply of high-value treats (canned chicken, rinsed and drained, works well), and sit next to the crate. When your dog alerts to a member of the trigger species (whether it is dog or human) passing at a noticeable but low-arousal distance, begin feeding him treats, non-stop, until that someone is gone. Each time the trigger appears, wait for your dog to notice, then start feeding him tiny tidbits of chicken, non-stop, until the trigger is gone.

Keep watching your dog's reaction. You're looking for his response to the appearance of the trigger to change from wary or alert to "Yay! Where's my chicken?" When you get the latter reaction consistently, move the trigger closer and repeat the lessons, until the trigger can pass next to the crate.

If *your* approach triggers an aggression response, do lots of practice sessions where you walk up to the crate and drop chicken into it, so your dog learns to associate your approach with good stuff. Never punish your dog for being aggressive in his crate—you're likely to make the behavior worse!

Crating Choices

Some dogs crate best in wire crates, others seem to prefer the plastic airline-style kennels. Portable, collapsible soft crates have become hugely popular. Some owners only crate through the puppy stage, others use crates throughout their dogs' entire lives. Both are acceptable.

Despite the potential for crating woes with some dogs, I remain a staunch fan of this invaluable management tool. We can educate owners about proper crate use to avoid overcrating and other abuses. The crate is so useful, it distresses me to hear that some well-meaning shelter folks have such a low opinion of it. Let's not throw the puppy out with the bath water!

Hyper Hounds

Identifying and (more importantly) dealing with overactive dogs

A disconcerting number of my clients preface the explanation of their dogs' undesirable behaviors with the pronouncement, "He is *really* hyper!!" The vast majority of the time, they have perfectly normal dogs. The explosion of apparently "hyper" dogs in our world can be traced to several factors:

- The popularity of breeds of dogs that are (when well-bred) genetically programmed to have enhanced environmental alertness, vigilance, and high activity levels. While high activity levels are distributed across all breeds (I am personally acquainted with a high-energy Basset Hound), they are especially prevalent in the sporting breeds (Labradors Retrievers, Golden Retrievers, etc.) and herding breeds (Border Collies, Australian Shepherds, etc.).

- The puppy-milling and retail sale of those popular breeds that result in poorly-bred, poorly-socialized pups ending up in the hands of owners under-prepared to care for and train them.

- Unreasonable expectations of dog behavior by owners who have a poor understanding of their dogs' needs and behaviors, which results in…

- Lack of adequate exercise and socialization.

Overdiagnosed

That said, hyperactivity *does* exist in dogs. It is, however, greatly overdiagnosed. Hyperactivity, otherwise known as "hyperkinesis," can be defined as dogs who display frenetic activity, abnormally short attention spans, and high impulsiveness. They can also demonstrate overbearing attention-seeking behavior. It is truly a canine form of **Attention Deficit Hyperactivity Disorder** (ADHD). Like some children who are prescribed Ritalin, it seems that dogs who are truly hyperkinetic can also benefit from the administration of stimulants to help them focus and pay attention.

What differentiates a normal, high-energy dog from one who has ADHD? Dogs with ADHD demonstrate exceptionally short attention spans and a high degree of impulsiveness that makes it impossible for them to focus on one task for long. They are easily distracted.

In contrast, most of the high-energy dogs that clients bring to me will focus very quickly on the click-and-treat game. They are normal, active dogs who haven't learned how to control their own behavior—but they can, if you show them how. In fact, owners are often amazed by the undivided attention their previously intractable canine companions will offer—as soon as we give the dogs a *reason* to focus; when we show them that focused attention makes good stuff happen. The truly hyperactive dog can't focus even if she *wants* to—everything she encounters, regardless of how trivial or irrelevant, is given equal and minimal, active but fleeting interest.

Paws is a highly active dog—you have to say that about a dog who romps on a trampoline all by himself! But he can demonstrate great powers of attention and concentration when properly motivated. He exhibits his best "manners" after really hard workouts.

Hyperactive dogs also tend to be especially sensitive to sudden environmental changes (SEC)—overreacting to the presence of a strange person or animal and apparently unable to adjust to the new stimulus. In addition, they seem to have little tolerance for boredom and an exaggerated need for novelty and variety. They don't do well with repetitive tasks (such as basic obedience drills), but may excel in situations requiring creative solutions, such as the Border Collie who often must think for himself and make his own decisions about how to move the sheep.

Hyperactive dogs also are likely to get into everything (bored, looking for creative opportunity), can be destructive, and are often emotionally unstable. They can become almost unmanageable if physically restrained, and may exhibit uncontrollable rage-like aggression if frustrated.

Causes and Effects

Like so many other behaviors, hyperactivity is believed to result from a mix of genes and environment—nature versus nurture. Certainly, the high-energy breeds previously mentioned are more *prone* to develop true hyperactive behaviors, but a dog's genes are just the canvas that his personality is painted on by life, training, and socialization experiences. Hyperactivity can be minimized or exacerbated from puppyhood on, depending on social and environmental factors.

Excitable dogs can often be identified early. They are frequently the puppies who continually bite at hands and fight any attempt to restrain or control them—not with just a mild struggle, but with violent resistance. An excitable puppy placed into a calm, structured environment, with an owner who provides adequate exercise, socialization, and training, has a good chance of growing up to be a well-behaved, albeit active, canine companion. In the wrong environment, this pup is a disaster.

Exposure to overly active and playful children can feed hyperactivity—just one of many reasons that interactions between children and dogs should be very closely supervised. Excitable children tend to do exactly the wrong things in response to an excitable puppy's inappropriate behaviors—hitting back, restraining, running, or screaming—all of which are guaranteed to escalate the pup's level of excitement. Even a pup with a moderate activity level can be induced into hyperactivity in the wrong environment.

As many trainers will testify, social isolation also makes a significant contribution to hyperactive behavior. We often encounter the conundrum of the owner who promises to bring Rex into the house as soon as Rex learns to be well behaved, but Rex can't learn to be well-behaved when he is experiencing the activity-increasing effects of social deprivation.

A 1961 study conducted by Waller and Fuller found that puppies raised in semi-isolation exhibited excessive social contact behavior when given limited access to other puppies. When kept with their litters, the number of social contacts reduced by 75 percent. One conclusion of this study is that dogs may possess a biological *need* for a certain minimum amount of daily social stimulation and activity, and if that need is not met, a dog compensates with excessive activity when placed in a social situation.

It is likely that the minimum amount of social stimulation needed varies from one dog to the next. When faced with a dog who has higher-than-anticipated social needs, some owners resort to routine isolation of the dog in order to deal with the unwanted behaviors. This results in inadequate attention, insufficient exercise, and excessive confinement, adding fuel to the fire and creating a vicious cycle. When the dog is released from his confinement his behavior is worse than ever, which results in more isolation, and further decline of behavior. Rex's chances of ever becoming a house dog grow dimmer and dimmer.

Some physiological conditions are believed to play a role in canine ADHD as well. In a study published in 1999 by Drs. Jean Dodds and Linda Aronson, in collaboration with Drs. Nicholas Dodman and Jean DeNapoli of Tufts University, 634 dogs were evaluated for thyroid dysfunction as it related to various behavior problems. Forty two of those dogs were determined to be hyperactive; thirty one percent of the hyperactive dogs (13) were diagnosed with thyroid dysfunction.

Of 95 dogs in the study whose behavioral responses to thyroid therapy were evaluated, 81 dogs (85.3 percent) showed at least a 25 percent improvement in their behavior. Thirty four of the dogs (35.6 percent) showed better than 75 percent improvement. Of 20 dogs treated with conventional methods and modification techniques over the same time period, only 11 (55 percent) improved by at least 25 percent.

Chronic lead poisoning is also a potential cause of hyperactivity in dogs. Two common sources are destructive chewing on linoleum, or surfaces painted with lead-based paints.

There is also evidence to suggest that inadequate nutrition, especially early in life, may permanently affect activity levels throughout the remainder of a dog's life. This means that the importance of proper nutrition during puppyhood cannot be overstated. Breeders must be sure that puppies in large litters or those born to mothers with insufficient milk receive adequate nutrition from other sources, and that the mother's dietary intake can meet the demands of a nursing litter. A diet high in protein, or containing elements to which a dog is allergic, may also contribute to hyperactive behavior.

Although the scientific jury is still out on the role that food additives and colorants play in hyperactive behavior, and, in fact, many studies have *not* found a direct correlation, a 1980 study did find a sharp decrease in hyperactive symptoms when dogs were put on a 28-day-additive free diet.

Conduct a 10 Minute ADHD Test

How can you tell if you have a "normal" high-energy dog or one with ADHD? The proof is in the Ritalin. Your veterinarian can administer a low dose of an appropriate amphetamine after measuring your dog's respiration, heart rate, and reaction to restraint. Most hyperkinetic dogs will show a marked decrease in excitement and activity level as well as a measurable drop in respiration and heart rate, and greater acceptance of restraint, some 30-120 minutes after the amphetamine is given. A normal-but-active dog will have the opposite response to those markers.

First, however, you might want to try an ADHD experiment at home. Make sure your high-energy dog hasn't eaten for at least four hours. Take him out for a good hard romp in a safely enclosed area to take the edge off—but don't run him into exhaustion. Then leash your dog, grab your clicker and a treat bag full of *very high value* treats, and take him to a place with minimal distractions (indoors) for some clicker-testing fun:

Step 1: Supercharge your clicker using a very high rate of reinforcement and tiny treats for one minute (30-60 treats per minute)—a smidgeon of chicken will do for each Click! Your dog doesn't have to do anything but focus on you—don't ask for sits, downs, stays, or any other good manners behaviors. If he tries to jump on you, just turn away, but keep clicking and treating. Be sure to deliver the treats at his nose level so he doesn't have to jump up to get them.

Step 2: After one minute, reduce the rate of reinforcement to 15-30 click/treats per minute, and start moving the treat over his head to lure a sit. If he does sit, briefly increase the rate of reinforcement for three to four clicks, then slow down again. Do this for two minutes.

Step 3: Continue at a reinforcement rate of 10-20 per minute, and when he sits, Click! but hold off delivering the treat for two seconds at first, *gradually* increasing the delay of treat delivery for up to four or five seconds. Do this step for two minutes.

Step 4: For two more minutes, Click! and treat on a variable/random schedule of reinforcement. That is, vary the number of seconds between clicks and treats—sometimes doing several click/treats rapidly in a row (remember to treat after *each* click) sometimes pausing for a second, or five, or two, or seven, between clicks. Try to keep it random—we humans are very good at falling into patterns!

Step 5: Now, stop clicking for 30 seconds.

Step 6: After 30 seconds, Click! *only* if he looks at you. If he keeps looking at you, keep clicking using the random reinforcement schedule for Step 4. If he looks away, stop clicking. If he looks back at you *or looks in your general direction,* Click! again. Do this for 2.5 minutes.

Step 7: Time's up—the test is over!

If your dog is willing to play this game with you for the entire 10 minutes with only occasional minor attention lapses, you probably have a normal high-energy dog. It's time to increase his exercise, socialization and training programs. (See "Working With The 'Normal' High-Energy Dog" pg. 161.)

If, however, you lost your dog's attention totally somewhere between Steps #2 and #4, there's a good chance you really do have a hyperkinetic dog. Time to call your vet to schedule that amphetamine test, and while you're there, have a full thyroid panel done as well as a blood test for lead poisoning. Remember that thyroid results within the clinically normal-but-low range can be a contributing factor to behavior problems. Your vet can contact Dr. Jean Dodds at www.hemopet.org to discuss the significance of your dog's thyroid test.

The ADHD Difference

What do you do if you conclude that your dog has ADHD? In some cases, these dogs exhibit behaviors that are so intrinsically driven by organic causes that behavior modification and positive training alone can't help. Fortunately, a high percentage of ADHD dogs can be helped with the judicious use of stimulants in combination with a behavior modification program. Hyperactive dogs tend to be very responsive to positive reinforcement shaping procedures in conjunction with brief time-out periods.

Think back to the results of your 10-minute ADHD test. At what step did you start to lose your dog? If he was with you through Step 2, and you lost him at 3, you know that he does well with a continuous schedule of reinforcement at a fairly high rate.

Go back to the step where he did well (Step 2), and work toward Step 3. Work even more gradually towards building the time between the "Click!" and the reward so you don't lose him with too big a leap.

Keep your expectations low. Shape most of his behaviors in very tiny increments with a high rate of reinforcement. Keep your training session brief (five minutes, maximum), with a short time-out to calm him before you start another brief session.

Sample Tasks for ADHD Dogs

With many dogs, lure-shaping a down is a simple matter, accomplished in short order by moving the treat toward the floor and clicking the dog for following into a down position. We often have success in just three or four clicks, as we hold the treat at the dog's nose and he focuses on it (Click! and treat), we move it halfway to the floor and he follows (Click! and treat), three-quarters of the way and his feet are sliding forward (Click! and treat) and he's down (Click! and treat).

In contrast, the hyperkinetic dog may need twenty or even a hundred clicks, over several sessions, before you reach your final behavior goal—down. Teaching "Down" to this dog might require the following:

- The dog is sitting. You hold a treat in front of dog's nose and he focuses on it. Click! and treat.

- He stays focused on the treat. Click! and treat.

- Lower the treat a half-inch. His nose follows. Click! and treat.

- He stays focused on the treat. Click! and treat.

- Lower the treat another half-inch. He follows. Click! and treat.

- Lower another half-inch. He follows. Click! and treat.

- He stays focused. Click! and treat.

- Release him from the sit, tell him he's a great dog—and both of you take a five minute brain break.
- Start with the sit again. As soon as he focuses on the treat, Click! and treat.
- Lower the treat an inch. His nose follows. Click! and treat.
- Lower the treat another inch. He follows. Click! and treat.
- He stays focused. Click! treat.
- Lower the treat another inch. Click! and treat.
- He stays focused. Click! and treat.
- Lower the treat another inch. Click! and treat.
- Take another brain break.

You get the idea: slow and steady. Anytime you increase the increment, say from 1 inch to 2 inches, and make sure he stays with you. If you lose him between 1 inch and two, go from 1 inch to 1.5 inches. Take frequent brain breaks, and don't make your total session more than about 15 minutes. If you lose his attention a lot, you are expecting too much. Use smaller increments, a higher rate of reinforcement (Click! him often just for staying with the game), and more breaks.

You never know; with patience, in the right positive environment, your "hyper" pal may turn out to be a great agility, herding, tracking or drug-sniffing dog!

Working With "Normal" High-Energy Dogs

Say you determine that you have a high-energy dog, rather than a hyperactive one. That may be good news, but you still need to deal with your out-of-control canine. Here are some tips to help you turn your Wild Willy into a Gentle Bill:

- **Increase the structure in his environment.** Teach him to "Say Please" (sit) to make good things happen. Have him sit for his dinner bowl. Have him sit for his leash to go for a walk. Have him sit to make the door to the back yard open. Have him sit to be petted, or get a cookie for coming back inside.

- **Increase his exercise.** Whatever he gets now, give him more, and make it *quality* exercise. Tossing him out in the back yard by himself is not quality exercise. Go out with him. Throw sticks, balls, play tug of war, get him to swim in the pond, take him to the dog park. And add structure to his exercise. Have him sit politely for you to throw the ball. Make sure he will "Give" you the tug toy when you ask him to. Have him sit before you open the gate into the park.

- **Increase his socialization time.** If you've been leaving him outside because he's too wild, grit your teeth and bring him in. Use leashes, tethers, crates, and baby gates as needed to preserve your sanity while inviting him into the family.

- **Increase his training time.** If you've already taken him to a basic training class, sign up for a Level 2. Or a tricks class, or agility—anything that will keep the two of you active and learning together. Keeping his brain occupied and busy is just as important as keeping his body working.

Touch Me, Touch Me Not

*This program will make your dog safer
to live with and easier to examine*

Canine massage therapists and human health officials often expound on the benefits of touching for dogs and people. I was graphically reminded of those benefits recently when our beloved 15 year old Dusty succumbed to an ulcerated cornea and eventual rupture of his left eye. This is an extremely painful condition, and given his failing ability to use his hind legs, refusal to eat, and signs of obvious depression, we sadly opted for euthanasia.

We spent our last afternoon together sitting in the sun, on the grass lawn of our new farm in Maryland. As I stroked Dusty's soft golden fur and massaged his limbs and frame, I could see the tension leave his small, frail body. His pain seemed to fade at my touching; he stretched out on the grass with a sigh, more relaxed than he had been since his eye ruptured three days earlier. I could feel my own tension lessen as well, as I savored what I knew were my last moments with this gallant little boy who had shown me that small dogs could be every bit as big in heart and mind as their larger brothers.

I'm grateful that our dogs enjoy being touched and that we can share the gifts that such healing contact offers. But not all dogs like—or even tolerate—being touched. Fortunately, a dog's negative association with touching can often be changed through the use of counter-conditioning and desensitization (CC&D).

Not all dogs are comfortable being touched, but most can be taught to enjoy and crave human contact. This is a useful life skill for all dogs, helping them get along in human society comfortably. It can be life-saving in a veterinary emergency.

Classical vs. Operant Conditioning

A negative reaction to being touched is usually a **classically conditioned response**. With classical conditioning, the environment acts on the dog. That is, the dog's brain contains a pre-programmed message that says, "Touch is BAD!"—and when the dog feels your touch he reacts, without stopping to think. The negative message could be a result of harsh handling and punishment, pain from a prior injury, or simply a lack of adequate handling and socialization when he was a pup.

This is very different from operant conditioning, where the dog acts on the environment. For example, if you say, "Sit!" the dog thinks, "Ah, I know what that means—if I put my bottom on the ground I might get a cookie!" and so he *chooses* to sit in order to make a good thing happen. When your dog reacts to your touch with distaste, perhaps even aggression, he's not *choosing* to react that way, it just happens, thanks to that pre-programmed message in his brain.

The most effective and successful way to change your dog's response to your touch is through counter-conditioning, which reprograms the message at a low level of stimulus that he can at least tolerate—perhaps briefly and softly touching his head. Then we use desensitization to help him accept the touching at gradually increasing levels of intensity—touching more of his body, or touching with more pressure, or for longer periods of time.

It's almost magical to watch an effective CC&D program in progress. Some behavior changes I've seen as a result of this kind of behavior modification have been nothing short of miraculous. One family's Chow mix and newly adopted Chow who wanted to tear each other to shreds became fast friends within three weeks when the owners implemented a CC&D program.

Reprogramming

Perhaps your dog will tolerate a light touch on the top of his head, and a gentle scratch under his chin, but he becomes very tense if you do more than that, and any efforts to touch his legs and feet or his hindquarters and tail elicit serious warnings about forthcoming aggression. You believe him, and wisely don't press the issue, but that means even simple but necessary procedures such as nail trimmings and baths will be stressful and potentially dangerous.

The first step in your program is to have a complete and thorough veterinary exam, and an adjunct visit to a chiropractor if indicated. Pain is a huge contributor to aggression—if he's hurting, all the CC&D in the world won't change his opinion of being touched—*it hurts!*

Of course, if the whole point is that your dog doesn't tolerate being touched, how do make him submit to a vet exam before you work on the problem?

Unfortunately, it's a necessary evil, so spend a week (or a few weeks) acclimating your dog to a comfortable cloth muzzle. Lend muzzle-wearing a very positive association by pairing its presence and application with *wonderful* treats. Then muzzle him before the vet or vet tech begins to examine him, in order to keep everyone safe.

Ask your vet whether using a sedative would help make the experience less traumatic. You might also consider products such as herbal calming agents, Rescue Remedy™, and DAP (Dog Appeasing Pheremones, sold as Comfort Zone™).

With a clean bill of health, you're ready to begin. You'll need a large supply of absolutely scrumptious treats—canned chicken, rinsed and drained, is my favorite for CC&D purposes; most dogs totally love it. Pick a comfortable spot on a bed that your dog loves, or lay down a cushion or a soft thick blanket for the two of you to sit on. Attach a leash to your dog's collar so you don't have to grab to keep him with you.

The sequence of the next part is very important. You will touch your dog's head *first*, very briefly—say for one second—then feed him a tiny bit of chicken. The touch must come first because you want him to understand that *the touch makes the chicken happen*. If you feed chicken first, then touch, he won't make that connection.

A "Where's My Chicken?" expression tells you that your dog has made the link between a stimulus and an enjoyable reward. Make sure you elicit this response several times before increasing the duration or intensity of the stimulus.

Keep repeating this step until your touch causes him to look at you with a smiling face as if he's saying, "Alright—you touched me. Yay! Where's My Chicken?" You want the "Where's My Chicken?" (WMC) response to happen reliably several times in a row before you proceed to the next step.

Good job! You've accomplished the first tiny step on a long road; he thinks being touched softly and briefly on the head is a wonderful thing. Now you must decide whether to stop the session—ending on a high note—or continue on because you both are having a wonderful time and don't want the session to end. If you're unsure how much longer he will work with you, it's better to stop sooner, while you're ahead, than to push it too far and suffer a setback.

If you proceed, the next step might be to touch him on the head, still very gently, but for two seconds. You may lose the WMC response at first as he adjusts to the increased time, but it will probably return quickly. Continue to increase the time, very gradually, so you don't lose the progress you've made. As your touches get longer, feed him several treats in rapid succession *while* you are touching. Remember to stop the treats when the touch stops.

Be sure to end the session before one or both of you gets bored, tired, stressed, or frustrated. You can always do another session later that day or the next. If you sense that he's getting restless, stop the session, feed him a few extra tidbits for being a wonderful boy, and release him with an "All done!" cue. Next time, stop a little sooner—you don't even want him to *think* about getting restless.

Taking the Next Step

When you begin again with your next session, back up a little at first. If you ended with five second gentle touches on your dog's head, start with three second touches. You'll be able to progress more quickly back up to five seconds, but be sure to start well within his comfort level and then work back to where you ended.

When he has a positive association with gentle touching up to perhaps ten seconds, you can increase the intensity of a different stimulus—the amount of pressure. Each time you raise the bar for a new stimulus, lower it for the others—in this case you might go back to two or three seconds, with a slightly stronger pressure when you touch. Work to get that positive WMC response with the new amount of pressure at each length of time before you increase the time again.

When he's responding happily to a moderate amount of touch pressure at 10-15 seconds, you can increase the intensity of the third stimulus in the touch package—the position of your hand. Up until now you've been touching him in his most accepting spot—the top of his head. Now you're going to begin to move your hand to more sensitive places—again reducing the intensity of the other two stimuli—time and pressure.

Perhaps you'll try ears first. Returning to a very gentle touch, stroke one ear for one to two seconds, then feed some chicken. Repeat this until you're getting his WMC response to the ear-stroking, then do the same with the other ear. Gradually increase the length of time you stroke each ear gently, and when you're getting positive responses to ten second ear stroking, it's time to increase the pressure. Shorten your ear strokes back to one to three seconds, but stroke the ear a bit more firmly.

Remember to be very generous with your chicken bits, feeding a morsel or two every time you stroke the ear, and several morsels as the touches get longer. When he's happy to have you stroke both ears firmly for 10-15 seconds or longer, you can move to a new spot on his body.

Don't forget to reduce the other stimuli each time you move to a new touching place. After the ears, you might run your hand down the back of his neck, gently and briefly. Treat! You should find that as you work toward various new spots around your dog's legs and body, he'll accept new touches more quickly in many places. Adjust your pace to his behavior. If he's giving you WMC responses very quickly, you can progress more rapidly in your program. If he seems slower to respond, you're probably working on or near a very sensitive place, and you need to slow the program down. He'll tell you how slowly or quickly you can progress. Listen to him. Attempts to force him to accept your touching will backfire, big time.

Sensitive Places

Many dogs, even those who are comfortable being touched elsewhere, are tense about having their feet handled. Take extra care as you begin to move down his legs. A few extra days—or weeks—now will pay you jackpots in the long run, when you can finally clip his nails without a violent struggle. Spend lots of time massaging the areas where your dog has come to enjoy being touched, and occasionally work on the more sensitive spots. In addition to the chicken, soothing massage sends a very positive association to the message that you are reprogramming in his brain.

It's critically important to avoid triggering the negative associations outside your CC&D sessions. If you forget about his sensitivities and grab him during a "real-life" moment you may set your program back. It won't hurt to skip one or two nail-trimming sessions while you work to get him to accept foot-handling without a fight.

Make sure that others are aware of the importance of respecting your CC&D program too. There's nothing like having a friend or family member think it's funny to see your dog's negative reaction when they play "grab your paws"—thereby undoing all the good work you've done. Grrrr! I've been known to banish human acquaintances from my household for less!

Do NOT punish or yell at your dog if you push too far and elicit a bad reaction. Keep giving him the treats whether he's being "good" or not; this is conditioning, not training. Proceed more slowly, though, to elicit more positive responses.

In His Own Time

How quickly you complete your CC&D program depends on several factors:

- Your dog's age and how long he has been displaying a negative response to being touched.

- The intensity of his negative association with touch.

- The cause of his sensitivity. Prior harsh handling is likely to be more difficult to overcome than lack of handling, since he has a negative association with the human presence as well as the sensitivity to touch itself.

- Status of physical contributors to the sensitivity. If your dog has a grass allergy that causes inflammation in his pads, for example, your constant struggle to reduce the discomfort in his feet will slow your CC&D progress.

- Your commitment to implementing the program on a daily basis. Several short sessions a day are generally more effective than one long daily session.

- Your skill at reading your dog's comfort level and moving the program forward at an appropriate pace without triggering negative reactions.

Success!

The success rate for touch CC&D programs is high. Unlike modification programs for things like dog reactivity, where it's difficult to control all the variables, you can manage the factors of a touch modification program with relative ease. Chances are good that even if you don't achieve 100 percent positive association with touching every part of your dog's body, you can accomplish a positive response for much of it, with agreeable acceptance for the highly sensitive parts.

Just ask our three-year-old Scottish Terrier. When we found him as a stray in Chattanooga as a six-month-old pup, his feet were raw and bloody, he had sores and scabs all over his body from a generalized dermatitis, and his ears were badly infected, all from a severe grass allergy—not uncommon to Scotties. He could barely tolerate being brushed, treating those infected ears was a real challenge, and touching his sore paws was out of the question.

Today, although he's still a little sensitive about his paws, he adores being touched elsewhere—there's nothing he loves more than lying on my lap, stretched out flat on his back for tummy rubs, and having the rest of his body brushed and massaged. We're still working on feet—it was 18 months before I could clip all his nails in one sitting—and his first instinct is to pull away when I touch them—but then he relaxes and enjoys a little foot massage as well.

And for me—there's nothing like a Scotty body in my lap to help ease the tensions of a busy day, and soften the grief of losing a beloved companion.

When a Voice is a Vice

How to prevent (or at least manage) your dog's nuisance barking

Quiet reigns in my house—for the moment, anyway. I look at young Lucy sleeping on her bed on the floor next to my desk and appreciate the rare moment of tranquility.

Like so many herding dogs, the year old Cardigan Welsh Corgi lying at my feet is vocal. She barks when she's excited. She barks when she's playing. She barks when she wants something. She barks to alert us to visitors. She barks out of frustration. She barks when she hears a dog bark on TV. Not just any bark, mind you, but a shrill, high-pitched bark that grates on your nerves.

When we were in the final stages of completing her adoption from the local Humane Society, the animal care supervisor approached me with an expression of concern on her face. "That little dog you're adopting . . . she's, um, pretty vocal," she warned.

I shrugged. Dogs bark. What's the big deal? I could train her to be quiet, I thought to myself confidently. Little did I know what a challenge it would be in this case.

Dogs do bark—some more than others. Like Lucy, they bark for a wide variety of reasons. Fortunately, like Lucy, most dogs can learn to control their barking—at least enough that we can live with them in relative peace and harmony. Some, however, are easier to teach than others.

Cross an active breed with a long, solitary day in the yard, and you will probably end up with a problem barker.

Why Bark?

While dogs are primarily body language communicators, they also use their voices to share information with other members of their social group. Compared to their wild brethren, however, our domesticated dogs use their voices far more—a tendency we have genetically encouraged. We've created herding breeds, including Shelties, Border Collies, Welsh Corgis, and others, who use their voices when necessary to control their flocks. We've bred scent hounds to give voice when they are on the trail of prey.

We've also created a lot of breeds whose predilection for barking is a side effect of their main purpose. For example, we created many terrier breeds for hunting small rodents. These dogs are often notoriously barky, perhaps from generations of excited pursuit of their prey. Likewise, many of the toy breeds are known to be "yappy," serving double duty as door alarms as well as lap warmers.

For what it's worth, we've also produced breeds that have a reputation for quiet. Many of the guarding breeds tend not to announce their presence, but instead carry out their duties with a quiet intensity. Chows, Akitas, and Mastiffs are more likely to escort you off the property with a low growl or a short warning bark rather than a canine chorus. And of course, Basenjis don't bark at all; they scream when they are displeased.

Hush Their Mouths

We'd probably all be pleased if our dogs limited their barking to those situations for which they were bred to give voice, but of course they don't. Those who have inherited a propensity for using their voices freely in one situation are highly likely to use them freely in others as well. And so, we end up with "nuisance" and "problem" barking.

Problem barking comes in a variety of flavors, each with its own unique triggers and solutions. Your dog might bark in several different situations, requiring a multi-pronged behavior modification program. Outlined below are the most common triggers and solutions.

Whatever the cause of your dog's barking, don't make the mistake of yelling "Quiet!" (or worse) at your dog. This is likely to increase his excitement and arousal, adding to the chaos rather than achieving the desired effect of peace in the kingdom. Even if you *do* succeed in intimidating him into silence, you risk damaging your relationship with him, as he learns to be quiet through fear.

Instead, use your human brain to figure out how to manage and modify your dog's penchant for pandemonium. Fortunately, with a commitment of time, effort, training, and management, most barking can be controlled. Start out by identifying the type of barking your dog practices most frequently and applying the appropriate solution.

Boredom Barking

The largest category of nuisance barking is caused by boredom. Boredom barkers are the dogs who are left out in their yards all day, and sometimes all night, with nothing to do but patrol their territory and announce the presence of anything and everything. Sometimes it seems they bark just to hear themselves bark; perhaps they do.

Boredom barking often has a monotonous tone, and can go on for hours. The greatest numbers of barking complaints received by animal agencies are generated by boredom barkers.

The Fix: Fortunately, there's an easy fix for outdoor boredom barking. Most of these dogs, if left *inside,* are happily quiet in their human's den. The complicating factor is the length of time a dog can be safely left alone in the house. Crates and exercise pens are good management solutions for dogs who haven't yet learned good house manners, and dogwalkers can be enlisted to provide mid-day potty breaks if owners work long hours. (Dogwalkers need not be professionals; you can often enlist the help of a friend, family member, or a neighbor.)

Boredom barking can also be reduced by enriching your dog's life, by increasing his physical exercise and mind-engaging activities. A good, tongue-dragging, off-leash run or fetch and some interactive games and toys such as stuffed Kongs™, Iqubes™, and Egg Baby Turtles™, *daily,* can minimize the tedium of a lonely dog's day.

Play Barking

These are the dogs who can't handle too much fun. They are the canine equivalent of cheerleaders, running around the edges of the game giving voice to their arousal while others play. Herding dogs are often members of this group. Bred to keep livestock under tight control, they often experience an inherited compulsion to control anyone or anything that moves.

The Fix: This is such a hardwired behavior that it's difficult to modify. You do have several options:

- **Accept and allow the behavior.** Determine a time and place where the barking is least objectionable, and let the dog do it.

- **Manage the behavior.** Remove the barker from the playing field when others want to engage in rough-and-tumble or chase-me games.

- **Use negative punishment,** a gentle, nonviolent form of punishment that can be effective *if applied consistently.* Negative punishment is the behavioral term for any situation in which the dog's behavior makes a good thing go away. If your dog is playing (an activity he enjoys) and starts barking (the thing you don't want), you remove his opportunity to play. Use a cheerful "Oops, time out!" and remove him from the game for a brief (perhaps one to five minutes) session in the penalty box (say, another room).

- **Teach a positive interrupt,** and use it when he barks to invite him to come to you and briefly stop the barking, then release him to go play again.

- **Encourage him to carry his favorite toy in his mouth** during play. As I discovered with Lucy, a mouth full of a highly valued toy makes it difficult to bark. If she does, at least the sound is muffled. *Caution: This is not a good option to select if your barking dog also "resource guards" his toys from other dogs.*

Demand Barking

This is less annoying to neighbors, but it can be very irritating to you. Your dog is saying, "Bow wow! GIVE it to me NOW!" Demand barking may be encountered in the early stages of positive training, as your dog tries to figure out how to make treats, play, and attention happen. It often starts as a low grumble or soft "whuff," and if not nipped in the bud can turn into a full-scale, insistent, persistent bark.

The Fix: It's easy to derail demand barking when it *first* starts by ignoring the dog. When your dog barks for treats, attention, or to get you to throw his ball, simply utter an "Oops" to mark the unwelcome behavior, turn your back on him until he is quiet, then say "Yes!" and return your attention to him. His goal is to get you to give him good stuff. Your goal is to teach him that barking makes good stuff go away.

At first, you'll need to say "Yes!" after just a few seconds of quiet, but fairly quickly extend the period of quiet so he doesn't learn a behavior chain of "Bark, be quiet for a second, get attention." At the same time, you'll need to reinforce quiet when he *doesn't* bark first, again, to prevent the behavior chain.

It's more challenging to extinguish demand barking when your dog has had lots of reinforcement for it. Remember, any attention you give him reinforces demand barking. Eye contact, physical contact, verbal admonishment—all of these give him what he wants: attention!

The process for modifying the behavior of a veteran demand barker is the same: remove all reinforcement. However, be prepared for an extinction burst—the period when the behavior gets worse rather than better. The behavior *used* to work, so the dog thinks if he just tries harder, surely it will work again. If you give in during an extinction burst, you reinforce the more intense barking behavior, and guess what happens next time? Right—your dog will offer the more intense behavior sooner, and it gets even *harder* to extinguish the barking. Oops!

Alarm Barking

This is Lassie's "Timmy's in the well!" bark. It means something is seriously wrong—or at least your dog thinks so. The alarm bark usually has a tone of urgency or ferocity that's absent in most other barks. Because your dog's judgment as to what constitutes a serious threat may differ from yours, after many false alarms you may fall into the trap of asking him to stop barking without investigating the cause. Don't! This may be the time a fire is smoldering in the kitchen.

The Fix: Always investigate. It could just be the UPS driver leaving a package on the porch, but it might be something serious. Sometimes Timmy really is in the well! Investigate, use a positive interrupt to stop the barking, and then reinforce the quiet. I also like to thank my dogs for letting me know something important is happening.

Greeting Barking

Dealing with inappropriate greeting behavior could be a whole chapter in its own right.

Your dog may be giving an alarm: "Danger! Intruder at the door!" Or he may be barking in excitement: "Huzzah! Dad's home!" or "Hooray! Company's here!" His tone—ferocious versus excited—will tell you the difference.

The Fix: If you have guests arriving, the management/modification program is complicated by the fact that you have to answer the door! Ideally, a second person answers the door while you use the positive interrupt to halt the barking. If there is no second person available, use the interrupt, secure your dog in another room or tether him, then go greet your guests. You may want to put a note on your door asking guests to be patient if it takes you a minute or two to come to the door!

You can also help minimize greeting barking by remaining calm when the doorbell rings, because otherwise, your dog may get excited and bark at *your* excitement. In families with children, you may have to spend some time training the *kids* not to rush excitedly to the door, too!

Often, people unwittingly train their dogs to bark when they come home, by greeting the dog in a boisterous manner. It's human nature to enjoy it when another being seems glad to see us! But it's one thing to be greeted by a wagging, wiggling dog, and another to be greeted by a cacaphony of loud, maniacal barking. And with some dogs, one often leads to the other.

If your dog is barking as you approach your door, wait outside until he is quiet for at least a few seconds. Then enter the house, remaining very calm and quiet yourself. If your dog starts barking as you enter, ignore him until he is quiet, and then greet him calmly. After you have been home a little while and he is calm, you can initiate a play or affection session.

Frustration Barking

Frustration barking can be identified by its tone of shrill insistence. When Lucy first joined our family and we used tethers to manage her cat-chasing, for a time she became a master at frustration barking. She still gives shrill voice to her frustration when we confine our dogs to the tack room while we move horses in and out of the barn, but she settles quickly, having learned that it doesn't get her released any sooner.

The Fix: Frustration barking is a close relative of demand barking, but is more likely to occur when you are a distance from the dog, or when it is directed at something other than you. You handle it the same way. Ignore the behavior you don't want (the barking) and reward the behavior you do want (quiet). A reward marker such as the Click! of a clicker, or a verbal "Yes!" is very useful to mark the quiet, since you are often at a distance from the dog when the barking and the moment of quiet happen.

As with demand barking, the more your dog has been rewarded for frustration barking in the past, the more committed and consistent you'll need to be to make it go away, and the more likely you'll have to work through a significant extinction burst. Frustration barking is also more likely to escalate to reactivity and/or aggression, so it's wise to modify it sooner, rather than later.

Anxiety Barking

Hysterical vocalization is just one of several manifestations of separation anxiety (SA), often accompanied by destructive behavior, extraordinary efforts to escape confinement, and/or inappropriate urination and defecation. Separation anxiety is a complex behavior—a full-blown panic attack. To modify SA barking, howling, or screaming, you must modify the entire anxiety complex.

The Fix: While it *can* be modified through a program of counter-conditioning and desensitization, SA barking usually requires the intervention of a professional trainer/behavior consultant, sometimes with the assistance of behavior modification drugs. If your dog's barking is related to anxiety, we suggest you contact a good, positive trainer/behaviorist to help you with the complex and difficult anxiety behavior.

Not All Barking is Bad

A dog's voice can be a useful thing, especially the bark that lets us know a dog needs to go outside, or is ready to come back in. Some service dogs are trained to bark to alert their owners. Dogs warn us of intruders and tell us of pending emergencies. I can think of numerous times when the Miller dogs' barking served a valuable purpose. There was the time they let me know that our horses had escaped and were trooping down our driveway toward the road. I smile whenever I remember Dusty, standing his ground, ferociously barking, preventing our 1,000-pound Thoroughbred mare from walking through a gate accidentally left open. When Lucy's shrill voice causes me to grit my teeth, I remind myself that there will be times when she, too, will use that same voice to tell me something important, and I'll be glad she has a voice to use.

They Need to Gnaw

But you can direct the behavior to appropriate chew toys

My office floor, ankle-deep in fluffy white stuff, looks like it's been struck by a blizzard. Lucy lies contentedly on her rug under my desk, pulling more cotton batting from her stuffed dog. As I sigh and kneel down to clean up the mess, I realize it's simply one of the joys of owning a young dog.

Dogs chew. They *need* to chew. Puppies chew to explore their world as well as to relieve the pain of teething. Adult dogs chew to exercise their jaws, massage their gums, clean their teeth, and to relieve stress and boredom. It's as basic a behavior to them as a human baby sucking on a pacifier. Humans, as they grow, transition to sucking on lollipops, straws, sports bottles, and perhaps cigarettes. Dogs, like us, can learn to transition to appropriate objects for mature oral satisfaction, but they never completely outgrow the need to gnaw.

I doubt there's a pet puppy in the universe who hasn't managed to destroy at least one of his owner's valuable possessions with those wickedly sharp baby teeth, despite scrupulous supervision and management. Just because they have a penchant for chewing anything they can find, however, doesn't mean we should let them.

Building Good Chew Habits

Puppies come to develop substrate preferences for elimination in the early months of their lives, and they similarly develop chew-object preferences. Hence the inadvisability of giving him old shoes or socks as chew toys! If you give your pup the run of the house and he learns to chew on Oriental carpets, sofa cushions, and coffee table legs, you will likely end up with a dog who chooses to exercise his jaws and teeth on inappropriate objects for years to come. You'll find yourself crating him frequently, or worse, exiling him to a life of loneliness in the back yard, where he can only chew on lawn furniture, loose fence boards, and the edges of your deck and hot tub.

If, instead, you focus your dog's fangs on approved chew toys at an early age and manage him well to prevent access to your stuff, he'll earn house privileges much sooner in life. By the end of his first year, you'll probably be able to leave him alone safely while you go out to dinner, shopping—even while you're away at work.

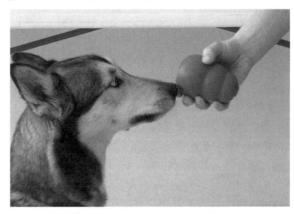

Your dog can be taught to give up inappropriate chew objects if you reward him for chewing only objects of your choosing, a stuffed Kong™, for example.

As long as your dog still snags the occasional shoe, knick-knack or other off-limits items for a gnaw, it's too soon to give him unsupervised freedom. When you're home, he needs to be under your direct supervision. Keep him on a leash or a tether, or simply close the door of the room you're in so he can't wander into the parlor and shred your grandmother's antique lace doily while your back is turned. If you're otherwise too occupied to supervise, put him in his crate or exercise pen to keep him out of trouble.

Be aware that some destructive chewing and other related inappropriate behaviors are a result of separation anxiety rather than "normal" chewing. Such chewing is often—but not exclusively—directed toward door and window frames, and occurs only outside of the owner's presence, by a dog who shows signs of stress at the signs of his owner's pending departure. Separation anxiety dogs often don't crate well either, which makes managing the destructive behavior even more challenging. If you think your dog's chewing is related to separation anxiety, you'll need to work with a qualified, positive dog training professional to modify the behaviors.

One of the keys to solving unwanted chewing is to supply the dog with "legal" chew objects to keep his needle-sharp puppy teeth appropriately occupied. Stuffed Kongs™, Goodie Ships™, Buster Cubes™ and Roll-A-Treat Balls™ are some of the many interactive toys available that can keep your dog's teeth and mind suitably busy. If you consistently supply him with desirable and acceptable objects upon which to chew, he'll eventually develop a strong preference for chewing on those objects. He'll seek them out when he feels the need to gnaw, and ultimately your personal possessions will be safe, even when your back is turned.

Because different dogs chew with different levels of intensity, it's impossible to make definitive statements about which types of chew products are appropriate for your particular dog. The safety of chew objects such as rawhide, various bones, pig ears and cow hooves is a hotly debated topic. Rope tugs are wonderful chew toys for some dogs, but others chew off and ingest the strings and risk serious gastrointestinal complications, even death. Check with your own veterinarian and follow his/her recommendations regarding the use of these and other chew items for your dog. Regularly check the condition of any chew toys you do give your dog, and discard them when they begin to show signs of wear and tear.

One of the basic tenets of positive training is that it's much easier to teach the dog what *to* do rather than what *not* to do. If you program your dog's chew preferences early in life by consistently directing his attention—and teeth—to appropriate objects and preventing his access to inappropriate ones, you won't have to constantly tell him he's chewing on the wrong things.

Interactive toys can help too. A stuffed Kong suspended just out of reach can help your dog work off excess energy as he jumps and grabs at the tempting prize. Instead of giving him his bowl of food in the morning, fill the Buster Cube or Roll-A-Treat Ball with his kibble and make him work for his meal by pushing the ball or cube around to make the food fall out. He won't have the time, energy or desire to shred your grandmother's antique afghan if he's out "hunting" for his breakfast!

The Trading Post

You can reduce the risk of damage to occasional ill-gotten items by teaching your pup to exchange toys for treats, using something he loves that he's allowed to have, such as a favorite chew toy, or a stuffed Kong. The goal of this trading game is that your dog learns that if he gives something up, he gets something *better* in return *and* he gets the original thing back as well. Two rewards for the price of one! Then, when he has a forbidden object, he's more likely to bring it to you to trade than to drag his prize to his cave under the dining room table for a leisurely gnaw. The rare occasion that he doesn't get "the thing" back, won't be enough to overcome the programming you've done by playing the "Trade" game with him frequently.

In order for this to work, you have to stop playing his game of "Chase the Puppy" when he grabs the sofa cushion or some other forbidden object. This is often an attention-getting behavior; he's learned that grabbing "your" toys and dashing off with them initiates a rousing play session.

Here's what you do:

Step 1: Offer him his well-stuffed Kong and say, "Take it!" Have him on a leash if you think he'll run off with it.

Step 2: Give him a little while to get fully engaged in chewing, and then say "Give!" or "Trade!" in a *cheerful* tone of voice and offer him a handful of irresistible treats, such as small bits of chicken or low fat cheese.

Step 3: Hold the treats under his nose and let him sniff. It may take him several seconds to think about it, but eventually he should drop his Kong and start eating the treats. Don't let him eat them in one gulp! Protect the tidbits in your hand a little so he can only nibble them one-by-one.

Step 4: When he drops the Kong, say, "Yes!"

Step 5: *While he is still nibbling*, reach down with your *other* hand and pick up the chew toy.

Step 6: Let him nibble a bit longer, then offer him the Kong again.

Step 7: Repeat the exercise several times, then end the game by giving him back his Kong and letting him chew to his heart's content.

Step 8: Play this game at every opportunity, whenever he's engaged in chewing on his toys on his own, or whenever you feel like initiating the game, until he'll give up his chew object easily, on your "Give" cue.

Troubleshooting

The game doesn't always go as smoothly as you might like. Here are some of the challenges you may face:

- Your dog may not be willing to drop his toy in exchange for the treats in your hand. Try dropping the treats on the floor in a little Hansel-and-Gretel-trail. Lots of dogs are more willing to give up their valued possession if the treats are within easy reach on the floor. Then, while he is following the trail to your hand that's still holding a reservoir of treats, pick up the Kong with your *other* hand.

- Your dog may lose interest in his toy after he realizes you have yummy treats in your hand. Try using less valuable treats, or a more valuable chew toy. Or simply play the game when he happens to be chewing on one of his toys.

- Your dog may be a resource guarder. If he growls, snaps, or even stiffens and looks angry when you try to trade with him, you should seek the help of a qualified and positive training professional to help you resolve the resource guarding challenge. Meanwhile, supervise him very closely to prevent his access to forbidden objects so you don't put yourself at risk for being bitten because you *have* to take something away from him.

Give the dog the Kong.

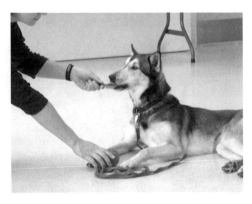

Offer treats, and when he takes them, pick up the Kong.

Give him back the Kong and repeat the exercise.

Leave It

You can also teach your dog to respond to your cue to leave a treasured possession alone *before* he sinks his sabers gum-deep into it. To teach "Leave it," have your dog on leash in front of you. Show him a tasty treat, tell him "Leave it!" and let him see you place it under your shoe. Freeze-dried liver cubes work well for this; they are high-value for the dog, but firm enough that they aren't easily squashed under your foot.

Your dog is probably going to dig, claw, and even chew at your foot to try to get the treat. Let him. This is an exercise in patience for you as well as an exercise in "Leave it!" for Fido. *Be sure to wear durable shoes for this exercise.* Sandals may leave you with bloody toes, and patent leather will be permanently scratched.

Your dog may give up easily when he realizes he can't get the treat, or he may be very persistent. Either way, just wait for him to give up. The instant he looks away from your foot, Click! your clicker (or say "Yes!") and feed him a very tasty treat. If he continues to look away from your foot, keep clicking and treating at a high rate of reinforcement—lots of clicks and treats. If he returns his attentions to the treat under your foot, just wait for him to look away again. Do *not* repeat the cue. When he looks away again, Click! and treat—again, at a high rate of reinforcement.

When he can control his urge to maul your foot for at least five seconds, carefully move your foot off the liver cube. If he tries to grab the treat, simply cover it back up with your foot. You don't need to repeat the "Leave it" cue. In a surprisingly short time, he'll ignore the treat on the floor. Now pick it up, show it to him again, repeat the "Leave it!" cue and try it under your foot again, still with a high rate of reinforcement when he ignores it. Remember to keep your cue cheerful—you're not trying to intimidate him away from the forbidden object; you're just giving him information.

When he's reliably ignoring the treat, you can move a few inches away from it. Don't get too confident! The farther you move from the treat, the more likely he is to think its okay for him to have it. Take it slow—set him up to succeed, and in time you'll be able to tell him "Leave it" and leave the object unattended.

You can translate this exercise to real life as soon as your dog understands to look away from the object when he hears the "Leave it!" cue. Set some tempting items on the floor, put him on leash, and walk him past, with the objects just out of reach. The instant he looks at an object, say, "Leave it!" in a cheerful tone, and stand still. He may stare at and strain toward the object. Just wait. When he gives up and looks away from the forbidden object, Click! and treat. Then continue toward the next object.

When he'll do this reliably without the leash tightening at all, you're ready to try it off-leash. As you supervise your pup's antics, if you see him coveting an inappropriate object, say, "Leave it!" in that cheerful tone, and be ready to Click! and treat when he turns back toward you.

Once you've taught your dog the "Trade" and "Leave it!" games, the rest is up to you. Of course, you'll continue to supervise him closely to minimize his access to forbidden objects and redirect his attention when you see him coveting an inappropriate one. If, however, he does happen to find something he's not supposed to have, odds are he'll bring it to you to exchange for something better. Next time you see your dog with Aunt Ida's antique lace doily in his mouth, instead of going into "Omidog the puppy has the doily!" panic mode, walk to the refrigerator, take out a bag of his favorite treats, and calmly initiate the Trade Game. You'll be surprised by how easy it is.

Finally, a well-run positive training class can assist in resolving behavior problems, chewing and otherwise, by helping you and your dog learn to communicate more clearly with each other. The better you understand how his mind works, and the better he understands what you expect of him, the stronger the relationship between the two of you. In the end, it's the strength of this relationship that will carry you through the challenges of dog care-taking and allow you to experience the joys and rewards of sharing your life with a canine companion.

Can You Dig It?

A natural behavior need not render your lawn a moonscape

With four dogs who spend a fair amount of time playing in the back yard, we have no expectations of an immaculately manicured lawn. Still, I was a bit taken aback one summer afternoon when I walked out to the yard to find a patch of previously respectable grass converted into a six-foot diameter bare-dirt, hole-pocked moonscape.

Dubhy's dirt-encrusted whiskers and paws betrayed him as the culprit. A closer inspection of the devastated area told the story: small rodent trails riddled the ground around the remnants of an old tree stump. A family of moles had moved in, and Dubhy was just doing what he was genetically programmed to do—seek and destroy small critters. Along the way, he destroyed a portion of our lawn.

It's the human's role in the dog-owner relationship to teach the dog how to behave appropriately in a world run by Homo sapiens. Far too often, owners seem to assume that dogs come already programmed with good manners. Then they become frustrated and angry when their dog engages in behavior that seems perfectly acceptable to him. If we're ever to make headway in reducing the seemingly endless numbers of dogs who end up looking for new homes in shelter kennels, it's critically important that canine caretakers gain a realistic perspective on what it means to be a dog.

Make the Effort

Dogs dig. They bark. They chew. They roll in smelly stuff and chase things that move. They eat garbage, and they poop and pee. Most owners understand that dogs *must* eliminate, and rather than trying to prevent them from doing it at all, they wisely redirect the behavior so that urine and feces are generally deposited in an acceptable location. Dog owners need to understand that dogs also must satisfy their needs to perform other natural dog behaviors. It's possible to teach your dog to restrict his digging to acceptable locations and objects, just as it's possible to housetrain him. You simply need to make the commitment to make the effort.

It is *always* easier to prevent an undesirable habit from developing than it is to change it once it is established. Good management is the key. If you don't want your dog to turn your back yard into a moonscape, don't give him unlimited access to the yard when you're not there to redirect his digging behavior.

Irresistible Motivator

Gophers and moles may be an irresistible motivator for digging, and a strong reinforcer if your dog ever actually catches one. If you don't want him to rototill the zucchini in your absence, fence off the garden so he doesn't have access to it. Soft garden soil is infinitely tempting to a dog who has an inclination toward excavation.

You accomplish prevention through management, with the judicious use of crates, baby gates, exercise pens, kennels, dog walkers, leashes, direct supervision, and if necessary, doggie daycare. If your dog spends the first six to twelve months of his life learning that digging without restriction is a fun, satisfying and rewarding behavior, you'll struggle with resolving or managing that behavior for a good long time. If on the other hand your dog spends the first year of his life learning to dig when and where it's appropriate, before long you'll be able to trust him home alone without worrying that he's re-landscaping the yard.

When faced with a digging challenge, your best route to success is understanding *why* your dog digs, and creating a combined management and training solution to the problem. Dogs are compelled to dig for a variety of reasons, including:

- Pursuing critters
- Attempting to escape
- Burying/retrieving valuable objects
- Making a den
- Creating a cool spot
- Having fun

In each case, you can take steps to reduce or eliminate the dog's *motivation* for digging, and use a combination of management and training to modify or extinguish the digging behavior.

Critter Digging

When a dog is pre-programmed to pursue rodents, as most of the Terriers are, your best solution is effective critter removal. In our back yard, a few days of Dubhy torment convinced the mole family to pack up and leave for parts unknown. We never found evidence that our Scottie actually caught one, and he hasn't dug a hole since. If your dog *does* capture and eat rodents, he's likely to acquire tapeworms—which can be treated with a de-wormer from your veterinarian.

You may choose to escort your rodent pests out of your yard more proactively than leaving it up to your digging dog. If so, manage your dog's behavior in the meantime by restricting his unsupervised access to the critter-affected area while you implement other rodent-control measures, such as flooding the little guys out with a hose down one of their holes so they run out their other holes.

Be cautious about using a commercial pest-control service. Many pest-control products are toxic to dogs as well as rodents.

Small burrowing animals are one of the motivations for your dog to dig. Evict the groundhog and remove the motivation.

If you decide to live-and-let-live, leaving the critters to flourish in your yard, you can still prevent digging by preventing your dog from inhabiting the same area as the rodents. Be aware that your dog's territory may continue to shrink as the rodent population expands. Because digging for rodents is such a hardwired, self-reinforcing behavior, humane training methods will generally be ineffective as a long-term solution—the behavior will continue to be re-triggered by the presence of the rodents.

Escape Digging

There's no doubt about it—some dogs are harder to contain than others. Dogs try to escape their yards because they're bored, because there's something of value to them attracting them to leave the yard, or because they're panicked about staying in the yard. You have one simple management solution for each of these causes: Don't leave your dog in the yard unattended. Not only are unattended dogs more likely to dig a tunnel to freedom, they're also subject to neighbor complaints about barking, accidental or deliberate release by someone entering the yard, and malicious teasing, poisoning, and other abuse.

If you must leave your dog in the yard, there are several strategies you can use to alleviate escape motivation:

- Provide interactive toys such as stuffed Kongs™ suspended from a sturdy tree branch, or toys such as the Buster Cube™ that you fill with treats (or his breakfast kibble) and give to your dog. He must push the cube around the yard to make treats fall out.

- Provide a canine companion—borrow a dog from a friend or neighbor—to keep him company in the yard. Be sure to check on him regularly the first few times you to this to be sure he's not teaching his pal how to dig out! If this works, you could consider adopting a second dog—as long as you really want a second dog!

- Give him lots more exercise when you're with him—a tired dog is less likely to try to escape. A tired dog is generally a better-behaved dog.

- Determine what's enticing him from outside the fence to escape. If he's tunneling out to pursue females in season, neuter him. If there are free-roaming dogs in the area, that he's digging out to join, ask your neighbors to keep their dogs home. If that doesn't work, ask animal control to patrol your street more regularly.

- Bury your fence a foot underground to block his escape efforts. Your dog may give up when he meets a barrier. Also, installing a privacy fence rather than chain link can reduce the visual stimulation outside the fence from dogs, cats, people, etc., that may generate frustration arousal and incite him to escape.

- Keep him confined in a large, chain-link kennel on a cement pad.

You cannot, however, come up with an easy management solution for a panicked dog who digs to escape his fear. It's simply cruel to leave a fearful dog in the back yard, subject to firecrackers, truck backfires, the fear of separation anxiety, or whatever triggers his panic attack. You must provide him with a safe environment, free from his triggers, while you work to desensitize him, if possible, to whatever torments him.

Burying/Retrieving Objects

Your dog may hoard his bones and toys, secreting them in caches that he happily digs. You can manage this behavior by not leaving your dog in the yard unattended, or modify it by teaching him to dig in a designated spot—his digging box. (See "Give Your Dog A Digging Box!" pg. 183.) If your dog has a strong need to dig, giving him a legal alternative to digging in your flowerbeds can be the best solution. Thwarting a strong, hardwired behavior can sometimes lead to other behavior problems. Providing him with an acceptable outlet for the behavior can fulfill his need to dig while keeping your lawn intact. Of course, you'll need to manage his behavior by preventing his access to his other preferred digging spots until he's fully trained.

Making a Den

Pregnant mother dogs will naturally look for, and create if necessary, a cozy birthing and nursery den for their pups. If you have pending puppies in your pack, it behooves you to set up a comfortable, secure spot for your mom-dog well in advance. Be sure it's protected from intruders—canine and otherwise—so she feels safe and won't go looking for her own spot.

Non-pregnant, unspayed female dogs may also go through false pregnancy, and succumb to the same den-creating urges as a pregnant dog. You can offer the same safe den spot for this dog—or better yet, consider spaying, to remove the motivation for den-digging.

Creating a Cool Spot

Just like us, dogs like to be cool on a hot day. If your dog digs up a spot on the ground the damp soil underneath is exposed, and cools as the dampness evaporates. Your dog lies on the spot and takes advantage of the cooling evaporation. Voila! He has solved his overheating problem—and made a mess of your lawn in the process. Northern breeds in particular have a natural inclination to dig to make depressions in the tundra to escape inclement weather.

Try providing an approved cool spot instead. There are products on the market—cooling pads, available at pet supply stores and online catalogs—that absorb water and evaporate the moisture over several days. One of those, placed in your dog's favorite shady spot, might ease his temperature-control needs for days at a time. Or, on the low-tech end, take your hose and soak a blanket for him to lie on before you leave for work, or create a hard-packed bare-dirt patch for him in an obtrusive spot and dampen it each morning.

Of course my favorite solution is for you to keep your dog indoors in your air-conditioned house so he doesn't *need* to dig a cool spot on a summer's afternoon. My cool-loving pack of dogs agrees wholeheartedly.

Having Fun

Some dogs just like to dig for the heck of it. It's fun. It feels good. You can tell these diggers by the expression of glee on their faces when they're digging up a nice plot of ground. Fun diggers are great candidates for the digging box. Rather than thwarting your dog's fun you're encouraging it. You can even join in and have fun with him!

Finally, a good positive training class can help resolve behavior problems by teaching you and your dog to communicate more clearly with each other. The better you understand how his mind works, and the better he understands what you expect of him, the stronger your relationship. In the end, it's the strength of this relationship that will carry you through the challenges of dog caretaking and allow you to experience the joys and rewards of sharing your life with a canine companion.

Give Your Dog a Digging Box

A digging box can be as simple as a designated spot in the yard, dug up and turned over to make it soft and inviting for your canine pal to dig in. Or it can be as elaborate as a four-sided wooden structure custom-designed to fit your dog, complete with a roof to protect it from rain and shade it from the sun, and filled with potting soil to allow for maximum digging pleasure. Once you have created your digging box, it's time to teach your dog to use it. This is the fun part.

Start by burying some of your dog's favorite toys in the dirt. Treats and stuffed Kongs are good here. Let him watch you bury the objects, and then encourage him to find them. Tell him "Go dig!" and help him if necessary—the two of you can have a great time digging together! Gradually give him the "Go dig!" cue from farther and farther away, until you can send him across the yard to his box to dig without your help.

When he seems to have the idea, bury objects when he's not looking. Then sometimes tell him to "Go dig!" and sometimes let him discover the buried treasures all on his own. Continue to supervise his yard activities, and if you catch him digging somewhere other than his box, interrupt his activity with a cheerful "Oops, Go dig!" and redirect him to his box.

When you no longer have to redirect his digging to his box, you can start giving him some unsupervised time in the yard—brief periods at first, then longer and longer as he continues to direct all of his digging in the appropriate place. If he lapses, you will need to return to supervised activity for a period of time. When you are ready to go back to no supervision, start with shorter periods and increase the length of time even more gradually than before.

Remember to address the other areas that motivate his digging, and before long, you should have a dog who can happily "dig it" with the best of them.

Your Dog Eats...WHAT?!

Stop them when the behavior risks their health

Even the most dedicated dog-lover has to admit that our canine pals have some habits that are totally alien to us. Okay, let's face it, not just alien but sometimes exceedingly gross and disgusting. Who can ever forget the once-in-a-lifetime experience of having your dog come and kiss your face just after he cleaned your cat's litter box?

Pica is the scientific word for the behavior of eating abnormal stuff. Even more graphic—and to us, repugnant—is a particular form of pica, known as coprophagia; the behavior of eating feces. Yes, some dogs eat poop—their own, as well as that of other dogs and other species.

The key word in the definition of pica is "abnormal." What may seem abnormal to us may be quite normal to dogs, or more specifically, to the particular dog in question. Pica really only becomes a problem when the abnormal eating behavior either presents a potential physical risk to the dog, or damages the relationship between dog and owner. Let's look at some examples.

Woody was an adolescent Golden Retriever who loved to eat sticks, rocks, and acorns that had fallen from the oak trees that flourished in his yard. By the time Woody was six months old his owners had already rushed him to the veterinarian twice to remove obstructions in his digestive system that, left untreated, could have killed him. This clearly presented a significant risk to Woody's health and long-term survival.

A friend of mine has an eight-year-old yellow Labrador Retriever who loves to eat paper, and occasionally snacks on other household objects. Daisy has eaten numerous books, countless pieces of mail, and volumes of personal papers. She once consumed an entire leather belt when Tim, her owner, let his vigilance lapse briefly.

Some dogs repeatedly eat grass until they vomit. Others will chew and swallow stones, causing excessive dental wear and risking bowel obstruction.

Many dogs chew on wood. While shredding an occasional fetch-stick is not a big deal, chewing on wood can become a problem if done obsessively, resulting in splinters to the mouth, possible obstructions, and lead poisoning if the wood has been painted with lead-based paints.

Finally, there are our special canine friends, the poop-eaters. Lots of dogs eat (and roll in) feces from herbivores. Deer and sheep pellets, horse apples and cow pies are favorites of dogs who live or hike in rural environs. Most dog owners begrudgingly accept this behavior in their canine pals, and expect to conclude their hikes with a doggie bath or a dip in convenient pond.

Closer to home and somewhat less acceptable to most humans, many dogs will sift flowerbeds and vegetable gardens for cat feces, or happily empty Felix's litter box of any solid feline waste. Most objectionable from the human perspective—as if cat-poop breath wasn't bad enough—are the dogs who eat canine feces—their own and/or that of other dogs.

What Causes Pica?

Is it a coincidence that both of the above real-life examples involved Retrievers? I don't think so. In his book *Applied Dog Behavior and Training, Volume Two*, Steven R. Lindsay, M.A., a dog behavior consultant and trainer in Philadelphia, Pennsylvania, suggests that this behavior is particularly evident in young sporting dogs. My personal theory is that through selective breeding we have *so* intensified the retrieving behavior in these dogs that they are compelled to pick things up in their mouths. Of course, once a young dog has something in his mouth the next obvious step is to chew, then swallow it.

Behaviorists and other scientists cite a number of possible causes for this sometimes benign, sometimes life-threatening behavior. As I've suggested, there clearly appears to be a genetic component, and, as with most behaviors, there are likely environmental factors as well. Nutritional causes are sometimes suspected, particularly deficiencies in some trace minerals such as zinc and iron. According to Lindsay, iron deficiencies may be related to low levels of dopamine receptors in the brain, which is believed by some authorities to have a significant relationship to pica activity.

An emotional component may also be at work. Dogs who are fearful, anxious, stressed or bored often resort to digging and chewing to resolve the situation. Their chewing can evolve into persistent and destructive habits to such a degree that they turn into pica behavior.

Finally, pica may be an attention-getting behavior. Some dogs learn that the quickest way to get their owner's attention is to grab, maybe chew on, something that the owner considers important. This is not done out of spite, but rather because the dog has been rewarded for this behavior by gaining his owner's attention for it. Because behaviors that are rewarded tend to increase, the pica worsens.

"Hmmmmmmm," thinks Rover. "Every time I eat sticks (or stones, or acorns) my owner comes and plays with me. Eating stuff is an effective cue to get my owner to come play. I think I'll go find an acorn to munch."

Of course, because of the potential harm to Rover from eating sticks, stones and acorns, or the potential for damage to the owner's valuable possessions in the case of the dog who eats paper, clothing or furniture, Rover's strategy works—his pica behavior *does* induce the owner to come and "play" with him.

In the case of feces-eating dogs, especially those who eat their own stools or those of other dogs, there is some evidence that the behavior *may* be related to a deficiency in a dog's naturally occurring digestive enzymes. In the wild, dogs are opportunistic carnivores who consume an omnivorous diet containing a significant proportion of unprocessed animal protein. In our homes, most dogs are made to eat an unvarying diet of processed kibble consisting of high levels of carbohydrates, with much of the protein content derived from plant sources. Whatever animal protein may be included is often of poor quality and/or highly processed, especially in the less expensive brands of kibble. However, because dogs on a starvation diet do not necessarily develop a predilection for stool-eating, there is some doubt in scientific circles about the enzyme deficiency theory.

Finally, it's important to remember that what we call pica and coprophagy may be very normal behaviors from the dog's perspective. Dogs are naturally scavengers and opportunistic feeders. If something looks like food to them it *is* food, even if it's something that we humans would consider totally inappropriate, such as a book, or a leather belt, shoe or purse. Leather is, after all, the skin of a dead animal, and dogs *do* naturally eat dead animals.

Even feces-eating is arguably normal in some circumstances. Mother dogs eat the feces of their young puppies to keep the den clean. At what point does it suddenly become "not okay" to eat feces?

Normal or not, some pica behavior is harmful to the dog, and some is truly unacceptable in the human world. Since our dogs have to live in human culture and we want them to be safe and healthy, how do we deal with the dog who eats bad stuff?

Pica Prevention

Behavior management is an important part of pica-prevention. Most stuff-eating habits are formed during a dog's puppyhood and adolescence. The use of crates, pens, leashes, tethers and proper supervision can go a long way toward preventing pica, as can the ready availability of *appropriate* chew objects. Regular removal of feces from the pup's primary confinement area can forestall poop-eating habits; some puppies who engage in coprophagia were raised in dirty, barren environments with no other play toys than pieces of feces.

If you can get through your dog's first year or two by directing chewing and eating to appropriate stuff, there is little likelihood that he will develop pica and coprophagy in his adult years. The exception to this is the eating of other species' feces—dogs do seem to be eternally attracted to horse manure, kitty poo, and some other inexplicably delicious (to them!) kinds of dung, even if prevented from doing so as pups.

If it's too late for prevention, management can also work to stop a dog from practicing his inappropriate eating behaviors. Woody, the adolescent Golden Retriever, was allowed to play in his yard wearing a muzzle that kept acorns and sticks safe from his insistent puppy mouth. Of course, his owners were careful to remove the muzzle frequently to allow Woody to drink water and cool down. A muzzle can restrict a dog's panting, which is his primary cooling mechanism. After two years of management, Woody's pica behavior seemed to wane, and he was given increasing amounts of muzzle-free time, while still monitored to be sure the habit didn't reappear.

Daisy's owner was not so successful. Whether her behavior was more firmly hardwired, or her owner wasn't as consistent at preventing the behavior, we're not sure—although I suspect some of both. To this day, Daisy will eat paper if given the opportunity. Dog and owner still make occasional trips to the emergency clinic when Daisy has eaten something, such as the belt, that Tim fears could cause a serious obstruction. In fact, Daisy is extremely fortunate that Tim is a very dedicated dog owner—in lesser hands Daisy's behavior might well have already caused irreparable damage to the relationship.

In addition to management, try increasing the pica dog's exercise. A tired dog is a well-behaved, happy dog—one less likely to be on the search for an inappropriate item to eat. Also, for dogs like the Retrievers who have an insatiable urge to put things in their mouths, orient them early in life to carrying around acceptable play objects too tough and too large to chew or swallow, such as an appropriate-sized Kong™ or a retrieving bumper.

Bumpers, made of canvas or vinyl, are frequently used to teach hunting dogs to retrieve on land and in water. The vinyl ones float and can be used for water retrieve. A bumper can occupy the mouth of a dog who wants to pick up inappropriate objects. The canvas ones have a nice feel—a soft give—in the dog's mouth.

If the pica appears to be attention-seeking behavior, try ignoring your dog by leaving the room to distract him from the inappropriate object, rather than focusing on trying to get it away from him. If he follows you, pay attention to him in a different location, and return to the room after playtime to pick up the object. Then make a commitment to supervise him more closely to prevent his access to inappropriate objects, and remove loose objects from his reach throughout the house.

Our four-legged friends will probably always find ways to mystify us with canine behaviors that are beyond our comprehension. Our behaviors are probably just as mysterious to them. Why do we insist on using the freshest water source in the house as our toilet? Why do we let big trucks come and haul away our large plastic containers of food scraps just when they are getting to their ripest and smelliest best? Why do we speak loudly when our dogs' hearing is so good that they can hear our whisper from across the room, and why do we use large gestures when our tiniest body movements have meaning to a species with a natural Ph.D. in body language?

When you think about our differences, it's a miracle that we get along with our dogs as well as we do. Next time your dog is eating something "inappropriate," consider it from his perspective, and decide whether it's really inappropriate or not before responding with your own knee-jerk human reaction to a good helping of liquid green cow pie. Then thank the powers that be for the amazing miracle that allows our two species to be best friends.

The Final Poop: 10 Tips to Discourage Your Dog from Dining on Dung

Management is your best tool to prevent pica and coprophagy, although there are some aversive products that sometimes work. Here are your best bets for out-foxing the feces-munching Fido:

1. Have your vet give your dog a complete physical to rule out any medical conditions that may contribute to the problem.

2. Take your dog out for potty breaks *on-leash*. Distract him from his own by-product after he goes by praising him, feeding him a treat and offering him a toy for a rousing game of tug or fetch.

3. Keep his yard scrupulously scooped so if he goes out between potty walks he won't find bonus piles to satisfy his habit.

4. Feed him twice a day rather than once, and include good sources of fiber in his meal to give him that satisfied "full" feeling.

5. Step up his exercise program. A tired dog is less likely to have the energy or desire to go on a poop hunt.

6. Add one of several deterrent products to his food to discourage him from eating his own feces. This works for some dogs, not for others, and it doesn't work, of course, to keep him from eating the feces of *other* animals.

7. Apply a topical deterrent such as Bitter Apple™ or Citronella™ to piles of his and/or other animals' feces. This works for some dogs, not for others.

8. If you are totally turned off by his horse, cow, sheep and deer dung consumption, simply avoid areas inhabited by those creatures.

9. Put cat litter boxes in locations inaccessible to your dog, or use baby gates to prevent his access to them. Your cat will thank you, too, for the peace and quiet in his lavatory space. There are few things more off-putting to a cat than having a canine stare at you intently while you relieve yourself, knowing that he is just waiting for you to finish so he can leap into your toilette.

10. Keep your cool. It may be disgusting to watch your canine pal wolf down a fresh, steaming turd, but yelling at him won't help. If anything, it will teach him to carry out his habit surreptitiously so he won't get in trouble for it, or to run away from you when you catch him *in flagrante delicto*. If he manages to sneak a snack, just reinforce your own commitment to manage his behavior so he doesn't have the opportunity to find his forbidden fruit.

Good Fences Make Better Dogs
Put a stop to fence-running, fence-fighting, and barking

As I sit here writing, I hear a ruckus coming from my back yard. Leaning forward, I look out my window to see Dubhy running the fence line and barking madly at two black Labs who have wandered over from a distant neighbor's house, still sporting the highly ineffective shock collars that are supposed to keep them home.

As I cuss under my breath yet again at my irresponsible neighbors and get up to call Dubhy in, I have a sudden epiphany. Three years ago when Dubhy's on-again, off-again dog aggression erupted for the first time, it was directed at a black Lab. I have always wondered why… and suddenly I see it. There's a good chance that Dubhy has a strong negative classical association with black Labrador Retrievers as a result of his irregular but frequent encounters-of-the-fence-kind with our neighbor's wayward dogs. Duh!

In his famous poem, "Mending Wall," Robert Frost starts out by saying, "Something there is that doesn't love a wall." We could revise that slightly to say "Something there is that doesn't love a fence." That "something" is our dogs.

Fence-running, and its close cousin, fence-fighting, are manifestations of barrier frustration, also called restraint frustration. The frustration that a dog feels when he can see—but not reach—his objective, can, and often does, give rise to **canine obsessive-compulsive disorders** (COCD) and aggression, both of which are serious behavior problems caused by stress.

Fence-running can quickly become a COCD. I see a mild version of it with Dubhy—stereotypic running along the fence line, accompanied by aroused barking, and spinning at the corners. He has a path worn around the interior of our large yard, which wasn't there prior to his joining our family.

If a dog has had ample opportunity to fence-run, fence-fight, or just bark madly when people or dogs pass by his yard, it can be challenging to stop these behaviors. Strict management of his environment to eliminate his "practice time" is critical.

I have no doubt that if Dubhy were a (shudder) back yard dog, he would have serious problems. Instead, he's only outdoors when we are home, and if he starts his fence-running behavior we interrupt it and bring him in. We are fortunate that our fence doesn't conjoin any of our neighbors' fenced-in dogs, or we would have to take much stronger steps to manage or retrain the behavior.

Restraint frustration also quickly turns into aggression. Aggression is caused by anxiety and stress, easily triggered by the arousal of fence-running. Some dogs who fence fight are fine if they meet the same dog sans barrier. Others, like Dubhy, may generalize their aggression to some or all dogs even when there's no fence present.

As dog owners become more and more responsible about keeping their dogs safe at home, the incidence of fence-related behavior problems rises. Even the unfortunately popular underground electronic (shock) containment system fences can give rise to the problem. The barrier is there, even if the dog can't see it, and the intense punishment of the shock the dog receives if he breaches the invisible barrier can intensify the resulting aggression.

Tying up a dog outside creates the same restraint frustration problem, and shares an additional major drawback with electronic fences. Neither prevents trespassers, human or otherwise, from invading the dog's territory, putting both the trespasser and the dog at serious risk.

What's an Owner to Do?

It sounds like you're damned if you do, and damned if you don't! If not confining your dog isn't safe or responsible, and confining him causes behavior problems, what are you supposed to do with him?

This is a case where prevention and management are much easier solutions than training. There are a number of things you can do to reduce the likelihood and opportunity for fence running and fighting. You can:

- **Install a solid fence.** This is the best solution, albeit expensive, and in an increasing number of shortsighted communities, prohibited. If you block your dog's visual access to the stimuli outside his fences, he's not likely to get aroused enough to begin the undesirable behaviors. If you live in a no-fence community, you might want to consider moving.

- **Keep your dog indoors.** Dogs who are permanent outdoor residents are at high risk for fence-related behavior problems. There are many reasons it's not wise to leave your dog outdoors when you're not home—this is just one of them. If he's out while you're away, he'll get lots of opportunities to practice fence-running and fighting. The more he practices, the harder the behavior is to modify.

  Do like we do with Dubhy: let your dog out in the yard for limited periods only when you're home, and bring him in immediately if he starts the unwanted behaviors.

- **Eliminate the stimuli.** Duhby's fence problems are triggered by stray dogs and itinerant cats. We eliminated the majority of Dubhy's fence running by adopting (with the neighbor's blessing) the neighbor's cat who had taken up residence in our barn. We had Barney vaccinated and neutered, and brought him indoors. A good percentage of Dubhy's problem was solved. (See "Barney Morphs Into Housie" pg. 193.) We're still working on the black Labs.

- **Modify your existing fence.** If you have a see-through fence, like the ubiquitous chain-link enclosures common in my neighborhood, do something to make it more solid. There are slats available that you can slide into the chain link to block some of the visual stimuli. This will work with mild fence problems, but won't deter a dedicated fence-runner or fighter if he can still see through the gaps between the slats.

  You can try the slats to see if they work, and if not, line the inside of the fence with something to block his view completely. FRP (fiberglass reinforced plastic) is probably the most durable option, also the most expensive but least visually offensive. Other options might be plywood, or tarps, at least temporarily.

- **Install an "airlock."** Also a fairly costly option, you can discourage fence fighting by putting up a second fence inside your existing one to create a "no-dog's land" between your dog and your neighbor's.

  As an added benefit, this protects your dog from neighbor children sticking fingers and potentially harmful objects through the fence. While a double barrier can reduce actual fence-*fighting*, I am confident that this option would not have put a dent in Dubhy's fence-*running* behavior.

Repair the Damage

If you have a dog who already manifests fence-related behaviors, you *can* do some training that will help you get a handle on the problem. You have probably already discovered how difficult it can be to call your dog to you when he is in a state of high arousal, racing along the fence in futile, frustrating pursuit of his adversary.

Your first challenge is to find a way through the fog in his brain so he can even acknowledge your presence. With Dubhy, I found that standing directly in his path didn't work. He simply darted around me and continued on his mission. I know better than to try the lunge-and-grab method, which would only serve to make him wary of me. Tossing something like a treat or a ball to try to break his focus was equally ineffective.

I began a two-pronged training program, one to counter-condition him to the presence of the arousal-causing stimuli, and the other to improve his recall response, even in the face of high distractions.

Come Again?

The recall training was easiest to implement, as I could do it any place, any time. Dubhy already had a rock-solid and speedy recall in the training center, but was somewhat less reliable in the back yard, and even less so in wide open spaces. I was already fed up with his "maybe" recall, after being forced on several occasions to go out and get him in the dark when he declined to come back indoors after the pack's bedtime bathroom break.

We embarked on back yard and long line recall training. Several times a day I would play with Dubhy in the back yard, calling him, giving him a high-value reward (such as canned chicken), and letting him go again. Especially since Dubhy prefers outdoors to indoors—first dog I have *ever* had who exhibited *this* bizarre preference—I didn't want his recall to be a predictor of "outdoors is over" by bringing him indoors every time I called him.

I would also call him to the back deck and cue him to do several of his tricks for high value rewards, since he likes to do tricks. And I called him and had him practice on several pieces of agility equipment; he *loves* his agility stuff. Gradually his recall responses improved.

I even used a little negative punishment on one occasion when he failed to come for dinner call. Rather than trekking out to get him, I let him stay out, and didn't serve him his meal when he finally did deign to come in. He hasn't missed dinner call since.

In addition, we worked on recalls in wide open spaces on his long line, until we started getting snappy responses, even spinning on his heels if he was heading the other direction. We now take a chance on our five acres and occasionally let him off-leash to practice recalls outside the yard. Most of the time, he comes when called. Every once in a while his Scottie brain takes over, and I have to retrieve him before he wanders off the property.

I also did counter-conditioning work with him. Whenever the opportunity presented itself—with the neighbor dogs, or Barney—I went out in the yard and waited for a brief lapse in Dubhy's fence-focused attention, then offered him yummy treats. At first he would grab a treat and go right back to his running and barking. My ability to keep him focused on me and the treats was in direct proportion to the distance to the stimulus. If the neighbor dogs appeared to just be passing through, Dubhy would stay more attentive to me as they moved away. Over time, as we worked on it, he would turn his attention to me—and keep it there, with the dogs in closer and closer proximity.

Barney, who loved to tease Dubhy by rolling around on the driveway six feet from the fence line, was more of a challenge. But with time and practice, I could even call Dubhy away from his feline nemesis.

Band-aid, Not a Cure

What I have accomplished with Dubhy is a compromise, not a cure. He still "goes off" when neighbor dogs pass by; it's just easier for me to interrupt his behavior and call him into the house. If I were to leave him in the back yard unattended he would continue his arousal behavior and the COCD nature of his actions, especially the spinning, would probably worsen.

I'm still dealing with the collateral damage of his fence behaviors; specifically his aggression toward some dogs, especially black Labs. When we are out in the real world and he sees another dog he will go on alert—tail up, ears pricked, eyes bright, leaning forward. Then, unless it's a Lab, he'll swivel his head toward me to ask for his treat—the positive result of lots of counter conditioning. With Labs, I still have to draw his attention to me; he doesn't offer it on his own. I can gauge how aroused or relaxed he is by the amount of pressure from his teeth when he takes the treat from my fingers. With Labs, his teeth definitely hurt.

It would be a very large challenge to counter-condition a dog's fence-running or fighting behaviors to the point that the behavior goes away. Even if you succeed in habituating your dog to the presence of the arousal-causing stimuli, the chances of spontaneous recovery are very high; the behavior is likely to resurrect itself with additional uninterrupted exposures to the stimuli.

Prevention is your best course of action, by not putting your dog in a position to develop the behaviors in the first place—not leaving him fenced and unattended. If it's too late for prevention, management is your next best bet—putting up a solid fence and/or not leaving in him the yard alone.

If at any time you feel that you and your dog are not making progress, or your dog is exhibiting signs of a serious COCD, contact a good positive behavior consultant or veterinary behaviorist. She can evaluate your training and help you investigate the possibility of using behavior modification drugs to control obsessive behaviors that may be interfering with the success of your program.

The property we are hoping to purchase in Maryland is in the middle of 80 rural acres, and the back yard is fenced with a solid wooden fence. Sounds like a great management plan to me!

Robert Frost's neighbor was right…good fences *do* make good neighbors, and especially better neighbor dogs!

A Challenge for a Former Cat-Chaser: "Barney" Morphs into "Housie"

Although my husband and I are strong advocates of indoor-only cats, after we adopted Barney it was our intention to allow him to continue his life as a barn cat until we moved, and then transition him into the house. It can be difficult to turn a full-time outside cat into a house resident, and we were reluctant to upset the equilibrium of our four-legged family while we were trying to sell the house. Stressed dogs and cats can find ways to make a house less marketable, if you know what I mean.

Barney, however, had other ideas. On a frigid rainy night just after Christmas, Barney sat outside our den windows and cried for an hour. Clearly, he wanted to come in. I tried to ignore him, but when he took to hanging on the window screens and meowing, I couldn't stand it. Barney came indoors.

One of the things that worried me about bringing him in was Dubhy's reaction. The feisty Scottie had developed a strong animosity toward Labs as a result of his fence running; would he generalize the same reaction to an indoor Barney? I had done scads of counter conditioning with Dubhy when I brought home a kitten 18 months prior; would that help?

Armed with stick cheese, I let Dubhy into the den with Barney. As I'd feared, Dubhy's radar was instantly on high alert. His tail went up, ears pricked, eyes bright, leaning forward…I held my breath—and he swiveled his head back toward me for his treat. The crisis was over—counter-conditioning wins again.

Interestingly enough, Barney's life as an outdoor cat made him fairly pugnacious. If a dog gives him a hard time, Barney holds his own—lunging at the dog and swatting with claws that are now kept clipped. Barney and Dubhy have invented a game that they play together. Dubhy will tease Barney into leaping at him, and then do puppy rushes around the dining room table, occasionally deliberately passing close enough to Barney to elicit another lunge. They both seem to derive great enjoyment from the game.

And I was worried.

Preventing Great Escapes

How to safely confine burrowers and bolters

Otis the Bloodhound was an opportunistic escapee. I discovered his talent one day while working at the front desk at the Marin Humane Society, early in my animal protection career. A woman came in asking if we might know where a certain Bloodhound lived, because he kept visiting her house every day. He was charming, she said, but she worried that he might get hit by a car.

A Bloodhound owner myself at the time, I was curious where this errant Bloodhound might live; it's not a very common breed. But when I asked the woman for her address, I was dismayed to hear she lived around the corner from me. Could it possibly be *my* safely-fenced dog who was making house calls around the neighborhood?

It was, indeed. Unbeknownst to me, Otis had discovered a hole in the fence behind some dense bushes. He waited every morning until I was gone, crawled out the hole, spent his day visiting neighbors, and returned home in time to greet me innocently at my back door.

I was lucky. Otis wasn't a dedicated escape artist—a solid patch to the fence ended his wanderings. Owners of other canine escapees often must work much harder to keep their errant dogs safe at home.

Escape Artists

Roaming is an innate behavior for dogs. They are hunters and scavengers, and left to their own devices will wander a territory far larger than the average back yard. Escaping, however, is a learned behavior. Dog who are given the opportunity to escape often do. Once they figure out how, they will try harder and harder, even when the fence is belatedly fortified. Dogs who become escape artists hone their skills to a fine edge. Keeping them safely confined at home where they belong can be a huge challenge. Our nation's animal shelters are full of escape artists.

The best avenue for managing a dog's wanderlust is to prevent him from wandering in the first place. The problem starts when you bring home the new puppy before you are fully prepared, promising to put up that fence before Rover grows up.

A tiny puppy won't wander far from the back stoop, even when you leave him out on his own for a bit. Before you know it, though, Rover is six months old, already has a habit of making neighborhood rounds, and you still haven't finished the fence. When Mr. Jones from down the road calls you up and threatens to shoot Rover if he chases his goats one more time, you rush to the hardware store to buy some metal fence posts and hog wire. Hastily you throw up a pen in the back yard that attaches to the back deck. "That should hold him until I get the rest of those post holes dug!" you think.

As you settle yourself back on the sofa to watch the last half of the football game, Rover is already testing the fence; he's late for his daily visit to the Smith's garbage can! He checks out the gate latch, but it doesn't yield to his tentative pawing and gnawing. He trots around the inside of the enclosure, searching for a way out.

In the far corner where the yard dips into a gully he finds a three-inch gap between the wire and the ground and pokes his nose under. Getting his nose on the other side of the fence encourages him to try harder. He starts to worm his way under. The soft ground gives way beneath his claws. He digs harder. Before you can say "end zone," he's free, headed for the Smith's omelet scraps and bacon drippings. You eventually retrieve him and fill the hole, but the damage is done. Rover is on his way to a lifetime career as a master burrower.

Burrowers, Beavers, Bounders, and Bolters

Whether your dog's escape efforts focus on tooth and claw or he excels in feats of aerial accomplishment depends both on genetics and learning. Dogs who are genetically pro-grammed to dig, such as Terriers, are likely to *burrow* under the fence, especially if a handy soft spot presents itself.

If, however, the first weak spot in the fence is a loose board, we can inadvertently train Rover and our Terrier to eat their way through fences, turning them into *beavers* rather than burrowers. Once Rover discovers that the fence is breachable, he'll test every spot where his teeth can gain purchase, and you'll forever spend your football-watching time patching his holes.

Herding breeds such as Border Collies, and Sporting breeds like Labradors have a natural ability to leap tall buildings in a single *bound*. Given the opportunity, they'll make jump-ing fences their specialty.

However, you can inadvertently teach a less athletic dog to bound over fences by starting small.

Confident that a four-foot fence will contain the Beagle-mix you just adopted from the shelter, you leave him in the back yard and go off to work. That night, your new dog greets you in the driveway after terrorizing cottontails in the neighbors' woods all day. You raise the fence six inches, positive that this will hold him. Flush from his exploits the day before, your dog has to struggle a little harder to make it over 4'6", but nothing breeds success like success. A little extra oomph, and he's out again for another rousing day of bunny-bashing.

You raise the fence to five feet this time, absolutely sure there's no way he can get over that. But again, even more confident of his jumping prowess, Snoopy tries a wee bit harder, and he's up and over. There's a good chance that if you had *started* with a five-foot fence Snoopy never would have tried to jump it at all. What you've done is taught him to jump higher and higher, consistently reinforcing his belief that if he just tries hard enough he can make it.

Bolters have learned to watch for a moment of human inattention, then charge through the tiniest crack in the gate or door.

While the other escape methods work best in the absence of humans, bolting requires the unintentional complicity of the visitor who doesn't know (or the family member who forgets) that Dash must be manacled and hog-tied before a door is opened to the outside world.

Once again, prevention is the better part of valor. If Dash is taught from early days to wait politely at a door until invited out, he doesn't learn the fine art of door-darting.

Prevention

You've heard this from me before, and I promise you'll hear it from me again. It's *al-ways* easier to *prevent* a behavior problem from happening than it is to fix it after the fact. There's no excuse for letting a puppy learn how to be an escape artist. Prevention measures are relatively simple. Don't let your puppy learn that roaming is rewarding—keep him at home, and stop any embryonic escape attempts in their tracks by taking the following prophylactic measures:

- Provide a safe, secure enclosure. Before the new puppy comes home, make sure your fence is flush to the ground, or even buried a few inches. Check for rotten spots, and crawl behind shrubs and brush to look for holes or loose boards.

- Go overboard on fence height. Raise the fence to at least five feet for a small dog (perhaps higher for very athletic small dogs like Jack Russell Terriers) and six feet for medium to large dogs. Make sure there are no woodpiles, doghouses, deck railings or other objects close enough to the fence to provide a convenient launch pad.

- Teach your pup to wait at doors until invited through. Use "Wait" at every door to the outside world, every time you open it, whether you are going to let him go through or not.

- Install dog-proof latches on gates. There's no point in waiting until after he's been hit by a car to discover that Rover can learn to work the latch. In fact, a padlock will prevent accidental release from the outside by a visitor or intruder at the same time it keeps Rover from practicing his latch-opening skills.

- Minimize Rover's motivation to roam by neutering at a young age (eight weeks or not long thereafter), and providing him with ample exercise and companionship at home.

- Consider keeping Rover indoors when you're not home. Boredom and loneliness provide strong motivation to escape, and Rover has plenty of time to plan and execute the great escape when you are not there to interrupt unwanted behaviors such as digging under and chewing through fences.

Repair any problems that you observe with your fence before your dog notices the weakness and takes advantage of it.

The Fix

What if it's too late for prevention? Maybe you adopted Rover from the shelter after his last adopter taught him to jump a six-foot fence, and then returned him because he kept escaping. Do you give up on Rover too? Not at all. There are lots of steps you can take to fortify your defenses and keep your escape artist at home, depending on his proclivities.

- **Bounders:** If you have a scaler, who hooks his nails in the chain link and climbs up and over, you can cover the inside of the fence with a flat, solid surface so his nails can't get a good footing for climbing. A relatively new material, fiberglass reinforced plastic (FRP), is now regularly used in animal shelters and can usually withstand tooth and nail, but it may be prohibitively expensive if you have a large fenced area.

  Or, you can install a "roof" at the top of the fence that comes in at a 90-degree angle; he won't be able to reach behind his head and pull himself backwards over the ledge when he gets to the top. Some people use wire mesh to create an angled-in barrier—similar to those at the top of prison fences, but without the razor wire!—that impedes jumping.

  Another option that I've seen work is to top your fences with a "roll bar" that prevents your dog from getting a purchase at the top of the fence and pulling himself over. This is easily installed by running a wire or rope through sections of fat PVC pipe and hanging them along the top of the fence.

  If you have a dog who gets a good running start and clears the fence with the greatest of ease, plant a hedge or place some other obstacle in his takeoff zone, interrupting his stride and making it impossible for him to jump. If you put your last fence extension inward at a 45-degree angle you may also fool his eye and foil his leap.

- **Bolters:** The dog who bolts through open doors needs an airlock—a system of double gates so that if he makes it through one, he is still contained behind the next. Self-closing gate springs are a must, to prevent visitors and family members from being careless twice in a row. A good solid recall—teaching Dash to come when called—taught with positive methods, of course, is an excellent backup plan for the door darter. Family members also need to remember not to panic and chase when Dash slips out—a good game of keep-away just makes door darting more fun for the dog.

- **Burrowers:** If you're going to bury the fence for a dedicated burrower, bury deep—at least six inches to a foot. If you bury it two inches, you'll just teach him to dig deeper. You might do better setting the fence in cement, or lining your fence trench with large rocks or small boulders. You definitely need a cement pad at the gate, since you can't bury the gate.

- **Beavers:** If Bucky has learned to gnaw his way through your fence you could be in big trouble. Lining the inside of the fence with heavy-duty wire—like chain link—may stop him. It may not, however, and he may break teeth in his attempts to eat his way out. Sheets of FRP are good for this also. Cement block walls can be effective, but may not be esthetically pleasing. Ceramic tiles can be glued to the blocks to make them more attractive, but they're not cheap.

It Can Happen to Anyone

I'm far more careful now than I was in the Otis days; my dogs are never left in the back yard if no one is home to monitor their activities. Still, that doesn't mean that accidents don't happen. Just the other day, my phone rang. I answered, and it was Helen, my assistant, calling from the training center a few hundred feet from the house.

"I have Lucy," she said.

WHAT?!

Lucy was supposed to be safely in the back yard! I dashed out to find the back gate open—left that way by the usually-very-careful guy who mows our lawn. Tucker was safely indoors, Dubhy and Katie were still in the back yard—only Lucy had made the great escape, and she hadn't gone far.

It can happen to the best of us. I was just thankful someone was home.

A Shocking Solution?

Many dog owners are turning to electric shock collars to keep their dogs contained. Non-visible electronic fences are quite the rage, especially in communities where shortsighted homeowner regulations prohibit the installation of physical fences. Many dog owners are pleased with the results—no unsightly fence to impede their view of the sunset, and Rover magically stays within his delineated boundaries. Many dog owners are not so pleased. There are a myriad of things that can fail with non-visible shock fencing systems. Here are just a few:

- For most dogs, there usually is some stimulus strong enough to entice the dog through the barrier. For some, it might be that bunny or squirrel venturing a tad too close. Once the dog is outside the fence line, he's rarely motivated to brave the shock to get back in.

- Some dogs learn that the shock stops once they cross the line. Dogs who are determined to escape can learn to grit their teeth and risk one shock to get to the other side.

- Shock collars are a punishment tool, and their use risks all the potential negative side effects of punishment. They can cause fear and/or aggression. If a dog receives a shock while a child is walking by, he may associate the shock with the child and become aggressive towards children. Or mail carriers. Or joggers. Or other dogs. Some dogs have become terrified and refuse to go into their own yards after receiving shocks from the collar during the training process.

- Electronic equipment can fail. Batteries die, and when the dog no longer hears the warning beep he is free to come and go as he pleases. Some collars have malfunctioned and delivered repeated shocks to hapless, helpless dogs until their owners arrived home from work at the end of the day to rescue them from their torture.

- The non-visible fence does not, of course, provide the dog with any protection from intruders, so Rover is at the mercy of other dogs or humans who may enter the yard and do bad things.

- As an advocate of positive, dog-friendly training methods, I simply reject the idea of shocking dogs around the neck for our convenience. I would much prefer a chain-link dog pen with a top, set on a cement pad, for the master escape artist. Most dog owners want to be able to give Rover the freedom to play in the yard, however, so when all else fails, I am a bit less loath to use electric shock in a situation where the dog learns by doing. I have on rare occasion, suggested the use of a single strand of battery-powered electric fence wire, installed at nose level on the inside of the physical fence. While a shock to the neck that comes out of nowhere seems to confuse and even terrify a good number of dogs, an "ouch!" to the nose when they touch something seems to make more sense. After one, or maybe two touches, most dogs leave the fence alone without apparent long-term psychological trauma. A last resort, perhaps, and a very aversive one, but preferable to being hit by a car.

Monster Appliances

Vroom! Whirl! Roar! Desensitize your dog to those noisy appliances

My mother used to say, "There are more important things in life than having a clean house." While I certainly didn't buy into everything my parents tried to teach me (much to their everlasting dismay), I embraced this one wholeheartedly. Still, from time to time, I face reality and acknowledge that a coating of dog hair on the carpeting is not everyone's idea of a Martha Stewart home decorating theme. I reluctantly drag the Hoover out of the back recesses of the closet, and watch my dogs' ears and tails droop as they slink off to far corners of the house. Taking pity on them, I escort them to the safety of our fenced back yard before I attack dog hair and dust bunnies with the odious machine.

I am fortunate that my dogs have only a mild distaste for the vacuum cleaner. I have seen dogs with much more violent reactions—ranging from those who turn into a quaking pool of Jello at the sight of the of the voracious sucking monster, to dogs who attack the machine with a ferocity that could make you fear for your own safety.

I am also fortunate that my canine pals don't seem to transfer their vacuum fears to other household appliances—some dogs react badly to everything from power tools and the sewing machine to blenders, hair dryers, dishwashers, and even electric shavers.

You may have seen a few of these dogs featured on the "Funniest" TV shows. Some folks may think a dogs' fear or stress-related behaviors are funny, but I don't. Chances are, neither do the dogs who, for the mere purpose of human entertainment, are being deliberately subjected to the stimuli that cause such stress.

Perhaps their humans aren't aware that repeated exposure to major stressors can exacerbate behavior problems, may cause canine compulsive disorders, and can even lead to serious aggression in some cases. I like to believe that if these humans realized how much this kind of stress can degrade the quality of their dogs' lives, they would stop teasing and tormenting their canine companions. In fact, they might even consider doing some **counter-conditioning** and **desensitization** to make their dogs' lives more enjoyable.

Natural Response

Classical conditioning is a learning process in which a dog's brain comes to make an association between a stimulus and a natural response. The story of Pavlov's dogs salivating at the sound of a bell, is a story of classical conditioning. It worked like this: Food was presented to the dogs, and the dogs began to salivate in natural response to the food. The dogs didn't have to think about salivating, it just happened.

Pavlov began to sound the bell each time prior to the presentation of the food. Eventually the dogs began to automatically salivate at the sound of the bell, because the sound had become a reliable predictor of the presentation of food. It was as if Pavlov had programmed a tape playing in the dogs' brains that now produced the "conditioned response" of salivation when the dogs heard the ringing of the bell. The dogs didn't have to think about salivating, it just happened.

Fear of the vacuum cleaner is also a conditioned response. A dog has no reason to fear a silent machine sitting unobtrusively in the corner, but many dogs have a natural fear response to something that makes as much noise as a vacuum when it is turned on. Because a dog owner is not likely to haul the Hoover out of its home in the closet just to admire its esthetic qualities, the appearance of the vacuum has become a reliable predictor of that awful cacophony of sound that it produces. Add the fact that the machine moves around when it makes noise and it becomes even more threatening. Plus, a conscientious house-keeper eventually vacuums every nook and cranny of the house, so no matter where the dog takes refuge, sooner or later the monster vacuum finds him and chases him. Pretty scary!

It doesn't take long for the dog to transfer his noise-fear response to the mere presence of the vacuum cleaner, even before the problem is compounded by the addition of a mis-guided human who thinks it's funny to watch a dog go into contortions trying to attack a machine.

If your dog experiences only mild discomfort, you can circumvent the problem simply by removing him from the environment prior to launching the monster. This is what I do. My yard is safely fenced and big enough that my dogs can be perfectly comfortable sitting far from the house under the old hickory tree, while the Hoover monster commences its infrequent invasions of their den. If their fear responses were more intense, if I lived in an apartment where there was no easily available safe refuge for them, or if I were a neat-freak and cleaned my house every day, I might begin a program of counter-conditioning in or-der to avoid making my dogs miserable with frequent vacuum-torture.

Reprogramming the Tape

The counter-conditioning and desensitization processes reprogram the tape playing in the dog's brain in relation to a particular stimulus—in this case, the vacuum cleaner—until the dog is comfortable with it at any level of intensity. Right now, the tape is saying, "Vacuum cleaner—BAD!" If the dog is fearful, his response is "RUN AWAY!" and/or "TURN TO JELL-O!" If the dog is more confident and assertive, his response is likely to be "ATTACK THE BAD VACUUM CLEANER." Either way, through counter conditioning, you want to reprogram that tape to say "Vacuum cleaner—GOOD!!!"

You can do this by having a helper present the stimulus, the vacuum cleaner, turned off, at whatever distance is necessary to avoid sending the dog into a tizzy. Have her bring the machine in from the opposite side of the room and park it there. As soon as the dog sees the vacuum cleaner, immediately begin feeding him something absolutely wonderful, such as tidbits of drained, canned chicken. Do this for several minutes, and then have the helper remove the machine from the room. The instant the cleaner is gone, stop feeding tidbits. Repeat this process several times, commencing tidbits each time as soon as the cleaner ap-pears, stopping as soon as it leaves.

You are trying to convince the dog's brain that the vacuum cleaner *makes chicken happen.* You will know you are making progress when the dog, upon noticing the vacuum cleaner, turns happily to you and says, in cheerful dog body language, "Where's My Chicken?" You may achieve this in one session, or you may have to repeat the lesson several times in one day, or over several days.

When your dog is quite comfortable in the presence of a quiet, motionless vacuum cleaner, you can help the process along by leaving Hoover out of the closet in an out-of-the-way corner, and occasionally setting yummy treats on and around it for your dog to find when-ever he happens to be in the vicinity.

Use counter conditioning and desensitization to give your dog a new association with scary appliances. Vacuum cleaner = yummy treats.

Raising the Intensity

When you get the "Where's My Chicken?" reaction consistently in response to the arrival of the vacuum cleaner, you are ready to raise the intensity of the stimulus. *No, don't turn it on yet!* That would be too big a leap. Instruct your helper to bring the vacuum cleaner in, and move it back and forth at the far end of the room. Again, begin presenting chicken as soon as the dog sees the machine. If the motion of the vacuum cleaner is too stressful for him, find a lower intensity; perhaps have your helper move it more slowly, or for shorter distances. Each time you up the ante, you need to find a step that is small enough that your dog can handle it. If you discover you have taken too big a step, back up and find a smaller one.

When your dog is comfortable with the silent machine moving back and forth at the far end of the room, you can begin to reduce the distance between the dog and the cleaner. Have your helper enter the room and move a few feet closer to the dog, on a diagonal, so it doesn't look like the vacuum cleaner is headed in for the attack. Work back and forth at that distance, for several sessions if necessary, until the dog is comfortable and you are ready to increase the intensity again. You might also keep the vacuum cleaner still, and move the dog gradually closer to it—always making lots of chicken happen, and always making sure the dog is moving voluntarily closer. Do not force him to approach.

When the dog is very comfortable moving around the quiet vacuum cleaner and having it move around him, you are ready to add a new stimulus—noise. Once again, you want to do this at an intensity the dog can handle, by having your helper turn the machine on in the next room, or perhaps several rooms away. Instruct her to do it briefly at first, to be sure your dog will tolerate the sound. As soon as the sound begins, start feeding high-value treats. As soon as the sound stops, stop the treats. If your dog does well at that level of intensity, have your helper leave the sound on for longer and longer stretches. Remember, you are looking for the happy "Where's My Chicken?" response when your dog hears the sound of the vacuum.

When you are getting that happy response consistently, have your helper bring the machine one room closer, or at least from the far side to the near side of the room she was in—whatever you think your dog can tolerate easily. Continue to gradually increase the intensity of the sound stimulus by bringing the vacuum closer, until your helper is in the same room when she turns on the machine, and your dog is happily looking to you for his chicken.

Congratulations! You have convinced your dog that a noisy vacuum cleaner is a reliable predictor of chicken, and you are well on your way to successfully reprogramming his vacuum cleaner tape. You have just one more step—putting all the stimuli together.

So far, he is comfortable with a quiet vacuum cleaner moving around in his presence, and with a noisy one sitting still. The last hurdle is getting a happy "Where's My Chicken?" response with a *moving and noisy* vacuum cleaner in his presence. Again, you will do this gradually, using the same techniques you have already applied so successfully. Have your helper turn the vacuum on at the far side of the room and move it slowly, a short distance, then stop and turn it off. Feed treats when the sound starts and as long as the vacuum is moving. End the treats when the sound and movement stop.

When your dog is quite happy with a noisy, moving vacuum cleaner, your last step is to switch places with your helper, so that *you* are the one pushing the machine, since that is what will normally happen when you clean. Go back to the beginning, and work through all your steps again, starting with a quiet vacuum cleaner motionless in the room with your dog, then moving in the room, then a noisy vacuum in the next room, a noisy one motionless in the same room, and finally a moving, noisy vacuum cleaner in the same room as the dog. The process should go much more quickly this time. You and your dog are home free. Happy cleaning!

Other Appliances

The amount of time it takes to successfully reprogram a canine brain varies widely from one dog to the next, depending on how severe the dog's reaction is, how much and how skillfully you practice, and the dog's own natural resilience. Some dogs require weeks or months of behavior modification; others get it in just a few sessions. You can use the exact same process of counter-conditioning and desensitization with any of those nasty household appliances that are cause unnecessary stress in your dog's life. Simply figure out how to refit the description of the various vacuum cleaner counter-conditioning and desensitization steps so they are appropriate to the appliance in question.

Or, if your dog's response is really not that dramatic, you can just figure out how to manage his environment to prevent him from being exposed to and stressed by the appliances that concern him.

We are going away for the weekend and a pet sitter will be staying at our house to care for our four-legged family. I'd better put the dogs outside and haul out that Hoover!

Tips for Using Appliances

Here are a few things to keep in mind when using appliances around your dogs:

1. Prevention is always easier than cure. Make sure your dog's introduction to new household appliances is safe and positive, and you probably won't have to worry about behavior modification.

2. Never force your dog to approach an appliance he is afraid of. Use treats and gentle reassurances at a distance where he is comfortable, to help him learn to accept new things.

3. Never tease him or allow him to be teased with appliances. It might seem funny at first, but can cause big behavior problems. It's really not funny.

4. When doing counter-conditioning and desensitization, it is best to err on the side of caution. Move slowly, in small increments, when increasing the stimulus level or changing the stimulus. The biggest mistake people make is trying to move forward too quickly with the program. Take your time.

5. Be patient. Remember that your dog has no control over a classically conditioned behavior. It doesn't do any good to get angry with him—he can't help it. Getting angry will only add to his stress and make it more difficult to counter-condition the behavior.

6. If the dog's reaction is mild, you can choose to manage the environment to prevent his exposure to the stressful stimulus. Move him outside if you have a fenced yard, or put him in a room far enough away from the offending appliance so it doesn't bother him while you use it.

7. If the dog's reaction is severe, you may need the help of a qualified, positive trainer/behavior professional to assist you with an effective behavior modification program.

Permanent Markers

How to change the ways of a dog who urine-marks in the house

A client recently e-mailed me about a problem she was having with her dog urinating in the house. Here's what she wrote:

"I'm having a problem with my Jack Russell Terrier marking in my house. He's 4 1/2 years old, and we have another older male dog, a 6 1/2 year old Collie. We adopted the Collie when he was 1 1/2, and he was already neutered. We adopted the JRT when he was 3, and had him neutered six months ago when he was 4. The marking happened once or twice before he was neutered, but has become much more of a problem lately, long after the procedure.

He always marks at the front door of our house, I think it's when someone is walking by, which makes me think it's a territoriality issue. It's very hard to catch him in the act and therefore hard to discipline him. I've tried putting our clothing on the spot where he marks to try to communicate that it does not belong to him, we put a doggie diaper on him when we think he is likely to mark, but that chafes him if we leave it on too long. I took him to the veterinarian to see if he has a physical problem and he does not. This is clearly behavioral.

I want him to be part of our family, so I won't confine him to his crate or to one room of the house when we're home and everyone else is together. I know that would control the problem but that's not the environment I want to create for him or for us. Not only is the problem harming our furniture, but it harms the bond between the dog and we humans because it makes our home unpleasant for us. I'm out of ideas! Any suggestions?"

A Common Problem

If it makes you feel any better, you are not alone. A surprising number of dog owners across the country find themselves faced with this challenge at one time or another. In fact, one of my apprentices has been struggling with it, with Newman, a Shih-Tzu/Terrier mix rescue dog she recently adopted. I understand the stress that your Terrier's behavior puts on your relationship, and applaud you for the commitment you are making to maintain his position as a full-fledged family member.

You have touched on many of the common suggestions for dealing with marking behavior, but I would like to explore some of them further.

You mentioned a veterinary exam, and kudos to you for this. Many behavior challenges have medical roots. It is always important to find these (or rule them out) prior to investing in behavior modification techniques that can't succeed if the dog has a physical problem that interferes with his ability to perform. You don't go into detail about what tests your veterinarian conducted on your dog, but some of the things that may contribute to a marking problem are urinary tract infections, medications such as Prednisone that can cause a dog to drink more water, or other medical conditions, such as hyperthyroidism or kidney malfunction, that can cause a dog to drink excessive water and/or urinate more than normal. I will assume that your vet checked for all of these, and more, in your dog's exam.

You hypothesize that your dog may be responding to the presence of someone walking by the house, which would indicate a possible territorial component—often a cause of inappropriate marking. It may also be that he is trying to get outside to urinate—dogs who soil at the door are often trying to tell us that they have to go out. It is impossible to really look into our canine companions' brains to know for sure what they are thinking. We can do interesting mental exercises and come up with some pretty good guesses, but to a large degree, the cause, if not medical, is far less important than the cure. I'm going to expand on the often-successful solutions you have already mentioned, and suggest a few new ones for you to try.

Managing the Environment

If your dog only marks at the front door, one easy answer is to find a way to routinely block his physical access to that spot, perhaps with one or more baby gates or exercise pens in strategic places. Of course, you may wish to actually modify the behavior, and blocking his favorite marking spot may simply induce him to mark elsewhere, so read on for some more in-depth solutions.

First, if you do manage to catch him in the act, try to interrupt, rather than discipline him. I use a cheerful "Oops! Outside!" interrupter instead of an angry "No! Bad Dog!" Trust me, I know how hard it is to be cheerful when you see your dog lifting his leg in the house, but too much discipline can teach him to do it only when you aren't looking. That's not the training goal here!

You are on the right track when you put your clothing on the spot, but you may need to use something more meaningful to him. He may think you and your clothing *do* belong to him, or are at least community property open for marking.

For starters, be sure you have *thoroughly* cleaned the area with one of the several products now on the market, such as Nature's Miracle™, that contain enzymes that destroy odor-causing bacteria in the dog's urine. Then try one or more of several different environmental changes to his marking zone. For example, dogs tend not to want to soil their own dens and eating areas, so you might put his bed or food and water bowls by the door.

You can also change his association with the spot by doing training, massage, and play sessions there. Drop treats around the previously soiled area on a random but high-frequency basis. Finding treats gives him something different to think about in that spot.

You can also tether him near the area for short periods, 10 to 20 minutes at a time, to help him think of it more as a living space than a marking zone, and even anchor chew toys near the spot with a length of sturdy twine to further the positive association.

You mention that the doggie diaper you used was causing chafing. Did your dog soil the diaper, or stay dry when it was on? If he stayed dry, then this can be an effective management tool for short periods when you don't feel like supervising him closely. You might also look for a different brand of diaper. There are several on the market and one might fit him better than others. You could also try lining the parts that chafe with a softer material.

I understand why you don't want to crate him away from the family and agree that this isn't a productive solution, but you do need to be able to supervise him more closely so he doesn't have the opportunity to make mistakes. Tethers and leashes are great for this. The leash works fine when you have free hands; the tether is perfect when you are too busy to hold the leash. You can set up tether stations all over the house, so your dog can always be a part of family activities. Of course, he mustn't be allowed house freedom when no one is home. It is appropriate to crate him for a reasonable period of time during the day when no one is around to supervise, and at night when you are all sleeping. If he can't be crated routinely for more than eight hours a day, or if he can't hold it that long, you will need to arrange for someone—family member, neighbor or pet sitter—to come by and let him out for a potty break during the middle of the day.

Housetraining Redux

Then, in conjunction with your program of closer supervision, go back to the housetraining schedule you would use for a young puppy. Take him out on leash, every hour on the hour at first, and reward him for going outside.

Your dog may benefit from having a couple of designated spots outdoors where he is not only permitted to mark, but also encouraged to do so. This small dog has been trained to use a "patio potty" made and sold by Nelson's Back yard.

After a week with no accidents, increase the time to two hours. After another successful week, go to three hours between outside trips. Any backsliding is a reminder to increase supervision, and a red flag to return to the previous week's potty schedule. When you get another pee-free week, you can increase the time again.

On the off-chance that his marking at the door is really related to *needing* to go outside, be sure to install a noticeable signal during this training period, if he doesn't already have one, so he can let you know he has to pee. If you get excited whenever you take him out for a potty break, he will learn to get excited as his cue to you that he has to go. If you encourage him to bark each time you take him out, he will learn to bark to tell you his bladder needs relief. If you teach him to ring a bell with his nose or his paw (by putting a bell on a string, or a portable wireless electric doorbell where he can reach it) before you take him out, then that will become his cue.

Other situations can provoke marking behavior in dogs, primarily males, but even an occasional female dog—usually a very assertive one—can present a marking challenge. The first line of defense with a male dog marking challenge is usually neutering. Unsterilized male dogs are much more likely to mark than neutered ones, since it is usually the testosterone that drives the behavior of compulsively claiming possessions and territory. Sometimes, neutering alone will solve the problem, once the hormones are gone and the dog has time to forget why he was so compelled to lift his leg on everything in sight. Many times, however, a behavior modification program is still necessary to help the dog unlearn the marking habit, particularly if he has been practicing the behavior for a long time. A good argument for juvenile spay/neuter, by the way…

Marking is often more generalized around the household, as opposed to being focused at one specific spot. For example, a dog may choose to mark the possessions of a particular family member, feeling for some reason that he needs to make a strong statement about identifying items belonging specifically to that person. It may be because he has a particularly strong attachment to that person, or perhaps that person comes in contact with scents in the outside world that are particularly provocative to the dog. Other dogs are prone to marking *any* new item brought into the household, as if it doesn't really belong there until he has "tagged" it. Again, the dog's reason for doing the marking is less important than our ability to put an end to the inappropriate behavior.

When marking is generalized, in addition to thoroughly cleaning of all spots, plus implementing the modification, management and training solutions already described, household members must be scrupulously conscientious about keeping the dog's likely marking targets put up out of leg-lift's reach. A critical part of a successful behavior modification program involves preventing the dog from practicing the behavior. If Dad insists on setting the grocery bags on the floor in the mudroom, the corn flakes are likely to get marked. If Mom leaves her briefcase on the floor in the corner while she hangs up her coat in the front hall closet, she can expect to come back later and find a sticky trickle staining the leather. Sometimes it's harder to train the humans than the dogs, but it's important that all family members make the necessary changes to their own behavior in order to help the dog succeed in changing his.

Yet another scenario that can evoke inappropriate marking is conflict between dogs within the household. This may be a short-term reaction to a new canine arrival, or an ongoing conflict between two dogs within the family. If you have a dog that you know has marking tendencies, revert to your management and supervision protocols the instant you bring a new dog into the home—don't wait until the marking starts up again. Hopefully, within a short time, your marker will accept the new family member and you can slowly relax your vigilance. If you are faced with a long-term canine personality conflict that is fueling the marking, then you will need to resolve the relationship problem before you can expect the marking to stop. Meanwhile, exercise all your modification, management and training talents to prevent the dog—or dogs—from having opportunities to practice their marking skills.

I know many dog owners and trainers who have been successful in ending their dogs' inappropriate marking with a combination of the behavior modification, closer supervision, and retraining techniques presented here. My apprentice's dog was diagnosed as hyperthyroid. Medication for that condition, plus the judicious use of a belly-band (doggie diaper) and retraining efforts, have succeeded in overcoming his marking behavior. If you, too, have the commitment to make the necessary effort, I'll lay odds that you, too, can do this!

Mounting Block

An embarrassing behavior? Yes, but it can be stopped

Luke had been at the shelter for more than a month, and staff was delighted when the 2-year-old Cattle Dog mix was finally adopted to what seemed like the perfect home. Introductions at the shelter with the adopter's other dog went reasonably well—although the two didn't romp together, they seemed perfectly willing to peacefully co-exist. Luke went to his new home just before Christmas. Before New Year's, he was returned.

Her cheeks damp with tears, the adopter explained that the two dogs were fighting. Luke insisted on mounting Shane. Shane would tolerate the rudeness for awhile, but when he finally let Luke know that he found the behavior unacceptable, a battle would ensue. The intensity of the fights was increasing, and the adopter was concerned that one or both of the dogs was going to be badly injured. I discussed the situation with her, and agreed that returning Luke was the right decision.

It's Not About Sex

First, we're not talking about sexual behavior displayed by intact male and female dogs used for breeding. High hormone levels and normal sexual responses to other intact dogs are different from "problem mounting." Sometimes, an owner will report that when her young dog plays with other dogs, he gets overstimulated and will attempt to mount another dog or even just "air-hump" for a few seconds. In pre-adolescent and neutered dogs, this is generally a product of physiologic arousal—an inappropriate response triggered by sensory stimuli, motor activity, and/or emotional reactivity.

The dog who is most likely to be reported as having a real mounting problem is the dog who routinely mounts people, or, like Luke, who mounts other dogs to the point of provocation. This sort of mounting behavior has nothing to do with sexual activity. Rather, it's often a social behavior, and sometimes a stress reliever. Nonsexual mounting of other dogs is generally a status, control or challenge behavior, although when practiced by puppies it's primarily about play and social learning, beginning as early as 3-4 weeks. Mounting of humans is strictly non-sexual; it may be about control, it can be attention-seeking, and it can be a stress-reliever.

Dogs will also mount inanimate objects. Our Pomeranian will get intimate with our sofa cushions if we leave the house and take all the other dogs with us. While dogs do sometimes masturbate for pleasure, in Dusty's case I am convinced he's not seizing a moment of privacy for self-gratification, but rather mounts the cushions as a way to relieve his stress of being left "home alone."

In fact, if dogs did wait for some private time to engage in their mounting behaviors, most owners would be far less concerned about it. But dogs, having no shame, are far more likely to take advantage of a visit from the boss, or the in-laws, to display their leg-hugging prowess. Regardless of how much you love your dog, it's embarrassing to have him pay such inappropriate attention to your guests.

Mounting Your Campaign

Like a good many canine behaviors that we humans find annoying, inconvenient or embarrassing, mounting is a perfectly normal dog behavior. And like other such annoying, inconvenient, and embarrassing behaviors, it's perfectly reasonable for us to be able to tell our dogs to stop!

Brief bouts that involve mounting of other dogs in canine social interactions might be acceptable, as long as it doesn't lead to bloodletting, or oppression of the mountee. Mounting of human body parts rarely is acceptable, nor is mounting that leads to dogfights, as in Luke's case.

So, if there's a Luke whose mounting behavior is wreaking havoc in your family pack, what do you do?

The longer the dog has practiced his mounting behavior, the harder it is to change. So it's logical that the sooner you intervene in your dog's unacceptable mounting, the better your chances for behavior modification success.

Neutering is an obvious first step. A 1976 study found an 80 percent decrease in mounting behavior following castration. (This is far more often a male dog behavior problem than a female one.) The same study determined that within 72 hours of surgery, the bulk of hormones have left the dog's system. Since mounting is partially a learned behavior as well as hormone-driven, the extent to which neutering will help will be determined at least in part by how long the dog has been allowed to practice the behavior. Just one more strong argument for juvenile sterilization, between the ages of eight weeks and six months, rather than waiting for your dog to mature.

Dog-Dog Mounting

Luke, at age two, had been practicing his mounting behavior for many months. In addition, as a mostly Cattle Dog, he was assertive and controlling. When Shane attempted to voice his objections, Luke let him know that he would brook no resistance. Shane, a Shepherd/Husky mix, also had an assertive personality, so rather than backing down in the face of Luke's assertions of dominance, he fought back. Neither dog was willing to say "Lassie," and so the battles escalated.

In contrast, we later introduced Shane to a somewhat timid but playful 4-month-old Lab puppy. Dunkin also attempted to mount Shane in puppy playfulness. When Shane snapped at Dunkin, the pup backed off apologetically; in a short time the two were playing together, with only occasional puppy attempts to mount, which were quickly quelled by a dirty look from the older dog. No harm, no foul.

Similarly, you will need to work harder to convince your adult, well-practiced dog to quit climbing on other dogs than you will a young pup, and there's more potential with adult dogs for aggression if the recipient of unwanted attentions objects.

With both young and mature dogs, you can use time-outs to let your dog know that mounting behavior makes the fun stop. A tab (short, 4 to 6-inch piece of leash) or a dragline (a 4 to 6-foot light nylon cord) attached to your dog's collar can make enforcement of time-outs faster and more effective when you have to separate dogs—as well as safer.

Set your dog up for a play date with an understanding friend who has an understanding dog. Try to find a safely fenced but neutral play yard, so that home team advantage doesn't play a role. If a neutral yard isn't available, the friend's yard is better than your own, and outdoors is definitely preferable to indoors.

When you turn the dogs out together, watch yours closely. It's a good idea to have some tools on hand to break up a fight, should one occur.

If there's no sign of mounting, let them play. Be ready to intervene if you see the beginning signs of mounting behavior in your dog. This usually occurs as play escalates and arousal increases, if it didn't happen at the get-go.

As a first line of defense, try subtle body-blocking. Every time your dog approaches the other with obvious mounting body postures, step calmly in front of your dog to block him. If you're skilled, you may be able to simply lean your body forward or thrust out a hip or knee to send him the message that the fun's about to stop. This is more likely to work with the younger dog, who is less intense about his intent to mount. Be sure *not* to intervene if your dog appears to be planning appropriate canine play.

If body blocking doesn't work, as gently and unobtrusively as possible, grasp your tab or light line, then cheerfully announce, "Time out" and lead your dog to a quiet corner of the play yard. Sit with him there until you can tell that his arousal level has diminished, and then release him to return to his playmate. If necessary, have your friend restrain her dog at the same time so he doesn't come pestering yours during the time out.

These two dogs enjoy roughhousing together, but the spayed female occasionally mounts the younger, neutered male in an effort to put and keep him in his place—lower than her in the chain of command. As long as he defers, their play continues.

Keep in mind that the earlier you intervene in the mounting behavior sequence, the more effective the intervention, since your dog has not had time to get fully involved in the behavior. Also, it's important that you stay calm and cheerful about the modification program. Yelling at or physically correcting your dog increases the stress level in the environment, making a fight more likely, not less.

With enough repetitions, most dogs will give up the mounting, at least for the time being. With an older dog for whom the habit is well ingrained, you may need to repeat your time-outs with each new play session, and you may need to restrict his playmates to those who won't take offense to his persistently rude behavior. With a pup or juvenile, the behavior should extinguish fairly easily with repeated time outs, especially if he is neutered.

Just keep an eye out for "spontaneous recovery," when a behavior you think has been extinguished returns unexpectedly. Quick re-intervention with body blocks or time-outs should put the mounting to rest again.

Dog-Human Mounting

This embarrassing behavior is handled much the same way as dog-dog mounting. One difference is that you must educate your guests as to how they should respond if your dog attempts his inappropriate behavior.

Another difference is that some dogs will become aggressive if you physically try to remove them from a human leg or other body part. It works best to set up initial training sessions with friends who agree to be human mounting posts for training purposes, rather than relying on "real" guests to respond promptly and appropriately, at least until your dog starts to get the idea.

For your average, run-of-the-mill human mounting, ask your guests to stand up and walk away if your dog attempts to get too cozy. Explain that it is not sexual behavior, but rather attention-seeking, and anything they try to do to talk him out of it will only reinforce the behavior and make it worse. You can also use a light line here, to help extricate your friends from your dog's embrace, and to give him that oh-so-useful "Time out." If the behavior is too disruptive, you can tether Luke in the room where you are all socializing, so he still gets to be part of the social experience without repeatedly mugging your guests.

If your dog becomes aggressive when thwarted, he should be shut safely away in his crate when company comes. Social hour is not an appropriate time to work on aggressive behavior—it puts your guests at risk, and prevents all of you from being able to relax and enjoy the occasion.

If your dog becomes growly, snappy, or otherwise dangerous when you try to remove him from a human, you are dealing with serious challenge and control behavior. You would be wise to work with a good behavior consultant who can help you stay safe while you modify this behavior. The program remains essentially the same—using time outs to take away the fun every time the behavior happens, but may also involve the use of muzzles, and perhaps pharmaceutical intervention with your veterinarian's assistance, if necessary.

Dog-Object Mounting

Dog owners are often surprised to discover that some dogs will masturbate. Our diminutive Dusty discovered early in life that he was just the right height to stand over a raised human foot and engage in a little self-pleasuring if the person's legs were crossed. We squelched that behavior as soon as we realized what the heck he was doing.

There's no harm in it, as long as the objects used are reasonably appropriate (say, a washable stuffed animal that's his alone, as opposed to your favorite sofa cushions), and it doesn't become obsessive. Removing an inappropriate object or resorting to time-outs can redirect the behavior to objects that are more acceptable.

I've also known dogs to engage in push-ups on carpeting as a way to enjoy self-stimulation. You can use the time out if your dog chooses to do it in front of your guests, or whenever he does it in the "wrong" room (such as on the living room Berber), and leave him alone when he's in the "right" room (such as on the indoor-outdoor carpeting on the back porch).

If your dog practices the behavior to the degree that is appears obsessive—a not uncommon problem in animals, especially in zoos—then you may need some help with behavior modification. A behavior is generally considered obsessive when it is causes harm to the animal or interferes with his ability to lead a normal life. If your dog is rubbing himself raw on the Berber carpet, or spends hours each day having fun in the bedroom, that's obsessive behavior. There are behavior modification programs that can help with canine obsessive-compulsive disorders, and they often require pharmaceutical intervention, especially if the obsession is well-developed.

Say Please

In addition to specific behavior modification programs for mounting behavior, the "Say Please" program can be an important key to your ultimate success. No, I'm not suggesting you allow your dog to do inappropriate mounting if he says "please" first—the "Say Please" program requires that he perform a behavior, such as sit, before he gets *any* good stuff, like dinner, treats, petting, going outside. This helps create structure in the pack, and constantly reminds him that *you* are in charge and in control of all the good stuff. Since a fair amount of mounting has to do with control, "Say Please" is right on target.

"Good Manners" classes are also of benefit when you are mounting your defense against your mounting dog's behavior. If he's trained to respond promptly to cues, the "ask for an incompatible behavior" technique can serve to minimize mounting. If you see your dog approaching a guest with a gleam in his eye, your "Go to your place" cue will divert him to his rug on the opposite side of the room. He can't "Down" and mount a leg at the same time. Nor can he do pushups on the rug if he is responding to your request for a "Sit."

If you start early and are consistent about discouraging your dog's inappropriate mounting, you should be successful in making the embarrassing behavior go away.

The Behavior Formerly Known as Begging

Redefine it as attention to food and use it to your advantage

Lucy lies at my feet with a shiny coat and happy smile while I eat dinner, her bright eyes following each forkful of food as it travels from my plate to my mouth. When I work with Lucy in the training center, I get the same rapt focus as she performs her exercises in anticipation of the occasional Click! and treat that mark a superlative performance. Is this focused stare simply a form of attention—coveted and prized by obedience competitors and other dog trainers? Or is it begging—a behavior often maligned?

It is, in fact, the exact same behavior—offering attention to a human in hopes that a tasty morsel might result. Lucy pays attention in the training center because I've highly reinforced that behavior. I also reinforce her for lying at my feet at mealtimes rather than demand-barking or whining for food, or chasing after our cats, two other family members who enjoy sharing our evenings.

Block Access

I appreciate and cultivate Lucy's attention at mealtimes, occasionally rewarding her for calm, quiet behavior with a morsel from the pile of dog treats I keep next to my own plate for that purpose. If she were to jump up, which she doesn't, I would mark the inappropriate behavior with an "Oops!" and block her access to my plate with my body while turning away from her. Just as the Click! of the clicker tells her when her behavior has earned a reward, the "Oops" tells her which behavior made the opportunity for a treat *go away*.

In past times, when food was scorned as a training tool and physical corrections with choke chains and prong collars dominated the training scene, attention for food—begging, if you will—was roundly discouraged. A dog who sat at your feet during a meal, attentive to the movement of food, was scolded and sent away to the corner, banished to another room, or worse, the back yard. "Inappropriate, rude dog behavior!" we claimed.

But appropriate behavior is in the dog owner's mind. Today's modern, positive trainers recognize the value of food rewards to elicit the canine trainee's willing participation and cooperation. No longer do we discourage attention for food. Instead, we cultivate, even treasure it. The last thing we want to do is scold a dog for attentive food-related behavior.

A dog's goal in life is to get good stuff, and dogs are naturally opportunistic eaters—most will eat good stuff just about any time they get the chance unless they are sick or stressed. They also learn to do what works, especially what works to get the good stuff. Dogs learn that if they watch humans long enough, sooner or later someone will drop a bit of food, either on purpose, or accidentally. It's natural, then, for dogs to watch us intently when we're handling food.

Rather than trying to discourage a very strongly hard-wired behavior—"watch food, eat food"—you can use it to your advantage by linking the "watch food" behavior to an appropriately polite behavior, such as "Lie quietly by my feet during meals," or "Sit perfectly straight at heel when on leash." You're reinforcing attentive food-related behavior when you toss a treat, while at the same time you're reinforcing good manners.

That doesn't mean you have to tolerate *inappropriate* behavior. If you too, as a member of the positive-training generation, recognize the value of your dog's food-focused attention, you can redefine begging. You can use positive methods to reinforce whatever appropriate mealtime behavior you want from your dog—part of the fun of being the human in the primate-canine relationship is that you get to decide.

The most successful way to achieve appropriate behavior is to use a combination of management—to prevent your dog from being reinforced for undesirable behaviors—and training—in which you reinforce the behaviors you want. First, you need to have a clear idea of what you want your dog to do. In the case of dinnertime behavior, you have several options.

Option #1: Lying At Your Feet

You can choose, as I have, to allow your dog to lie politely at your feet. Of course, you get to define "politely" for your own dog, but for Lucy and me it means no whining, barking, pawing, climbing onto my lap, or helping herself to items on my plate or fork. To accomplish this, I steadfastly ignore any of those impolite behaviors while using body blocking to prevent her from helping herself to my dinner, not even giving her the satisfaction of my eye contact if she makes noise.

Body blocking consists simply of occupying the coveted space—in this case near my dinner—with my body any time I see her about to try to get closer to my meal. If that didn't work, I'd use a cable tether to secure her just out of reach so I could enjoy my food without having to defend it. Don't get me wrong—Lucy was never a persistent plate-surfer. A few minor body blocks early in our relationship successfully thwarted her efforts to help herself to my meals.

At the same time I ignore any unwanted behavior, I make sure to reinforce desirable behavior by occasionally rewarding her for lying quietly at my feet. I usually use tiny bits of her dog food or treats for this, but may occasionally slip her a snippet of my own meal. This makes her no more—or no less—likely to perform the attentive behavior previously known as begging. It's all treats to her. (See "The 'People Food' Myth" pg 217.)

This Cattle Dog mix has been trained to lie quietly and attentively during meals without whining, barking, pawing, or table surfing.

Option #2: Lying Somewhere Else In the Room

If it makes you uncomfortable to have your dog staring up at you while you dine, or if other family members can't be relied on to ignore undesirable behaviors, it may make more sense to have your dog share your mealtimes from afar, from a place you've designated as his dinner spot.

Teach your dog a "Go to Your Rug" exercise separate from dinnertime at first. Set a comfortable dog bed or throw rug where you want his spot to be, a fair distance from the dinner table. Say "Rug" or Go to your rug" and lead him to his spot. Have him lie down on the rug, then Click! or say "Yes!" and feed him a tasty treat. If he doesn't lie down easily for you on cue, just Click! and treat for going to his rug at first, work on the "Down" separately, and put them together later.

Click! and treat him several times for staying on his rug—you want him to understand that *staying* on the rug is a very rewarding behavior, not just *going* to his rug. Throughout the day, you can also secretly drop treats onto his rug, so he never knows when he will find a yummy surprise there. If you happen to find him lying on his rug of his own accord, be sure to give him an extra special Click! and treat. The more you can get the message to him that lying on his rug is a very rewarding behavior, the better.

When you first incorporate this exercise into the actual dinner routine, you may need to use a tether to prevent him from reverting to his old table-attention behavior. When you tether him, give him a stuffed Kong™ or some other delectable goodie that will hold his attention for the duration of dinner. Occasionally during the meal, tell him "yes" or Click! your clicker, walk over to his rug and feed him a treat—human food or a doggie treat. As long as he's being rewarded for lying quietly on his rug and not hanging out at the table, you're reinforcing your version of polite canine table manners. Eventually you'll be able to remove the tether, and if you remember to occasionally reward him for his good rug behavior, he'll be happy to stay there for dinner.

If you want to share his company for dinner but not have to worry about keeping him in his place, simply keep him tethered. Alternatively, you can provide him with a crate in the corner of the dining room, where he can happily eat his dinner from a stuffed Kong while you eat your own, unmolested, from your plate.

Body blocking can be a successful strategy to reduce begging behavior.

Option #3: Being In Another Room, Or As a Last Resort, Outside

If you prefer not to have your dog share the dinner hour with you, I encourage you to re-think this choice. Dogs are highly social creatures, and this is a relatively easy way to satisfy a significant part of his social needs, but if a family member is dead set against having a doggie diner, you can use physical barriers to bar your dog from the room during meals. A baby gate across the dining area door can block his physical presence but allow him visual contact with the family. A closed door shuts him out completely, as does crating him in another room. In each of these cases, you can help him be more accepting of the separation and reinforce polite away-from-family behavior by providing him with a tasty chew object that will occupy him during your meal.

I suggest "outside" as your very last choice. Isolating your dog in the back yard during the dinner hour may frustrate him and lead to barking, digging, jumping on or scratching at the back door in efforts to rejoin his family. You are less likely to remember to reinforce appropriate behaviors when he's shut outside, so he's more likely to resort to attention-seeking behaviors to let you know you've forgotten him. If you treat him as a beloved fam-ily member in other aspects of his life with you—as is ideal—this is a poor time to change the rules on him.

Want some great news? Polite dinner behavior transfers easily to other food situations: the family eating buttered popcorn on the sofa while watching a movie; the toddler holding a dripping ice cream cone on a warm summer day; or preparing the holiday turkey on your kitchen counter. In each of these cases, your dog can quickly realize that his best chance of getting some—popcorn, ice cream, turkey—is to lie quietly at the feet of the one who is in control of the good stuff.

Lucy isn't the only one of our dogs who shares our meals. Katy the Kelpie, Tucker, Dubhy, and Bonnie all understand the value of polite food-related behavior. They can all sit or lie quietly near us as we eat, hoping for a morsel to fall their way. Not one is doing what I'd define as begging—they are simply attentive for an opportunity to get good stuff—as nature made them.

The "People Food" Myth

More times than I care to count, new Peaceable Paws students have resisted my suggestions for using foods like canned chicken, turkey franks and string cheese as training treats. "If I feed my dog people food," they insist, "he will learn to beg."

What kind of bizarre logic is this? A dog has no idea who manufactured his train-ing treats or whether they're labeled for sale to humans or canines. If your dog shares a noted former president's well-known disdain for broccoli—a vegetable commonly viewed as "people food"—and you feed him only broccoli from the table for giving you his attention, he'll learn that giving you his attention at the table is singularly unrewarding; he's not likely to "beg" for broccoli. If you also use broccoli for his training sessions, your efforts to gain his attention are likely to meet with little success.

The commercial dog food industry claims scientifically-supported superior food formulas. At the other end of the food discussion, a growing number of dog owners are converting partly or exclusively to feeding their dogs "raw" or "natural" diets consisting, at least in part of—you guessed it—fresh meats, fruits and vegetables. In other words, "people food."

In between the two ends of the doggie-diet continuum, a relatively new segment of the commercial dog food industry produces high-end, commercially processed foods using human-grade ingredients. Open a few cans of this class of dog food and you'll find identifiable chunks of carrots, potatoes, peas, chicken, turkey, duck, and more, in a savory sauce or gravy. Sure looks like people food. You may be tempted to eat some yourself!

It's true that a regular diet of hot dogs, cheese or fatty pieces cut off your pork chops isn't good for your dog. But using good quality foods for your dog's training treats and meals, whether marketed for use by dogs or humans, will keep him healthy.

Some Foods to Avoid

Some "people foods," however, have the potential to do serious harm to dogs, even in small amounts. Regardless of where you fall on the doggie diet debate, it's wise to studiously avoid feeding your dog items from this short list:

- Chocolate: Contains theobromine, which is highly toxic to dogs—the darker the chocolate, the more toxic. If your dog consumes chocolate, seek immediate advice from your veterinarian.

- Onions and garlic: Can cause hemolytic anemia in dogs. Small amounts are generally not harmful, but it's better to be safe than sorry.

- Grapes and raisins: Can cause kidney damage and even death in some dogs. While the exact reason hasn't been identified, they're best avoided in *any* quantity.

- Pork products: Dogs' systems don't deal well with fatty foods; excessive amounts can cause pancreatitis. If you must feed your dog some of your pork chop, feed him a bit of the center meaty portion.

Part Five
AGGRESSION

Our society is developing an increasing intolerance for dogs who bite—even dogs who bite appropriately, with lots of provocation. This section will help you gain a better understanding of that natural, normal (but socially unacceptable) behavior—biting—that every living, breathing dog is capable of. Learn what to do if your own dog has aggression or reactivity issues, and how to protect yourself if you encounter someone *else's* dog who takes a dislike to your presence.

Bite-Me-Not

One of the most important things a puppy needs to learn: bite inhibition

Animal care professionals are fond of saying, "All dogs will bite, given the right (wrong) circumstances." If that's the case, how have I managed to suffer only two punctures in a 30-plus-year career working with dogs? Partly through reading and responding to canine body language well enough to avoid provoking an attack. Partly, I'm sure, through luck. But largely, I suspect, because many dogs possess a wonderful quality known as "bite inhibition."

Unconscious Control

Bite inhibition is the ability of a dog to control the force of his bite. Without it, even a playful grab at your sleeve when you are wrestling with your dog or a quick snap of shocked self-defense (when you accidentally step on his tail, for example) can result in a serious or painful puncture. In contrast, a dog in those same circumstances who has well-developed bite inhibition can grab your wrist and even gently shake it, or bite at the ankle of the foot that is planted on his tail—without leaving a mark or causing you more than a moment's minor discomfort.

Canine behaviorists theorize that dogs have evolved to normally develop bite inhibition for good reason. In canine society, dogs normally use escalation of force effectively to get their messages across without inflicting grievous injury upon each other. This is important from a survival standpoint; if pack members consistently punctured each others' skins they'd risk their own injury and debilitation, even death, as well as that of the pack mates they depend upon for mutual protection, food gathering, and survival. Even when encountering canines from an "alien" pack, the less actual physical engagement, the better the chances of survival for all concerned.

Fortunately for humans, this bite inhibition behavior often transfers to us, as honorary members of our canines' social groups.

How to Get It

Bite inhibition is clearly a desirable thing. So how do you get it? Or more correctly, how does your dog get it? It's not something you'll find on the shelf of your local pet supply store!

Bite inhibition has both genetic and environmental components. That is, a dog can inherit the potential to use gentle bite pressure from parents who are also genetically programmed to mouth softly, and he can also learn to bite softly. Of course, the more strongly a desirable behavior trait is encoded in the genes, the easier it is to nurture appropriate behaviors. If your pup lacks good genes for bite inhibition, he'll need lots of environmental influence—the sooner, the better.

Genetics of bite inhibition is one of the very important reasons to meet a pup's parents, if possible, when you purchase from a breeder. While sometimes one or both parents simply aren't available for legitimate reasons, if the breeder declines because either of the parents aren't friendly, have bitten in the past, or cautions you to be careful when interacting with them, you may not want to risk purchasing a puppy from those lines. Make it a point to specifically ask if either parent has ever been bitten and if so, the severity of the bite, and how the breeder would characterize both dogs' levels of bite inhibition. If she's not willing to discuss the topic, doesn't understand the question, or seems not to be forthcoming with information, make your puppy purchase decision accordingly.

If you're adopting from a shelter, Mom and Dad aren't likely to be around. When you can't meet parents, your personal observations during puppy selection—always important anyway—become even more critical. Most puppies will engage in some degree of mouthing—it's how they explore their world. However, if you play with a number of puppies, you'll discover that some mouth your hands very gently, others will repeatedly bite hard enough with their wickedly sharp baby teeth to cause pain, and still others will even draw blood.

Those who consistently mouth gently have a healthy degree of innate bite inhibition and or have learned their lessons well from Momdog and siblings who let them know when they bite too hard. Those who cause pain or draw blood need more lessons. There's a good chance they can still turn into great dogs—and it will take more input on your part to teach them to be gentle with their teeth. The older a pup is, the more effort it will take to install bite inhibition, and the greater the likelihood that you'll be less successful.

One of the reasons it's such a tragedy to remove a pup from his litter too soon is that he'll miss those all-important bite-inhibition lessons from Momdog and sibs. This is also one of the big drawbacks of adopting a singleton pup—one who had no littermates. I strongly recommend you wait to take your new pup home until he's at least seven weeks, preferably eight, regardless of how eager the breeder is to give him up. Your own bite inhibition lessons can never be as effective with your pup as those from his own kin. No matter how hard we try, we just can't speak dog as well as dogs can.

There is a good reason to put up with those needle-like teeth. Puppies learn lifelong "bite inhibition" from consistent consequences for too-hard and just-right chewing and mouthing. If it is forbidden altogether, they may never develop a "soft" mouth.

Don't Punish!

In past times, and unfortunately sometimes still today, dog owners were counseled to use aversives to try to teach bite inhibition. If a puppy gnawed on your hands, some trainers suggested holding his muzzle closed as punishment, "cuffing" him under the chin with an open palm, or worse, shoving a fist down the pup's throat. In a word…"Don't!"

Not only are these methods abusive and have the potential to teach your pup to fear your hands, they can also trigger aggressive responses from assertive or fearfully defensive pups. If they do succeed in putting a stop to the mouthing, you may have taught the pup that his only options are to "Not Bite" or to "Bite Really Hard" rather than the third important "If You Must Bite, Bite Gently" option.

Remember, all dogs bite, given the right (wrong) set of circumstances. With enough provocation, even the most tolerant and gentle of dogs might be induced to put her mouth on human skin. With good bite inhibition, provocation is likely to result in a polite, "Please don't do that" mouth-on-skin warning. Without it, the provoked dog is likely to leap to cause serious damage when he puts his teeth on someone.

Things to Do

The older a dog is when you start trying to teach bite inhibition, the greater the likelihood that, while you may succeed in teaching the dog to consciously use his mouth more gently, he will still fall back into hard biting during times of stress and arousal.

If you have a pup with naturally good bite inhibition, consider yourself blessed, and take steps to preserve this valuable natural resource. If not, start immediately to cultivate bite inhibition.

Play fetch games with your pup to direct his mouth toward appropriate toys to take some of the "wild puppy" edge off his bite. Be sure to give him plenty of exercise daily. A tired pup is a well-behaved pup. Consult your vet for guidance on how much exercise is appropriate for your pup.

Work with his bite inhibition while he's in an ex-pen or on a tether so you can calmly escape his shark teeth. Begin petting him and playing gently. As long as he's not causing pain, even if he's putting his mouth on you with some pressure, continue playing.

If he bites and hurts you, calmly say "Ouch" and walk away from him. Step outside the reach of the tether, or exit the ex-pen so he can't follow you and continue to bite. The "Ouch" isn't intended to stop the biting; it only marks the behavior—tells him what he did that made you leave. This is negative punishment, his biting behavior makes a good thing—you—go away.

Wait 20-30 seconds to give him time to calm down, then go back to him and calmly resume playing. If he's barking and aroused, wait to return until he settles. As long as he bites softly, continue playing. Any time his bite hurts, say "Ouch" and leave.

If several repetitions don't seem to reduce hard biting, give him longer timeouts to give him more time to settle. Over time, as he learns to control his hardest biting, you can raise the bar—use the same methods to gradually shape a softer and softer mouth. When he's no longer biting hard enough to hurt, use your "Ouch" technique for moderately hard bites, then medium ones, then finally, as he outgrows the puppy stage at 5-6 months, for any bites to skin at all.

If you must handle him when he's being "bitey" to groom, trim nails, attach leash, etc., keep his teeth busy nibbling at treats you hold in one hand while you work with the other, or have a helper feed treats so you have both hands free to groom, trim or leash.

This method of marking the inappropriate behavior and walking away from the pup imitates, to some degree, the behavior of Momdog and littermates when a pup bites too hard. If needle-sharp teeth clamp too hard on Momdog's tender teats, she may stand up and exit the den. Pups learn to nurse gently to keep the milk bar open. Similarly, when pups play together, if one is too rough his playmate may "Yipe!" and decline to continue the game. Pup learns to inhibit his bite to keep the fun happening.

Some trainers teach owners to give a high-pitched "Yipe" or "Ouch!" to mimic a littermate's protestations. While this can work with some pups, others find it more arousing—perhaps because we don't really know what we're saying when we try to speak Dog.

I tell my clients to skip trying to imitate a puppy "Yipe!" and just use the calm "Ouch" as a marker. If you do try the "Yipe!" once or twice and it works, great. If it doesn't, don't keep doing it! Simply replace it with a more composed marker.

More Tips

Pups with poor bite inhibition can exhibit exceedingly frustrating behaviors. It's easy to lose patience when those needle-sharp puppy canines sink into your skin. Remember that these "sharky" little guys usually *love* reactions; you're playing into their paws when you lose your temper with them.

Use management solutions such as crates and baby gates so your pup doesn't have access to you when you're dressed up. Have treats and toys handy so you can toss them away from you and divert him when he's approaching with mayhem on his mind. Do lots of work on the tether so you can repeatedly send the message that hard bites make the good stuff go away.

Young children should play with a shark-pup only under direct supervision, and only when the puppy is in a mellow mood. Most pups develop predictable cycles—if you know he's calmest early to mid-afternoon, that's when he can play with the kids. Controlled games only—no running around the back yard squealing while puppy tries to latch onto chubby, tender toddler legs!

If you're doing positive training, with treats—and of course we hope you are—a hard-mouth puppy can bring you to tears and leave your fingers bleeding as they clamp down on treats. It's reassuring to know it gets easier when they lose their sharp baby canine teeth at five to six months, but meanwhile you're tempted to stop training, or at least stop using treats! Try these temporary solutions:

- Keep the treat hidden in your closed fist until you feel your pup's mouth soften. Then open your hand and feed the treat from the palm of your hand like you would feed a horse. This teaches the pup he gets the treat when his mouth is soft, and prevents finger-shredding because he's taking it from your palm.

- Use metal finger splints. Available over-the-counter at pharmacies, these handy gadgets protect your fingers and teach him to be soft because most dogs don't like to bite on metal.

- Blend up a soft solution of treats and feed it from a camping food-tube.

- Feed treats from a metal spoon. This keeps your fingers out of his mouth, and teaches him to be gentle.

- Toss treats on the floor instead of hand-feeding. This is a temporary solution, as there are many times in training when it's far preferable to feed from the hand than the floor. On occasion though, it can save your fingers—and your sanity.

It may take a while to see the positive results of your gradual bite inhibition lessons, but it's worth it. Lucy came to us at five months of age with a pretty hard bite—you knew when she took a treat from your fingers! It took months, and a lot of patience, to get her bite to soften.

At first it seemed we made no progress at all. Then for several months she'd start to bite down, I'd say "Ouch," and feel her pause and relax her mouth before taking the treat. Now at age 18 months she takes treats sweetly, leaving fingers behind, intact, without a reminder. That alone was worth the effort, and I pray that it translates to true bite inhibition and nothing more than a Level 2 bite (see below) should the occasion ever arise that she feels compelled to put her teeth on human skin in earnest.

Dr. Ian Dunbar's Bite Hierarchy

The following descriptions were developed by Dr. Ian Dunbar, veterinary behaviorist and pioneer in the field of gentle puppy training. They are often used by trainers and behavior professionals as a shorthand method of referring to the severity of a bite that a dog has inflicted. Rather than having to describe injuries in gruesome detail, we can just say, "The 90-pound Labrador has inflicted Level 4 bites on three separate occasions." (Yikes!)

Level 1: Harassment but no skin contact

Level 2: Tooth contact on skin but no puncture

Level 3: Skin punctures; 1-4 holes from a single bite (all punctures shallower than length of canine)

Level 4: 1-4 holes, deep black bruising with punctures deeper than length of canine (dog bit and clamped down), or slashes in both directions from puncture (dog bit and shook head)

Level 5: Multiple bite attack with deep punctures, or multiple attack incident

Level 6: Killed victim and/or consumed flesh

The Gift of Growling

Why you should <u>never</u> punish a dog for growling

Clients always appear a bit stunned at first when I tell them their dog's growl is a *good* thing. In fact, a growl is something to be greatly treasured.

These are my aggression consultation clients, who are in my office in desperation, as a last resort, hoping to find some magic pill that will turn their biting dog into a safe companion. They are often dismayed and alarmed to discover that the paradigm many of us grew up with—punish your dog harshly at the first sign of aggression—has contributed to and exacerbated the serious and dangerous behavior problem that has led them to my door.

It seems intuitive to punish growling. Growling leads to biting, and dogs who bite people often must be euthanized, so let's save our dog's life and nip biting in the bud by punishing him at the first sign of inappropriate behavior. It makes sense, in a way—but when you have a deeper understanding of canine aggression, it's easy to understand why it's the absolute wrong thing to do.

Communication Efforts

Most dogs don't want to bite or fight. The behaviors that signal pending aggression are intended first and foremost to warn away a threat. The dog who *doesn't want to* bite or fight tries his hardest to make you go away. He may begin with subtle signs of discomfort that are often overlooked by many humans—tension in body movements, a stiffly wagging tail.

"Please," he says gently, "I don't want you to be here."

If you continue to invade his comfort zone, his threats may intensify, with more tension, a hard stare, and a low growl.

"I mean it," he says more firmly, "I want you to leave."

A professional dog trainer or behavior consultant can help you learn to see and interpret the signals your dog uses to try to tell you that he is uncomfortable, so you can remove the stressor—or at least, remove the dog from a stressful situation.

If those are ignored, he may become more insistent, with an air snap, a bump of the nose, or even open mouth contact that closes gently on an arm but doesn't break skin.

"Please," he says, "don't *make* me bite you."

If that doesn't succeed in convincing you to leave, the dog may feel compelled to bite hard enough to break skin in his efforts to protect self, territory, members of his social group, or other valuable resources.

Caused by Stress

What many people don't realize is that aggression is caused by stress. The stressor may be related to pain, fear, intrusion, threats to resources, past association, or anticipation of any of these things. An assertive, aggressive dog attacks because he's stressed by the intrusion of another dog or human into his territory. A fearful dog bites because he's stressed by the approach of a human. An injured dog lacerates the hand of his rescuer because he's stressed by pain.

When you punish a growl or other early warning signs, you may succeed in suppressing the growl, snarl, snap, or other warning behavior—but you don't take away the stress that caused the growl in the first place. In fact, you *increase* the stress, because now you, the dog's owner, have become unpredictable and violent as well.

Worst of all, and most significantly, if you succeed in suppressing the warning signs, you end up with a dog who *bites without warning*. He has learned that it's not safe to warn, so he doesn't.

If a dog is frightened of children, he may growl when a child approaches. You, being a conscientious and responsible owner, are well aware of the stigma—and fate—of dogs who bite children, so you punish your dog with a yank on the leash and a loud "No! Bad dog!" Every time your dog growls at a child you do this, and quickly your dog's fear of children is confirmed—children *do* make bad things happen! He likes children even less, but he learns not to growl at them to avoid making you turn mean.

You think he's learned that it's not okay to be aggressive to children, because the next time one passes by, there's no growl. "Phew," you think to yourself. "We dodged *that* bullet!"

Convinced that your dog now accepts children because he no longer growls at them, the next time one approaches and asks if he can pat your dog, you say yes. In fact, your dog has simply learned not to growl, but children still make him very uncomfortable. Your dog is now super-stressed, trying to control his growl as the child gets nearer and nearer so you don't lose control and punish him, but when the scary child reaches out for him he can't hold back any longer—he lunges forward and snaps at the child's face. Fortunately, you're able to restrain him with the leash so he doesn't connect. You, the dog, and the child are all quite shaken by the incident.

It's time to change your thinking.

"Help!"

A growl is a dog's cry for help. It's your dog's way of telling you he can't tolerate a situation—as if he's saying, "I can't handle this, please get me out of here!"

Your first response when you hear your dog growl should be to calmly move him away from the situation, while you make a mental note of what you think may have triggered the growl. Make a graceful exit. If you act stressed you'll only add to his stress and make a bite more, not less, likely. Don't worry that removing him rewards his aggression; your first responsibility is to keep others safe and prevent him from biting.

If the growl was triggered by something *you* were doing, stop doing it. Yes, your dog learned one tiny lesson about how to make you stop doing something he doesn't like, but you'll override that when you give him lots of lessons about how that thing that made him uncomfortable makes *really, really good stuff* happen.

This is where counter-conditioning comes in. Your dog growls because he has a negative association with something—say he growls when you touch his paw. For some reason, he's convinced that having his paw touched is a bad thing. If you start by touching his knee, then feeding him a smidgen of chicken, and keep repeating that, he'll come to think that you touching his knee *makes* chicken happen. He'll *want* you to touch his leg so he gets a bit of chicken.

Please make sure your dog's discomfort with you touching his paw is not related to an association with pain. If it hurts when you touch him there, counter-conditioning won't work. It's a good idea to get a full veterinary workup if there's any chance your dog's growling may be pain-related.

When you see him eagerly search for chicken when you touch his knee, you can move your hand slightly lower and touch there, until you get the same "Where's my chicken?!" response at the new spot. Gradually move closer and closer to his paw, until he's delighted to have you touch his foot—it makes chicken happen! Now practice with each foot, until he's uniformly delighted to have you touch all of them. Remember that the touch comes first, so it consistently predicts the imminent arrival of chicken.

If at any time in the process—which could take days, weeks, or even months, depending on the dog and how well you apply the protocol—you see the dog's tension increase, you've moved too quickly. Back up a few inches to where he's comfortable being touched and start again. Or, there may be other stressors present that are increasing his tension. Conduct an environmental check to be sure nothing else is happening that's adding to his stress. Have the rowdy grandkids leave the room, give him a little time to relax, and start again.

Remember, dogs can't tell us in words what's bothering them, but they can communicate a lot with their body language and canine vocal sounds. Pay attention to what your dog is telling you. Listen with heart and compassion. Be gentle when your dog tells you he needs help. Come to his rescue. Treasure his growl.

No Warning?

Contrary to popular belief, dogs only rarely—if ever—bite someone without plenty of warning signals. The problem is, not enough dog owners are alert to or educated about those signals and precursors to biting. A dog's escalation of force often includes the following behaviors, frequently in the following order:

1. Non-contact body language: freeze, hard stare, a "whale-eye"—a quick sideways looks with the whites of the eyes flashing—growl, snarl, air-snap

2. Mouth-closed contact: a hard bump of the nose, no tooth contact; the dog's way of politely saying, "Please don't do that…"

3. Mouth-open contact: mouth closes on skin with gentle to moderate pressure, as if the dog is saying, "I said don't *do* that!"

4. A dog with excellent bite inhibition stops here, unless given extreme provocation to bite. Dogs with lesser bite inhibition may skip some or all of the early warning steps and will eventually or quickly proceed to Level 3 bites that break skin, and perhaps higher.

Bully for You

Why (and how) you should intervene if your dog picks on others

You can find them everywhere—at dog parks and doggie daycare centers, in dog training classes, in your neighbor's yards. Perhaps even in your own home. "They" are canine bullies—dogs who overwhelm their potential playmates with overly assertive and inappropriate behaviors, like the out-of-control human bully on the school playground.

Jasper is a nine-month old Labradoodle from an Amish puppy mill, currently enrolled in one of my Peaceable Paws Good Manners classes. He was kept in a wire cage on a Pennsylvania farm until he was four months old, when his new owners purchased him. Katy Malcolm, their class instructor, asked me to sit in on the first end-of-class play session with Jasper because she was concerned that his lack of early socialization could present a challenge. She was right.

Sam was a 10-week old Golden Retriever puppy, well bred, purchased from a responsible breeder by knowledgeable dog owners who immediately enrolled him in one of my Peaceable Paws Puppy Good Manners classes to get him started on the right paw. Sam unexpectedly also turned out to be a challenge at his first end-of-class puppy play session.

These two dogs had considerably different backgrounds, but when it came time to play, both dogs exhibited bullying behaviors: Jasper because he never had a chance to learn how to interact appropriately with other dogs; Sam because—well—who knows? Genetics, maybe? Early experiences in his litter, maybe? Regardless of the reasons, both dogs required special handling if they were ever to have a normal canine social life.

Bullying Defined

In her excellent book *Fight!*, dog trainer and author Jean Donaldson defines bullying dogs (not to be confused with "Pitbull-type dogs") as those dogs for whom "roughness and harassment of non-consenting dogs is quite obviously reinforcing." Like the human playground bully, the bully dog gets a kick out of tormenting less-assertive members of his playgroup. Donaldson says, "They engage at it full tilt, with escalating frequency, and almost always direct it at designated target dogs."

When released with permission to "Go play," the poorly-socialized Labradoodle, Jasper, immediately pounced on the back of Mesa, an easy-going and confident Rottweiler who was playing nicely with Bo, a submissive but exuberant Golden Retriever. Jasper barked insistently, nipping at Mesa's back as she tried to ignore his social ineptness. Finally, fed up with his boorish behavior, she flashed her teeth at him one time, at which point he decided Bo was a better target for his attentions. Indeed, Bo found him overwhelming, a response that emboldened Jasper to pursue him even more energetically.

We intervened in his play with Mesa several times by picking up Jasper's dragging leash and giving him a time-out when his behavior was completely unacceptable, then releasing him to "Go play!" when he settled a bit. Each time we released him he promptly re-escalated to an unacceptable level of bullying, until Mesa herself told him to "Back off, Bud!" with a quick flash of her teeth.

Human controlled time outs were making no impression on Jasper. The canine corrections were more effective, but didn't stop the behavior; they only redirected it to a less capable victim. Because Bo wasn't assertive enough to back Jasper off, we ended the play as soon as Jasper turned his attentions to the softer dog.

Bully #2

Like Jasper's preferred victim, Sam's favorite bullying target was *also* a Rottweiler—not a breed you'd expect to find wearing an invisible "Bite me!" sign. Max was a pup about Sam's own age, who outweighed Sam considerably but was no match for the smaller pup's intensity.

Sam had given us no indication during class that he had a play problem. In fact, he was a star performer for his clicks and treats. However, when playtime arrived his demeanor changed from an attentive "What can I do to get you to click the clicker?" pupil to an "I'm tough and you just try to stop me" bully. Several seconds after the two pups began frolicking together, Sam suddenly pinned Max to the ground with a ferocious snarl, then released him briefly, just to pin him again in short order. Needless to say, we also intervened quickly in *that* relationship!

Appropriate Play

Owners often have difficulty distinguishing between appropriate and inappropriate play. Some may think that perfectly acceptable play behavior is bullying because it involves growling, biting, and apparently pinning the playmate to the ground. Appropriate play can, in fact, look and sound quite ferocious.

The difference is in the response of the playmate. If *both* dogs appear to be having a good time and no one's getting hurt, it's usually fine to allow the play to continue. Thwarting your dog's need to play by stopping him every time he engages another dog, even if it's rough play, can lead to *other* behavior problems.

With a bully, the playmate clearly does *not* enjoy the interaction. The softer dog may offer multiple appeasement and deference signals that are largely or totally ignored by the canine bully. The harassment continues, or escalates.

Anytime one play partner is obviously not having a good time, it's wise to intervene. A traumatic play experience can damage the softer dog's confidence and potentially induce a life long fear-aggression or "Reactive Rover" response—definitely not a good thing!

Some bullies seem to spring from the box full-blown. While Sam had, no doubt, already been reinforced for his bullying by the response of his softer littermates, he must have been born with a strong, assertive personality in order for the behavior to be as pronounced as it was by the tender age of 10 weeks. Jasper, on the other hand, may have been a perfectly normal puppy, but months of social deprivation combined with a strong desire to be social turned him into an inadvertent bully.

There can certainly be a learned component of any bullying behavior. As Jean Donaldson reminds us, the act of harassing a "non-consenting dog" is in and of itself reinforcing for bullies.

By definition, a behavior that's reinforced continues or increases—hence the importance of intervening with a bully at the earliest possible moment, rather than letting the behavior become more and more ingrained through reinforcement. As with most behavior modification, prognosis is brightest if the dog is young, if he hasn't had much chance to practice the unwanted behavior, and if he has not been repeatedly successful at it.

Four shots of the same playground bully, taken over a 20-minute period at a dog park. In the first photo, the Boxer-mix bully has blindsided a dog who just entered the park. In the next three, she focuses her attention on the same victim, a young Lab-mix. She clearly enjoys holding him down as variety of other dogs come over to investigate.

Oops!

Successful modification of bullying behavior requires attention to several elements:

- Skilled application of intervention tools and techniques: Leashes and long lines, no-reward markers (NRMs—see below) and time-outs.

- Excellent timing of intervention: Application of NRMs and time-outs.

- Reinforcement for appropriate behavior: Play continues or resumes when dog is calm or playing nicely.

- Selection of appropriate play partners: dogs who are not intimidated or traumatized by bullying behavior.

The most appropriate human intervention is the use of negative punishment in which the dog's behavior makes a good thing go away. In this case, the most appropriate negative punishment is a time-out. Used in conjunction with a **no-reward maker** (NRM) or "punishment" marker, this works best for bullying behavior.

NRM

The opposite of the clicker (or other reward marker such as the word, Yes!"), the NRM says, "*That* behavior made the good stuff go away." With bullying, the good stuff is the opportunity to play with other dogs. Just as the clicker *always* means a treat is coming, the NRM *always* means the behavior stops immediately or good stuff goes away—it's *not* to be used repeatedly as a threat or warning.

My preferred NRM, the one I teach and use if/when necessary, is the word "Oops" rather than the word "No" which is deliberately used to shut down behavior—and as such is usually delivered firmly or harshly and unfortunately often followed by physical punishment. "Oops" simply means, "Make another behavior choice or there will be an immediate loss of good stuff." An NRM is to be delivered in a non-punitive tone of voice. It's almost impossible to say "Oops" harshly.

Timing is just as important with your NRM as it is with your reward marker. It says, "Whatever you were doing the exact instant you heard the 'Oops!' is what earned your time-out." You'll use it the *instant* your dog's bully behavior appears, and if the bullying continues for more than a second or two more, grasp his leash or drag-line (a long, light line attached to his collar) and remove him from play. Don't repeat the NRM. Give him at least 20 seconds to calm down, more if he needs it, then release him to go play again. If several time-outs don't dampen the behavior even slightly, make them longer and make sure he's calm prior to returning to play.

If a half dozen time-outs have absolutely no effect, end the play session for the day. If the NRM *does* stop the bullying, thank your dog for responding, and allow him to continue playing under direct supervision, as his reward.

Another sometimes-effective approach to bully modification requires access to an appropriate "neutral dog"—a dog like Mesa who is confident enough to withstand the bully's assault without being traumatized or responding with inappropriate aggression in return. A flash of the pearly whites as a warning is fine. A full-out dogfight is not.

It's important to watch closely during interactions with the bully. Any sign the neutral dog is becoming unduly stressed by the encounters should bring the session to an immediate halt. A neutral dog may be able to modify your bully's behavior, and have it transfer to other dogs—or not. If not, you may be able to find one or two sturdy, neutral dogs who can be your dog's play companions, and leave the softer dogs to gentler play pals. Not all dogs get along with all other dogs.

Outcomes

Sam's owners were exceptionally committed to helping their pup overcome his inappropriate play behaviors. We continued to allow him to play with one or two other sturdy, resilient puppies, using an NRM and his leash to calmly but firmly remove him every time his play intensity increased, moving him away from the other pups until he was calm, then allowing him to resume his play. By the end of his first six week class he was playing appropriately most of the time with one or two other pups, under direct supervision. After two more six-week sessions he played well with a stable group of four other dogs, under general supervision, without needing any NRMs or time outs.

The last time I saw Sam was an incidental encounter, at Hagerstown's Pooch Pool Plunge event. Every year when the city closes their community pool for the winter, they open it up on one Saturday for people to bring their dogs for a pooch pool party. Sam, now a full-grown adult dog, attended the Plunge at the end of Summer 2005, with more than 100 dogs in attendance. His behavior was flawless.

Jasper may have a longer road, but I'm optimistic that he'll come around as well. We plan to continue having him play with Mesa, as long as she's handling him as well as she did in last week's class. Between Mesa's canine corrections and our timeouts, we're hopeful that he'll learn appropriate social skills and be able to expand his social circle to other appropriate dogs. Is there a Pool Plunge in Jasper's future? We'll just have to wait and see.

Say No to Saying "No!"

Dog owners are often puzzled when I suggest they not use the word "No!" with their dogs. "How else," they wonder, "will my dog know what he's *not* supposed to do?"

A dog's goal in life is to get good stuff, and his mission is to do whatever makes good stuff happen. You can teach your dog what *not* to do by controlling the consequences of his actions. If inappropriate behaviors consistently make good stuff go away, your dog will stop those behaviors. His goal is to make good stuff *happen,* not make it go away.

If you're good at managing your dog's environment, then he'll learn to do appropriate things to get good things, without your use of the word "No!" If you're poor at management, he'll be reinforced for his inappropriate behaviors, like jumping up on counters or tipping over garbage cans to look for food, and those behaviors will persist. That said, there are plenty of trainers who *do* use the "No" word, in various ways.

I use it on rare occasions, for extreme emergencies, and when I do it comes out as a loud roar, indeed intended to stop all behavior. When I'm compelled to use it, I always try to pause afterwards, analyze the situation, and figure out where I need to shore up my management and/or training to avoid having to use it in that situation again.

In contrast, trainer and behaviorist Patricia McConnell uses "No!" as a positive interrupt. She teaches her dogs that "No!" means "Come over here for a treat"—no matter what tone of voice is used. When her dogs hear "No!" they happily run to her to see what she has for them, necessarily interrupting whatever inappropriate behavior they may have been engaged in.

If you *do* still use "No!" as an aversive in your training program, be sure to avoid coupling your dog's name with the loud, harsh "No!" It takes only a few repetitions of "Fido, NO!!!!" for your dog to start having a negative association with his *name*—and you absolutely want to preserve the sanctity of your dog's positive association with his name. "Fido!" should always mean very, very good stuff!

Let Us Prey

Few people want their dogs to act on their inherited predatory drives

Tiffany approached me shortly before the start of her weekly training class recently, clearly distraught. "Newton did something very bad this week," she said.

My heart skipped a beat as I glanced down at Newton, the black and white Border Collie/Basset mix sitting calmly by her side. In my dog trainer brain, "very bad" usually equates with serious aggression to humans. Newton and his vivacious, committed owner are two of my favorite clients, and I didn't want to hear that Newton had done something irredeemable.

"What did he do?" I asked.

"He chased and killed a bunny in my back yard!" Tiffany wailed. "My roommates and I were so upset. He dropped it immediately when I told him too, but it was too late, the bunny was dead!"

I breathed a silent sigh of relief, and reassured her that while I understood her distress, Newton's behavior was natural and normal. Bassets were bred to chase rabbits, after all, and Border Collies were bred to chase things that move. More often than not when our dogs chase small beings like squirrels and rabbits the little critters manage to escape. This poor bunny wasn't so lucky, and Newton just did what dogs do.

Predatory Behavior: Aggression or Not?

Our dogs' predatory instincts are one of the things that make them fun to play with. When you throw a ball or a stick and he chases it, you are triggering his natural predatory desire to chase things that move. In fact, some behaviorists argue that predatory behavior should not be called aggression at all—that it is more appropriately interpreted as a form of food-getting behavior.

Indeed, the motivation to chase prey objects is vastly different from other forms of aggression, which are based on competition for resources, status, and/or self-protection. It is distinguished from other forms of aggression by a marked absence of "affective arousal" (anger), and is a social survival behavior, not a social conflict behavior. Predatory behavior is indicated by distinct behavior: hunting (sniffing, tracking, searching, scanning, or waiting for prey; stalking); the attack sequence (chase, pounce/catch, shaking kill, choking kill); and post-kill consuming. The underlying motivation for chasing things that move is to eat them.

Dogs who challenge, bark, snarl and chase skateboarders or joggers who pass the house are generally believed to be engaging in territorial aggression—individual predators don't usually openly advertise their intent by making lots of noise (although anyone who has ever followed a pack of baying hounds knows that group hunting can be quite noisy!) Dogs who hide in ditches or behind bushes and silently launch their attack on unsuspecting passers-by are exhibiting more classic predator behavior. However, the frustration of restraint on a chain or behind a fence combined with constant exposure to the trigger of rapidly moving prey objects can push a dog from predatory behavior to real aggression. Both behaviors, of course, are dangerous.

Just because predatory behavior is natural doesn't mean that it's acceptable in its inappropriate manifestations. It was not acceptable to Tiffany and her roommates for Newton to chase and kill a bunny, and it certainly wasn't acceptable to the rabbit. Predatory behavior has been responsible for the death of many unfortunate pet cats and rabbits; chickens, sheep, goats, and other livestock; even humans. (See "What About the Baby?" pg. 238.) While it often can be expressed in harmless, even useful outlets such as games of fetch, retrieving ducks and herding sheep, chase behavior can be dangerous to dog and prey alike. It is our responsibility, as caretakers for our canine companions, to be sure their natural predatory instincts don't get them into trouble.

Manage Manage Manage.

As with so many other undesirable dog behaviors, if your dog has a strong prey drive, your first line of defense is management. Make sure you have a secure fence from which your dog cannot escape. Don't leave him in the yard unattended if he will be constantly tantalized by lots of fast moving prey objects—squirrels, deer, skateboarders, or small children running and playing.

Use leashes and long lines to prevent your dog from taking off after deer, rabbits and squirrels when you are on walks and hikes. Especially keep him on leash at dawn and dusk, when the deer and the antelope—and other wild things—are most likely to play. Look for ways to minimize his visual and physical access to prey in his own yard—a solid fence will prevent him from seeing things moving quickly by, and will prevent many potential prey animals (including small children) from entering easily. A non-visible underground electronic fence will not. Nor will a non-visible fence necessarily prevent him from leaving the yard if he is highly motivated to chase prey.

A muzzle can also be useful on a limited basis. Since muzzles restrict a dog's ability to drink water and pant normally, you cannot leave one on your dog while you are away all day at work. But if he's devastating the squirrel population in your back yard, or you want to give a litter of baby bunnies a chance to grow up and get wiser and faster, you can put a muzzle on him for brief fresh air/potty trips to the yard. Be sure to take time to desensitize him to wearing a muzzle first, by associating it with yummy treats while you put it on him for gradually longer periods of time.

Training

You will never train most herding dogs not to chase things that move, given the chance. Similarly, you'd be hard pressed to convince many terriers not to go after rats and other small creatures when the opportunity arises. Their brains are hardwired to chase and you can't change that.

A slightly less imposing goal is to change the predatory response into an incompatible behavior response. For example, you could teach your Border Collie that the appearance of a deer is the cue to lie down. She can't "down" and "chase the deer" at the same time. Or, as we taught our own Scottie, the appearance of your kitten could be the cue for your dog to sit at your feet. This type of training can be difficult because the dogs are so highly motivated to chase—it is quite a challenge to convince them that they'd rather do something else. You must find something highly rewarding in order to make it work. For our Scottie, it was food. For a Border Collie, it might be the opportunity to chase a tennis ball—after she lies down—*instead of* the deer.

This approach works best *in your presence,* and only if you practice it regularly rather than just expecting it to work in the heat of the moment. Although we are quite comfortable leaving our now-grown kitten alone with Dubhy, it was several months and several pounds worth of kitten-growth before we stopped shutting her in her own room when we weren't there to supervise. You might not ever be able to expect that your Border Collie will leave the deer (or the skateboarders) alone if she is outside, unrestrained, and left to her own devices.

A solid foundation of good manners training can also be helpful, combined with vigilance on your part. If you are out hiking with Bess and see the deer before she does, you can call her to you and snap the leash on. Even if she sees it first, a really reliable recall will bring her back to your side, especially if you call her pre-launch, before she is headed hell-bent-for-leather after the fleeing deer.

A well-trained emergency "Down!" can also save the day, even if your dog is in full stride. Many dogs will "Down!" even when they won't "Come!" because they can still watch the prey. Stopping the charge gives the dog's arousal level and adrenaline time to recede, and you may be able to call her back from the down or calmly walk up to her and snap her leash on her collar.

Dangers of Thwarting

Dogs who have strong, hardwired behaviors are usually happiest if they are allowed to engage in those behaviors in some form. Greyhounds chase mechanical rabbits on the track—and while I abhor the abuse that is rampant in the Greyhound racing industry, there is no question that the dogs love to run and chase. Jack Russell Terriers are in heaven when they get to play in Earthdog trials. Katie gets a huge charge out of running circles around our horses in the pasture, even though they are impervious to her attempts to direct their movement.

In fact, if hardwired behaviors are constantly thwarted (prevented from occurring), you risk having your dog develop obsessive-compulsive disorders. A canine obsessive-compulsive disorder (COCD) is a normal coping behavior that becomes exaggerated to the degree that it is harmful to the dog. Some common examples are excessive licking, spinning and tail-chasing. Some dogs are genetically predisposed to COCD, but it usually takes an environmental trigger—stress—to cause the behavior to erupt. The breeds known to have a high prey drive (See "It's In The Genes" pg. 237) are often the most susceptible to developing stereotypical spinning behavior when kept in high-stress kennel environments.

Many people are attracted to certain breeds of dogs because of certain traits, such as a Labrador's genial temperament and athletic prowess. They conveniently forget that the dogs also frequently come with an intense desire to hunt and fetch.

If you are the owner of a dog with strong predatory inclinations, it behooves you both to find an outlet for the behavior rather than simply trying to shut it off. Encourage your dog to chase and fetch balls, sticks and toys, and take the time to engage in several fetch sessions with him per day.

Use these strong reinforcers to incorporate training in your play sessions and strengthen your dog's good manners. If your dog rudely jumps up and tries to grab the Frisbee™ from your hand, whisk it behind your back until he sits, then bring it out again, and only throw it if he remains sitting until you throw. You are using two of the four principles of operant conditioning here. The dog's behavior—jumping up—makes the Frisbee go away, which is "negative punishment"—the dog's behavior makes a good thing *go away*. When he sits and stays sitting, you throw the Frisbee. This is "positive reinforcement"—the dog's behavior makes a good thing *happen*. Works like a charm.

If you have a terrier, provide an outlet for his prey-seeking behavior by creating a digging spot—a box filled with soft soil or an area you have dug up where he is allowed to dig. Bury his favorite toys and encourage him to "Find it!" Toys that squeak and wiggle are especially suited to terrier games.

Come Chase With Me

One of the most useful applications of chase behavior is in conjunction with teaching your dog to come when called. Lots of dog owners make the mistake of moving toward their dogs—or even chasing after them—when they won't come. In dog language, a direct frontal approach is assertive, even aggressive, and dogs naturally move away from it.

It's much more effective to do the exact opposite—run away from your dog! Start playing chase/recall games when your dog is a pup. Get excited, call your pup, and run a short distance away. Let him catch up to you while you are still facing away from him, then turn sideways, kneel down (*don't* bend over him), praise him, feed him a treat or play with a tug or fetch toy, and pet him (if he enjoys being petted—not all dogs do). If your dog is no longer a pup, you can still play this game to strengthen his response to the "Come!" cue.

Teach your dog from early on that "Come!" means "Chase me and play," keep up the games as he matures, manage him so he doesn't get to practice inappropriate predatory behavior, find acceptable outlets for his natural chase behaviors, and you'll have a much better chance of getting those incompatible behaviors later on when you are faced with the challenge of competition from *real* prey.

It's In the Genes

It should come as no surprise that some breeds seem to have a much stronger predatory instinct than others. Dogs who were purposely bred over the centuries to chase and kill small animals are much more likely candidates for strong chase behavior than those with enhanced genes for lap-sitting. While there are exceptions in every breed and group, and any individual dog, from Chihuahuas to Newfoundlands, can display predatory behavior—or not; in general the following dogs are exceptionally likely to display strong predatory behavior:

- Herding Breeds (such as Border Collies, Kelpies, Australian Shepherds, Cattle Dogs, etc.)

- Sporting Breeds (Retrievers, Spaniels, Setters, Pointers, etc.)

- Hounds (Beagles, Bassets, Bloodhounds, Coonhounds, Greyhounds, Salukis, etc.)
- Terriers (Jack Russells, Scotties, Westies, Rat Terriers, Bull Terriers, etc.)
- Northern Breeds (Huskies, Malamutes, etc.)
- Wolf Hybrids

Interestingly, *because* of the specialized purposes for which these dogs have been bred, many of these breeds will display *parts* of the predatory sequence of behaviors more strongly than others. The Herding breeds have a strong stalk and chase behavior, but the kill-and-consume part of the sequence has been greatly inhibited. Sporting breeds are strong on sniffing, scanning, watching, and grabbing, but again, have been bred not to actually destroy the prey—they are supposed to gently bring it back.

The Hounds are split into two groups. Scenthounds are low to the ground, with long ears to catch scent particles, and who are very big on the sniffing and chasing aspects of the sequence. They may sometimes actually catch and kill, but it's not their primary purpose. Sighthounds, on the other hand, are long-legged to enhance their ability to scan—to *look* for prey rather than finding it by smell—and to run after it, *fast*, when they see it.

Terriers have had the grab-and-kill part of the predatory sequence genetically enhanced, giving them a well-deserved reputation for a pugnacious personality. Their owners didn't just want them to *find* the rats in the barn; they really wanted the dogs to *kill* the rats. Or, historically, in the sad case of the Pit Bull Terrier, people wanted the fighting Terriers to kill the opposing *dog*.

The Northern breeds have been the least genetically manipulated, which is why, in part, they most closely resemble their wolf ancestors. Thus they, and the Wolf Hybrid, are most likely to display the complete predatory sequence.

What About the Baby?

One of the very real concerns I hear expressed from new or soon-to-be parents is that of the family dog's predatory behavior being elicited by the baby. There is some evidence to support the belief that at least some dogs may view an infant more as a prey object than as a little human. New babies move strangely, and make funny noises that can resemble prey distress sounds.

The Centers for Disease Control in Atlanta, Georgia, published figures from the 25 dog-bite-related fatalities in the two-year period from 1995-1996. Of those 25 deaths, 20 of the victims were children (80 percent). Three of the children were less than 30 days old, one was under five months, and ten were from one to four years old. The remaining six child victims were under 11 years old. It is likely that the three neonates and perhaps the five-month old were victims of prey-related behavior, while the others were at least as likely to have somehow elicited a true social conflict/aggression attack.

I strongly recommend that all parents-to-be, but *especially* owners of dogs with strong predatory behavior who plan to bring an infant into the home, work with a trainer/behaviorist to desensitize the dog to baby sights and sounds, and to create a good training and management plan to ensure that Fido and Junior will be comfortable with each other.

There are CDs and audio tapes of baby noises available, which can be used to teach the dog that a baby's cries are the cue to lie down on his bed—or do a Lassie trick and go get Mom or Dad.

It goes without saying that dogs should *never* be left alone with infants and young children, but that warning goes *triple* for dogs who have demonstrated any propensity toward predatory behavior. A family dog mauling or killing a child is a horrible tragedy that just doesn't have to happen.

Rage Without Reason

Idiopathic aggression is (thankfully) quite rare,
but also quite dangerous

The term "rage syndrome" conjures up mental images of Cujo, Steven King's fictional dog, terrorizing the countryside. If you're the owner of a dog who suffers from it, it's almost that bad—never knowing when your beloved pal is going to turn suddenly, without warning, into a biting, raging canine tornado.

The condition commonly known as rage syndrome is actually more appropriately called **idiopathic aggression**. The dictionary definition of idiopathic is: "Of, relating to, or designating a disease having no known cause." It applies perfectly to this behavior, which has confounded behaviorists for decades. While most other type of aggression can be modified and reduced through counter-conditioning and desensitization plus some operant conditioning, idiopathic aggression can't. It is an extremely difficult and heartbreaking condition to deal with.

The earmarks of idiopathic aggression are:

- No identifiable trigger stimulus/stimuli.

- Intense, explosive aggression.

- Onset most commonly reported in dogs 1-3 years old.

- Some owners report that their dogs get a glazed or "possessed" look in their eyes just prior to an idiopathic outburst, or act confused.

- Certain breeds seem more prone to suffer from this condition, including Cocker and Springer Spaniels (hence the once-common terms—Spaniel rage, Cocker rage and Springer rage), Bernese Mountain Dogs, St. Bernards, Doberman Pinschers, German Shepherds, and Lhasa Apsos. This would suggest a likely genetic component to the problem.

Glimmer of Hope

The good news is that true idiopathic aggression is also a particularly uncommon condition. Discussed and studied widely in the 1970s and 80s, it captured the imagination of the dog world, and soon every dog with episodes of sudden, explosive aggression was tagged with the unfortunate "rage syndrome" label, especially if it was a spaniel of any type. We have since come to our senses, and now investigate much more carefully before concluding that there is truly "no known cause" for a dog's aggression.

A thorough exploration of the dog's behavior history and owner's observations often can ferret out explainable causes for the aggression. The appropriate diagnosis often turns out to be status-related aggression (once widely known as "dominance aggression") and/or resource guarding—both of which can also generate very violent, explosive reactions.

An owner can easily miss her dog's warning signs prior to a status-related attack, especially if the warning signs have been suppressed by prior physical or verbal punishment. While some dog's lists of guardable resources may be limited and precise, with others it can be difficult to identify and recognize a resource that a dog has determined to be valuable and worth guarding. The glazed look reported by some owners may also be their interpretation of the "hard stare" or "freeze" that many dogs give as a warning signal just prior to an attack.

Although the true cause of idiopathic aggression is still not understood, and behaviorists each tend to defend their favorite theories, there is universal agreement that it is a very rare condition, and one that is extremely difficult to treat.

Theories

A variety of studies and testing over the past 30 years have failed to produce a clear cause or a definitive diagnosis for idiopathic aggression. Behaviorists can't even agree on what to call it! (See "The Evolving Vocabulary of Aggression," pg. 242)

Given the failure to find a specific cause, it is quite possible that there are several different causes for unexplainable aggressive behaviors that are all grouped under the term "idiopathic aggression." *Some* dogs in the midst of an episode may foam at the mouth and twitch, which could be an indication of epileptic seizures. The most common appearance of the behavior between 1-3 years of age also coincides with the appearance of most status-related aggression, as well as the development of idiopathic epilepsy, making it even impossible to use age of onset as a differential diagnosis.

Some researchers have observed abnormal electroencephalogram readings in dogs suspected of having idiopathic aggression, but not all such dogs they studied. Other researchers have been unable to reproduce even those inconclusive results. Another theory is that the behavior is caused by damage to the area of the brain responsible for aggressive behavior. Yet another is that it is actually a manifestation of status-related aggression triggered by very subtle stimuli. Clearly, we just don't know.

The fact that idiopathic aggression, by definition, cannot be induced also makes it difficult to study and even try to find answers to the question of cause. Unlike a behavior like resource guarding—which is easy to induce and therefore easy to study in a clinical setting, the very nature of idiopathic aggression dictates that it cannot be reproduced or studied at will.

Treatment

Without knowing the cause of idiopathic aggression, treatment is difficult and frequently unsuccessful. The condition is also virtually impossible to manage safely because of the sheer unpredictability of the outbursts. Prognosis, unfortunately, is very poor, and many dogs with true idiopathic aggression must be euthanized, for the safety of surrounding humans.

Don't despair, however, if someone has told you your dog has "rage syndrome." First of all, he probably doesn't. Remember, the condition is extremely rare, and the label still gets applied all too often by uneducated dog folk to canines whose aggressive behaviors are perfectly explainable by a more knowledgeable observer.

Your first step is to find a skilled and positive trainer/behavior consultant who can give you a more educated analysis of your dog's aggression. A good behavior modification program, applied by a committed owner in consultation with a capable behavior professional *can* succeed in decreasing and/or resolving many aggression cases, and help you devise appropriate management plans where necessary, to keep family members, friends and visitors safe.

A behavior consultant's investigation will reveal discernible triggers and warning signs if a dog has a more common form of aggression; not so with idiopathic aggression.

If your behavior professional also believes that you have a rare case of idiopathic aggression on your hands, then a trip to a veterinary behaviorist is in order. Some dogs will respond to drug therapies for this condition, many will not. Some minor success has been reported with the administration of Phenobarbital, but it is unclear as to whether the results are from the sedative effect of the drug, or if there is an actual therapeutic effect.

In many cases of true idiopathic aggression, euthanasia is the only solution. Because the aggressive explosions are truly violent and totally unpredictable, it is neither safe nor fair to expose yourself or other friends and family to the potentially disfiguring, even deadly, results of such an attack. If this is the sad conclusion in the case of your dog, euthanasia is the only humane option. Comfort yourself with the knowledge you have done everything humanly possible for him, hold him close as you say good-bye and send him gently to a safer place. Then remember to take good care of yourself.

The Evolving Vocabulary of Aggression

Different behaviorists and trainers have used and continue to use different terms for what was once commonly known as "rage syndrome." The confusion over what to call it is a reflection of how poorly understood the condition is:

- **Rage Syndrome.** This once popular term has fallen into disfavor, due to its overuse, misuse, and poor characterization of the actual condition.

- **Idiopathic Aggression.** Now the most popular term among behaviorists; this name clearly says "we don't know what it is."

- **Low-threshold Dominance Aggression.** Favored by those who hold that idiopathic aggression is actually a manifestation of status-related aggression with very subtle triggers.

- **Mental Lapse Aggression Syndrome.** Attached to cases diagnosed as a result of certain electroencephalogram readings (low-voltage, fast activity).

- **Stimulus Responsive Psychomotor Epilepsy.** Favored by some who suspect that idiopathic aggression is actually epileptic seizure activity.

"Rage Syndrome" is not the only aggression term that has undergone a metamorphosis in recent years. Even the way we look at aggression is changing. Where once each "classification" of aggression was seen as very distinct, with its own distinct protocols for treatment, it is becoming more and more widely recognized that most aggressive behavior is cause by stress or anxiety.

It is now generally accepted by the training and behavior profession that physical punishment should not be used in an attempt to suppress aggressive behavior. Rather, aggressive behavior is best *managed* by preventing the dog's exposure to his individual stressors, and *modified* by creating a structured environment for the dog—through a "Say Please," or "Nothing In Life Is Free" program—and implementing a solid protocol of counter-conditioning and desensitization to reduce or eliminate the dog's aggressive reaction to those stressors.

We also now recognize that aggressive dogs may behave inappropriately and dangerously as a result of imbalances in brain chemicals, and that the new generation of drugs used in behavior modification work help rebalance those chemicals. This is in stark contrast to older drugs, such as Valium, that simply sedated the dog rather than providing any real therapy. As a result, many behaviorists recommend the use of pharmaceutical intervention sooner, rather than later, in appropriate aggression cases.

Here are some of the newer terms now in use:

- **Status-related aggression.** Once called dominance aggression, a term still widely used. Status-related aggression focuses more on getting the confident high-ranking dog to behave appropriately regardless of status. Old methods of dealing with dominance aggression often focused on trying to reduce the dog's status, often without success.

- **Fear-related aggression**. Once called submission aggression. A dog who is fearful may display deferent (submissive) behaviors in an attempt to ward off the fear-inducing stress. If those signals are ignored and the threat advances—a child, for example, trying to hug a dog who is backing away, ears flattened—aggression can occur.

- **Possession aggression.** Previously referred to as food guarding and now also appropriately called resource guarding, this name change acknowledges that a dog may guard many objects in addition to his food—anything he considers a valuable resource, including but not limited to toys, beds, desirable locations, and humans.

How to Save Yourself

In case of a dog-attack emergency, make like a rock or a tree

The tragedy of a 12-year-old boy killed by his family's Pit Bulls in San Francisco in 2006 highlights the importance of providing information that will help people survive such dog attacks—and perhaps the need for laws that encourage and require dog owners to be responsible for their dogs.

Any large, powerful breed of dog may, occasionally, cause serious injury, even death. Small dogs can certainly bite, too, though they just normally have less potential to do serious harm (the Pomeranian who killed a 6-week-old infant girl in California in 2000 notwithstanding). You and your family members would be smart to learn how to stay safe around aggressive dogs, by knowing how to avoid provoking an attack, and how to protect yourself should one occur.

Easy to Say, Difficult to Do

When I was a humane/animal Control Officer in Marin County, California, I once handled a report of an aggressive male Rhodesian Ridgeback who was running at large in an upscale suburban neighborhood. As I walked up the front sidewalk toward the house where the dog was reported to live, a reddish-brown flash came speeding around the corner of the house, headed menacingly and directly at me.

I averted my eyes and held my breath, then froze myself in place as he charged up and bumped me with his nose, hard.

I have no doubt that if I had moved when he punched me with his nose, he would have bitten me, probably badly. Instead, I passively held my ground and he backed off, staring at me intensely. Still without making direct eye contact, I backed slowly to my truck and climbed in, reached behind the seat for my control stick, stepped out, slipped the loop over his head and pulled it tight. Then I breathed. In her excellent book *The Other End of the Leash*, Patricia McConnell makes the important point that, as primates, humans tend to automatically do exactly the wrong things when confronted by a dog. Instinctive, genetically programmed primate behavior causes us to make direct eye contact and confront a threat with full-face aggression—stare at the dog, facing him directly, perhaps yell, reach or move toward him or make other defensive moves, escalating rather than defusing aggressive behavior.

Programmed by decades of living and working with dogs, I knew to avoid eye contact and movement, and I froze instead. Lucky for me. Many people either scream in fear (or in an attempt to attract attention and help) or shout to try to scare or bluff the dog into leaving. Unfortunately, this usually further provokes the dog.

You can reduce the risk of being attacked, and reduce the likelihood of serious injury if you *are* attacked, by doing the right things, pre- and post-confrontation. Next time you feel threatened by a dog, remember these tips:

1. **Be a Tree.** If a dog approaches you with assertive/aggressive body language, be a tree. Stand perfectly still but relaxed. A tense, unnatural position looks weird to the dog; weird can trigger an attack. Avoid direct eye contact, but keep the dog in your peripheral vision. Keep your arms at your sides, and don't speak—and certainly don't scream, which can further excite a dog who is already aroused. By offering ap-

peasement behaviors and not doing anything assertive or provocative, you increase the odds that the dog will back off and move away without attacking.

2. **Be a Rock.** If the dog *does* attack despite your inoffensive body language, you have two choices. If the dog is small or just nipping at you rather than launching an all-out attack, seek safety—climb up on a fence or tree, the hood of a car, or any object large enough to provide sanctuary. You can unobtrusively scope out the landscape for such objects while you're being a tree. On the other hand, if you feel you're being overpowered by the dog, be a rock. Drop to the ground in the fetal position with your hands behind your neck and legs pulled up to your chest, protecting your spine, face and vital organs. If there are people nearby who could help you, screaming to get their attention could save your life. On the other hand, screaming may also further provoke the dog. If you feel certain that no one will be able to hear you, don't yell.

3. **Find a Shield.** While you're being a tree, carefully scan the area for possible shields—a gate you can slip through, a garbage can lid you can hold between you and the dog. If you think the dog will allow it—like the Ridgeback that came after me—back carefully to your shield, keeping the dog in view, and use it as needed to protect/defend yourself.

4. **Find a Weapon.** In no way do I advocate hitting dogs in the name of training, but if you're being attacked and have access to a club or other weapon of some kind, do what you need to do to save yourself. Don't attempt to use a weapon, however, unless you're prepared to use it with full commitment. Waving a stick feebly at an attacking dog may only antagonize him further. If you use it, either offer it as a target for the dog to bite or use it as hard as you can. If you walk in an area with free roaming dogs, consider carrying a club with you, or a shield, such as an umbrella, to help ward off dogs.

5. **Report Incidents.** Even if you escaped unscathed, report the incident to animal control and the police department; the dog's *next* attack may be fatal. If you don't feel the local officials are taking you seriously, talk to their supervisors, and, if necessary, your local elected representative and the media. You may save the life of the next person the dog would accost.

Be alert in places where dogs are running loose and possibly aroused enough to behave aggressively—especially when you have small children with you. Teach your children how to "be a tree" if approached by a scary dog and how to "be a rock" if attacked.

Complications

The first four tips listed above are much more difficult to implement if you're walking your own dog(s) on a leash, or are accompanied by a child, senior citizen, or disabled person. You may need to use your own body as a shield by calmly moving into position between your dependent dog or person and the attacking dog.

You may be able to lift a child or your dog onto a raised surface for safety, and then climb up yourself. You can still use the fetal position, either while coaching the other person to do the same, or by folding a small child or small-to-medium-sized dog between your chest and knees, or wrapping them in a jacket if you happen to have one with you. You might practice these maneuvers in advance with lots of positive reinforcement so no one panics if it happens in a real life encounter. Carrying a weapon of some kind is still an option.

I'm sorry to say there are no guarantees that the above suggestions will save you from being bitten, or even mauled, but it's a good bet that if you do the wrong things when a dog accosts you, or do nothing at all if you're attacked, the damage will be greater. It's sort of like the terrorist threat: you don't want the risk of being attacked to alter your regular activities or enjoyment of life, but it pays to be on heightened alert, and to be prepared to defend and retaliate in case of attack.

Fatal Dog Attacks

It's important to keep dog-bite deaths in proper perspective. Dog usually cause fewer than thirty deaths each year in the United States. According to the Centers for Disease Control in Atlanta, Georgia, dogs killed 22 people in 2004. In 2003, nearly twice as many (43) people died after being struck by lightning, while in 2002, 113 people died in traffic collisions with deer.

Because dogs are our trusted and loyal companions, a dog-related fatality is more sensational and seems more sinister than most other accidental deaths. There are thousands of non-fatal dog bites each year, but statistically, the chance that you're at risk of being mauled to death by a dog is very low. Of course, that's small comfort to anyone who is approached or attacked by an aggressive dog, or to the families of those who were killed by one.

An Accident Waiting to Happen

What you should do if you have a run-in with a dangerous dog

At the end of November 2003, a 40-year-old woman in a small ranching community southeast of Denver, Colorado was killed by a pack of three dogs belonging to a neighbor. What made the gruesome event more shocking was the news that the dogs responsible for the attack were well known for roaming free in the community and threatening the safety of residents. In fact, the pack reportedly had also seriously injured a neighbor of the dead woman the previous April.

Maybe we're just paying more attention since the infamous fatal mauling of Diane Whipple outside her apartment door in San Francisco. But it seems we are increasingly hearing about serious and fatal dog attacks where a subsequent investigation determines that the attacking dogs had been an identified problem in their community for quite some time.

"I've been an expert witness in two fatal dog bite cases, one in Wyoming and one in Kansas," said Suzanne Hetts, Ph.D., a Denver-based, Certified Applied Animal Behaviorist, in the December 2003 issue of Animal Behavior Associates e-zine. "There were breakdowns in both situations where interventions should have been done, but weren't. Both were accidents waiting to happen."

The news reports on the Colorado tragedy contained similar quotes, such as, "The people in the area had their own sort of emergency phone network to warn each other if the dogs were loose before they would go out," said Fire District Chief Dale Goetz. "A few weeks earlier they had come to our house and bared their teeth at me, and I called the owner and told her I would shoot them if they came back."

And, of course, following the death of Diane Whipple in January 2001, *dozens* of people, including neighbors, postal carriers, delivery-persons, and other dog owners from the neighborhood, testified in court about numerous occasions when the two dogs that killed Whipple had threatened them. *None* of those incidents were reported to animal control or police. "The Whipple case underscores the community's obligation to report dangerous dogs to animal control authorities," said Los Angeles Lawyer Kenneth Phillips, a national expert on dog bite law who runs a website: www.dogbitelaw.com.

Responsible Dog Neighborship

There are many reasons why a person might tend to look the other way when confronted with a potentially dangerous dog. You may be busy; you may be fearful of the dog's owner or potential retaliation; you may be friends with the owner and reluctant to cause hard feelings between you; you may worry about being responsible for the dog's impoundment and possible euthanasia; or you may simply feel that it's none of your business.

The thing is, it *is* your business if the dog lives, plays or wanders in your community. It could a member of *your* family—human or animal—that gets killed by the dangerous dog. And even if the next victim is not someone near and dear to you, how will you to feel if the dog finally mauls someone and you had done nothing of substance to prevent that attack, even though you recognized that the dog presented a threat?

Loose Cannons

The following are suggestions for action if you are aware of a potential problem dog that roams your neighborhood:

1. **Talk to the dog's owner** (if the owner is known). Be friendly, non-threatening, tactful and educational. Try something like: "You may not realize this, but when your dog roams the neighborhood he acts a little (or a lot) aggressive. He probably is very loving at home, but he chased my son on his scooter and ripped his pants. I wonder if there's something you could do to keep him more securely confined to your yard."

2. **Follow up your first visit** *quickly* if the owner seemed friendly and receptive to your concerns but the dog continues to roam. This time you might offer some suggestions: "We just talked the other day about your dog, and you seemed to understand my concerns, but he's still getting loose. If you are having a problem keeping him contained, perhaps I can help."

3. **If it's a confinement problem**, you can offer suggestions for keeping the dog at home, such as an overhead runner if there's no fenced yard, or repairing an aging fence. You can also call the owner and politely ask him to come get his dog every single time you see him loose. Document everything you do, for possible future use as evidence if needed.

4. **It's time to call the animal control authorities.** If the owner was friendly on the second visit but fails to follow through on your suggestions, there's probably no point in a third visit. Similarly, there is probably no point in a second visit if the owner was *not* friendly or receptive the first time.

   Be prepared to be identify yourself—many agencies won't act on anonymous complaints. Be specific in your information: give the name and address of the owner, a description of the dog, and dates, times, and detailed descriptions of any incidents that have occurred. It's even better if you have photos or video of the dog acting in a threatening manner. You can also advise them of the owner's schedule, if you know it, so they don't make wasted trips to the owner's home. Ask the agency how long it might take for them to contact the dog owner, and to let you know when your complaint has been handled, and how.

   If the person you speak to at the agency seems receptive to your complaint, you'll need to wait a reasonable period—a week is good—for the complaint to be handled. Meanwhile, every time you see the dog at large, call them so they can (at least) put the reports on the record, and (better yet) patrol for him if they have adequate staff.

5. **Ask to speak to a supervisor** if the person you speak to does not seem receptive, tells you they don't go out on such complaints, says that it's low priority and could take several weeks, or if the person seemed receptive but a week goes by and when you call to check on the status of the complaint you are told no action has been taken.

6. **Politely explain the situation** to the supervisor, emphasizing your concerns about the dog's potential to injure someone. Try to extract a commitment from the supervisor that the complaint will be handled within a specific time frame.

7. **Step up the ladder**. If the supervisor appears unsympathetic, or time passes and the complaint still has not been handled, ask to speak to that person's supervisor. Continue to move up the administrative ladder until you reach the top. For a private, non-profit humane society the top would most likely be the executive director, then the board of directors. For a municipal agency it's probably a director, followed by one or two layers of city or county administration, and then your elected representative—a city councilperson or county commissioner. Meanwhile, you (or your fellow concerned neighbors) should still file a report every time you see the dog is loose.

8. **It's time to go to the media** if you reach the top of the animal control administration and still haven't gotten resolution. Let administrators know that you're going public with your concerns, this may spur them into action. Sometimes a well-placed call or articulate letter to a local television station or newspaper reporter can pressure a lazy or ineffective agency into taking action.

9. **Ensure your own safety** until you start to see some fruits of your labors. A neighborhood watch system that alerts the community when the dangerous dog is loose is a good idea.

   Also consider the very real possibility that you may need to defend yourself from a serious attack. This could involve the carrying and/or strategic placement of mace sprays, golf clubs or other weapons, in easily accessible places so that one is always within reach if needed. While we would never advocate abusing an animal, there may come a time when physical violence against a dog is required to save a life.

   If all goes well, the dog's owners will be forced to become more responsible for their dog, or lose the privilege of owning him. Yes, the dog may be impounded and even euthanized if his owners refuse to take appropriate steps to confine his dog, but that's the owner responsibility and guilt, not yours.

Dangerous Dogs on Leash

Of course, not all dangerous dogs are roaming free. Take the case of the infamous Presa Canarios in San Francisco, for example, who terrorized many people in their community while on leash and ostensibly under the owner's control. What do you do if you are walking down the street and a leashed dog lunges aggressively toward you? Or you and your dog are at a dog park and you see a dog whose behavior is threatening the safety of other park users? You need to file a report with the appropriate authorities—the police, sheriff, animal control department, or whatever agency handles the dangerous dog reports in your community. To file a report, you'll need to give authorities as much information as possible about the event, the problem dog, and his owner. You *can* politely ask the owner for his name and address, but depending on the circumstances, you may or may not get it.

In these situations, unless you're extremely lucky, it's probably not realistic to expect even the most efficient animal control or police officer to arrive in time to apprehend the culprit, even if you immediately call to report it.

In these and other "dog-with-owner" scenarios there's a good chance that you are near either the dog owner's home or his car. Try following discreetly at a distance and getting a license plate number or street address when the offenders arrive at their destination. If you have a camera handy, take a picture, to provide for positive identification of dog and his handler later.

You can also ask other witnesses if they are familiar with the dog and owner. The culprits may be well-known for previous misdeeds. While you're at it, get those witnesses' names and contact information, and add this information when you call the appropriate authorities to file a report.

Even if you are unable to provide the identity of the dog and person in question, call the appropriate authorities and give them a complete description of the offending parties. The officials may recognize the offenders from your description or photo. If not, they may be able to identify the dog and handler later if there are future incidents.

Be a Legal Beagle

You may be told that there are no laws to address your concerns. If so, you'll need to either do some legal research yourself, or ask an attorney for help. First, ask the animal control agency to send you a copy of the local animal control ordinance. Read it for yourself, to see if you agree that existing law offers no relief from the threat of dangerous animals.

If you believe that it does have relevant provisions, make an appointment with your district attorney, and ask for his interpretation of the local ordinance. If he agrees with you, get his opinion in writing and ask him to notify animal control that the law provides for them to deal with the dangerous dog, and encourage them to do so.

If you agree that the ordinance is too weak, or your district attorney tells you it doesn't apply to your local dangerous dog, ask about any dangerous dog laws at the *state* level that could be enforced locally. If authorities in Colorado had filed charges against the owner of the loose dogs after their April attack using the stronger state dangerous dog law rather than the weaker county ordinance, one death might have been prevented.

If you find an applicable state law, take it back through the chain of command, district attorney opinion in hand, and ask that it be enforced. Again, ask the district attorney to urge the appropriate agency to enforce it as well.

If there are no existing laws that deal effectively with dangerous dogs, it's time to work with local authorities to create effective but fair animal control ordinances. Many jurisdictions have incorporated a definition for "potentially dangerous" to address dogs who present a threat but haven't actually bitten, as well as a "dangerous dog" category for dogs who have committed more serious acts. Kansas City is currently considering such a law, the provisions of which would require dogs deemed "potentially dangerous" to wear an orange collar, be muzzled and leashed when outside, and require their owners to carry added liability insurance.

A Danger to Other Dogs

If you are working on changing laws, make sure your ordinance language also includes dogs who threaten and/or attack other animals as well as humans. Some existing laws only address dogs who attack people or livestock. If your local or state laws don't address dogs who attack other animal companions, start lobbying in your community for a new ordinance. Leave petitions to be signed at places where responsible dog owners congregate, such as groomers, veterinarians' offices, and dog parks. Educate lawmakers to the fact that an aggressive dog poses an unacceptable risk to human and animal lives in the community.

If your community *has* laws providing for the control of dangerous dogs but the animal services department is not staffed or funded adequately to enable the officers to enforce them effectively, it's time to mount a campaign to pressure your elected officials to make animal control a higher priority at budget time. The media can help you here too, if you feel that your requests and demands are falling on deaf ears.

Don't Do Nothing

Please make a commitment to do *something* the next time you see a canine accident waiting to happen. If not all the suggestions and strategies listed above appeal to you, select the ones that do, and enlist the assistance of family, friends, and neighbors to implement them. Some people need someone else to take the lead and help motivate them to become involved. If you do it, you, and those who join forces with you, will all sleep better at night, knowing you are working to make your community safer for your loved ones.

What Does a Dangerous Dog Look Like?

Despite the prevalence of certain breeds of dogs being in the headlines, laws addressing specific breeds are far less effective than dangerous dog laws that do not mention breed. Breed-specific legislation applies unfairly to dogs who may be no threat whatsoever, and doesn't help a community with dangerous dogs who are mixed-breeds or not of the breed mentioned in the legislation.

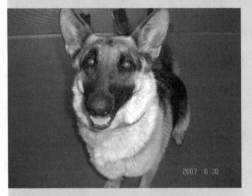

A dangerous dog may be of any breed or size. A dog that has attacked and seriously injured a person or another dog is obviously dangerous. More difficult to identify are potentially dangerous dogs.

Dangerous dogs are better identified by their behavior than shape and size. The sort of canine menace to society we are talking about includes:

- A dog who shows aggression warning signs: freezing and giving a hard, direct stare; leaning forward, ears pricked, growling, perhaps with hackles raised; issuing one or more challenging barks; bared teeth, snarling, and/or snapping; stiff, rigid appearance and movements.

- A free-roaming dog or pack of dogs who have stalked, chased, or threatened people and/or animals.

- A dog on leash who lunges aggressively toward other animals or people, and whose owner appears in danger of losing control of the dog.

- A dog who gets in a fight and punctures or lacerates another dog, or bites a person who is trying to break up the fight. *Note:* Many dogs get into scuffles in group interactions. Dogs who have good bite inhibition may be involved in a fight that looks and sounds awful, but leaves no visible traces of injury on the participants. A truly dangerous dog in the same fight punctures or lacerates her opponents, or causes serious damage by grabbing and shaking.

- A dog who bites another person or animal, puncturing or lacerating the skin.

Fight!

Ritual display or real deal? Counter-conditioning can avoid fierce dog fights

If you look closely, you can see the pea-sized divot in the outer edge of our Australian Kelpie's right ear—souvenir of a battle between Katie and our Scottish Terrier over a coveted resource—my attention. We had already successfully resolved the food-guarding issues between these two assertive members of our family, so this brief but fierce battle took me by surprise.

Perhaps if my attention hadn't been distracted by the fact that I was showing our new pet sitter the animal care routines I would have heeded the warning signs, but instead I failed to intervene when I caught a glimpse of Dubhy bristling at Katie. The next instant her blood was splattering the walls.

Dogs fight. It's a natural and normal behavior for them. They engage in ferocious displays of growling, snarling, snapping and teeth-on-fur to settle differences and make political statements about social order. The good news is that most fights are only ritual display and rarely result in serious injury or death. This is important for any species that lives in social groups—the ritualized fight communication actually benefits both parties. An appropriate outcome is achieved, with no harm to either party.

Healthy Pack Members

Pack survival depends on the robust good health of all pack members. An injured or debilitated member diminishes the pack's hunting effectiveness and ability to defend itself.

In the wild, a normal level of fight-willingness and ability is an important survival mechanism. If a dog is unable or unwilling to defend himself, his offspring, his pack mates, his food, or his territory, he's not likely to stay alive long enough to reproduce successfully and pass on his genes.

Domestication has done little to reduce the fighting instincts of *Canis familiaris*. In fact, while some breeds are quite social, such as the scent hounds (think Beagles) who have been bred to hunt in large groups, others, notably many of the "bull breeds" and some Terriers, are exceptionally pugnacious because instincts for aggression have historically been selected for and genetically enhanced.

In addition, we humans often have unreasonably high expectations about our canine companions' social skills. We are a social species, but we don't get along well with every human we meet. Yet we expect our canine pals to get along with other dogs in constantly changing social groups, with artificially small territories and countless other unnatural stressors. It's a wonder our dogs get along at all!

Our challenge, as our dogs' caretakers and protectors, is to help them be as socially adept as possible, while protecting them from situations in which they may be attacked or feel compelled to attack others. To do that, we need to understand why dogs fight, how to prevent inter-dog aggression, and how to react when a fight does occur.

It's very distressing to see your dog in a fight. Fortunately, the majority of fights—the ritualized ones—are normally over before you have a chance to react. An occasional brief scuffle between canine family members that doesn't result in injury is not a major concern, as long as fights aren't increasing in number and/or intensity. If they are, then the ritual isn't resolving the conflict. You need to intervene.

This usually involves a management program to prevent fights, and behavior modification to diminish the likelihood fights will continue. The following management and modification suggestions are for information only—most dog owners will need the help of a positive behavior counselor to resolve serious dog-dog aggression issues.

Note: many trainer/behaviorists call themselves "positive." Be sure to interview a potential counselor carefully to be sure you are comfortable with the methods and training philosophies. Good positive trainers and behaviorists generally agree that the use of force and physical punishment or rough handling is not appropriate for basic training or most behavior modification programs.

Here are some of the reasons dogs fight, and what you can do about it.

Poor social skills. Dogs who miss out on the opportunity to meet, greet, and play with other dogs during the important socialization period from about 4 weeks to 4 months often don't know how to behave properly around others of their own species. This can manifest itself in clumsy, oafish social overtures that offend other dogs, resulting in fights. The oaf doesn't know how to read and respond properly to other dogs' complex and subtle signals, and like the overly-friendly cocktail party swinger who bestows unwanted affections on other partygoers, he may get slapped for his efforts by the irritated recipient of his attentions. If the oaf is willing to back off after the "slap," such reprimands may help to teach him appropriate social skills. If the oaf takes offense in return, a fight is likely to ensue.

The solution. The best way to teach an oaf proper social skills is to introduce him to a tolerant but socially appropriate adult dog who will let him know that he is out of line, without doing damage. This is best done while the oaf is still a youngster, and done only by a person experienced and skilled at reading dogs properly and handling them in difficult situations. The oaf problem can often be *prevented* by providing lots of socialization for dogs during the first year of their lives and beyond with other pups and adult dogs of *appropriate* age and social skills. Inappropriate encounters can have the opposite effect, producing dogs with fear-related aggression.

A bully who traumatizes other dogs isn't a good choice for your dog's playmate.

Fear-related aggression. This, too, be a result of poor socialization during a pup's first several months of life. It can also result from one or more incidents in which an "innocent" dog is attacked by one or more other dogs. One incident can be enough to make a dog wary of others of his kind, resulting in defensive aggression when he sees other dogs.

The solution. Dogs who are aggressive due to fear respond best to programs of counter-conditioning and desensitization to change their association with the presence of other dogs from "Bad/Scary!" to "Yay, good stuff!" To do this, determine your dog's threshold distance—the distance at which he'll notice the presence of another dog but not go off the deep end.

This distance may be 10 feet or 150; it's different for every fearful dog. If your dog's threshold distance is 20 feet, you'll begin by introducing a dog at 21 feet. The instant your dog notices the other dog, being feeding him, non-stop, tidbits of something wonderful, like chicken. When the other dog leaves, the chicken stops. Your goal is to have your dog understand that "Other dogs makes chicken happen!" You'll know you've accomplished this when, if a dog appears at 21 feet, your dog—instead of bristling defensively—looks to you with a big grin, as if to say, "Yay, a dog! Where's my chicken?" Then decrease the distance slightly, introducing the other dog at 20 feet, gradually moving closer each time your dog consistently gives you the "Where's my chicken?" response at the new distance.

Genetic programming to enhance dog-dog aggression. The Pit Bull is the common scapegoat for this behavior in light of his fighting dog heritage. These dogs may not acknowledge cut-off signals. Even when the other dog gives all the right responses to stop a fight, the aggression continues, often to the death.

There are, sadly, plenty of other breeds that have been deliberately bred for pugnacious behavior. The Scottish Terrier is one. Scotties are encouraged by their handlers to "spar" outside the breed ring so they'll display the characteristic feisty Terrier attitude in front of the judge.

The solution. You can't change a dog's genes—but you may, through training and counter-conditioning as described above, be able to have your dog safely under control around other dogs—or not, depending on the strength of the genetic influence. These dogs are not likely to ever be good candidates for the local dog park. They *may* develop a group of playmates that they can safely socialize with, or they may always have to be kept apart from other dogs.

Play aggression. In this case, two or more dogs appear to be happily engaged in rowdy play when suddenly a fight breaks out. One dog may continue to get increasingly aroused during play, and, as the intensity escalates, ignores the other dog's signals that he'd like things to calm down, thank you. When the less enthusiastic dog tries to protest in self-defense, the more aroused one, rather than recognizing and acceding to the social "settle down!" signal, continues his rough play, and a fight breaks out.

The solution. The good news with play aggression is that you can usually see it coming as the level of arousal escalates. The key here is to consistently intervene before the fight happens with a cheerful "Too bad, time out!" Put the dogs in a gentle time-out to give them time to calm down, then allow them to play again. This is known as negative punishment, in which the dog's behavior makes a good thing (playtime) go away. Over time, the dogs may learn to control their arousal in order to be able to continue playing, or you may always need to supervise and step in before things get too rough.

Bully dogs. These dogs, similar to playground bullies, are looking for a fight—not with the intensity of a genetically-enhanced aggressive dog, but just for a little Saturday night fun. They tend to target as their victims dogs who are clearly not in their league, as opposed to the fighting dog, who will take on all comers. This can be very traumatic to the canine victim—and the victim's owner—as these bullies tend to harass dogs who have soft temperaments.

The solution. These tough guys can't be allowed to terrorize less assertive dogs. Allow them to play only with dogs who can withstand their bullying tactics, and perhaps put them in their place in return. Again, this should only be done under the supervision of a skilled and experienced professional, who can determine if your bully dog is an appropriate candidate for behavior modification, or if management is a better choice. These dogs, too, are not good dog park dogs, where they might pounce on an unsuspecting victim.

Resource Guarding. The instinct to protect one's resources from others is a normal canine behavior. The ritual hard stare and tooth-exposing lift of a lip are normally enough to counter an outsider threat to a dog's food bowl, chew-bone or favorite toy. Sometimes, however, the guarder is overenthusiastic in his defense, launching his attack before the other dog can respond, and sometimes the dog making the threat refuses to heed the ritual warnings. In either case, a fight may occur.

The solution. The first line of defense here is management. If dogs are battling over food bowls, crate or tether to feed, or feed them in separate rooms. If they are guarding valuable chew objects, pick the objects up and put them away, only returning them when the dogs are separated. If they are guarding their humans, interact with them one at a time, while you are working on modifying the behavior. Modification can be done through counter-conditioning—teaching the guarder that the presence of the other dog makes great stuff happen. You can also use operant conditioning—teaching the guarder that the presence of another dog is the cue to do something non-aggressive, such as go lie down on his rug, or teaching the challenging dog to avoid the guarder when that dog has a valuable resource.

Status-Related Aggression. Also known as "dominance aggression," much more is made of this than necessary. In fact, the majority of status disputes are resolved through ritualized display, not through serious combat. When a status-related fight does occur, it's often brief, with lots of noise and flashing of teeth, and ultimate voluntary submission of one party, but little real damage. When damage does occur, it's most likely because one or both of the participants lack the appropriate social skills to allow for an injury-free resolution, or, on rare occasion, because there really is an irresolvable dispute over social rank.

The solution. If you have a case of true status-related aggression, you need to convince both dogs that *you* are the highest-ranking member of the social group, and that their behavior is not acceptable. Teach both dogs basic good manners—sit, lie down and stay—and put both on a "Say Please" or "Nothing In Life Is Free" program, wherein they must sit or lie down in order to make all good things happen: petting, treats, dinner, walks on leash and other privileges.

When a status battle occurs, *both* dogs are at fault, so *both* dogs get a cheerful "Too bad, time out!" in crates or separate rooms. Take care not to leave these dogs alone together when you are not home to intervene if necessary, unless and until you are confident that their status dispute has been resolved.

Dubhy and Katie haven't had a resource guarding battle in almost a year—not since Katie lost that piece of her ear. They have learned not to challenge each other over food bowls—

or me! For my part, I am more vigilant about watching for sideways glances between the two of them that predict potential conflict, and more prompt with intervention when I see tensions building.

Now we have a new challenge. The latest addition to the Miller family is a 7-month Cardigan Corgi, who also has resource guarding tendencies. So far, it's just at the scuffle level. I am watching closely to see if it starts to escalate, in which case I'll need to go into trainer mode and get to work.

Break It Up!

You can't always prevent incidents of serious inter-dog aggression. You can, however, be prepared to intervene to protect your dog—and yourself—should the necessity arise. Familiarize yourself with various tools and techniques that have the greatest chance of successfully quelling doggie disputes with the least injury to all parties. Then determine which are most appealing to you, and be sure to have them on hand should you need them.

Remember that none of these tools and techniques are foolproof. They all involve some inherent risk to the dogs who are fighting and to the humans who are trying to intervene, and they all can be applied with varying degrees of success. You'll need to weigh the odds and decide, in each case, if the risk outweighs the potential for injury from the fight.

Aversives

Aversives are tools that a dog finds offensive to the senses, and that are strong enough to stop a behavior. They generally are most effective if used to interrupt fighting dogs prior to full arousal. Their effectiveness decreases as arousal levels increase—although they may still succeed in stopping some full-scale fights. Aversives should also be considered primarily a tool for crisis intervention—not as basic training tools. Here are some options:

Blasting dogs with water from a nearby hose is a tried and true method of separating fighting dogs. It often works—assuming a hose happens to be nearby with a powerful enough spray. A good tool to keep in your arsenal for the right time and place –not particularly useful, however, when there's no hose handy!

One of the easily portable aversive sprays, such as Direct Stop™ (citronella) or Halt!™ (pepper spray) might be an effective alternative to the hose. Of the two, Direct Stop, available from Premier Pet Products, is the safer choice, since pepper spray products are more corrosive, and the spray can drift and affect innocent bystanders—humans as well as dogs. There are laws in some jurisdictions requiring that users of pepper spray products complete a training course and carry a permit. In a pinch, even a fire extinguisher might just happen to be a handy and effective aversive tool.

Some doggie daycare providers swear by air horns. Available at boating supply stores, air horns can be effective at warding off attacking dogs, but your own dog has to be desensitized to the cacophony, or you are likely to lose him as well! You also risk damage to eardrums, both canine and human, and take a chance of frightening your own dog beyond repair.

Physical Intervention with Objects

Another route is intervention with a physical object. If fights are a regular problem in your household you might attach a couple of handles to a sheet of plywood so you can lower it between two sparring dogs.

Dogfighters—and some Pit Bull owners who don't fight their dogs but know the breed's potential—always carry a "parting stick" or "break stick" with them. This is usually a carved hammer handle, tapered to a rounded point at one end. When two dogs are locked in combat, the parting stick can be forced between a dog's teeth and turned sideways to pry open the jaws. Parting sticks can break a dog's teeth, and a dog whose jaws have just been "parted" may turn on the person doing the parting. Like many other techniques offered here, this method should only be considered for dire emergencies.

A blanket can also be useful. Tossed over the fighters, one over each, blankets muffle outside stimuli, reducing arousal. This also allows humans to physically separate the combatants by picking up the wrapped pooches with less risk of a serious bite—the blanket will cushion the effect of teeth on skin if the dog does whirl and bite.

When a dog's life and limb are at stake, extreme measures may be called for. You can wrap a leash around the aggressor's neck or get hold of a collar and twist to cut off the dog's airflow until he lets go to try to get a breath of air, then pull the dogs apart.

This could be more difficult than it sounds. It might be difficult to get a leash around the neck of a dog who is "attached" by the mouth to another dog without getting your hands in harm's way. Grabbing a collar to twist also puts hands in close proximity to teeth.

Physical Intervention by Humans

One method I heard about recently is a rather drastic technique observed at a dog show 20 years ago. Two dogs got into it, ready to cause major damage. The elderly judge, a tiny woman, had the handlers both grab their dogs and hold on *tight*. Then she went up and took the dog on top by the tail and jammed her thumb up his rectum. He let go in an instant and whirled around to see what was happening. The judge excused the two dogs, calmly washed her hands, and continued her classes without a hitch—just as if it happened every day.

Although this is an amusing anecdote, remember that it's *never* advisable to try to grab or otherwise physically separate fighting dogs. Angry dogs, even your own, may whirl and bite you without realizing what they're doing, or who they're biting.

Armed and Ready

Now, all you need to do is stuff a canister of Direct Stop in your pocket, attach a parting stick to your belt, carry a blanket over your arm, balance a sheet of plywood on your head, wear an air horn around your neck, be sure you have at least two friends with you to hold dogs while you put your thumb in private places, and you're ready for anything.

Seriously, if and when that next fight happens, take a deep breath, resist your instincts to yell or leap in the middle of the fray, quickly review your available options, and choose the one—or ones—that are most likely to work in that place and time. When the fight is over and no one is being rushed to the hospital in an ambulance, remember to take a moment to relax and breathe, and then congratulate yourself for your quick thinking.

Nuclear Reactors

*Dealing with dogs who "go off" or "lose it"
in certain circumstances*

At least 85% of the time, Dubhy is laid-back and phlegmatic. He methodically solves every training challenge I give him (although I don't expect him to break any speed records on the agility course). His low-key approach to life won our hearts and earned him a permanent home after we found him running loose in a Chattanooga neighborhood in January of 2001 at the tender age of 6 months. Residents said he had been roaming the area for at least six weeks. A search for his owners proved fruitless. His uneventful introduction to the rest of our pack sealed his fate, and Dubhy joined the Miller family.

Thus his behavior at a Tennessee trainers' meeting some 16 months later came as a complete shock to me. I arrived early at the Knoxville location, and was sitting on the far side of the training room when fellow trainer Claire Moxim entered with her Labrador Retriever, Pete. Dubhy knew Pete well—they had played happily together at my training center on several occasions. Dubhy looked up as Claire and Pete entered, then went nuclear, raging and snarling at the end of his leash.

My trainer brain immediately leaped to the obvious "restraint frustration-aggression" conclusion. Here was a dog that Dubhy knew from prior positive play experiences. Dubhy was excited to see Pete, and his frustration at not being able to greet his friend was manifested in a display of aggression. Or so I thought.

"Let's have them meet on loose leashes," I suggested to Claire. "Once Dubhy gets to say hi to his pal, he should be okay."

Fat chance. As Dubhy and I approached Pete on a loose leash, Dubhy did, indeed, seem to settle down. I mistook his *controlled* behavior for *calm* behavior. As we came near the big black dog, Dubhy redoubled his hostilities. When I reached down and touched my dog's hip in an attempt to interrupt his attack, he whirled around and punctured my hand with his teeth in a classic display of redirected aggression. Yikes! Overnight, seemingly without warning, Dubhy had turned into a reactive dog.

Talkin' Bout Excitation

"Reactive" is a term gaining popularity in dog training circles—but what is it, exactly? In her *Clinical Behavioral Medicine for Small Animals,* Applied Animal Behaviorist Karen Overall uses the term to describe animals who respond to normal stimuli with an abnormal (higher-than-normal) level of intensity. The behaviors she uses to ascertain reactivity (or arousal) are:

1. Alertness (hypervigilence)

2. Restlessness (motor activity)

3. Vocalization (whining, barking, howling)

4. Systemic effects (vomiting, urination, defecation)

5. Displacement or stereotypic behaviors (spinning, tail- or shadow-chasing)

6. Changes in content or quantity of solicitous behaviors

The key to Dr. Overall's definition is the word "abnormal." Lots of dogs get excited when their owners come home, when they see other dogs, when a cat walks by the window, when someone knocks at the door, and so on. The reactive dog doesn't just get excited, he spins out of control to a degree that can harm himself or others around him. In his maniacal response to the stimulus that has set him off, he is oblivious to anyone's efforts to intercede. He goes nuclear.

Dubhy has demonstrated reactive behavior in other situations as well. Our neighbor's black-and-white tuxedo cat has appointed himself Official Rat Patrol in our barn. The cat's casual strolls outside the back yard fence send the Scottie into a frenzy. Dubhy runs the fence line like a maniac; barking hysterically and doing stereotypic spins at each corner. When I place myself in Dubhy's path and wave liver treats in his face I might as well be invisible; he darts around me and continues on his mission. If I let him, he would run himself into heat stroke.

Causes of Reactive Behavior

There is definitely a genetic component to Dubhy's out-of-control level of excitation. If I had researched Scottish Terriers before I decided to keep him, I would have learned that this behavior is a desired trait for the breed. Hard to believe?

The excuse, of course, is that good breeding maintains the original temperament and behaviors of purpose-bred dogs. Labrador Retrievers should be able to retrieve ducks; Border Collies should be able to herd sheep; and Scotties and other terriers should display the pugnacious behavior that makes them good vermin-killers. I had heard this all my life, and was quite familiar with the Terrier reputation for feistiness. I now have an intimate understanding of what that really means.

As with most behaviors, environment also plays a role in the responses of reactive dogs. With careful handling, a dog with reactive tendencies may never exhibit the abnormally intense reaction to stimuli that lies dormant in his genes. A dog who could have been a reasonably self-controlled canine in normal conditions, might be induced into reactivity if kept in a highly stimulating environment.

Had I been smarter and realized Dubhy's propensities earlier, I might not have taken him to doggie daycare, where he experienced a heightened level of stimulation in the presence of other dogs that *might* have contributed at to his Jekyll and Hyde reaction to Pete. He might never have been able to "play well with others," which he did nicely for over a year, but we might also have avoided the "can't even control himself in the presence of other dogs" behavior that I found myself dealing with in Knoxville.

Managing Reactive Behavior

Even if you have a highly reactive dog, all is not lost. A reactive dog may be a challenge, but there are things you can do that will help you cope with the stress of living with a dog who has a tendency to flip out. Let's start with management:

1. **Identify his triggers.** Make a complete list of all the environmental stimuli that set off your dog's nuclear reactions. Be specific. For Dubhy that would be: (a) A cat flaunting himself on the other side of the fence; and (b) *Some* other dogs—mostly those who are taller than Dubhy. Since I can't successfully predict which dogs will set Dubhy off, I assume all dogs will, and act accordingly.

2. **Prevent his access to the stimuli.** Change the environment so your dog's reactive behavior isn't constantly triggered. For example, you can block his visual access

with barriers, control it with training tools, or simply move your dog to another environment when the stimulus is likely to be present. For Dubhy that might mean: (a) Asking the neighbor to keep his cat home (which probably won't happen) or erecting a solid wooden privacy fence so he can't see the cat; and (b) Using a control harness, perhaps even a head halter, when I walk Dubhy in public so I can easily turn him away from other dogs, breaking the visual contact that triggers his reactive behavior.

Modifying Reactive Behavior

If you are particularly successful at managing your dog's environment, that may be all you need to do. Lots of dog owners get by on management without ever retraining the dog. If, however, you'd prefer to change your dog's behaviors in case your precautions should slip, or if you'd like to be able to relax when you take him out, you can learn to put a behavior modification program in place.

The most powerful tools you can use to reprogram your dog's reactive responses are classical and operant conditioning. Don't be frightened off by the technical terms, these behavior modification tools are easy to put into practice.

Say your dog is reactive to people walking their dogs past you when she is inside, and she barks hysterically and scratches at the windows whenever she sees a dog walking past. You *manage* the behavior by closing drapes, moving the sofa to the other side of the room so she can't jump up and see out, or putting up a baby gate to prevent her access to the front room. But if you really *like* having the drapes open, the sofa fits perfectly under the front window, and you enjoy your dog's company when you are watching TV, you might be more motivated to undertake a behavior modification program to change your dog's annoying response for the long term.

Here's what Mokie does if he's left alone in a car—even if I'm just gassing up the car. If he sees a stranger approaching, he lets out ungodly shrieks, hysterically rattling his teeth against the windows.

Think of it this way: There's a little switch in your dog's brain that gets flipped whenever she sees a dog outside your window. She likely sees each dog-human pair as a trespassing threat. The instant one appears, her brain kicks into overdrive and she goes nuclear. This is a classically conditioned behavior. She is *not* thinking, "If I bark hysterically and run in circles, climb the walls and claw the curtains, something good might happen." Her brain is screaming, "Alert! Alert! Intruders!!!!!" and her body reacts accordingly.

Of course, her behavior *is* reinforced by the fact that every time she does this, the intruders leave. Her canine brain doesn't comprehend that they would've left anyway—she may well think *she* made it happen. This negative reinforcement (dog's behavior makes a bad thing go away) only increases the likelihood that the behavior will continue, or even escalate.

This is operant conditioning. In reality, classical and operant conditioning work together all the time to mold our dogs' behaviors. We use food to operantly condition our dogs to respond to our cues with a desired behavior. At the same time we give our dogs a very positive classical association with the whole training experience because they love food (and playing with us), so they come to love training too.

To change your dog's classical association with the presence of a dog walking by from negative to positive, you need to convince her brain (the automatic response part, not the thinking part) that the presence of dogs walking by something *wonderful* happen. This is called counter-conditioning.

Build an Unconscious Positive Association

To succeed at counter-conditioning, begin by preventing your dog's access to the windows when you are not there so she can't practice the undesirable behavior. Plan your training sessions for a time of day when you'll have high traffic pass your window. If there is no such time, convince several of your dog-friends to leash their canine companions and—at different times—march back and forth past your window for 15 to 20 minutes. You can take them all out to dinner afterwards as a reward!

Be sure your friends know they need to march out of sight in each direction before they turn around. Mark the place on the sidewalk where you want them to turn, just to be sure.

Meanwhile, back in the house, have your dog on leash, using a front-clip control harness or even a head halter, if necessary. As soon as the marchers come into view, start feeding your dog something totally irresistible, such as tiny morsels of canned chicken. Be sure your dog has noticed the pair before you begin feeding, but don't wait for her to work herself up into a frenzy. The *instant* she notices them, begin feeding. Feed the morsels non-stop as long as the marchers are in view—treats raining from the heavens! As soon as the dog and human are gone, stop feeding your dog. When they reappear and your dog notices them, start feeding her again.

Your goal is to convince your dog that a dog walking by *makes* chicken happen. You will know you're making progress when you see your dog notice the walkers and, instead of getting tense and alerting, she turns to you with a smile and a "Where's my chicken?" expression. When she realizes that chicken *only* happens in the presence of a dog outside the window, she'll *want* them to be there, rather than wanting to chase them away.

Building a Conscious Positive Association

When you have successfully changed your dog's automatic or unconscious association with the stimulus, you can start using operant conditioning to teach her that the presence of the previously offensive stimulus is a cue to sit and look at you.

It's easier than you might think—just ask her to sit when she gives you the "Where's my chicken?" look, before you feed her a treat. Slow your rate of reinforcement (how fast you feed treats) and reward her only for the desired behavior, rather than shoveling treats non-stop.

Eventually you can fade the verbal "Sit" cue, the mere appearance of a dog walking by your house will become the operant cue for your dog to sit and look at you.

All is Calm

Counter-conditioning is definitely more challenging with a reactive dog than with one who responds to stimuli with a normal level of intensity. It may take you longer than it would with a "normal" dog, but it does work. Don't give up! The more you can saturate the reactive dog's environment with the *concept* of "calm," the more successful you will be at managing and modifying her nuclear reactions.

Help your dog understand that calm behavior is universally rewarded. Keep your own interactions with her calm and cool, even when you are tempted to scream at her to startle her out of the high-intensity behavior pattern. Your own intense behaviors are more likely to elevate her energy level than tone it down.

Learn about calming massage, acupressure and TTouch™ techniques to help your dog relax. Consider using DAP™—Dog Appeasing Pheromones—a product recently released in the U.S. under the brand name "Comfort Zone™," which mimics the pheromones released by a mother dog while she is nursing her puppies and has a calming effect. Research herbal, homeopathic and flower essence remedies to see which ones might be appropriate for your dog. You may need a holistic veterinarian to help you with this—go to the website of the American Holistic Veterinary Medical Association at www.ahvma.org for a directory of holistic vets in the U.S., listed by state, to find one near you.

It is possible to make progress with a reactive dog. While my Scottie is not yet ready to show off his piano-playing technique at the next big dog trainer conference I attend, I *am* much more comfortable taking him to relatively small gatherings where other dogs might be present.

We recently helped staff a booth at a fair. Our two-hour stint was uneventful despite dozens of dogs walking by on leash—except for the bad moment when a thoughtless lady allowed her dog to run 25 feet to the end of her retractable leash and get right in Dubhy's face. I did a quick about-turn with Dubhy to avoid disaster and a setback to his modification program, and then proceeded to explain to the lady why retractable leashes weren't a good idea in a crowd. She was offended and indignant. I was just thrilled that Dubhy had come so far with his reactive behavior.

Breeding (and Selecting) Dogs for Behavior

For those of us who deal with ordinary pet dogs, selected and trained to be pleasant, safe family companions, the concept of intentionally breeding reactive dogs seems ludicrous. However, there are many breeds whose "standards"—the signature traits of the breeds—include some functional variant of reactivity.

One of the functions of a responsible breeding program *is* to retain certain breed qualities. Terriers, therefore, more than any other breed group, seem prone to reactive behavior. The herding breeds are probably second. (This isn't an absolute, however. I've known mellow terriers and laid-back Border Collies.)

However, in my opinion, there's a much larger market in today's society for dogs who can be good companions than there are for dogs who can display aptitude for their original purpose, killing rats in a barn, for example. Perhaps breeders need to rethink the paradigm that says dogs have to be able to do exactly what they were once bred for. How many of today's Border Collies, kept in suburban homes as pets, suffer because they have no sheep to herd? How many Jack Russell Terriers will ever be called upon to kill a rat? Pit Bulls were once bred to kill other dogs. Who needs that?

A dog with all of my dog's *great* Scottie qualities but with his terrier pugnacity turned down a couple of notches would be a terrific family pet, and a breed that I would recommend to people who call asking me to suggest a breed of dog that's good with children. As it is now, much as I adore Dubhy, Scotties would be way down my list because of their high potential for reactivity. Even pre-warned, I doubt many pet-owning families are equipped to manage the environment well enough to prevent the behavior. Nor are they likely to want to deal with it once it erupts—especially if their child suffers a serious puncture to the hand—or worse—while walking MacDuff around the block.

I frequently remind clients to thoroughly research whatever type of dog they are interested in *before* they get one. My intention is not to discourage them from getting certain types of dogs; I want them to be prepared to prevent or deal with the behaviors that are endemic to certain breeds. Attend a number of dog shows where your favorite dogs are exhibited or call breeders and ask about the behavior and personality they seek to perpetuate in their own dogs. Ask, too, about the behaviors that a novice dog owner might find challenging.

Responsible breeders are forthright about their favorite dogs, even warning away individuals who seem all wrong for the breed. For example, an honorable breeder of Labradors should tell that frail senior citizen that a Labrador from hunting bloodlines is a poor candidate for quiet apartment living. A family with toddlers might be steered away from breeds like the Australian Shepherd, which may have a compulsion to "herd" children and may nip the kids in an attempt to keep them in line.

Alternatively, you can look for a breeder who has a reputation for producing the exact type of dog—in looks *and* behavior—you are looking for, even if it doesn't exactly meet the breed standard. I had a client in Santa Cruz, California, with the sweetest Jack Russell Terrier I've ever met. Skippy's owner, Marianne, tells me that when she and husband Tom were walking their dog in New York City, they ran into a man walking a JRT that looked a lot like Skippy. They stopped to chat, and discovered that this dog was also unusually calm for a JRT. Upon further discussion, it turned out that both dogs had come from the exact same breeder! Chances are, if you ask around and search long enough, you could find a breeder who has the same "taste" in dogs you do, and who will help you find a dog with the best potential for becoming the dog of your dreams.

Reform School

The latest developments in remedial classes for reactive dogs

We used to call them growl classes—a term that, in hindsight, was perhaps a poor choice—likely to intensify feelings of apprehension in the human member of the training team before dog and owner even walked through the door into the classroom for the first session. These were classes designed for dogs whose aggressive on-leash reactions to dogs or other environmental stimuli made them inappropriate candidates for regular companion dog classes. They were simply too disruptive, even dangerous, to be in mixed company.

While the term "growl class" may have mostly gone by the wayside, fortunately the concept of a class for difficult dogs has not. It is a tribute to dog owners of today that many of them are unwilling to give up on their canine companions, even when faced with behavior challenges that can shake the foundations of the dog-human bond. It's as much a tribute to the modern dog training profession that trainers continue to seek out and develop innovative, positive, and effective solutions for owners who are committed to helping their dogs "be nice." From east coast to west, trainers are increasingly offering classes that now go by friendlier names, such as "Rowdy Rover," the goal of which is to help owners help their difficult dogs be more manageable in the real world.

Do You Have a Rowdy Rover?

Candidates for difficult dog classes are generally those who tend to react more intensely than the situation calls for. They may bark aggressively at other dogs on leash, lunge uncontrollably after joggers, or claw at car windows when someone passes by. While some of this is normal dog behavior—chasing things that move *is* a hardwired canine response—difficult dogs are distinguished by their owners' sense of frustration and helplessness—they have tried all the remedies that worked just fine for their friends' and neighbors' dogs to no avail…Rover is still intimidatingly rowdy. If you are reluctant to take your dog to a training class because of his embarrassing or frightening behavior, or the two of you have been excused from a regular class for the same reason, then you are good candidates for a canine "special education" class.

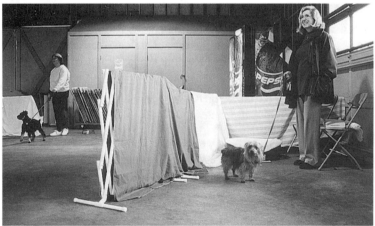

In today's "difficult dog" classes, the focus is on gradually teaching dogs new and more appropriate responses to increasingly proximate contact with other dogs. Pupils begin learning new skills behind visual barriers, which help prevent triggering relapses.

Most trainers who offer classes for Rowdy Rovers agree that, while dog-dog aggression is an allowable behavior problem for class participants, dog-human aggression is not. Ali Brown, CPDT, of Great Companions in Allentown, Pennsylvania, says, "If the owner tells me the dog is aggressive, fearful, etc., we explore further. If the dog hasn't made bite contact, I will accept them—but we do a minimum of three private sessions first, focusing on calming and control exercises. If the dog has actually bitten, mauled or attacked a person, then no, they don't come to our Reactive Dog classes."

Trish King, Director of Behavior and Training for the Marin Humane Society in Novato, California, suggests that her difficult dog classes are as much a support group for owners as they are vehicles to achieve the goal of helping the dog be civilized in the presence of other dogs. "The owners really encourage each other," she says. "After a dog who used to be outrageous succeeds at a previously 'impossible' exercise, the other participants often break out in applause. No one can appreciate the progress of these dogs as much as owners of similar dogs!"

At the Marin Humane Society, instructor Trish King walks a strange dog past an opening in a student's alcove, as the owner rewards her dog for staying calm.

Later in the class, students walk their dogs—at a distance that does not set them off—past other students, rewarding the dogs for maintaining focus on their handlers.

Caren Salisbury of Warner Robins, Georgia, agrees. "I offer classes for difficult dogs because I have found that owners are embarrassed to have an 'out of control' dog. They think they are alone with the behavior, but they quickly learn that they are not!" she says.

Methods and Tools

Brown and King both emphasize the importance of using positive tools and techniques, and they are not alone. Overwhelmingly, trainers use positive training and behavior modification tools and methods to work with Rowdy Rovers. Owners bring their dogs' soft beds to class, and the dogs relax in them between more active exercises, giving each dog a chance to "practice" calming down from a more aroused state, even in the presence of other dogs. Treats, toys and touch are used to encourage and reward progress. These work to classically condition the dogs to form more positive associations with being around other dogs.

"All our courses depend on positive, non-aversive, reward based methodology," says Jackie McGowan, of Click Starts Dog Training in Alberta, Canada. "Clicker training is used, unless the dog has a strong aversion to the sound of the clicker. We use canine and human positive relationship building, dog on owner focus, relaxation techniques, coping skills, alternate behavior skills and management skills."

Physical barriers are commonly used in these classes, to block visual stimulation until dogs are ready for more interaction. King starts each dog in class in its own alcove to provide a safe, quiet environment. As dogs learn to relax, the "walls" of the alcove can be gradually opened.

Oops! These dogs have gotten a little closer than is comfortable for them at this stage. Both stiffen and begin to "wind up" into an aggressive confrontation. Their owners stay calm (very important), keep the dogs from actually being able to touch, give a calm "Off!" cue, and offer a tasty lure to lead the dogs away from each other. It works beautifully, and the owners lavish praise and treats on the dogs as they retreat.

Other trainers use physical distance to keep the dogs' reaction to stimuli at a comfortable level. Brown uses the dogs' own cars as barriers—the equivalent of large portable crates. Her clients park as far away from each other in the parking lot as possible and work with their dogs one at a time in and near their cars, very gradually working toward bringing the dogs closer together, still calm and controlled.

Another frequent tool of choice in these classes is the use of calming massage and touch. A number of trainers will, like Brown, require one or more private sessions to give them an opportunity to meet and work with dog and owner outside the stress and confusion of a group class. In these private sessions, trainers teach owners new techniques to respond to, redirect, and control inappropriate behaviors that will help lower the dogs' arousal and reactivity rather than exacerbating it. Often, teaching the *owner* to remain calm is a huge step toward helping the dog maintain his mental equilibrium.

While some still use head halters, many trainers have ceased using them for difficult dogs in recognition of the increased stress level this tool may cause. King suggests that if you need a head halter to control the dogs in class or a muzzle to ensure safety, perhaps the dogs are too close and too aroused anyway. She does, however, enthusiastically promote the use of the front-clip control harness.

Class Goals

In the "olden days"—just a few years ago!—the goal of a growl class was often expressly to get all the dogs in the class playing together by the end of the six or eight weeks. Trainers have come to realize that for the most part this is an unrealistic goal, and one that places entirely too much stress on dogs and humans alike—trainers as well as owners! Today's goals are inclined to be much more modest and humane.

"My biggest goal is to educate the owner on proper dog handling techniques: Preventing the dog from practicing the undesired behavior; being proactive and alert instead of reactive; teaching desensitization and counter conditioning skills," says Carole Lawson, CPDT, of the Classic Academy of Canine Learning in Cleveland, Ohio. "My goal for the dog is to help create a relationship between owner and dog where the dog is confident in the human and willing to be attentive to the owner regardless of the fear stimulus or other distraction."

Valerie Pollard, of Valerie Pollard Dog Training, Orange, California wants her difficult dog clients to learn to trust and enjoy focusing on their handlers, and be able to function calmly in social situations involving other dogs and people.

Different Classes for Different Types of Rowdy Rovers

Like most trainers who provide this type of service, King agrees that owner education is a vital part of the program. She offers three different types of classes for dogs with challenging social behaviors, to create positive learning environments for the humans that are most conducive to addressing their dogs' specific behaviors:

- **Difficult Dogs.** For dogs who are seriously aggressive toward other dogs.
- **Feisty Little Fidos.** For difficult dogs who weigh 25 pounds or less.
- **ADD Dogs.** For young adult dogs who are displaying "Adolescent Dog Disorder"—frustration/aggression on leash as a direct result of their strong desire to go play with other dogs.

The goals are similar but different for each type of class. For the Difficult Dogs, the aim is to increase the owner's level of confidence and control as well as modify canine behavior so their dogs are safe and civilized around other dogs. There is no expectation that these dogs will come to love and frolic with each other by the end of the eight-week program.

Feisty Little Fidos are also expected to learn to be civilized around others, although because of their smaller size, actual physical control is less of an issue.

ADD dogs are the group most likely to learn how to "play well with others" by the end of their classes. Their inappropriate behavior is driven by the thwarting of their strong desire to socialize, as opposed to truly aggressive motives. When owners are taught how to appropriately redirect and reward their dogs' focus and attention the frustrated arousal recedes. Owners in this class are often gratified by the ultimate miracle of seeing their dogs romping happily together with no signs of aggression.

Janet Smith, Behavior Program Manager for the Capital Area Humane Society in Lansing, Michigan, offers two different types of classes for difficult dogs. Smith's "Shy Dog" class is for dogs who have issues with humans, and the "Growls and Howls" program is for dogs who are reactive to other dogs. Her goal for her owners is education—helping them understand their dog while improving their management, training, and relationship. Her goal for the dogs is simply *improvement.*

Like most trainers, and especially those who work in or closely with shelters, Smith's perennial goal is to keep the dogs in their homes. Owners who can see even small improvement in their dogs' behaviors are more motivated to keep working with their dogs rather than giving up on them.

Finding a Class Near You

Once a rarity, difficult dog classes can now be found in many communities. (See "Difficult Dog Classes Around North America".) Even better, *good* difficult dog classes can be found in many communities.

If you aren't conveniently located to one of the trainers listed here, try calling the one nearest you and asking if she knows anyone who may be offering the classes closer to your town. You can also pick up your phone book, call the trainers listed there and ask if they offer such classes.

You can also go to the website for the Association of Pet Dog Trainers (www.apdt.com) and click on the "Trainer Search" button. The site allows you to search by city and state for trainers near you, and while not all APDT members may fit my definition of a positive trainer, and not all of them offer classes for Rowdy Rovers, it's a good place to start.

Not Just *Any* Class Though…

Once you have located a class near you, you will need to investigate further. Ali Brown makes the following suggestions for evaluating your potential difficult dog instructor:

- Observe a class in progress. If a trainer won't let you observe a class, don't bother to pursue it any farther.

- Listen to the trainer speaking. She should discuss the science of behavior and learning, and explain concepts such as counter conditioning and desensitization, and stress levels. She should not just tell people *what* to do with their dogs, but how, and especially *why.*

- Be absolutely sure the training is *all* positive. Handlers should be using buckle collars, leashes, harnesses, treats, clickers, etc. Anything that applies force is counterproductive. No choke chains, no prong collars, no shock collars.

Trish King offers other suggestions:

- Be sure the instructor is experienced at teaching difficult dog classes. Everyone has to learn somewhere—usually as an assistant or apprentice—you don't want you and your dog to be guinea pigs.

- Look for safety controls throughout the class. Dogs and owners should be set up to succeed safely. Equipment, methods, exercises and environments should all be designed to ensure safety; anything in the environment that puts dogs or humans at risk is not acceptable.

- Be absolutely sure the training is *all* positive reinforcement.

Patricia McConnell's booklet, *Feisty Fido*, is included as a textbook by many trainers who teach difficult dog classes, and is an excellent adjunct to the information in this chapter. While hands-on assistance from a skilled trainer in the nurturing environment of a group class of owners facing the same challenges you are with your Rowdy Rover is ideal, McConnell's book is a great backup tool that can start you in the right direction while you track down a suitable class.

Finally, don't despair. You are *not* alone, and your dog's behavior is probably *not* beyond all hope and help. Find yourself a good Rowdy Rover class, and you just might be pleasantly surprised to find that it's easier and far less painful than you thought to turn your difficult dog into a reliably good canine citizen.

"Difficult Dog" Classes Around North America

E-mail list for owners of reactive dogs:

http://groups.yahoo.com/group/pos-4-reactivedogs

CALIFORNIA

Trish King
Marin Humane Society
Novato, CA
(415) 883-4621
www.marinhumanesociety.org

Valerie Pollard
Valerie Pollard Dog Training
Orange, CA
(714) 771-8431
vpollard@socal.rr.com

GEORGIA

Caren Salisbury
Warner Robins, GA
(478) 328-1716/(478) 284-1900
kritterkrnr@watsononline.net

MARYLAND

Tressa Everts
Training by Tressa
Silver Spring, MD
(443) 995-8907
http://hometown.aol.com/bluedevilalumni/myhomepage/dog.html

Pat Miller, CPDT
Peaceable Paws, LLC
301-582-9420
www.peaceablepaws.com

MASSACHSETTS

Kathy Fardy, CPDT
Dog's Time
Billerica, MA
(978) 667-6607 (line #1)
www.dogstime.com

MICHIGAN

Janet A. Smith, Behavior Program Manager
Capital Area Humane Society
Lansing, MI
(517) 626-6821 Ext. 24
www.cahs-lansing.org

MONTANA

Jackie Loeser, CPDT
Black Dog Ranch Training Center, Inc.
Bozeman, MT
(406) 686-4948
www.blackdog.cc

NEW HAMPSHIRE

Dee Ganley, CPDT
Dog Training Services
East Andover, NH
www.lunnflutes.com/deesdogs.htm

NEW JERSEY

Pia Silvani, CPDT
St. Hubert's Animal Welfare Center
Madison, NJ
(973) 377-0116 Ext. 223
psilvani@sthuberts.org

OHIO

Carole Lawson, CPDT
Classic Academy of Canine Learning
Cleveland, OH
(216) 475-9558/216-272-1995
www.classick9academy.com

PENNSYLVANIA

Ali Brown, CPDT
Great Companions
Allentown, PA
(610) 737-1550
www.greatcompainons.info

WISCONSIN

Patricia McConnell, Ph.D.
Dog's Best Friend Ltd.
Black Earth, WI
(608) 767-2435
www.dogsbestfriendtraining.com

CANADA

Jackie McGowan, CPDT
Click Start Dog Training
Calgary, Alberta
(403) 273-6735
lallylegs@telus.net

Resources

Recommended Reading

Aggression in Dogs: Practical Management, Prevention & Behavior Modification, Brenda Aloff, 2002. In-depth explanation of aggressive behavior in dogs.

Canine Body Language: A Photographic Guide, Brenda Aloff, 2005. Hundreds of images accompanied by helpful commentary to help those who own, work with and love dogs to better understand their canines' communications.

The Cautious Canine: How to Help Dogs Conquer Their Fears, Patricia B. McConnell, Ph.D., 2005. Useful words of wisdom in a concise booklet for owners of fearful dogs.

Click for Joy! Questions and Answers From Clicker Trainers and Their Dogs, Melissa Alexander, 2003. Everything you always wanted to know about clicker training.

Clinical Behavioral Medicine for Small Animals, Karen Overall, 1997. An extensive review of behavioral problems from a veterinary perspective.

Coaching People to Train their Dogs, Terry Ryan, 2004. An excellent resource for trainers, contains good information on the science of behavior and learning as well as the art of teaching people.

Control Unleashed, Leslie McDevitt, 2007. In-depth volume on modifying behavior of dog-reactive dogs.

The Culture Clash, Jean Donaldson, 2005. Understand how your dog's brain works. Explore scientific principles of behavior and learning, and commonly held myths.

Doctor Dunbar's Good Little Dog Book, Dr. Ian Dunbar, 2003. Excellent puppy book; illustrates basic training using lure-and-reward methods.

Dog Detectives: Train Your Dog to Find Lost Pets, Kat Albrecht, 2007. A fascinating look at how dogs can be trained to find a variety of lost pets.

Dog Whisperer: A Compassionate, Nonviolent Approach to Dog Training, Paul Owens, 1999. This book predates TV's dog whisperer, and is a thoughtful discussion of gentle methods of dog guardianship.

Dogs Are From Neptune, Jean Donaldson, 1998. Case histories illustrate protocols for modifying aggressive behavior using counter conditioning and desensitization, in an easy-to-read Q&A format.

Don't Shoot the Dog: The New Art of Teaching and Training, by Karen Pryor, 1999. The book that launched the dog training culture's shift to positive training methods.

Feisty Fido: Help For the Leash Aggressive Dog, Patricia B. McConnell, Ph.D., 2003. Incredibly useful booklet for owners of dog-reactive dogs.

Fight! A Practical Guide to the Treatment of Dog-Dog Aggression, Jean Donaldson, 2004. Essential reading for anyone who wants to understand canine aggression.

For the Love of a Dog: Understanding Emotion in You and Your Best Friend, Patricia B. McConnell, Ph.D., 2006. Enjoyable volume that supports the belief that dogs feel very much same range of emotions as do humans—and how this effects our relationships with them.

Help For Your Fearful Dog: A Step-By-Step Guide to Helping Your Dog Conquer His Fears, Nicole Wilde, 2006. A comprehensive guide to the treatment of canine anxiety, fears, and phobias.

Living with Kids and Dogs…Without Losing Your Mind, Colleen Pelar, 2005. Simple, realistic advice for busy parents to help ensure that the relationship between their kids and the family dog is safe and enjoyable for all.

Mine! A Practical Guide to Resource Guarding in Dogs, Jean Donaldson. Resource guarding is perhaps the most common form of aggression you might encounter with your dog.

On Talking Terms With Dogs: Calming Signal, Turid Rugaas. 2006. The ground-breaking work that first introduced this fascinating element of canine communication to students of dog behavior.

The Other End of the Leash: Why We Do What We Do Around Dogs, Patricia B. McConnell, Ph.D., 2002. Explores communication differences between humans and canines.

Parenting Your Dog, Trish King, 2004. Solid information on dog-parenting, training and behavior modification using a positive approach.

Positive Perspectives: Love Your Dog, Train Your Dog, Pat B. Miller, CPDT, CDBC, 2004. Collection of articles from *Whole Dog Journal* and Tuft's University's *Your Dog,* reworked into a comprehensive volume about training and behavior for the committed owner who wants to have a positive and successful relationship with her dog.

The Bark Stops Here, Terry Ryan, 2000. Helpful hints for owners whose dogs are a little too willing to speak their minds.

The Power of Positive Dog Training, Pat B. Miller, 2001. Explains positive training philosophies and methods including clicker training; common behavior challenges; offers a 6-week, step-by-step training program.

Right on Target: Taking Dog Training to a New Level, Mandy Book and Cheryl S. Smith, 2006. In-depth book on a wide variety of ways to use targeting in training and play with your dog.

Videos and DVDs

Click and Go! Deborah Jones, 2006. A great introduction to clicker training.

Clicker Magic, Karen Pryor, 2007. Learn what clicker training is all about if you're a beginner, fill in the gaps if you've been working on your own, get inspiration if you're an experienced instructor or trainer.

The Language of Dogs: Understanding Canine Body Language and Other Communication Signals, Sarah Kalnajs, 2006. Extensive footage of a variety of canine breeds showing hundreds of examples of canine behavior and body language, accompanied by insightful commentary from Kalnajs.

New Puppy, Now What? Victoria Schade, 2006. Everything you need to know about living with your new puppy—a friendly, positive approach!

Really Reliable Recall, Leslie Nelson, 2004. Easy to follow steps to train your dog to come when it really counts, in an emergency.

Periodicals

Bark, 1-877-227-5639; www.thebark.com

The Whole Dog Journal, 1-800-829-9165; www.whole-dog-journal.com

Your Dog, 1-800-829-5116; www.tufts.edu/vet/publications/yourdog

Web Sites

Association of Pet Dog Trainers, www.apdt.com
This is a professional organization for dog trainers, with useful information for dog owners.

Certification Council for Professional Dog Trainers, www.ccpdt.org
The CCPDT is an international testing and certification program for professional pet dog trainers. The website includes a listing of certified pet dog trainers around the world.

Clicker Teachers, www.clickerteachers.net
Extensive listing of clicker trainers around the world. Search by state or by country.

Doggone Good, www.doggonegood.com
Training tools, soft crates, jewelry, and gift items.

Dogwise, www.dogwise.com
Great source for dog books, videos, training products, food, toys and supplies.

Karen Pryor, www.clickertraining.com
Karen Pryor is the "Queen Mother" of clicker training – her website is a "must visit."

The Kong Company, www.kongcompany.com
Originator of the Kong, an exceptionally durable and versatile toy; other ultra-tough and interactive products.

Missing Pet Partnership, www.missingpetpartnership.org

Search-and-Rescue for lost pets; learn how to be a Pet Detective!

Patricia McConnell, www.patriciamcconnell.com
Offers class schedules (Madison and Milwaukee, Wisconsin), private consultation services, and information/ordering on books, booklets, DVDs, and seminars.

Peaceable Paws/Pat Miller, www.peaceablepaws.com
Author's website. You can also join the author's email discussion list by sending a message to: peaceablepaws-subscribe@yahoogroups.com.

Premier, www.gentleleader.com
Source for the Easy Walk harness, the Calming Cap and various other *very* useful dog products.

Truly Dog Friendly, www.trulydogfriendly.com
A group of trainers who are committed to pain-free, positive training. Website includes a long state-by-state listing of "truly dog friendly" trainers around the U.S.

White Pine Outfitters, www.whitepineoutfitters.com
Exceptionally well-designed leashes, collars, harnesses, hands-free belts and more.

Index

Author Biography

Dogs and dog training have been a consistent thread throughout Pat Miller's life. Beginning at age six with the family Beagle, continuing on in her teenage years when she showed her Rough Collie and into her professional life, Pat has enthusiastically shared her world and her heart with dogs. She has titled her canine companions in Obedience and Rally, trained dogs in a wide variety of dog sports and built her career around animals. Pat is a columnist for *Whole Dog Journal, Your Dog Magazine* and *Popular Dogs,* and she is the author of *The Power of Positive Dog Training* and *Positive Perspectives. Love Your Dog, Train Your Dog.* Working now with people and their dogs, Pat has her own training establishment "Peaceable Paws, LLC" on 80 acres near Hagerstown, Maryland where she offers dog training classes and one-to-one behavior consulting to pet dog owners as well as boarding services. Peaceable Paws also hosts a number of courses and programs for both the professional dog trainer and those wanting to become a professional. Pat is past president of the Association of Pet Dog Trainers, APDT, the largest professional organization for dog trainers in the world and is a Certified Dog Behavior Consultant (CDBC) and Certified Pet Dog Trainer (CPDT). As a 20-year veteran of the Marin Humane Society in California, Miller knows too well that when normal, healthy dogs aren't given the time and attention needed to become well-mannered family members, the results can be tragic. Pat and her husband live with their canine, feline, and equine family in Fairplay, Maryland. Learn more about Pat and her programs at www.peaceablepaws.com

Author Pat Miller and Josie.

The Dog Trainer's Resource: The APDT Chronicle of the Dog Collection.
Mychelle Blake (*ed*)
Therapy Dogs: Training Your Dog To Reach Others.
Kathy Diamond Davis
Training Dogs, A Manual (reprint). Konrad Most
Training the Disaster Search Dog. Shirley Hammond
Try Tracking: The Puppy Tracking Primer. Carolyn Krause
Visiting the Dog Park, Having Fun, and Staying Safe. Cheryl S. Smith
When Pigs Fly. Train Your Impossible Dog. Jane Killion
Winning Team. A Guidebook for Junior Showmanship. Gail Haynes
Working Dogs (reprint). Elliot Humphrey & Lucien Warner

HEALTH & ANATOMY, SHOWING
An Eye for a Dog. Illustrated Guide to Judging Purebred Dogs. Robert Cole
Annie On Dogs! Ann Rogers Clark
Canine Cineradiography, DVD. Rachel Page Elliott
Canine Massage: A Complete Reference Manual.
Jean-Pierre Hourdebaigt
Canine Terminology (reprint). Harold Spira
Dog In Action (reprint). Macdowell Lyon
Dogsteps DVD. Rachel Page Elliott
Performance Dog Nutrition: Optimize Performance With Nutrition.
Jocelynn Jacobs
Puppy Intensive Care: A Breeder's Guide To Care Of Newborn Puppies. Myra Savant
Harris
Raw Dog Food: Make It Easy for You and Your Dog. Carina MacDonald
Raw Meaty Bones. Tom Lonsdale
Shock to the System. The Facts About Animal Vaccination...
Catherine O'Driscoll
The History and Management of the Mastiff. Elizabeth Baxter & Pat Hoffman
Work Wonders. Feed Your Dog Raw Meaty Bones. Tom Lonsdale
Whelping Healthy Puppies, DVD. Sylvia Smart

Dogwise.com is your complete source for dog books on the web!

2,000+ titles, fast shipping, and excellent customer service.

Phone in your Order! 1.800.776.2665 8am-4pm PST / 11am-7pm EST

Search Dogwise

Everything ▼

GO

Browse Dogwise

Books & Products
* By Subject
* Dogwise Picks
* Best Sellers
* Best New Titles

Book Reviews
* Find Out How

Resources & Info
* Dogwise Forums
* Dogwise Newsletters
* Dogwise Email List
* Customer Reading Lists
* Dog Show Schedule
* Let Us Know About Your Book or DVD
* Become an Affiliate
* APDT, CPDT
* IAABC
* CAPPDT

Help & Contacts
* About Us
* Contact Us
* Shipping Policy

Employee Picks!
See which books the Dogwise staff members love to read.
* Click Here!

Dog Show Supplies from The 3C's
* Visit the 3c's Website
* View our selection of 3c products.

Save up to 80% on Bargain Books! Click here for Sale, Clearance and hard to find Out of Print titles!
* Click Here!

Prefer to order by phone? Call Us!
1-800-776-2665
8AM - 4PM M-F Pacific Time

Be the First to Hear the News!
Have New Product and Promotion Announcements Emailed to You.
Click Here To Sign Up!

Free Shipping for Orders over $75 - click here for more information!

Win a $25 Dogwise credit - click here to find out how!

Featured New Titles

STRESS IN DOGS - LEARN HOW DOGS SHOW STRESS AND WHAT YOU CAN DO TO HELP, by Martina Scholz & Clarissa von Reinhardt
Item: DTB909
Is stress causing your dog's behavior problems? Research shows that as with humans, many behavioral problems in dogs are stress-related. Learn how to recognize when your dog is stressed, what factors cause stress in dogs, and strategies you can utilize in training and in your daily life with your dog to reduce stress.
Price: $14.95 more information...
DIG IN

SUCCESS IS IN THE PROOFING - A GUIDE FOR CREATIVE AND EFFECTIVE TRAINING, by Debby Quigley & Judy Ramsey
Item: DTO230
The success is indeed in the proofing! Proofing is an essential part of training, but one that is often overlooked or not worked on enough. We all know the story of the dog who can perform a variety of behaviors perfectly in the backyard but falls apart in the obedience ring. This book is full of great ideas and strategies to help your dog do his best no matter what the distractions or conditions may be. Whether competing in Rally or Obedience, trainers everywhere will find this very portable and user friendly book an indispensable addition to their tool box.
Price: $19.95 more information...
DIG IN

REALLY RELIABLE RECALL DVD, by Leslie Nelson
Item: DTB810P
From well-known trainer Leslie Nelson! Easy to follow steps to train your dog to come when it really counts. In an emergency. Extra chapters for difficult to train breeds and training class instructors.
Price: $29.95 more information...
DIG IN

THE DOG TRAINERS RESOURCE - APDT CHRONICLE OF THE DOG COLLECTION, by Mychelle Blake, Editor
Item: DTB880
The modern professional dog trainer needs to develop expertise in a wide variety of fields: learning theory, training techniques, classroom strategies, marketing, community relations, and business development and management. This collection of articles from APDT's Chronicle of the Dog will prove a valuable resource for trainers and would-be trainers.
Price: $24.95 more information...
DIG IN

SHAPING SUCCESS - THE EDUCATION OF AN UNLIKELY CHAMPION, by Susan Garrett
Item: DTA260
Written by one of the world's best dog trainers, Shaping Success gives an excellent explanation of the theory behind animal learning as Susan Garrett trains a high-energy Border Collie puppy to be an agility champion. Buzzy's story both entertains and demonstrates how to apply some of the most up-to-date dog training methods in the real world. Clicker training!
Price: $24.95 more information...
DIG IN

FOR THE LOVE OF A DOG - UNDERSTANDING EMOTION IN YOU AND YOUR BEST FRIEND, by Patricia McConnell
Item: DTB890
Sure to be another bestseller, Trish McConnell's latest book takes a look at canine emotions and body language. Like all her books, this one is written in a way that the average dog owner can follow but brings the latest scientific information that trainers and dog enthusiasts can use.
Price: $24.95 more information...
DIG IN

HELP FOR YOUR FEARFUL DOG: A STEP-BY-STEP GUIDE TO HELPING YOUR DOG CONQUER HIS FEARS, by Nicole Wilde
Item: DTB878
From popular author and trainer Nicole Wilde! A comprehensive guide to the treatment of canine anxiety, fears, and phobias. Chock full of photographs and illustrations and written in a down-to-earth, humorous style.
Price: $24.95 more information...
DIG IN

FAMILY FRIENDLY DOG TRAINING - A SIX WEEK PROGRAM FOR YOU AND YOUR DOG, by Patricia McConnell & Aimee Moore
Item: DTB917
A six-week program to get people and dogs off on the right paw! Includes trouble-shooting tips for what to do when your dog doesn't respond as expected. This is a book that many trainers will want their students to read.
Price: $11.95 more information...
DIG IN

THE LANGUAGE OF DOGS - UNDERSTANDING CANINE BODY LANGUAGE AND OTHER COMMUNICATION SIGNALS DVD SET, by Sarah Kalnajs
Item: DTB875P
Features a presentation and extensive footage of a variety of breeds showing hundreds of examples of canine behavior and body language. Perfect for dog owners or anyone who handles dogs or encounters them regularly while on the job.
Price: $39.95 more information...
DIG IN